COMPARATIVE RELIGION
A History

ERIC J. SHARPE

Comparative Religion
A History

SECOND EDITION

DUCKWORTH

This impression 2003
Second edition 1986
First published in 1975 by
Gerald Duckworth & Co. Ltd.
61 Frith Street, London W1D 3JL
Tel: 020 7434 4242
Fax: 020 7434 4420
inquiries@duckworth-publishers.co.uk
www.ducknet.co.uk

A catalogue record for this book is available
from the British Library

ISBN 0 7156 1081 3

Printed in Great Britain by
Antony Rowe Ltd, Eastbourne

Contents

For

BIRGITTA

We are dealing with a topic, complex and many-sided. It comprises the deliverances of the understanding as it harmonises our deepest intuitions. It comprises emotional responses to formulations of thought and to modes of behaviour. It comprises the direction of purposes and the modifications of behaviour. It cuts into every aspect of human existence. So far as concerns religious problems, simple solutions are bogus solutions. It is written, that he who runs, may read. But it is not said, that he provides the writing.

Alfred North Whitehead

Preface to the second edition

More than a decade has elapsed since the publication of the first edition of this book, which now has been out of print for some time. I have been pleasantly surprised in recent years to find how widely it has been, and is still, being used in universities and colleges as a first introduction to the history of the multicultural study of religion, and I welcome this opportunity to reissue it in an updated version. The updating has proved problematical, not least because of the vast amount of relevant material published since my original cut-off date of 1970. Occasionally I have been left with the feeling that a volume of considerable size could easily be written solely on the developments of the past fifteen or so years. This being out of the question, in the end I have been even more severely selective than in the earlier part of the book. I have added only one more short chapter, in which I have attempted to sketch a few recent trends in the field. I have also revised the bibliography.

Of those I had most occasion to thank in the first edition, Professor C. Jouco Bleeker and Miss Grace Perigo have since passed away. Both are remembered with affection. I should like however to take this opportunity to acknowledge the help of a large number of other colleagues and friends in many parts of the world in providing comments, encouragement, criticism, books, articles and offprints. Although I have in the end been able to make explicit use of only a fraction of this material in my last chapter, I should not wish any to think me ungrateful. In Australia I owe much to my co-workers at the University of Sydney, William Jobling, Arvind Sharma and especially Garry Trompf; in Sweden to Carl-Martin Edsman, Jan Bergman and Åke Hultkrantz; to Ugo Bianchi in Italy, Peter Antes in Germany and Jacques Waardenburg and J.G. Platvoet in the Netherlands; to Gerald Larson, Hans Penner and Jonathan Z. Smith in the USA; and in Canada to Hans Mol, Klaus Klostermaier, Reinhard Pummer, Roger O'Toole, Willard Oxtoby, Donald Wiebe and the graduate students at McMaster University.

A very special word of thanks is due, finally, to my English publishers, Duckworth. That this book was attempted in the first place was their idea rather than mine; and since then, some sixteen years ago, they have provided the kind of support that all writers hope for, but not all find.

Sydney   Eric J. Sharpe
July 1986

Preface to the first edition

A Science of Religion, based on an impartial and truly scientific comparison of all, or at all events, of the most important, religions of mankind, is now only a question of time. It is demanded by those whose voice cannot be disregarded. Its title, though implying as yet a promise rather than a fulfilment, has become more or less familiar in Germany, France and America; its great problems have attracted the eyes of many inquirers, and its results have been anticipated either with fear or with delight. It becomes therefore the duty of those who have devoted their life to the study of the principal religions of the world in their original documents, and who value religion and reverence it in whatever form it may present itself, to take possession of this new territory in the name of true science.[1]

These words were spoken on 19 February 1870 at the Royal Institution in London by the expatriate German philologist and man of letters Friedrich Max Müller, and were later reprinted in what one might reasonably identify as the foundation document of comparative religion in the English-speaking world, Max Müller's *Introduction to the Science of Religion* (1873). They do not, it is true, mark an absolutely new departure. There had long been those in the West who had looked upon religion in all its diversity as an object to be studied rather than as a creed to be followed. But for reasons which we shall examine in due course the last decades of the nineteenth century saw the first attempt to systematise the material which was emerging from this study, to subject it to a definite method, and thus to make of it a 'science'. By 1870 what Max Müller called 'this new territory' was beginning to be mapped out, and to assume firm outlines. Some followed Max Müller and his Continental mentors in speaking in this connection of 'the science of religion' (in French *la science de religion*, in German *Religionswissenschaft*); while others preferred to emphasise the necessary

[1] Max Müller, *Introduction to the Science of Religion* (1873), p. 34f.

aspect of comparison, and to refer to the study simply as 'the comparative study of religion', or, more simply still, as 'comparative religion'.

Between 1870 and the end of the century it came to be more and more widely accepted that quite apart from the individual's personal beliefs, to understand religion inevitably involved comparison—of material from different traditions, different parts of the world and different periods of human history. To this end the religious traditions of the world, past and present, were scoured for every scrap of evidence that might throw light on the origin and evolutionary development of religion as an apparently universal human activity.

Thirty-five years later, in 1905, the time having come for the writing of a first provisional chronicle of the subject, the tireless Louis H. Jordan found it appropriate to define comparative religion as

... that Science which compares the origin, structure, and characteristics of the various Religions of the world, with the view of determining their genuine agreements and differences, the measure of relation in which they stand one to another, and their relative superiority and inferiority when regarded as types.[2]

Today we look back, not without a certain nostalgia, at the age which produced such a confident definition. Today there would appear to be no such 'Science'. Not that we have ceased altogether to compare 'the origin, structure, and characteristics of the various Religions of the world'; but we do so with great caution, and we have ceased almost entirely to concern ourselves with 'relative superiority or inferiority' of religions on the criteria provided by the Darwinian-Spencerian theory of evolution. That is to say, that whatever image comparative religion may once have presented to the world, it has since undergone a radical transformation. Although the thirty-five years between Max Müller's lecture and Jordan's chronicle were dominated by the comparative (i.e. evolutionary) method in the study of religion, the seventy or so years which separate us from the world of 1905 have seen its virtual abandonment. No new method accepted by all has arisen to take its place. In this, comparative religion is by no means a special case. Academic specialisation is no respecter of synthetic sciences. Anthro-

---

[2] Jordan, *Comparative Religion, its Genesis and Growth* (1905), p. 63. But it is worth noting that he found even then little agreement as to method, writing: 'Every investigator is a law to himself' (p. 208).

pology, for instance, was once confidently characterised as 'the science of man' pure and simple, but is now studied under such varied headings as prehistoric archaeology, physical anthropology, ethnology, social anthropology, folklore, linguistics, and the rest. Similarly, the sheer weight of material which has accumulated under the general heading of 'comparative religion' is now sub-divided into the history of religion, the psychology of religion, the sociology of religion, the phenomenology of religion and the philos-ophy of religion (not to mention a host of auxiliary disciplines), the pursuit of any one of which might occupy a normal scholar for a normal lifetime. Each of these now has its own approaches and its own appropriate methods.

In practice it has, however, often been found necessary to con-tinue to use some form of words which on the one hand describes the multi-disciplinary and non-confessional approach to the study of religion, and on the other separates such a study from those theo-logical or other assessments which are entirely proper when applied within a single tradition. For a variety of reasons, which we shall examine in due course, scholars in some countries came in time to look with suspicion on the term 'comparative religion', which they felt to be too weighted with evolutionary associations to be of further value. But it has not been easy to find an alternative. Gener-ally speaking, the tendency in recent years has been to speak instead of 'the history of religions' or perhaps *Religionswissenschaft* (though in non-German-speaking countries this is not easily justified). In Britain, although the general term 'religious studies' has been gain-ing ground, there are still professors, lecturers and departments of comparative religion in a few universities, and it still seems feasible to use this form of words. It perhaps remains, its shortcomings not-withstanding, the only term which suggests the study, in the round, of the religious traditions of the world—including, of course, the Judaeo-Christian traditions—as phenomena to be observed, rather than as creeds to be followed. It is the only term broad enough to serve as a heading for the very disparate material which this book sets out to discuss, and to those who still object to it, I would simply plead that there is no obvious alternative. Since the 1950s, as I have said, 'the history of religions' has been the current term; how-ever, it is significant that here and there, the term 'comparative religion' has recently begun to enjoy a new lease of life. Depart-ments in Swedish and Finnish universities, for instance, use it freely, while the pan-Scandinavian journal *Temenos*, which com-menced publication in the 1960s, carries the subtitle, 'Studies in Comparative Religion'.

Given, then, that 'comparative religion' implies the serious and, as far as possible, dispassionate study of material drawn from all the accessible religious traditions of the world, there are certain obvious limitations which have been forced upon me in writing about its history. This book makes no claim to be an exhaustive chronicle of every aspect of comparative religious study. Nor does it pretend to include historical data about the development of studies in any specific geographical or cultural area. A volume of this size could easily be written about, say, the study of Hindu religion in the West,[3] or about the study of comparative religion in any one country (or even in one university, as Professor Rudolph has demonstrated with regard to Leipzig).[4] What I have tried to do is to write in broad outline, and occasionally in detail, about significant—or what appear to me to be significant—personalities, themes, stages and landmarks in the comparative study of religion, and to refer to specialist studies only insofar as they illuminate this larger methodological theme, and advance the wider argument by a step or two.

It would also be as well to point out at the very beginning that I do not adhere to a consistent chronological scheme. When I began to write, several years ago, I tried to do so; but I rapidly discovered how impossible it was, particularly in respect of more recent developments. Comparative religion has always been made up of many strands, many approaches and many methods, and I have regarded it as a first priority to attempt to disentangle these strands. This has involved dealing with each more or less separately, particularly in the second half of this book, and has meant that the reader must be prepared to make some chronological leaps. I regret the necessity; but a straightforward chronicle would have done justice to few of the issues, and would inevitably have involved much distortion.

Clearly a single writer cannot pretend to possess more than a nodding acquaintance with the specialist methods and literature of *all* the areas which are now recognised as forming part of comparative religion. In some of these areas I have felt it advisable for this reason to venture little comment. For instance the sociological tradition (from which the sociology of religion is not easily separable) has already found its chroniclers, to whom I am content to defer.[5] Again, as we approach our own day, the reader will notice a gradual narrowing of approach, towards a discussion of

---

[3] On the lines of, for instance, Welbon, *The Buddhist Nirvāna and its Western Interpreters* (1968).

[4] Rudolph, *Die Religionsgeschichte an der Leipziger Universität* (1962).

[5] Nisbet, *The Sociological Tradition* (1967). See also Wach, in RGG² (1930), cols. 1929ff.

some of the problems attending the study of religion in a religiously pluralist world. In the earlier part of the book, on the other hand, I have thought it best to aim at comprehensiveness.

I should not have made the attempt to write about these developments at all had I not felt it important to do so, and I freely acknowledge a host of second-hand insights. For mistakes of interpretation and errors of fact (which a study of this breadth cannot but contain) I am of course solely responsible.

This book grew out of lectures given to students in the Universities of Manchester and Lancaster, and in writing, I have tried as far as possible to keep the needs of students in mind. Professionals—professors and lecturers in the subject—will no doubt be accustomed to tracing their own course through one or another branch, or tributary, of comparative religion (or whatever else they may care to call it). I have not really written this book for them, though I hope they may find it useful. Bearing in mind those for whom it *has* been written, I have tried, though I fear not always successfully, to keep technicalities (and references) to a minimum. I have not, however, thought it proper to limit this account to developments in the English-speaking world. Again, this does not mean that note has been taken of all the significant literature in all the major languages; such a task would be entirely outside the competence of one person. But since there is nothing parochial about comparative religion, and since its history is in part the history of Western culture in interaction with cultures in other parts of the world, as well as within the bounds of the West, I have tried to exhibit some of the long views.

I first began the study of comparative religion in Manchester, under the late Professor S. G. F. Brandon, and I should like to quote a few lines from a book which he published exactly a century after Max Müller's statement with which I began, as a justification, not of this book, which must stand and fall on its own merits, but of the study it describes :

It is realised that to have an intelligent understanding of our common humanity and its problems today, it is necessary to know something of its religions as well as its political and economic affairs, its scientific and cultural achievements. For, whatever may be one's evaluation of the metaphysical aspects of religion, the significance of religion as a social phenomenon is fundamental. The ways in which other peoples today and in the past have sought to solve the problem of human nature and destiny have a deep and abiding interest . . . Moreover, the problem, which others have thus tried to solve, is a continuing one and it confronts each of us, whatever our age or the society in which we live.[6]

Although most of those who have helped me in the preparation of this book are unaware, and perhaps would prefer to remain unaware, of that fact, there are some personal debts of gratitude which I cannot allow to go unacknowledged.

I should never have begun to work in this field at all, had it not been for the late Professor S. G. F. Brandon; he knew that this book was being written, and encouraged and advised me during those early months when I was still feeling for an adequate form of treatment. I hope he would have approved of the final shape the book has taken.

I owe a particular debt of gratitude to my colleagues at the University of Lancaster, and especially to Professor Ninian Smart and Mr Michael Pye (now of the University of Leeds), for compelling me to ask—and to attempt to answer—some questions of method which I would otherwise have passed over in ignorance. I have also benefited greatly from the friendship and advice of Professor Edmund Perry of Northwestern University and Professor C. Jouco Bleeker of Amsterdam, though perhaps neither would agree with all my final conclusions.

Miss Grace Perigo of Penrith read a great deal of the first draft of my manuscript, and preserved me from many stylistic faults; I thank her for that valuable service. And finally, I must mention all the help I have received from my wife Birgitta. As well as doing most of the typing, and bringing a librarian's critical eye to bear on the bibliography, she nursed me through a serious illness when the book was less than half finished, and kept me from falling into the fits of depression which accompany a task of this size. In the circumstances, I can only echo the nineteenth-century writer who said : 'No metaphysician ever felt the deficiency of language so much as the grateful.'

Lancaster   Eric J. Sharpe
September 1974

---

[6] Brandon, *A Dictionary of Comparative Religion* (1970), p. 1.

I

The Antecedents of Comparative Religion

Comparative religion, that is, the historical, critical and comparative study of the religions of the world, first came widely to public attention in the sixties and seventies of the nineteenth century. It was not, however, created instantaneously at that time, as the result of a sudden blinding flash of insight on someone's part. Rather, its emergence represented the germination of seeds planted and watered over many centuries of Western history. For in a sense the entire history of the study of religion in the Western world may be seen as an extended prelude to the short period of study of which this book sets out to give some account.[1]

The antecedents of comparative religion were far more numerous, and far more diverse, than is commonly realised. It might perhaps be claimed that the first 'comparative religionist' was the first worshipper of a god or gods who asked himself, having first discovered the facts of the case, why his neighbour should be a worshipper of some other god or gods. Regrettably, we cannot study this entirely hypothetical pioneer. When our studies begin, we find that few historical situations of social encounter have entirely

---

[1] The most comprehensive study of the beginnings and early development of the comparative study of religion is still the magisterial work of H. Pinard de la Boullaye, *L'Étude comparée des religions* 1 (4th ed. 1929), to which I have made constant reference. I have also made considerable, though for the most part unacknowledged, use of the two painstaking works of L. H. Jordan, *Comparative Religion: its Genesis and Growth* (1905) and *Comparative Religion: its Adjuncts and Allies* (1915). Both contain a mass of bibliographical information, together with reports of the transactions of earlier congresses, details of journals, lectureships and learned societies; it has been entirely impracticable to reproduce more than a minute fraction of these details in this book.

I am also indebted for basic information to Lehmann, *Religionsvetenskapen* 1 (1914), to Mensching, *Histoire de la science des religions* (Fr. tr. 1955), and to de Vries, *The Study of Religion: a Historical Approach* (Eng. tr. 1967). Waardenburg, *Classical Approaches to the Study of Religion* 1 (1973) came into my hands only at the eleventh hour, when the greater part of this book was already written. I have therefore not been able to use it widely, though I have verified a number of facts with its help.

cf. also Sharpe, 'The Comparative Study of Religion in Historical Perspective', in Hinnells (ed.), *Comparative Religion in Education* (1970), pp. 1–19.

failed to produce some degree of curiosity, however slight and perfunctory, about the religious beliefs and practices of the 'barbarians'. Low-level solutions of the problem were apt to be abrupt and drastic; but on a higher level, there came in time to be much theological and philosophical speculation about the problem of religious plurality. This process inevitably involved at least a modicum of comparative religion.

It would seem that the existence of comparative religion, at its simplest, is dependent on the fulfilment of three elementary conditions. First, there must be a *motive* for comparative study : this might be no more than old-fashioned curiosity, though in practice it might well involve (and in later situations often did involve) a degree of dissatisfaction with inherited religious traditions. Secondly, *material* must be available : first or second-hand information about the religious beliefs and practices of persons not belonging to one's own dominant domestic tradition. And thirdly, there must be an acceptable *method* by which to organise the material into an intelligible pattern. Indeed, the history of the comparative study of religion is very much a matter, given the existence of adequate motivation, of rapidly increasing accumulations of material in search of a method.

Comparative religion, then, usually presupposes, if it does not absolutely require, a certain degree of detachment from a dominant religious tradition, and a degree of interest in the religious beliefs and practices of others. On these criteria, a good case might be made out for tracing the origins of comparative religion back to classical antiquity. Both elements were certainly present in the philosophical and historical traditions of Greece and Rome, though unevenly and not always in conjunction. The overall attitude of the classical cultures to the religious traditions of other peoples was one of indifference; and the exceptions—Herodotus, Plutarch and others—merely serve to emphasise the general rule. It was generally accepted that differences of country and race and language would inevitably mean differences of religion. This was part of the natural, and therefore unremarkable, order of things, and it was only as cultural contacts became more extensive during the Hellenistic and subsequent periods that individual writers felt drawn to describe the beliefs and practices of the 'barbarians', and to draw conclusions from the material thus assembled.

On the whole the methods employed for the study of religion in the ancient world were not as different from our own as might be supposed. There was an underlying current of criticism of accepted forms of religion at home; there was an attempt to record and describe what was seen and read and experienced; and there was an attempt to compare and contrast this material with familiar traditions and accepted ideas.

The first impulse was that of criticism. The Ionic philosophers of the sixth century B.C., attempting to explain the world as the manifestation of one indestructible principle, were led to criticise the inadequacy of Greek popular religion.[2] Perhaps they did not mean to cast doubt upon the simple and unreflecting faith of the common people; but their scientific researches and philosophical speculations inevitably tended in this direction. The astronomical calculations of Thales (*fl.* 585 B.C.) tended to rob the gods of their authority; his pupil Anaximander (610–*c.* 540 B.C.) ignored the gods altogether, announcing that the sun and moon were not deities, but circles of fire, twenty-eight and nineteen times respectively larger than the earth. But it was with the work of Xenophanes of Colophon (*c.* 570–475 B.C.) that serious battle was joined between philosophy and religion.[3]

Xenophanes held that no one knows, or can know, anything about the nature of the gods : all is a matter of opinion (*doxa*). He attacked popular religion on two fronts : first, for its anthropomorphism; and secondly, for its immorality. But he did not work out his ideas consistently or logically, operating rather within the sphere of creative intuition. His 'remains' are fragmentary, but entirely to the point. Witness this celebrated passage on the subject of anthropomorphism :

> If oxen, or lions, or horses had hands like men,
> they too,
> If they could fashion pictures, or statues they
> could hew,
> They would shape in their own image each face
> and form divine—
> Horses' gods like horses, like kine the gods of
> kine.
> 'Snub-nosed are the Immortals, and black,' the
> Ethiops say;
> But 'No,' the Thracians answer, 'red-haired,
> with eyes of grey.'[4]

With Xenophanes there thus begins the long tradition of criti-

---

[2] On this subject generally, see Decharme, *La Critique des traditions religieuses chez les Grecs* (1904). On its beginnings, cf. Stawell, 'Ionic Philosophy', in *ERE*, VII (1914), pp. 414ff.

[3] Decharme, op. cit., pp. 43ff; cf. Bowra, *Landmarks in Greek Literature* (1966), p. 161; *RGG*,[3] VI, cols. 1853ff.

[4] Lucas, *Greek Poetry for Everyman* (1951), p. 256f.

cism of native religion which was so characteristic of Greek philosophical thought. It is to be seen in practically all philosophers, at some stage or other; and in the dramatists. It was irreverent, and unpopular (as Socrates discovered); but without it, the study of religion would perforce have remained narrow and local.

A different type of Greek tradition was represented by the much-travelled historian Herodotus (*c.* 484–425 B.C.), who described many of the religious customs of the Egyptians, Babylonians and Persians. Not only did he describe what he saw and was told (apparently with accuracy); he exhibited more than a passing interest in exotic religious phenomena. He was an initiate into the mysteries of Osiris, and believed that Greek culture and religion had been derived in large measure from Egypt. He identified Greek gods and goddesses with their Egyptian 'prototypes'—Zeus with Amon, Apollo with Horus, Hephaistos with Ptah, and many more—and has been called one of the first syncretists.[5] In his desire to observe and describe the religion of a foreign culture with the help of data from his own culture, he anticipated one of the fundamental attitudes of comparative religion through the ages.

The period of the Persian Empire and the subsequent campaigns of Alexander the Great helped to produce a situation in which this concern could best be exercised. Culture met culture, and there were bound to be those who attempted to interpret the one to the other. A number of descriptive works date from this period. Berosus, a priest of the Babylonian god Bel-Marduk, published his *Babylonika*, or 'Chronicles of Babylon'; Megasthenes, a diplomatist on the staff of Seleucus Nicator, wrote in his *Indica* of India and Indian gods. Like Herodotus, he identified Indian deities with Greek prototypes in a manner which has caused much speculation among later scholars.[6] Manetho, an Egyptian priest and courtier of the first Ptolemies, wrote a chronicle of Egypt which, though valuable, is not altogether impartial, since he was an adherent of the new composite cult of Serapis.

It was, however, with the Stoics that the study of religion first became in a real sense 'cosmopolitan' (a Stoic word). A pioneer in this area was Chrysippus (280–206 B.C.), to whom Cicero paid tribute in this fragment of comparative study:

The Egyptians embalm their dead and keep them in their houses; the Persians dress theirs over with wax, that they may preserve

---

[5] Decharme, op. cit., p. 77.

[6] For a discussion of, and theories concerning, this problem, see Dahlquist, *Megasthenes and Indian Religion* (1962).

their bodies as long as possible. It is customary with the Magi to bury none of their order unless they have been first torn by dogs. In Hyrcania the people maintain dogs for the public use; their nobles have their own; we know they have a good breed of dogs, but every one, according to his ability provides himself with some, in order to be torn by them; and they hold that to be the best interment. Chrysippus, who is a painstaking student of every kind of history, has collected many other things of this kind . . .[7]

As well as classifying cults in accordance with their place of origin, the Stoics also referred to certain beliefs common to all cults (*omnibus innata et in animo quasi insculpta*); these constituted what they called *natural* religion—thus originating a well-known phrase. The Stoic line of study culminated in the celebrated works of Cicero, *De natura deorum* (Concerning the Nature of the Gods) and *De divinatione* (Concerning Divination).

Impelled by the same spirit were the fragments of Varro (116–27 B.C.), *Antiquitates rerum divinarum*, preserved by Augustine; and the more comprehensive work of Pausanias (*c.* 150 A.D.) on the subject of the religious topography of Greece—a source still used with appreciation by historians of Greek religion. These were local histories; but the *Geography* of Strabo (*c.* 63 B.C.–A.D. 21) contains references to the Celtic Druids and to the Brahmins of India, while from the wider areas of contact between the Roman imperial forces and the tribes of Northern Europe come Caesar's description of Germanic and Celtic religion in *De bello Gallico* and Tacitus' account of Teutonic religion in his *Germania*.[8]

The subject of mythology was also one which interested many writers in antiquity, and a number of attempts are known to have been made to organise current myths into coherent systems. Unfortunately, few of these systematic treatises have been preserved, and those which have, are of dubious origin. Worthy of mention is, however, the *Fabulae*, attributed to the Augustan Hyginus (but certainly of much later date), which was still being read with approval in the Renaissance period and later.

An alternative approach to the myths was to explain them in allegorical terms—a method in which the Stoics in particular excelled. Thus it was possible for them to explain the traditional gods as natural phenomena : Zeus as the sky, Hera as the air,

---

[7] Quoted in Baillie, *The Interpretation of Religion* (1928), p. 110f.

[8] But this was mere description. Roman writing on the subject of, for instance, Judaism shows how far the Romans were from attempting to understand other religious traditions. Cf. Reinach, *Textes d'auteurs Grecs et Romains relatifs au Judaisme* (1895).

Demeter as the earth, and so on—a method which was to arouse distant echoes in the work of Max Müller and the 'nature mythology' school at the end of the nineteenth century. Stoic allegorical moralism was primarily concerned with the native Greek material; but in one case, that of Plutarch's *De Iside et Osiride*, we can see it to some extent being applied to 'foreign' data. Plutarch certainly showed great knowledge of the religious material of Egypt and Persia, and without Plutarch, we should scarcely be able to claim to understand the important Egyptian myth of Osiris; but his constant comparisons between Greek and Egyptian myths are less than convincing, particularly when he uses supposed etymological derivations and connections.[9]

It was in opposition to the Stoic method that Euhemerus (*c.* 330–*c.* 260 B.C.) had written his fantastic novel *Hiera anagraphê* (The sacred inscription). In it he had told of a sea-voyage, on which he had visited the land of Panchaia, in the Indian Ocean; there he had found a temple of Zeus, containing a pillar on which had been written (by Zeus himself) the story of the gods. The burden of the inscription was that the gods had been men and women of ancient times, who had distinguished themselves in various ways, and had come to be worshipped as gods even while still living, a practice which continued after their death. So Aphrodite had been the first courtesan, worshipped by her lover Cinyras; Cadmos was cook to the king of Sidon; Harmonia was a flautist. The explanation was ingenious, and came to be widely accepted as a feasible account of the origin of religion. 'Euhemerism' in one or another form is found in Cicero, in the Church Fathers, in Snorri Sturluson, in David Hume, in Herbert Spencer and in Sigmund Freud.[10]

By the dawn of the Christian era, then, the Mediterranean world was already able to draw on a long tradition of critical examination of accepted religion, particularly in Greece, and had seen many attempts to provide a a rational explanation of religious phenomena—sometimes with the help of external traditions, sometimes without. The classical Olympian tradition of Greece was long moribund; and its Roman equivalent, though it provided a useful focus for patriotism, was scarcely better placed. In their stead, a stream of cults, drawn from every part of the then known world, was beginning to penetrate the popular mind. Some of the foreign religions, as they had become known to the successive empires of Greece and Rome, had already aroused the interest of intellectuals, and useful

---

[9] Jastrow, *The Study of Religion* (1901), p. 5.

[10] On the subject of the extraordinary tenacity of Euhemerism, see Seznec, *The Survival of the Pagan Gods* (Eng. tr. 1953), pp. 11ff.

descriptive work had begun. The Greek mind was characterised by its quality of curiosity, and perhaps as Dr. Johnson suspected, by not taking its religion too seriously;[11] the Hebraic mind, which entered the lists of world history with the spread of Christianity, took its religion very seriously indeed, and as a result had quite different priorities.

*   *   *

The Judaeo-Christian attitude of exclusiveness and intolerance in matters of religion contrasted sharply with the Hellenic attitude of curiosity and intellectual hospitality. The roots of this are to be traced far back into the history of Israel, to the period when the existence of Israel as a nation, being bound up with the maintenance of the pure worship of Yahweh, was considered to be threatened by the worship of 'other gods', notably the gods and goddesses of Canaan.

The Old Testament represents the Israelites as inveterate idolaters, despite the divine injunction, 'You shall have no other gods before me . . .' (Ex. 20 :3-4). And throughout the Old Testament there is an intensive polemic against such apostasy. To be sure, there is a measure of recognition of the *existence* of gods other than Yahweh, and of their proper sphere of influence within their own nations (in e.g. Micah 4 :1-5); but what might be tolerable in the non-Israelite world was utterly intolerable in the nation to whom Yahweh had revealed himself, and with whom Yahweh had made his covenant.

Accordingly the prophets in particular castigate the worship of other gods as 'adultery' (Ezek. 16), while the images of the gods themselves are called by Jeremiah 'scarecrows in a cucumber field' (10 :5)—useless and powerless objects which can neither walk, speak nor stand without support (cf. Ps. 115 :3-8).

Alternatively, the other gods might be regarded as daemons or evil spirits, as in Psalm 106 :

[11] 'Sir, they disputed with good humour, because they were not in earnest as to religion. Had the ancients been serious in their belief, we should not have had their Gods exhibited in the manner we find them in the Poets. The people would not have suffered it. They disputed with good humour upon their fanciful theories, because they were not interested in the truth of them: when a man has nothing to lose, he may be in good humour with his opponent.' Boswell, *The Life of Dr. Johnson*, vol. 2 (Everyman ed. 1949), p. 10.

> They did not destroy the peoples,
>   as the Lord commanded them,
> but they mingled with the nations
>   and learned to do as they did.
> They served their idols,
>   which became a snare to them.
> They sacrificed their sons
>   and their daughters to the demons . . .
>
> (Ps. 106 : 34–7)

It is unnecessary to point out that such attitudes virtually ruled out even the possibility of objective study of other religions. Such data as the Old Testament provides about the beliefs and practices of surrounding peoples come entirely incidentally in the context of polemics, aimed at demonstrating the worthlessness of idolatry in relation to the pure and spiritual covenant relationship between Yahweh and his chosen people.[12] In other words, the Jewish scriptures offer only an *interpretatio Israelitica* of other forms of religion as means of salvation. As such, they are inevitably found wanting.

The Christian Church took over this view of other religions, and developed it in relation to the new covenant established by God with the Church as the New Israel. Again, there is in the New Testament a total lack of objective interest in other religious traditions as such. Although the Christian Gospel, as the good news of the new aeon, is addressed 'to you and to your children and to all that are afar off' (Acts 2 :39), salvation is to be gained only through faith in Jesus Christ; '. . . there is salvation in no one else, for there is no other name under heaven given among men by which we must be saved' (Acts 4 :12).

The tendency in the New Testament, then, is not to contest the *existence* of other gods and forms of worship, but to stress that for the Christian, it is fatal to enter into any kind of relationship, however superficial, with them. An illustration of this attitude is provided by Paul's condemnation of Christian participation in the Hellenistic mystery cults :

Consider the practice of Israel : are not those who eat the sacrifices partners in the altar? What do I imply then? That food offered to idols is anything, or that an idol is anything? No, I imply that what pagans sacrifice they offer to demons and not to God. I do not want you to be partners with demons. (1 Cor. 10 :18–20).

---

[12] Kaufmann, *The Religion of Israel* (Eng. tr. 1960), pp. 13ff.

It might be argued that, theologically speaking, such practices were the result of 'ignorance' (Acts 17 :30) as long as they were carried out by non-Christians, and that in some obscure way the non-Christian was worshipping the Christian God without knowing it; or that the *logos* ('word') of God was working in some way in other forms of religion; but there is never the slightest suggestion in the New Testament that other religions *as actually practised* could ever be other than competitors to Christianity.

Competition there was, of course, and the early Church found it necessary to be constantly defending its frontiers against alternative soteriologies—either by defining its own position with greater and greater exactness, or by attacking other religions, and particularly the Hellenistic mysteries. The period of the great apologists, commencing in the second century, saw considerable interest taken by Christianity in the pagan cults (the writings of the apologists indeed serving as a valuable source for our knowledge of those cults), and witnessed a proliferation of theories to account for them.

The chief of these theories was thoroughly biblical—that other religions were the work of fallen angels or other evil spirits; such is the view expressed by, among others, Justin Martyr, Tatian, Minucius Felix, Tertullian and Cyprian.[13] Only in the case of the Alexandrian school of Clement and Origen, at a somewhat later stage, was this theory complemented (but not replaced) by an interpretation of truth as the operation of the *logos spermatikos*, 'the seminal word' (a concept borrowed from the Stoics); this led to a more favourable interpretation of at least the more ethically respectable among the non-Christian philosophers. But even the eirenic Clement of Alexandria could be severe in his attacks on the mystery cults, which he expounds only to expose :

> The wicked, crawling wild beast makes slaves of men . . . he rivets them to stocks, stones and suchlike idols, by the miserable chain of daemon-worship; then he takes and buries them alive . . . until they also, men and idols together, suffer corruption.[14]
> The mysteries . . . are mere custom and vain opinion, and it is the deceit of the serpent that men worship when, with spurious piety, they turn towards these sacred initiations that are really profanities, and solemn rites that are without sanctity.[15]

Further, although Clement certainly believed that 'there is one river

---

[13] Pinard de la Boullaye, op. cit., p. 55.
[14] *Exhortation* I (Loeb edition p. 19).
[15] *Exhortation* II (Loeb edition p. 45).

of truth, but many streams fall into it on this side and on that',[16] and that philosophy is '. . . the clear image of truth, a divine gift to the Greeks',[17] nevertheless he found it necessary to stress that even philosophers '. . . are children, unless they have been made men by Christ'.[18] Religions and mythologies are great irrelevancies, or worse :

> So, then, the barbarian and Hellenic philosophy has torn off a fragment of eternal truth not from the mythology of Dionysus, but from the theology of the ever-living Word.[19]

Clement was prepared to admit the greatest Greek philosophers, foremost among them Plato, to the fellowship of the Truth, and in this he was followed in large measure by the Greek-speaking branch of the Church. The Latin Fathers, on the other hand, taking their lead from Augustine and Tertullian, rather than from Clement, followed Paul along the path of strict exclusiveness, 'Hebraic', rather than 'Hellenic'. It was this Hebraic view which was to determine the future of comparative religious studies in the West for centuries to come, by ensuring that comparison should lead only to radical contrast.

At this point the conflict which is already apparent between an 'open' and a 'closed' view of other religions can perhaps be defined as one of philosophy *versus* cult. The Greek philosophers were committed to a quest for information, and a quest for truth; the Christian theologians were committed to a soteriology, and within a cultic framework to a quest for perfection. Both found themselves in contact with other forms of belief, and reacted in radically opposite ways, one positively, the other negatively. Although it may be something of an over-simplification, it might perhaps be maintained that in so far as Western civilisation is a product of these two forces—forces from the first in tension—so the comparative study of religion has tended to oscillate uneasily between two poles, depending on whether the study has been carried out from inside or from outside the Christian (or other) cultic community. At all events, the potential conflict should not be underestimated. We shall meet it repeatedly in the pages that follow.

*   *   *

In the Christian Church, the Middle Ages were characterised by doctrinal debate, by conflict with the rapidly expanding Islam in

[16] *Strom.* 1,5,29.
[17] *Strom.* 1, 2.
[18] *Strom.* 1, 11.
[19] *Strom.* 1, 13.

the south, and by steady missionary progress among the Germanic and other tribes in the north. Practically no study of other religions was carried out during these centuries, other than for purposes of refutation and ultimate conquest. The biblical and post-biblical theories of the origin of the non-Christian religions as devilry or as the work of fallen angels held sway throughout. Not that the Church was not prepared to use certain features of 'paganism', however. Pope Gregory the Great's celebrated letter to Abbot Mellitus in 601, containing instructions for the missionary Augustine of Canterbury, may serve as a case in point:

> [Bishop Augustine] is to destroy the idols, but the temples themselves are to be aspersed with holy water, altars set up, and relics enclosed in them. For if these temples are well built, they are to be purified from devil-worship, and dedicated to the service of the true God . . .[20]

The devil might not share in the truth, but why should he have all the watertight buildings?

Although Christians were not seriously interested in other religions, except as opponents to be overcome, there were a number of Muslim writers of the period whose work is deserving of mention—writers who attempted to describe or otherwise confront those religions to which Islam was opposed. Tabari (838–923) wrote about Persian religion; Mas'udi (d. 956) about Judaism, Christianity and the religions of India; and Alberuni (973–c. 1050) about India and Persia. The honour of writing the first history of religion in world literature seems in fact to belong to the Muslim Shahrastani (d. 1153), whose *Religious Parties and Schools of Philosophy* describes and systematises all the religions of the then known world, as far as the boundaries of China. This outstanding work far outstrips anything which Christian writers were capable of producing at the same period.[20a]

The first relatively accurate descriptions of the religions of northern Europe are, however, to be found in the work of Christian chroniclers, such as Adam of Bremen, whose *Gesta Hammaburgensis ecclesiae pontificum* was written in about 1075, and Saxo Grammaticus, whose *Gesta Danorum* dates from around 1210. Of somewhat later date is the *Gylfaginning* (or *Prose Edda*) of the Icelandic courtier Snorri Sturluson (d. 1241), in which an attempt is made to

[20] Bede, *A History of the English Church and People* (tr. Sherley-Price, 1955), p. 86.
[20a] Mention might also be made of Ibn Kammuna's *An Examination of the Three Faiths* (1280), written by a Baghdad Jew. The 'three faiths' are Judaism, Christianity and Islam.

describe the origins and nature of the Scandinavian mythological tradition, partly with the help of the theory of Euhemerism. Snorri was writing as a Christian; nevertheless his work has always been invaluable for the study of Nordic mythology.

Otherwise, Christian philosophers and theologians had little to offer to the study of religion 'in the round'. One of the few partial exceptions was the Franciscan Roger Bacon (1214–1294), whose *Opus majus*, completed in 1266 (but not in fact published until 1733) contains a classification of the adherents of all known religions into six categories: Pagans, Idolaters, Tartars, Saracens, Jews and Christians. It is perhaps not without significance that Bacon produced this work as a defence against charges of sorcery and heresy, for as Basil Willey has written, in the Middle Ages, '. . . Nature was full of pagan divinities turned devils, and to meddle with it was to risk damnation'.[21]

On the political front, the chief religions which Christianity was facing were, of course, Judaism and Islam, neither of which was viewed at all dispassionately. Judaism in Christian eyes was regarded with a mixture of pity and disgust; Islam with a mixture of fear and hatred : neither was known accurately. It is hardly surprising, for instance, that the Crusades failed to provide anything save fresh stores of fuel with which to feed the flames of old controversy; nevertheless, their very failure to achieve anything of lasting political or religious worth led indirectly to attempts to understand Islam. It seems that the first step in this peaceful crusade was taken in 1411 by Peter the Venerable, Abbot of Cluny, who, while travelling in Spain, commissioned Latin translations of the *Qur'an* and a *Disputation of a Saracen and a Christian of Arabia concerning the Law of the Saracens and the Christian Faith.*[22] Determined attempts to achieve a more accurate understanding of Islam were also made, along roughly the same lines, by the celebrated Ramon Lull[23] and by Ricoldo da Monte di Croce, author of *Liber peregrinacionis* and *Confutatio Alcorani*—though the latter's description of Muhammad as an epileptic robber chieftain does not suggest that sympathy was a necessary prelude to understanding.

The period from the thirteenth to the fifteenth centuries, beginning with the travels of Marco Polo, saw the extension of the missionary effort of the Church of Rome into the Far East, notably through the labours of the Franciscan and Benedictine Orders. The result was a new influx into the West of material concerning the religions of peoples from Persia to China, material which, when

---

[21] Willey, *The Eighteenth Century Background* (1962), p. 12.
[22] Pinard de la Boullaye, op. cit., p. 126.
[23] Allan, *Christianity among the Religions* (1961), pp. 14ff.

combined with new modes of inquiry into the foundations of religious philosophy, posed considerable problems for Christendom. The Scholastic philosopher-theologians had their own way of meeting this challenge; as a rule, the imperfectly-known non-Christian religions of the world were relegated to the categories of idolatry, superstition and falsehood, in contrast to the one true revelation of God which was to be found in the teachings of the Christian Church. John Baillie notes that '. . . the scholastic doctors were rather fond of engaging in a sort of dialectical thrust-and-parry with an imaginary Jew or Saracen or sometimes even with an imaginary pagan'. But he adds that '. . . on the whole the Middle Ages preferred the sword to dialectics when dealing with such opponents'.[24] Nevertheless St. Thomas Aquinas was one who held that the faults of these religions sprang from defective reasoning, and might be corrected. The Greek philosophers, on the other hand, needed less correction.

Thus throughout the Middle Ages, 'paganism' was a vast empty space on the religion map of the world, on which might be written, 'here be monsters', while one practical illustration of the lengths to which ignorance might go is to be seen in that hideously garbled version of the life of the Buddha which resulted in the creation of the entirely fictitious Christian Saints Barlaam and Joasaph.[25]

* * *

By the scholarly world of the Renaissance and the Reformation, the non-Christian religions were still regarded, as the Middle Ages had regarded them, as consisting essentially of Judaism, Islam and paganism. But two new elements were introduced into the picture with, first, the revival of interest in the world of classical mythology, and secondly, the great voyages of exploration. In Italy, interest in Roman antiquity had always been latent, but became explicit during the fifteenth century, particularly after the fall of Constantinople in 1453 and the subsequent influx of Greek scholars into Italy. The humanism of the Renaissance was founded on the belief that the individual could best develop under the guidance of the masters of classical culture, and thus took the form of a largely literary movement. Renaissance values were primarily aesthetic rather than religious; so while a vast body of classical material was added to the storehouse of Western learning, even such an outstanding representative of the tradition as Erasmus of Rotterdam (1466–1536) did

[24] Baillie, *The Interpretation of Religion* (1928), p. 111.
[25] Probably the work of St. John Damascene. See the edition of Barlaam and Joasaph in the Loeb Classical Library (1953). cf. *DCR*, p. 130.

little but note parallels between Christian and classical beliefs and practices, and recapitulate the arguments of Clement of Alexandria for allowing a place for the Greek philosophers within the Christian scheme of things. When the religions of Greece and Rome were studied, this study centred on the developed and sophisticated mythologies—seen at its best in such a work as Boccaccio's *De genealogis deorum gentilium* (written in 1375 but first published in 1532).

The great voyages of exploration of the fifteenth, sixteenth and seventeenth centuries took Christians into a far different and much more real world—the world of 'paganism', previously believed to be scarcely worthy of attention.[26] America in particular held its surprises : brilliant and highly developed cultures, described graphically by Spanish and Portuguese writers such as Sahagun, Acosta and Garcilasso de la Vega. Of course religion received much attention, though little sympathy. In fact these writings remained until the nineteenth century almost our only source of knowledge about pre-Columbian American civilisation. The East Indies, too, were being opened up, and elsewhere worlds of pagan belief and custom were coming more and more into the purview of the West.

Despite its great services in the area of Greco-Roman literature and philosophy, the Renaissance did little to provide the West with a more broadly-based study of religion. The Reformers did even less. Although Martin Luther developed more than a casual interest in Islam, and had Ricoldo's *Confutatio Alcorani* translated into German, he did so less out of any desire to understand Islam as such than simply to counteract the influence of a phenomenon which was in his view emphatically not the Gospel of justification by faith alone.[27] Of the other great Reformers, it was perhaps Zwingli who showed most interest in at least the Greek philosophical tradition, very much in the spirit of Erasmus. But the Reformation was a concern of Christian Churches, and so much energy was expended on the reconstruction of Christian belief that the world outside was apt to receive little attention. A similar observation might be made, with even more justification, of the post-Reformation period in the Protestant Churches, dominated as it was, first by what has been called 'post-Reformation Scholasticism' or 'Orthodoxy', and somewhat later by the increasing Pietist reaction. However, the Pietist movement was to lead in due course to a development of the utmost

---

[26] Geoffroy Atkinson, *Les Relations de voyages de 17e siècle et l'évolution des idées* (1926).
[27] On this subject, see Holsten, *Christentum und nicht-christliche Religion nach der Auffassung Luthers* (1932), esp. pp. 126ff.

importance for the comparative study of religion—the rise of the modern missionary movement.[28]

*   *   *

On the Roman Catholic side, one of the results of the Counter-Reformation was the establishment of the Society of Jesus and the extension of Christian missionary work into North America, the Far East, India and China. The Indian mission is of only slight importance in this context, though the name of Roberto de Nobili is deserving of honourable mention as one of the first Christian missionaries ever to identify himself thoroughly and unquestioningly with a non-Christian tradition, in this case Brahmanical Hinduism.[29] Of much greater importance was the China mission inaugurated by the Jesuit Matteo Ricci (1552–1610), because it provided the Age of Reason with material on which to base a thoroughgoing comparison of religions.[30]

Ricci was impressed from the very first by the rational mind of the Chinese, and was convinced that the teachings of Confucius on the nature of God were essentially similar to those of the Christian Church; he believed that Confucius had instructed his followers to worship, not the visible sky, but the invisible God, the Lord of Heaven, and that this could without difficulty be interpreted in Christian terms. Ricci was only the first of a number of Christian commentators who made similar observations about the nature of Chinese religion, and the Sinological literature of the seventeenth century flourished. Not only were books written about China : the classical Chinese scriptures were translated, with or without commentary, and came to occupy a position as important as it was unexpected in the religious debates of Western Europe.[31] For the 'religion' of China, without mysteries, without 'priestcraft', and inculcating a lofty moral ideal, provided—or appeared to provide—a welcome proof that, as certain European savants were claiming, the essence of religion was of precisely this nature, and that all later elaborations on this simple theme were both unnecessary and undesirable.[32]

---

[28] cf. below, pp. 151–4.

[29] Vincent Cronin, *A Pearl to India* (1959).

[30] On Ricci, see Vincent Cronin, *The Wise Man from the West* (1955).

[31] Among the most outstanding of the seventeenth-century books on China and Japan may be mentioned Trigautius, *Literae Soc. Jesu e regno Sinarum* (1615), Varen, *Descriptio regni Japoniae* (1649), and Kircher, *China monumentis qua sacris qua profanis* (1667).

[32] On Deism, see Pinard de la Boullaye, pp. 215ff., and Willey, *The Seventeenth-Century Background* (1962), pp. 111ff.

Deism, as this European theological fashion is named, began as a coherent form of theology with the publication, in 1625, of Lord Herbert of Cherbury's *De veritate*. In considering Lord Herbert, writes Basil Willey :

> It must be remembered that the old simple situation, in which Christendom pictured itself as the world, with only the foul paynim outside and the semi-tolerated Jews within the gates, had passed away for ever. Exploration and commerce had widened the horizon, and in many writers of the [seventeenth] century one can see that the religions of the East, however imperfectly known, were beginning to press upon the European consciousness. It was a pioneer-interest in these religions, together with the customary preoccupation of Renaissance scholars with the mythologies of classical antiquity, which led Lord Herbert to seek a common denominator for all religions, and thus to provide, as he hoped, the much-needed eirenicon for seventeenth-century disputes.[33]

This 'common denominator' was partly to be discovered by a neo-Stoic process similar to the 'inner light' of later Quakerism, and not altogether different from the 'witness of the Holy Spirit' in the Calvinist tradition; but it also meant seeking for the *quod semper, quod ubique, quod ab omnibus* of all the accessible religions of the world. The content of this common denominator, which Lord Herbert attempted to outline in his book *De religione gentilium* (1663; Eng. tr. 1705), resolved itself into five points : (i) that there is a Supreme Power external to the world; (ii) that this Power is to be worshipped; (iii) that worship consists not in outward ceremony, but in piety and holiness; (iv) that sin can be expiated; and (v) that there will be rewards and punishments after this life.

The Deist position came later to be reinforced by the work of the versatile Gottfried Wilhelm Leibniz (1646–1716), whose studies began in philosophy and law, but who subsequently branched out into many other areas, scientific as well as humanistic. In his *Essai de théodicée* (1710) and other works, he expressed the confident view that, since this is the best of all possible worlds, evil can only be a temporary shadow on a bright landscape : the world, with all its variety and *inter alia* all its religious traditions, is bound for perfection within the laws of God.[34] With Leibniz we come to the threshold of that period in Western intellectual history which we label the Enlightenment (*Aufklärung*), with its typical emphases on

[33] Willey, op. cit., p. 114.
[34] Leibniz also corresponded with missionaries in China.

individual freedom of intellectual inquiry and personal commitment to reason; while among subsequent scholars influenced by Leibniz we may mention in particular Friedrich Max Müller.

Deism as a whole was important in the prehistory of comparative religion in that it seriously put forward a set of criteria by which religion might be judged, without calling in any kind of belief in revelation. Chinese religion was for many decades its paradigm. It came to be believed all over Europe, and especially in France and Germany, that China had actually *lived* 'natural religion'. Mosaic and Chinese chronologies were compared, not always to the former's advantage. In 1721, an outstanding representative of the German *Aufklärung*, Christian Wolff of Halle (1679–1754), a disciple of Leibniz, devoted a festival oration to the subject *De sapientia Sinensium*, stressing that Confucius was merely the restorer of ancient Chinese wisdom. Later admirers of China included Goethe and Voltaire, who stated in his *Essai sur l'esprit et les moeurs des nations* (1754) that in his opinion, Confucius was as noble and as strict as Epictetus, and wrote in 1770 to the Emperor Frederick II of Prussia : 'Sire, vous et le roi de la Chine vous êtes à présent les deux seuls souverains qui soient philosophes et poètes.'[35]

Apart from their predilection for *Chinoiserie*, the seventeenth and early eighteenth centuries saw the publication of an increasing stream of books dealing with some of the other newly-discovered religions of the world. Persia came to the notice of the West as a result of the travels of Henry Lord, Chinon and Chardin, all of whom published books on the subject. Edward Brerewood published in 1614 *Enquiries touching the diversity of Languages and Religions through the chief Parts of the World*, John Selden *De diis Syriis* in 1617; in 1653 appeared Alexander Ross's *Pansebeia, or a View of all Religions in the World*, and in 1685 John Spencer's *De legibus Hebraeorum ritualibus*, a book which W. Robertson Smith later claimed—though with some exaggeration—'to have laid the foundations of the Science of Comparative Religion', by virtue of its method of comparing Biblical evidence with other Semitic material.[36]

It was, however, characteristic of European rationalism, from Leibniz to Lessing and Voltaire, that it was interested in other

---

[35] Quoted by Nathan Söderblom, *Gudstrons uppkomst* (1914), p. 314. The chapter 'Frambringaretron i Europa' (pp. 286–324) covers this entire subject. Note especially the comment on p. 322: 'It was not by chance that belief in reason entered the courts of Europe at the same time as rococo, the pig-tail and Chinese pavilions.'

[36] W. Robertson Smith, *The Religion of the Semites* (3rd ed. 1927), p. xiv. cf. H. P. Smith, *Essays in Biblical Interpretation* (1921), pp. 106ff.

religions less for their own sake than for the support which it found, or claimed to find, in them for its own theories. The rationalists were concerned only with what could be demonstrated by reason, explaining away other elements in religion as best they might; their interest in history was less genuine than it was claimed to be, and they had very little capacity for placing religious traditions in their proper cultural contexts.

Among the religious traditions of the world, on the whole least was known about what the West had so far been content to describe as 'paganism'—that vast and murky area of the religious beliefs and practices of the world's pre-literate peoples. But although the doctrine of the Great Chain of Being (still widely accepted in the eighteenth century) made it appear doubtful whether the pre-literate peoples should be regarded as human beings at all,[37] factual information about their customs and beliefs was constantly coming to the notice of the West. To take only one example, the work of the Jesuit missionaries in Nouvelle France, as embodied in the seventy-one volumes of the *Jesuit Relations*, shed a flood of light on religion in the Iroquois and Algonkian cultures. One of their number, Father Lafitau, published in 1724 a book entitled *Moeurs des sauvages Amériquains comparées aux moeurs des premiers temps*, which attempted, with some success, to treat this new material along comparative lines. It was, as Hultkrantz has pointed out, Lafitau's version of North American Indian religion which was accepted by eighteenth-century Europe.[38]

However, it was Charles de Brosses' book *Du culte des dieux fétiches* (1760), which provided the West with a word for it all. That word was 'fetishism', and was to prove extraordinarily long-lived as a description of the religion of pre-literate man, based as it appears to be on 'fetishes' (manufactured or found objects).[39] It was finally displaced in the 1860s by E. B. Tylor's term 'animism', though it was subsequently resurrected by Sigmund Freud as a des-

---

[37] 'No history of the biological sciences in the eighteenth century can be adequate which fails to keep in view the fact that, for most men of science throughout that period, the theories implicit in the conception of the Great Chain of Being continued to constitute essential presuppositions in the framing of scientific hypotheses.' A. O. Lovejoy, *The Great Chain of Being* (1936), p. 227. The observation is equally applicable to the field of the social sciences—and the study of religion—before the coming of evolutionism.

[38] Hultkrantz, 'North American Indian Religion in the History of Research', in *History of Religions* (1966), p. 93.

[39] Fetishism '. . . is simply the worship of nature, not in its grandest and most sublime aspect as seen in the movements of the heavenly bodies, but in the common objects that everywhere present themselves around us.' J. Gardner (ed.), *Faiths of the World* (n.d., c. 1890), I, p. 890.

cription of something quite different. Another significant book from
the same period is Bergier's *L'Origine des dieux de paganisme* (1767),
which in a sense anticipates the later theory of animism. De Brosses
and Bergier agree on one thing, that paganism is characterised by
infantile folly, and that whatever else they may or may not need,
certainly the 'savages' need to grow up.

Only a few years earlier than the appearance of de Brosses' book,
David Hume had published his *Natural History of Religion* (1755),
which was a determined attempt to break free from current speculations about natural religion. Hume held that, so far from religion
having originated in a sublime moral sense of deity, it had begun
on a barbaric level, with the barbaric emotion of fear. 'The primary
religion of mankind,' he wrote, 'arises chiefly from an anxious fear
of future events.'[40] The emotions which give rise to religion he elsewhere lists as '. . . the anxious concern for happiness, the dread
of future misery, the terror of death, the thirst of revenge, the
appetite for food and other necessaries.'[41] This lowest stage of religion
is polytheism, which Hume illustrates partly from 'primitive' races,
but more from classical sources. On the whole he was not impressed,
characterising polytheism as 'sick men's dreams', and (in the context
of the Great Chain of Being) as 'the playsome whimsies of monkies
in human shape'.[42] Eventually, however, in the history of mankind
nobler notions prevailed :

> The mind rises gradually, from inferior to superior : By abstract-
> ing from what is imperfect, it forms an idea of perfection : And
> slowly distinguishing the nobler parts of its own frame from the
> grosser, it learns only to transfer the former, much elevated and
> refined, to its divinity.[43]

Here we are approaching one side of the later evolutionary hypothesis.

The Age of Reason also saw some of the first of those compendia
of comparative religious study which were to become so common in
the late nineteenth and early twentieth centuries. For obvious
reasons, few of these early compendia have more than historical
interest. Examples include Picard and Bernard, *Cérémonies et
coutumes religieuses de tous les peuples du monde* (1723–43), C. F.
Dupuis, *Origine de tous les cultes* (1795), and somewhat later, the
five volumes of Benjamin Constant, *De la religion* (1824–31).

*   *   *

[40] Hume, *The Natural History of Religion* (ed. Root, 1956), p. 65.
[41] ibid., p. 28.
[42] ibid., p. 75.
[43] ibid., p. 24.

The first decades of the nineteenth century saw a widespread reaction against the rationalism of the *Enlightenment* : instead of reason and liberty, enthroned by the French Revolution, the new age decreed that 'feeling' and imagination, intuition and personal integrity were to be the pillars of human life. These qualities were all such as to inspire voyages of discovery into remote corners of the human mind : not only into strange and exotic cultures, such as that of India, but into the equally strange and exotic world of the European past. Instead of being interpreted purely in terms of reason, religion came to be seen as an inward experience, self-authenticating, conditioned subjectively and determined by feeling. This was a corrective which rationalism needed; but it was soon apparent that it could lead to much distortion in the opposite direction. However, the 'romantic revival' did supply the West with a sense of history, and with a feeling for the irrational in religion.[44]

The former was supplied by Herder and Hegel on the philosophical level, and by Sir Walter Scott and his lesser imitators on the popular level; the latter supremely by Schleiermacher. Herder's *Ideen zur Philosophie der Geschichte der Menschheit* (1784–91) (Ideas concerning the philosophy and history of mankind) introduced the idea of progress into the study of religion, placed the secular and religious phases in human history on the same footing, and accorded equal importance to the irrational as to the rational in human history. Herder claimed that the mind perceives the world intuitively, and that history is the study of the self-expression of minds. In Hegel's vast historical and philosophical synthesis the religious traditions of the world were placed on various rungs of a developmental ladder, culminating in Christianity as 'the Religion of Absolute Finality'.[45] A similar view was expressed by Schleiermacher, who, apart from defining religion in terms of absolute personal dependence, also ranged the religions on an evolutionary ladder, again with Christianity at its peak. He also established the principle by which each religious tradition should be viewed as a *necessary* manifestation of the encounter between man and the infinite; although Schleiermacher himself was of course writing for Christians, and recommending them to evaluate religion from within their own particular brand of Christianity (a piece of advice later taken with great seriousness), his work had one further important consequence : in time students of religion were led along these

---

[44] For a discussion of this element in relation to the work of Rudolf Otto, see below, pp. 162–6.

[45] Chantepie de la Saussaye, *Lehrbuch der Religionsgeschichte* (1887), p. 3; Schmidt, *The Origin and Growth of Religion* (Eng. tr. 1931), p. 33.

paths to attempt to understand each separate religious tradition on its own specific premises.

If the fifteenth and sixteenth centuries are to be seen as the great pioneer age of classical studies, and the seventeenth and eighteenth centuries as a period of vast, though often uncritical, interest in China and Chinese religion, the early nineteenth century was the period of the discovery of the ancient Near East and the Indo-European awakening.

The last two years of the eighteenth century were the years of Bonaparte's Egyptian expedition. It was in the course of this expedition that Bouchard discovered the Rosetta Stone, which permitted Champollion to decipher Egyptian hieroglyphics; the monumental *Description de l'Egypte* was published in twenty volumes between 1809 and 1822. The floodgates were thereby opened, not only to scholarship, but also to all manner of speculation about the Egyptian origins of Western civilisation and religion. The disclosure of the ancient cultures of Assyria and Babylonia began in 1811 with the visit of James Rich, and continued under Botta and Layard, while Rawlinson and Oppert had deciphered the cuneiform script by the middle of the century. Similar patterns repeated themselves throughout the century in various parts of the world; but by the nature of things, philological and archaeological studies were liable to become highly compartmentalised and (bearing in mind the dominant Christian orthodoxies of the West, in which the attitude of the Middle Ages toward non-Christian religions was being effectively perpetuated) there were few scholars prepared to draw wide conclusions from the mass of accumulating evidence.

However, a potentially far different situation, containing far greater possibilities for comparative historical understanding of specific religious traditions, was developing in Indian, Persian and Germanic studies. Britain had had a secure foothold in India since the middle of the eighteenth century, and towards the end of the century, thanks to the work of such scholars as Sir William Jones, H. T. Colebrook, Charles Wilkins and (a little later) Horace Hayman Wilson, certain of the Hindu religious classics were beginning to be edited and translated. Wilkins published the first English translation of the *Bhagavad Gītā* in 1785, Jones a translation of *Shakuntala* in 1789 and of *The Laws of Manu* in 1794; the French adventurer Anquetil du Perron published a Latin translation (from the Persian) of some fifty *Upanishads* in 1802; in Pinard de la Boullaye's words, 'L'élan était donné.'[46] 1808 saw the appearance of Schlegel's *Ueber*

---

[46] Pinard de la Boullaye, op. cit., p. 249. On the development of Indological studies, see also L. von Schroeder, 'Ueber die Entwicklung der Indologie in Europa,' in *Reden und Aufsätze* (1913), pp. 128–46.

die Sprache und die Weisheit der Indier (Concerning the language
and the wisdom of the Indians), a confused work, but one in which
a real intellectual relationship between Europe and India was
mooted, and a second Renaissance prophesied. The first Chair of
Sanskrit was established at Paris in 1814, and in 1822 the Paris
Société asiatique was founded. But it was the publication in 1816 of
Bopp's comparative grammar of the Sanskrit, Greek, Latin, Persian
and Germanic languages that ushered in the new age of comparative
'Indo-European' studies, and ultimately the still newer 'science of
religion', or comparative religion. Here for the first time was a
demonstrable scientific link between the old and respected discipline
of Classics, and the newer areas of Indology and Germanic studies,
which was capable of replacing the dilettantism and haphazard
quality of past comparative work. The link was one of language;
but establish a link between language and culture, and who could
tell what might not be achieved.

The third of these constituents, Germanic studies, or *Germanistik*,
began (and in many ways continued) as an offshoot of North
German and Scandinavian nationalism, and as an element in that
romantic concern for the past which is so well illustrated in the
English-speaking world by the work of Sir Walter Scott and in the
German-speaking world by Grimm's *Deutsche Mythologie* (Teutonic
mythology, 1832). Interest was often centred on the tradition of
myths, and on their interpretation, particularly in the continuing
tradition of popular belief. This was the main concern of 'folklore', in many ways a typical Romantic science.

Of the more general works written at this time we may mention
Georg Friedrich Creuzer's *Symbolik and Mythologie der alten
Völker* (Symbolism and mythology of the ancient peoples, 1810
et seq.); Christian August Lobeck's *Aglaophamus* (1829), which laid
the foundations of much later work on the Greek mysteries;
Christoph Meiners' *Allgemeine kritische Geschichte der Religionen*
(General critical history of religions, 1806-1807), which Gerardus
van der Leeuw reckoned as the first work of the phenomenology of
religion[47]; and Karl Otfried Müller's *Prolegomena zu einer wissen-
schaftlichen Mythologie* (Prolegomena to a scientific mythology,
1825), a book which deserves its title, being genuinely scientific in
method, though it deals with only the Greek material. Throughout
the early years of the nineteenth century, then, more and more far-
reaching comparisons were being made on a general basis of the
Indo-European material—a trend the religious implications of which

[47] G. van der Leeuw, *Religion in Essence and Manifestation* (Eng. tr.
1948), p. 690.

were there for all to see, and which was to reach its climax in the middle of the century in the work of Friedrich Max Müller.

Taken as a whole, these developments had the effect of concentrating the thought of Europe, and particularly Germany, on its own past. Historical method was in the process of being refined and strengthened by such men as Niebuhr and von Ranke, under whose leadership the subject was achieving an entirely new precision, and a more sensitive conscience. But the new European past was not a past in isolation. The past of Europe was the past of Greece and Rome, and also (for those whose horizons were sufficiently wide) the past of India and Persia. The grand synthesis, not unconnected with the fact that India was now the proudest jewel in the British imperial crown, and that one of the official languages of India was still Persian, was intoxicating. It no longer seemed strange that India might have much to contribute to the cultural history of mankind. Just how much was a moot point. But a generation of romantic philosophers was convinced that the study of India, and especially of Indian religion, was a *sine qua non*. To illustrate this, we must retrace our steps slightly, to Anquetil du Perron.

Du Perron's edition of the *Upanishads* had contained much more than mere translation : in true eighteenth-century eclectic style he had advanced elaborate arguments to demonstrate that all true wisdom is one. His text he had expounded with the help of examples drawn from Kant, Adam Smith, the Chinese classics, the religion of the Lapps and (no less significant, in view of one of the directions comparative religion was eventually to take), 'the famous Swedenborg of Uppsala'.[48] Among du Perron's many admirers the best known was undoubtedly Schopenhauer, who saw in this version of the Upanishads not only the deposit of the purest Indian wisdom, but also a means by which the soul might be washed clean of Judaeo-Christian superstition. The Upanishads provide, he wrote in a celebrated passage of *Parerga und Paralipomena*, '. . . the most rewarding and the most elevating reading (the original excepted) the world has to offer. It has been the consolation of my life and will be my consolation when I come to die.'[49]

Sentiments of this order were echoed by little groups of free-thinkers, Unitarians, Transcendentalists and romantics here and there in the Western world. Most represented 'the Romantic Move-

---

[48] Swedenborg, '. . . cujus mysticorum dogmatum cum Indorum doctrina, praesertim quod ad mundorum rationem, comparatione, philosophi 59° 54' latitudinis septrionalis gradu in Suevia, anno 1688 nati, et sapientum in Kaschmiro 33 et 34 gradu, a 4000 annis degentium, systemati, lux quaedam forte affulgebit.' Quoted by Söderblom, *Gudstrons uppkomst* (1914), p. 335.

[49] *Parerga und Paralipomena*, II (1888), p. 427.

ment' in literature; many had been influenced, directly or indirectly, by Swedenborg. In Germany there was Schelling; in Scotland Carlyle; from India came the authoritative voice of Rammohun Roy. Across the Atlantic, the New England Transcendentalists, Emerson, Thoreau and Alcott, read everything the East had to offer by way of translated wisdom, and everything published in which the East was mentioned. But the interest which the Romantics showed in the East was in large measure determined by the support which it gave (or appeared to give) for a certain kind of individual, intuitive philosophy of life. Thoreau wrote, for instance, that

> While the commentators are disputing about the meaning of this word and that, I hear only the resounding of the ancient sea, and put into it all the meaning I am possessed of, the deepest murmurs I can recall, for I do not in the least care where I get my ideas, or what suggests them.[50]

This statement was symptomatic of the Transcendentalists' lack of interest in the history or cultural context of the ideas they were so fond of using; and it may perhaps serve as a paradigm of one (not, in the opinion of many scholars, wholly respectable) type of 'comparative religion'—eclectic, intuitive, frequently inaccurate, resting on the foundations of a highly individual personal philosophy.[51]

But as the nineteenth century advanced, it became increasingly clear that the real focus of the study of religion was to be located, not in transcendental philosophy, but in the altogether this-worldly categories of history, progress development and evolution. The idea of progress was, of course, far from being a new one.[52] Its roots were to be found in the Renaissance, and early exponents were Descartes and Bacon in the early seventeenth century; in the eighteenth and early nineteenth centuries it won ground throughout Europe as a philosophical idea, and notable philosophies of history were constructed on developmental lines by Fichte, Schelling and Hegel in Germany, and by Saint-Simon and Comte in France. Hegel and

[50] Thoreau, *Journal*, VIII, p. 134f., quoted by Christy, *The Orient in American Transcendentalism* (1932), p. 6. cf. Matthiessen, *American Renaissance* (1941), p. 117f.

[51] At the same time it must be allowed that the Transcendentalists made reasonable use of the scholarly opportunities that presented themselves, though these were not great. For instance, Alcott expressed in 1842 the wish that 'a collection of the Sacred Books of all races would be made, that we might have the fullest revelation of God's word, as uttered by the inspired writers of all past time.' Christy, op. cit., p. 10.

[52] See J. B. Bury, *The Idea of Progress* (1920), written from the positivist point of view; and cf. John Baillie, *The Belief in Progress* (1950), the presuppositions of which are Christian.

Comte in particular, in their different ways, established patterns of progress which were to be of the greatest significance for the future course taken by the comparative study of religion. The essential difference between them has been described as follows:

> Hegel's interest in the past was that only through an understanding of its movement could he grasp the eternal nature of reality, while Comte's interest was that it provided him with such laws of historical movement as enabled him at the same time to predict and to influence the future. Hegel writes as if he were standing at the end of historical development, whereas Comte writes as if he himself were preparing the way for its most significant period.[53]

It is arguable that the influence of Hegel upon comparative religion was indirect, though a Hegelian theme came eventually to the surface in the phenomenology of religion; that of Comte, however, was mediated more directly, through the French sociologists and anthropologists, particularly Durkheim and Lévy-Bruhl.

Comte's *magnum opus, Cours de philosophie positive*, was published between 1830 and 1842. There were other reasons why these were highly significant years in the development of nineteenth-century thought. They saw the publication of Lyell's *Principles and Elements of Geology*, in which existing ideas on the origins of the world were virtually turned upside-down. In 1831 Charles Darwin—whose subsequent work was to take up many of the theories of the French natural historian Jean Baptiste Lamarck (d. 1829)—had set sail in the *Beagle* for the South Seas. On a somewhat different level, bearing in mind past controversies and polemics, in 1840 Thomas Carlyle had delivered a celebrated lecture on Muhammad, giving reasons why he should be regarded as a 'hero', rather than as a rogue. But it was the appearance in 1859 of Darwin's book *The Origin of Species* that set the seal on the new evolutionary age. In effect, scientific theory had joined hands in the theory of evolution with a dominant philosophy of history. Neither, on its own, could have made the impact on the popular mind that 'evolution' was so rapidly to achieve; together they conquered the nineteenth century —thanks not least to the use made of them by the great synthesiser Herbert Spencer. The West became obsessively historical, bent on drawing its parallels and pointing its morals on the largest of all canvases, that of the evolution of the world, and within the world, of mankind. The whole of human culture was examined afresh on new principles, with a view to discerning the origins, development and goals of each separate manifestation of the human spirit.

[53] Baillie, *The Belief in Progress*, p. 136.

Religion was no exception; indeed, evolutionary theory was prosecuted in the field of religion with an energy and intensity second to none.

As we shall see, it was approximately a decade before the full impact of the scientific revolution was felt in the field of religious studies. But with Comte, Darwin and Spencer we have come to the threshold of the hundred years of comparative religion which we are to survey. We have seen something of the variety of approaches to the religions of mankind which could be held before the coming of evolutionism : the Christian theological approach, which dealt with the religions under the all-embracing category of divine revelation; the philosophical approach, in which suitable material was pressed into service in the demonstration of a theory or theories; and what we might call the scholarly approach, that of the philologists, historians, archaeologists and others, who were content to cultivate a limited area intensively, perhaps making comparisons along the way, perhaps not.

What was lacking in all this was, however, one single guiding principle of method which was at the same time able to satisfy the demands of history and of science. Evolution was—or seemed to be—precisely that principle.

II

'He who knows one, knows none'

The decade from 1859 to 1869 witnessed the rapid development of an entirely new situation in the world of religious study, a situation over which may be set as a rubric one word, 'evolution'. Before 1859 the student of the religions of the world, although he might have ample motive for his study, and more than enough material on which to base his researches, had no self-evident method for dealing with the material; after 1869, thanks to the developments of the intervening decade, he had the evolutionary method.[1] It would be wrong to assume that all his doubts and perplexities had been swept away overnight (however much this impression might be conveyed by the overconfident writings of some of the early comparative religionists); but he was able to proceed on the assumption that there was no further need for random or haphazard judgements. As the outstanding New Testament scholar and Iranist James Hope Moulton later put it, 'A revelation of the Reign of Law invaded every field of thought.'[2]

The decade began, of course, with the publication of Darwin's *Origin of Species*. Before its end, Herbert Spencer was well started on his elaborate *System of Synthetic Philosophy*, Thomas Huxley had confronted Bishop Wilberforce before the British Association in the name of science, E. B. Tylor had launched his theory of 'animism, Benjamin Disraeli had announced that he was on the side of the angels, J. F. M'Lennan had borrowed the term 'totemism' and set it adrift in the scholarly world, and an expatriate German philologist resident in Oxford, Friedrich Max Müller, had begun to publish a definitive edition of the Sanskrit text of the *Rig Veda*, written a celebrated book on *Comparative Mythology*, and suggested to the English-speaking world that, so far from science and religion being

---

[1] Although challenged in the 1920s, the doctrine continued to dominate studies of religion throughout the inter-war years. S. A. Cook wrote in 1927 that '. . . one can but say that the study of beliefs and customs can only be pursued along evolutionary lines' (Intro. to W. Robertson Smith, *The Religion of the Semites*, 1927, p. xlviii). And in a statement dating from the 1940s the classicist M. P. Nilsson defended the evolutionary position, saying: 'The anti-evolutionists cannot deny evolution in religions which are known historically without falsifying facts . . .' (*Opuscula selecta*, 1960, p. 346f).

[2] Moulton, *Religions and Religion* (1911), p. 7.

irreconcilable opposites, there might be a 'Science of Religion' which would do justice to both. In short, comparative religion (at first a synonym for the science of religion) did not exist in 1859; by 1869 it did.

A few words are necessary at this point about the internecine feud between science and religion, since comparative religion as originally conceived owed much to the positions it created; and also because the 'image' of comparative religion has traditionally been determined, at least in the eyes of the orthodox, by the circumstance that it once appeared to be a variety of unbelief, having (apparently) sided with science in this war. It rested squarely on the evolutionary hypothesis; and the evolutionary hypothesis, because it refused to accept the finality of the then current Christian view of revelation, was anathema.

Broadly speaking, one might 'take religion seriously', then as now, or one might not. In the Europe of the 1860s, to take religion seriously meant taking seriously the need for divine revelation, and the fact of divine revelation. Religion was a divine dispensation, guaranteed either by an infallible book or by a near-infallible church, or by a combination of the two. Certainly the Age of Reason had left its mark, particularly in Britain and Germany, but Pietism had left a much deeper mark, and the name of Schleiermacher pointed (at least in Germany) to a theory of revelation which rested neither on book nor on church, but on the direct testimony of personal experience. But to the religious world generally, 'religion' was something unchangeable, save in externals : a static deposit of the faith once and for all delivered to the saints, capable of accounting with authority for the entire history of mankind and the world. Archbishop Ussher's chronology of the antediluvian world was still in possession of the popular mind, despite the publication, thirty years earlier, of Lyell's *Principles and Elements of Geology*, and despite the spectacular developments in the study of prehistory associated with such names as those of the Danes Thomsen and Worsaae, the Frenchman Boucher de Perthes, and the Englishmen Pengelly and Prestwich. Non-Christian religions, whether ancient or modern, could still for the most part be dismissed (albeit with pity) as the work of the devil, or as proofs of the depths to which the human mind could sink if deprived of the light of Gospel truth. In short, outside the tiny company of the speculative philosophers and theologians, the religions were still judged entirely according to the data of revealed truth. From the Roman Catholic point of view, this meant in practice that the dictum *extra ecclesiam nulla salus*, as expounded in 1302 by Pope Boniface II and confirmed in the fifteenth century by the Council of Florence, was rigidly applied, not only to non-Christian religions, but also to alternative expressions of Christianity. For the Protestant, it was axiomatic that mankind as a whole was fallen, in a state of sin and rebellion, and hence under the condemnation of God; it was held as a matter of theological fact that the heathen in his darkness was doomed, unless he turned in faith to the sole remedy for his sin, the atoning death of Jesus Christ. Although, as we have seen, there had already been attempts made by Christians to place a more generous and favourable interpretation on the religious phenomena of the non-Christian world, these had made practically no impact on the compactly exclusive Christian attitude to these beliefs and practices. Christianity (in whatever form) was revealed truth; other religions, by contrast, were compounded of human error and sin, though conceivably containing some distant reminiscences of primeval revelation. This, broadly speaking, was the view of those who 'took religion seriously'.

The ultimate point at issue in the debate between science and religion was precisely the question of divine revelation. Scientific inquiry was reaching back into the remote past, and finding there something far different from the beliefs of the orthodox, as propounded in Holy Writ and guaranteed by the ongoing tradition. The data of Genesis were being systematically challenged, in the name of an alternative cosmogony. As John Tyndall said in 1874:

> We claim, and we shall wrest from theology, the entire domain of cosmological theory. All schemes and systems which thus infringe upon the domain of science must, in so far as they do this, submit to its control and relinquish all thought of controlling it . . . Every system which would escape the fate of an organism too rigid to adjust itself to its environment, must be plastic to the extent that the growth of knowledge demands.[3]

Scientists could make such claims as these because they firmly believed themselves to have been emancipated from bondage to *a priori* theories. Instead of using some deductive method they worked by induction, from the specific instance to the general law— a method which seemed to be diametrically opposed to that of Christian theology. And partly because of their spectacular successes in the mechanical and technological spheres—as evidenced by the Great Exhibition of 1851, among other things[4]—partly because of the very boldness and all-embracing quality of the new laws that were being formulated on the theory that *natura non facit saltus*, they began to be carried on a great wave of popular support.

[3] Quoted by Brown, *The Metaphysical Society* (1947), p. 236.
[4] Briggs, *Victorian People* (1963), pp. 15ff.

Science seemed to be sweeping all before it, and in the intoxication of success it seemed capable of explaining all things. In the minds of many there was the conviction that a new age was about to dawn; that man by his unaided powers was about to triumph over all obstacles to happiness and progress. As for God and religion, there would no longer be any need for them.[5]

Perhaps there would not. But—and here we come to one of the main points of departure of comparative religion—there would always be a problem to be explained. Why had humanity *ever* found it necessary to be religious? Why were so many still unable to emancipate themselves from religion? What was there in the human make-up which made it seemingly imperative for man to perceive, or postulate, or imagine, a world beyond the senses? Were these impulses indeed being superseded by the insights of the new age, or was the new age merely altering presuppositions in such a way as to provide better and more reliable data on this question than the information previously provided by confessional theology? Might divine revelation itself be progressive, and might it be capable of interpretation on evolutionary principles? These were important questions, and they fascinated the late nineteenth century.

Few of those who were most captivated by the growing body of evidence concerning the religious history of mankind belonged wholeheartedly to any orthodox Christian tradition. Many, on the other hand, wished to call themselves Christians even under the new dispensation. But these men were forced to formulate new theories, or to refurbish old ones, to account for the persistence of religion as an element of human culture, and for the actual plurality of religions in the world. In either case appeal was made entirely to the inductive, historical method, in short, to 'science'.[6]

From the mass of writing on this subject we may take this statement, from the introduction to Friedrich Max Müller's *Chips from a German Workshop* (1867), as representative of the new alliance which was being proposed between religion and science :

It was supposed at one time that a comparative analysis of the languages of mankind must transcend the powers of man : and yet by the combined and well directed efforts of many scholars, great results have been obtained, and the principles that must

---

[5] Elliott-Binns, *Religion in the Victorian Era* (1936), p. 165.

[6] From the Christian point of view, one of the most important of the writers who attempted to reconcile religion and science was the Scottish scientist-evangelist Henry Drummond (1851-1896), author of *Natural Law in the Spiritual World* (1883) and *The Ascent of Man* (1894). See George Adam Smith, *The Life of Henry Drummond* (1899).

guide the student of the Science of Language are now firmly established. It will be the same with the Science of Religion. By a proper division of labour, the materials that are still wanting, will be collected and published and translated, and when that is done, surely man will never rest until he has discovered the purpose that runs through the religions of mankind, and till he has reconstructed the true Civitas Dei on foundations as wide as the ends of the world. The Science of Religion may be the last of the sciences which man is destined to elaborate; but when it is elaborated, it will change the aspect of the world, and give new life to Christianity itself.[7]

But as in language, as in any science, the absolutely vital principle is that of comparison. To argue from one single religious tradition is to cut oneself off from the springs of the new knowledge. To be a devoted Christian, Jew, Muslim or Hindu is admirable; but it is not science. In the science of religion, in short, as Max Müller so often said, 'He who knows one, knows none.'[8]

Now, by the 1860s, there was no need for anyone to complain that material for comparison was lacking. The developing science of archaeology was laying bare the monuments of vanished civilisations, particularly in the Near East. Advances in linguistic study were opening the way to first-hand examination of literary sources in many fields. Documents and inscriptions were constantly coming to light. The German historical school had already developed a new critical method in which 'facts' and 'primary sources' were all-important. And over all was being spread the Darwinian canopy. The method that resulted can be characterised as scientific, critical, historical and comparative : scientific because of its inductive pattern and its belief in universal laws of cause and effect, and because of its distrust of obvious *a priori* arguments; critical because of its fundamental attitude to evidence; historical because of the new sense of continuity between the past and the present to which it gave rise; comparative because it claimed comparison to be the basis of all knowledge. It compared the known with the unknown, it compared phenomena in apparent temporal sequence, it compared

---

[7] Müller, *Chips from a German Workshop* 1 (1867), p. xix. It is not claimed that Müller invented the term : in French, the expression 'la science des religions' had been used some years earlier, by l'abbé Prosper Leblanc, *Les Religions et leur interprétation chrétienne* (1852-54), and again by Émile Burnouf in 1864—though in neither case with the general acceptance it was later to gain. The German term *Religionswissenschaft* dates back to the first decade of the nineteenth century. For documentation, see Pinard de la Boullaye 1, p. 548.

[8] Müller, *Introduction to the Science of Religion* (1873), p. 16.

phenomena belonging to different areas but having features in common. In all this, in true scientific spirit, it set out to determine, with regard to religion, the genus 'religion' which underlay the species 'the religions'.

The feud between science and religion continued to rage. Across the Atlantic, its climax was still some way off, and *The Fundamentals* had not yet been written. But an attempt was beginning to be made to view religion on the criteria provided by science, to judge its history and growth and evolution as one would judge the history, growth and evolution of any organism—and to dissect it as one would dissect any organism. It is that attempt at *rapprochement* which established the principle of comparison, and to which the name 'comparative religion' first came to be applied.

* * *

In turning now to Herbert Spencer (1820–1904) we pass from general questions of background and method to particular exponents of this new non-confessional approach to the study of religion. Charles Darwin himself need not concern us, since, although he was by no means indifferent to questions of religion, his contribution was not made specifically in this area.[9] But among the earliest evolutionists, Spencer occupies a special position with regard to religion, since it was pre-eminently he who widened the boundaries of evolutionary theory so as to take in the phenomenon of religion. And for this reason if for no other, he occupies an important position at the threshold of comparative religion.[10]

Beginning with an indistinct theism, Spencer's personal religion progressed to absolute agnosticism. Beginning his career as a civil engineer, he gradually came to devote himself almost entirely to what he himself called synthetic philosophy—an attempt to achieve one vast synthesis of human history, human thought and human evolution. Here we are concerned only with the position occupied by religion in his theories, however.

Like many another Victorian, Spencer rejected, without really understanding, the Christianity on which he had been brought up. He spoke of the Christian God as '. . . a deity who is pleased with the singing of his praises, and angry with the infinitesimal beings

---

[9] 'I do not attack Moses,' he once wrote, 'and I think Moses can take care of himself.' F. Darwin (ed.), *The Life and Letters of Charles Darwin* III (1887), p. 288.

[10] For recent estimates of Spencer, see Rumney, *Herbert Spencer's Sociology* (1966), and Burrow, *Evolution and Society* (1966).

he has made when they fail to tell him perpetually of his great-ness'[11]—an unworthy caricature. He had no time for such a deity. Nevertheless, when writing his *First Principles* (1862) he was still prepared at least to consider that there might be some 'fundamental verity' in the universal phenomenon of religion; that 'verity' he suggested might consist in 'that element common to all religions, which remains after their discordant peculiarities have been mutually cancelled'.[12] But on examination, he could find no religious 'truth' other than 'that the Power which the Universe manifests to us is utterly inscrutable'.[13] To the end of his life he remained firm in his agnosticism, maintaining that he knew nothing about the ultimate nature of things, and that delving into such ultimate questions was on the whole a profitless activity.[14]

Among Spencer's early statements on religion, a special place is occupied by an article on 'Manners and Fashions' which he had published in 1854 in the *Westminster Review*. In it he had claimed that the three areas of Law, Religion and Manners were closely related, and that in the dawn of human history all three areas were cared for by one man. In respect of law, he was the Chief; in respect of manners the Master of Ceremonies, and in respect of religion the Deity. But he had been human, and worship had come only after this powerful leader had died. In a word, then, 'the aboriginal god is the dead chief'.[15] Put slightly differently, mankind's earliest deity was '. . . the first man sufficiently great to become a tradition, the earliest whose power and deeds made him remembered'.[16] The underlying theory is of course that of Euhemerism. It was neither original, nor particularly important, but Spencer was to develop it in other places in his writing.

In his *First Principles*, however, he stated more elaborately in what ways he was applying the evolutionary theory. Things develop uniformly, he maintained, from simple to complex forms : 'Evolution is a change from an indefinite, incoherent homogeneity, to a definite, coherent, heterogeneity; through continuous differentiations and integrations'.[17] This was in fact a basic axiom. And he went on :

Now I propose in the first place to show, that the law of organic

---

[11] Spencer, *An Autobiography* 1 (1904), p. 152.

[12] Spencer, *First Principles* (1st edition 1862), p. 23. Later editions were much revised, in both content and arrangement of material.

[13] ibid., p. 46.

[14] Spencer, *An Autobiography* 1, p. 346.

[15] Spencer, *Essays* 1, p. 67.

[16] ibid., p. 82.

[17] *First Principles*, p. 216.

evolution is the law of all evolution. Whether it be in the development of the Earth, in the development of Life upon its surface, in the development of Society, of Government, of Manufactures, of Commerce, of Language, Literature, Science, Art, this same advance from the simple to the complex, through successive differentiations, holds uniformly.[18]

True, he does not mention religion specifically in this context; but it soon becomes apparent that he is looking upon religion less as an entity in itself than merely as an aspect of the government of society, as an alternative and a parallel to civil government. What, then, is the 'homogeneous' form of religion? In a word, the principle he had expounded in his 1854 essay : the worship of the revered dead.

As all ancient records and traditions prove, the earliest rulers are regarded as divine personages. The maxims and commands they uttered during their lives are held sacred after their deaths, and are enforced by their divinely-descended successors; who in their turn are promoted to the pantheon of the race, there to be worshipped and propitiated along with their predecessors; the most ancient of whom is the supreme god, and the rest subordinate gods.[19]

Spencer does not pursue further this inadequate line of reasoning in his *First Principles*. Later he returned to it, however. In his *Principles of Sociology* he attempts to explain the primitive cult of ancestors as arising from a man's dream of his dead father's double or ghost; having seen the vision, he presumes the father to be still alive in some other world. This material was dealt with much more convincingly by Tylor in *Primitive Culture*, and Spencer makes little of it. He asserts simply that 'The rudimentary form of all religion is the propitiation of dead ancestors, who are supposed to be still existing, and to be capable of working good or evil to their descendants.'[20]

It is not for what has since been called 'the ghost theory of the origin of religion' that Spencer deserves his place in this record, but rather for his role in helping to convince the nineteenth century that religion, along with every other area of human culture, ought to be—indeed must be—treated in evolutionary terms. Thanks not least to Spencer, evolution, from being a theory, rapidly became an atmosphere.

[18] ibid., p. 148.
[19] ibid., p. 158f.
[20] 'The Origins of Animal-Worship', in *Essays* iii (1874), p. 102.

He had no followers of importance within the field of comparative religion, save perhaps the scientist and man of letters Grant Allen, a close friend of Andrew Lang, who in 1897 published a book called *The Evolution of the Idea of God*, which set out to prove that 'corpse-worship is the protoplasm of religion'. Most scholars in the field were liable to agree with A. M. Fairbairn of Mansfield College, Oxford, that '. . . if Mr. Spencer had studied at first hand a single historical religion, we should never have had the theory which forms the basis of his sociology'.[21] Nevertheless he helped create a climate of opinion. Along with Darwin and Huxley, he must be acknowledged as one of the fathers of evolutionism.[22] And it was in the climate of opinion thus created that comparative religion was to emerge and flourish.

*   *   *

There are perhaps only two serious contenders for the title 'the father of comparative religion'—the Dutch Egyptologist C. P. Tiele and the great philologist, German by birth, British by adoption, Friedrich Max Müller (1823–1900).[23] In choosing to give the accolade to the latter, we have no wish to minimise Tiele's outstanding work. But Max Müller was the more universal figure, much of whose work was carried out during the critical decade, 1859–1869; we have already quoted him on two occasions : from what we have presumed to identify as the foundation document of comparative religion, his *Introduction to the Science of Religion* (1873), and from the slightly earlier preface to *Chips from a German Workshop*. In both we see him not only as the scholar, but also as the advocate of the new science—and it is for his advocacy we select him. Far more effectively than any other among his contemporaries, he was

---

[21] Fairbairn, *The Philosophy of the Christian Religion* (1902), p. 209.

[22] It has been said that in America Spencer became 'the philosopher of those who ordinarily did not read philosophy', while dominant American behaviour became 'a vast caricature of his doctrines'. Matthiessen, *Theodore Dreiser* (1951), p. 39f.

[23] There is regrettably no comprehensive modern biography of Max Müller. After his death his wife edited *The Life and Letters of the Right Honourable Friedrich Max Müller* in two volumes (1902). See also Müller, *My Autobiography* (1901), and cf. Sharpe, *Not to Destroy but to Fulfil* (1965), pp. 43ff; Windisch, *Geschichte der Sanskrit-Philologie* (1920), pp. 207ff; Baetke, *Geist und Erbe Thules* (1944), pp. 145ff; Rudolph, Die *Religionsgeschichte an der Leipziger Universität* (1962), pp. 12ff; Trompf, 'Friedrich Max Müller: Some Preliminary Chips from his German Workshop', in *Journal of Religious History* 5 (1968-9), pp. 200ff.

able to convince the Western world that in matters of religion, as in matters of language, 'he who knows one, knows none'. In Max Müller, three streams met. First, the stream of German romantic idealism; secondly, the stream of comparative Indo-European philology; and thirdly, the stream of post-Hegelian philosophy of history (not to be identified without more ado with the evolutionism of Darwin, Huxley, Spencer and the anthropological school, which Max Müller mistrusted).

Friedrich Max Müller was born in 1823. His father was Wilhelm Müller (1794–1827) the Romantic poet, who is chiefly remembered outside Germany as the writer of the poems set to music by Schubert as *Die schöne Müllerin* and *Winterreise*.[24] Max Müller began his academic career at the University of Leipzig, first in classics and then in philosophy, completing his doctoral dissertation in 1843 on the third book of Spinoza's *Ethics*. His debt to the German idealist-romantic tradition, as represented by his father, was enormous. He also owed much to Klopstock, Lessing, Schiller and of course Goethe.

A closer and more personal influence on Max Müller's work was that of Baron Bunsen (Christian Carl Josias Freiherr von Bunsen, 1791–1860), cousin of the celebrated chemist.[25] Baron Bunsen was a scholar turned diplomatist, an Orientalist by inclination who was forced to spend much of his time in the company of the fashionable, the cunning, the unscrupulous and the silly. But as well as being a man of the world, Bunsen was also a passionate nationalist, who divided the world into 'Germans' and 'Philistines', and in 1853 congratulated Max Müller on his work in 'the Oxford Mission of German Science'. Bunsen's best-known scholarly work was his *Gott in der Geschichte* (1856–9; Eng. tr. *God in History*, 3 vols. 1868), a vast comparative study in which he endeavoured to show, with examples drawn from every part of the world, that the story of mankind is the story of a moral evolution towards Humanity, but stressed at the same time that the priorities must be observed : 'The individual for the nation, the nation for Humanity, Humanity for God . . .' Max Müller was in constant touch with Bunsen throughout his formative years following his arrival at Oxford. It was Bunsen who, together with the celebrated Sanskritist H. H. Wilson, persuaded the East India Company to bear the cost of printing Max Müller's *Rig Veda*, and until his death he served the younger man as guide, philosopher and friend.

---

[24] For Max Müller's estimate of his father, see 'Wilhelm Müller', in *Chips from a German Workshop* III (1870), pp. 103ff.

[25] 'Bunsen', in *Chips* III (1870), pp. 358ff.

After graduating from Leipzig, Max Müller worked for a time in Berlin under Schelling, where he acquired an interest in India. He also met Schopenhauer, with whom he discussed the relative importance of the Vedic hymns and the Upanishads for an understanding of the Indian religious traditions. Not surprisingly, Schopenhauer was entirely on the side of the Upanishads, dismissing the Vedas summarily and unfairly as *Priester-wirthschaft* ('priestly rubbish'). Perhaps because of this encounter, Max Müller's interest in the *Rig Veda* was aroused (or at least confirmed), but it was not until he went to Paris in 1845 to study under Burnouf that he determined on his great project. Learning there that the Sanskritist Frederick Rosen had died after producing only the first volume of his edition of the Sanskrit text of the *Rig Veda*, he took up the fallen mantle. For a variety of reasons, not the least of them being that the Oxford University Press had an excellent fount of *Devanāgarī* Sanskrit characters, the publishing venture was transferred from St. Petersburg to Oxford. Bunsen and H. H. Wilson persuaded the Directors of the East India Company to defray the not inconsiderable costs of publication, and Max Müller came to London in 1846 to supervise the work. The four huge volumes of the Sanskrit text of the *Rig Veda*, with Sayana's commentary, appeared in 1849, 1853, 1856 and 1862 respectively, marking not only a milestone in the study of Indian religion in the West, but also arguably marking an important step in the direction of the revitalisation of Hinduism itself.

Max Müller never returned to Germany, other than for short visits (nor, oddly enough, did he ever visit India). The remainder of his career was spent in England. He was never again to publish any work of pure scholarship to compare with his *Rig Veda*. Instead he devoted himself to a comprehensive and many-sided task of interpretation, aimed at explaining the intricate relations he believed to exist between religion, mythology, language and the human mind. The first step had been taken before his edition of the *Rig Veda* was complete, as he published the widely-read essay on *Comparative Mythology* (1856). There followed *Lectures on the Science of Language* (1861–1864), and the first of his four volumes of his collected occasional essays, *Chips from a German Workshop* (1867). In 1873 he published his *Introduction to the Science of Religion*— which we have already had occasion to mention—delivered a celebrated and controversial *Westminster Lecture on Missions*, in which he entered a plea for comparative religion as a vital piece of missionary equipment, and experienced the first of Andrew Lang's many attacks on his theories of the origin of mythology. The 1870s, too, saw the launching of the invaluable *Sacred Books of the East* series—fifty volumes of texts and translations under his general supervision and editorship. In 1878 there appeared *Lectures on the Origin and Growth of Religion, as illustrated by the Religions of India*, in 1883 *India, What Can it Teach Us?* and in 1884 *Biographical Essays*, which included pioneer studies of Rammohun Roy and Keshub Chunder Sen, and reflected his intense interest in the Indian renaissance, which he had been in part responsible for bringing about. His last major works were the three volumes of Gifford Lectures, *Natural Religion, Physical Religion* and *Anthropological Religion* (1888–92) and *Contributions to the Science of Mythology*, which appeared in 1897, and in which '. . . he massed the arguments of his lifelong researches for a personal clash with Lang, repeated everything he had previously written, and repeated his repetitions throughout the twin volumes'.[26] He died in 1900.

* * *

In all Max Müller's work on the subject of religion, there is a fundamental distinction to be borne in mind. He was in fact asking two quite different sets of questions : on the one hand about the *origin* of religion in the heart and mind of man, and the way or ways in which religion has been associated with morals and myths; and on the other, questions about the method by which it is appropriate to study the phenomena of religion. But the questions were seldom kept altogether separate, since an understanding of the former process must necessarily determine the steps which the modern scholar must take in order to disentangle and interpret the evidence.

To take first the question of the origin of religion, Max Müller held that all human knowledge begins with *perceptions* of finite entities, capable of being registered by the senses. However, such perceptions he considered always to imply something beyond themselves. To perceive any object it is necessary at the same time to perceive that which is *not* the object in question, that against which the object outlines itself, as it were; hence, in effect, '. . . in perceiving the finite we always perceive the infinite also'.[27] This perception of something which is not the immediate object of the senses Max Müller regarded as the *Urdatum* of religion : 'I hold that before man could speak even of the infinite sky of Dyaus, he must have been brought in sensuous contact with something not finite like everything else . . .'[28] This, then, is the origin of religion : the

[26] Dorson, *The British Folklorists* (1968), p. 166.
[27] Müller, *Natural Religion (Collected Works* I, 1899), p. 123.
[28] ibid., p. 129.

perception of the infinite. But such a perception is not religion *per se*; for that, something more is necessary, namely the moral sense. When the moral sense enters into an instinctive alliance with the sense of the infinite, religion is born :

> When . . . men began to feel constrained to do what they do not like to do, or to abstain from what they would like to do, for the sake of some unknown powers which they have discovered behind the storm or the sky or the sun or the moon, then we are at last on religious ground.[29]

Religion, therefore, is

> . . . the perception of the infinite under such manifestations as are able to influence the moral character of man.[30]

This is 'Natural Religion'—a possession common to the whole of mankind, and the substratum of every developed form of religion. In this, as in so much else, Max Müller was a true son of the Enlightenment, and a genuine disciple of Kant.

Scarcely less striking in this regard was his detestation of anything which might be called 'priestcraft'; this he regarded as the bane of all true religion. In fact, his own formal religious affiliation was determined by this. He was a devoted member of the Church of England, not because he held any particularly strong views on the Reformation Settlement or Apostolic Succession, but '. . . because I think its members enjoy greater freedom and more immunity from priestcraft than those of any other Church'.[31] Fundamentally, he believed that religion was subject to inevitable decline under the dead hand of institutionalism, and that the nearer one could approach to the fountainhead of any particular tradition, the nearer one approximated to the ideal of Natural Religion.

It was in the religion of Vedic India that this ideal was most nearly realised, in Max Müller's view. There the original state of man, perceiving the infinite beyond the phenomena of nature, appeared to be accessible to the scholar; there he could see what man made of nature before the decline set in with the elaboration of mythology. Of the many contexts in which he expounded this theme, we may take this entirely typical statement :

> We see in the Vedic hymns the first revelation of Deity, the first expressions of surprise and suspicion, the first discovery that

---

[29] ibid., p. 169.
[30] ibid., p. 188.
[31] *Life and Letters* I, p. 391.

behind this visible and perishable world there must be something invisible, imperishable, eternal or divine. No one who has read the hymns of the Rig-veda can doubt any longer as to what was the origin of the earliest Aryan religion and mythology. Nearly all the leading deities of the Veda bear the unmistakable traces of their physical character. Their very names tell us that they were all in the beginning names of the great phenomena of nature, of fire, water, rain and storm, of sun and moon, of heaven and earth. Afterwards, we can see how these so-called deities and heroes became the centres of mythological traditions, wherever the Aryan speakers settled, whether in Asia or in Europe. This is a result gained once for all, and this light has shed its rays far beyond the Vedic mythology and religion, and lightened up the darkest corners in the history of the mythological and religious thoughts of other Aryan nations, nay of nations unconnected by their language with the speakers of the Aryan speech.[32]

*   *   *

The other side of Max Müller's work is concerned with the method by which the study of religion is to be prosecuted, and with the nature of the Science of Religion. His ultimate aim was to elaborate a complete science of human thought : and this he chose to do in four stages, beginning with the science of language, and passing through the science of mythology and the science of religion to the final goal of the science of thought.

Max Müller had inherited from his philosophical mentors, principally Hegel and Schelling, the conviction that there can be no speech without reason, and no reason without speech. In his *Science of Language* he wrote that '. . . strictly speaking, it is as impossible to use words without thought, as to think without words'.[33] Therefore, the growth of language and the growth of the human mind are only two aspects of the same process. But how did language begin? Briefly (for this is not a subject we can undertake to discuss in detail) with the formation of *roots*, the 'ultimate facts' of language, which are themselves signs that man was rational from the very first. In this respect Max Müller was an anti-Darwinian. In his *Comparative Mythology* he had said :

Yet more and more the image of man, in whatever clime we meet him, rises before us, noble and pure from the very beginning . . .

---

[32] Müller, *Three Lectures on the Vedanta Philosophy* (1898), p. 25f.
[33] Müller, *The Science of Language* i (1861), p. 72.

As far as we can trace back the footsteps of man, even on the lowest strata of history, we see that the divine gift of a sound and sober intellect belonged to him from the very first; and the idea of a humanity emerging slowly from the depths of an animal brutality can never again be maintained again in our century.[34]

He continued to find some of the assumptions of the evolutionary anthropologists unwarranted on the basis of any evidence known to him; indeed, his debates with the anthropologists (and particularly with Andrew Lang) were made excessively difficult by the protagonists' different points of departure.

Thought, then, begins with language. The first period of linguistic formation, when words were invented for the most necessary ideas (pronouns, prepositions, numerals, household items) he called the *Rhematic Period*. This was followed by a *Dialectic Period*, in which the three main families of language (the Semitic, Aryan and Turanian) separated, and grammatical forms became more secure. Thirdly there came the *Mythological* or *Mythopoeic Period*—that in which the celebrated 'disease of language' makes its presence felt, and which Max Müller noted wryly is 'the most likely to shake our faith in the regular progress of the human intellect'.[35] It is the investigation of the strange events of this period which constitutes the science of mythology.

Building upon the previous work of such scholars as Karl Otfried Müller and Adalbert Kuhn, whose book *Ueber die Herabkunft des Feuers und des Göttertranks* (Concerning the origin of fire and of the drink of the gods) had appeared in 1859, Max Müller traced his subject back to man's apprehension of natural phenomena. Kuhn had done as much, claiming simply that the gods are personifications of the great powers of nature—sun, moon, stars, thunder, lightning, storm and the rest. However, Max Müller went farther. The problem, in his view, was to explain the original personification process. This he could only account for by postulating 'a period of temporary insanity' in the human mind—the product of the aforementioned 'disease of language'. But what was this disease?

Max Müller's starting point was the observation that Indo-European languages originally had no abstract words : only verbal roots and simple nouns. But 'nature-words', like day and night, spring and winter, storm and thunder, are really abstract nouns, and must therefore have been of relatively late formation; so far so good, but the structure of ancient language also gave these same

---

[34] *Selected Essays* 1 (1881), p. 306.
[35] ibid., p. 308.

words *gender*. Therefore, since language and thought are so closely linked,

> As long as people thought in language, it was simply impossible to speak of morning and evening, of spring and winter, without giving to these conceptions something of an individual, active, sexual, and at last, personal character . . .[36]

The disease, then, was the process by which the noun 'dawn' (feminine) became 'she of the dawn' (a person) about whom stories could begin to be told. There are other processes involved, but this is unquestionably the most important.

For comparative purposes, the mythology of Vedic India appeared to represent an earlier stage in the process than that of Greece :

> The Veda is the real theogony of the Aryan races, while that of Hesiod is a distorted caricature of the original image. If we want to know whether the human mind, though endowed with the natural consciousness of a divine power, is driven necessarily and inevitably by the irresistible force of language as applied to supernatural and abstract ideas, we must read the Veda . . .[37]

In comparison, the gods of Hesiod and Homer are no gods; 'They are masks without an actor—the creations of man, not his creators; they are *nomina* not *numina*; names without being, not beings without names.'[38]

For Max Müller, it seemed possible in virtually every Aryan instance (and in many other instances) to trace human thought on this subject back to man's fascination with the sun. Virtually every myth appeared to him to be a solar myth :

> What we call the Morning, the ancient Aryans called the Sun or the Dawn. . . What we call Noon, and Evening, and Night, what we call Spring and Winter, what we call Year, and Time, and Life, and Eternity—all this the ancient Aryans called *Sun*. And yet wise people wonder and say, How curious that the ancient Aryans should have had so many solar myths. Why, every time we say 'Good morning', we commit a solar myth. Every poet who sings about 'the May driving the Winter from the field again' commits a solar myth. Every 'Christmas number' of our newspapers—ringing out the old year and ringing in the new—is brimful of solar myths. Be not afraid of solar myths.[39]

[36] Müller, *Comparative Mythology* (1856), p. 72f.
[37] *Selected Essays* I, p. 318f.
[38] ibid., p. 382.
[39] Quoted, with many other examples, by Dorson, *The British Folklorists* (1968), p. 163.

Regrettably, other nature-mythologists, though agreeing with Max Müller on so many things, claimed with equal confidence that the lightning, or the stars, or some other natural phenomenon, was the original unit of mythological thought. The discrepancies were seized on with joy by Andrew Lang, who, beginning in 1875, for some years conducted what almost amounted to a personal vendetta against Max Müller, and succeeded, rightly or wrongly, in virtually discrediting him in many quarters.

However, for Max Müller, the relationship between mythology and religion was incidental, rather than essential, myths being in every case degenerate expressions of obscured truth. The perception of the infinite behind and beyond the solar and other phenomena of nature constituted religion; the necessity to use words to describe those same phenomena engendered mythologies, solar or otherwise. Hence it was and is necessary to penetrate the myths in order to reach the heart of the religion which they conceal. Of course, the given data are confused, but close examination and comparison can give information leading beyond the data to the nature of religion. This is the province of the 'science of religion'. Its methods were to be those of the sciences of language and mythology, but its focus lay as it were on the far side of mythology. But the science of religion is not for that reason any the less scientific; in religion, as in language and mythologies, 'he who knows one, knows none', and more specifically,

> . . . all higher knowledge is acquired by comparison and rests on comparison. If it is said that the character of scientific research in our age is pre-eminently comparative, this really means that our researches are now based on the widest evidence that can be obtained, on the broadest indications that can be grasped by the human mind.[40]

In his *Introduction to the Science of Religion*, the first of Max Müller's books to discuss the new science in detail, he divided it into two parts. Their names are, interestingly enough, compounded with the word 'theology'—perhaps a sign of parentage or at least of respectability. 'Comparative theology' is that part of the science of religion which deals simply with the historical forms of religion; 'theoretic theology' (corresponding more or less to an amalgam of dogmatic theology and the philosophy of religion) attempts to explain the conditions under which religion, in any form, is possible. To all intents and purposes, however, Max Müller's interests were centred on the first of these sections, and it is this which has devel-

[40] Müller, *Introduction to the Science of Religion* (1873), p. 12.

oped into the comparative study of religion as we know it. The comparative element needs no further justification; with it Max Müller combined the element of classification, on the basis of the motto *divide et impera*, 'classify and conquer'—the classification used being that which he had already applied to the science of language, i.e. into the great families of Aryan, Semitic and Turanian. In this way he avoided speaking of 'true' and 'false' religions, or even of 'revealed' and 'natural' religions, both pairs of terms being in his opinion of no value for scientific purposes.

Actual empirical religions, whether living or dead, provide objects of study, and insights into the nature of religion, into the nature of man, and into the nature of human thought. The science of religion could therefore take its place proudly as an element in idealistic humanism, since in studying religion, we are studying man at the various summits of his thought and experience :

> However imperfect, however childish a religion may be, it always places the human soul in the presence of God; and however imperfect and however childish the conception of God may be, it always represents the highest ideal of perfection which the human soul, for the time being, can reach and grasp.[41]

Thus the science of religion passes over by imperceptible degrees into the science of thought (the title, incidentally, of a large and not very significant book of Max Müller's old age).

Max Müller grew up in the atmosphere of German romantic idealism. It was probably this heritage which made him more than a mere historian, more than a mere philologist. To Max Müller, the attempt to understand religion was an attempt to understand man, and an attempt, too, to persuade men to understand one another. It is not irrelevant to record in this connection his enthusiastic advocacy of the Chicago World's Parliament of Religions in 1893, nor to note that in India today he is regarded as a pioneer of East-West understanding, honoured in the institution of the *Max Mueller Bhavan*. This, one feels, he would have found gratifying, since it belonged to the pattern of the religion of the future as he saw it. He believed that the future held the promise of a new form of religion, derived not from historical Christianity as he knew it, but from all the various repositories of truth that are to be found scattered over the face of the earth. It will be the 'true religion of humanity', since humanity is the sphere of divine revelation; and it will be the essential result of the historical process, leading beyond Christianity, though in some sense perhaps still to be called Christ-

41 ibid., p. 263.

ianity. 'The true religion of the future will be the fulfilment of all
the religions of the past.'[42]

This religion exists potentially at the heart of Christianity, he
believed, as the ethical and moral ideal taught by Jesus Christ, but
now overlaid by the accretions of centuries. And it is this central
religious ideal which is to be the final answer to the religious aspirations implanted in the mind of man by the working of God's Spirit.
It is here that the true God is to be found, and after this ideal that
all religions yearn.

* * *

What, we may ask in conclusion, had Max Müller done? He had
of course popularised a term—'the science of religion'—but this
was in a sense the least of his achievements. It was far more important that he had given the comparative study of religion an impulse,
a shape, a terminology and a set of ideals. He had recruited an
entire generation of scholars to his cause, as editors, translators and
commentators in his *Sacred Books of the East* enterprise; and in his
own chosen field of Indology had set standards as high as he knew
how to make them. Almost incidentally, he had prepared the Western world for what has since come to be called the dialogue of
religions, insisting not only on accuracy with regard to dead traditions, but sympathy with regard to living traditions. These are contributions which deserve to be remembered when his excursions and
excesses in the field of the interpretation of myth are forgotten.

This is not to say that Max Müller founded the science of religion,
or comparative religion, single-handed; he himself made no such
claim, and it would be unwise to claim for him more than he would
have claimed for himself. In 1905 Louis Jordan wrote of him that
he 'did infinitely more for this new discipline as one of its Prophets
and Pioneers than he was ever privileged to do for it as one of its
Founders and Masters',[43] and quoted C. P. Tiele's judgement that
'as the foundation of the new Science had only just been laid, he
[Max Müller] could but submit the plan of the building to his
readers and hearers . . . [His *Introduction to the Science of Religion*]
dealt with the preliminaries rather than with the results of the
Science, and was an apology for it more than an initiation of it.'[44]
This is all true enough, in its way. But it fails to take into account
the general *impression* made by his life and writings, that here

[42] *Life and Letters* II, p. 135.
[43] Jordan, *Comparative Religion, its Genesis and Growth* (1905), p. 522.
[44] ibid., p. 523.

indeed was a new power in the scientific world. It overlooks such a simple matter as the stylistic elegance with which Max Müller presented his material to the world, the lack of which has always been such a stumbling-block to the scholar. Before Max Müller, in fact, the field of religious studies, though wide and full, was disorganised. After him, the field could be seen as a whole, subjected to a method, and in short treated scientifically.

But as we have hinted, Max Müller's star had begun to wane long before the end of his career. There were various reasons for this, but the most important were that, on the one hand, he was subjected to a series of severe criticisms from the Darwinian anthropologists, and from Andrew Lang in particular; and on the other, that the science of comparative philology was moving rapidly into a new phase, which left many of his linguistic assumptions behind.

In the circumstances, it was doubly unfortunate that Max Müller had disciples, particularly in the field of mythology, who were characterised by an excess of enthusiasm and a lack of common sense. We have no reason to recall these in detail; but we may mention Rev. George William Cox (1827–1902), author of *Manual of Mythology* (1867), *The Mythology of the Aryan Nations* (1870) and *Introduction to the Science of Comparative Mythology and Folklore* (1881).[45] Cox had carried Max Müller's 'solar mythological' interpretation of the externals of religion to such extremes, that even Max Müller himself was turned slightly dizzy, and Andrew Lang exulted that the Lord had delivered them both into his hands. Partly as a result of such excesses, over which he had no control, Max Müller became in the last decades of his life something of an anachronism, supplanted in the popular esteem by men whose concerns lay less with the sophisticated data of language than with the crude and ambiguous products of Darwinian anthropology.

Nevertheless his work had been done, and foundations had been laid : perhaps not as firmly as Max Müller himself believed, but none the less capable of being built upon.

---

[45] On G. W. Cox, see Dorson, op. cit., pp. 174ff.

III

'Darwinism makes it possible'

During the first twenty or so years of its existence the emergent science of comparative religion was dominated by Max Müller's philological approach to the material. The most notable interests, and the most outstanding achievements, of the philologists were in the area of mythology, that is, of religion as conceptualised and expressed in words and stories. This is not to say that the few scholars who were interested in religion 'in the round' were all necessarily philologists; but most, having been trained in either Classics or Semitics, found this to be a natural approach. The philologists were of course interested only in textual material, and their working methods as historians of religion were essentially those which had been developed for the purpose of dealing with Semitic and Indo-European texts. Other data concerning the earliest history of mankind, and man's earliest religions, interested them hardly at all. It tended in these circles to be supposed that the 'lower' religions—which were then still classified, following de Brosses, as 'fetishism'—were the end product of a long process of degeneration, and therefore scarcely worthy of serious scholarly attention.

Max Müller, although a convinced believer in progress, had been suspicious of the Darwinians. By about 1880, however, the Darwinian hypothesis was becoming virtually impossible to resist. Spencer had in theory brought every aspect of human culture into its unfolding pattern, and now it was a matter of working Spencer's insights out in detail. The label under which this was to be done was still very much a matter of choice, but by this time the term 'anthropology' was gaining ground rapidly as the best label for comprehensive evolutionary science as it concerned man, and as the umbrella under which most evolutionary theories, including those involving religion, might most easily be accommodated. Ideally, anthropology claimed not to be concerned with the truth and falsehood of religion. T. H. Huxley had said in 1878 that it 'holds itself absolutely and entirely aloof' from such questions; but he had also claimed that '. . . the natural history of religion, and the origin and growth of the religions entertained by the different kinds of the human race, are within its proper and legitimate province'.[1]

[1] For an excellent survey of this question, see Dillenberger, *Protestant Thought and Natural Science* (1961), esp. pp. 219ff.

Value judgements of one kind or another were nevertheless common, as we shall see.

Viewed in Darwinian perspective, religion became something which it had never really been before. From being a body of revealed truth, it became a developing organism. To the scientific mind, there was something slightly intoxicating about this whole process of discovery, as though the cobwebs of centuries had been swept away in an instant, disclosing scenes of great depth, intricacy and beauty. 'Not since the material world became an object of human study and reflection,' wrote one anthropologist in 1908,

> has there been accomplished such a complete and far-reaching revolution in current philosophical opinion. From the standpoint of evolution, the entire organic world, not excluding man, reveals a unity, a harmony, and a grandeur never before disclosed under any system of speculative philosophy.[2]

Three years later the Oxford anthropologist R. R. Marett was able to put the whole matter in a nutshell when he wrote :

> Anthropology is the whole history of man as fired and pervaded by the idea of evolution . . . Anthropology is the child of Darwin. Darwinism makes it possible. Reject the Darwinian point of view and you must reject anthropology also.[3]

Before the Darwinian revolution there had of course been many attempts made to describe and map out various 'uncivilised' areas of the world, as these had come within the purview of the West. In this respect the antecedents of anthropology are virtually identical with those of comparative religion, and failed at precisely the same point. Having adequate motive and more than adequate material, the early students of mankind lacked a suitable method by which to systematise their material. Partly for this reason, their work had a certain haphazard quality, as well as tending, understandably enough, to focus on the spectacular, the grotesque and the bizarre. Hence there was a certain *odium* attending the work of the anthropologist. As Andrew Lang put it, 'Anthropologists were said to gloat over dirty rites of dirty savages . . .'—an occupation which commended itself to practically none of the respectable classes from which scholarship came. But the coming evolutionism changed the picture radically. In the new evolutionary perspective, the mind of 'primitive' man was removed from the lower rungs of the hierarchical ladder, and could be seen to be human, if childish, and therefore

[2] Munro, 'Anthropology', in *ERE* I (1909), p. 572b.
[3] Marett, *Anthropology* (1911), p. 8.

worth studying. His religion could also be seen to be eminently worthy of attention, if only as a means of demonstrating the earliest stages through which the faiths of mankind had passed on their way to the heights of ethical monotheism, or the heights of agnosticism, whichever was preferred.

Various elements went into the making of late-nineteenth-century anthropology. First, of course, there was the actual contact with 'primitive' peoples, which was increasing rapidly in an age of European colonial expansion. Across the Atlantic, the frontier of civilisation was being pushed westward thoughout the century, and although anthropology was perhaps not uppermost in the frontiersmen's minds, by the turn of the century much valuable work had been done on the religion of the North American Indian tribes. Then there was the development of prehistoric archaeology; the 'three-age' system of Thomsen and Worsaae was particularly important in providing a basis of approximate chronological classification for previously unclassifiable material. Thirdly, there was the theory of survivals, which postulated a simple equation between what was primitive and what was prehistoric. Thus a 'survival' was some element or component of culture, such as religion, which had in some way failed to evolve in a certain area or among a certain people, and which therefore might be made to serve as a sort of living fossil, capable of being studied *in situ* for the sake of the light it was able to throw on questions of origin and early history.[4] So, for instance, it became a popular pastime to study the religious beliefs and practices of the Aboriginal tribes of Australia in the firm belief that what was being studied was neither more nor less than 'the religion of Stone Age Man'.

However, it was not necessary to go to the ends of the earth in order to find 'survivals'. The popular beliefs of the European peasantry—or of the common people in any part of the world, for that matter—provided an equally fruitful field of study for the energetic and enterprising investigator. This was *folklore*—the term coined (though the study was of course not invented) by the antiquary William John Thoms in 1846. And although by 1913 G. L. Gomme was defining folklore with Teutonic precision as the study of

> customs, rites and beliefs belonging to individuals among the
> people, to groups of people, to inhabitants of districts or places;

---

[4] Marett described the process as '. . . a tendency to procrastinate on the part of some elements that are as it were unable or unwilling to maintain the pace of the rest', and as involving 'a sort of inverse method of assessing an evolutionary process'. *Tylor* (1936), p. 26. On the subject as a whole, see Hodgen, *The Doctrine of Survivals* (1936), passim.

C

and belonging to them apart from and oftentimes in direct antagonism to the accepted customs, rites and beliefs of the State or the nation to which the people and the groups of people belong.[5]

Andrew Lang had some years previously defined folklore more succinctly, if more tendentiously, as 'the study of survivals'. By the turn of the century folklore had come to serve as a kind of home missions department of anthropology, and it served comparative religion in more or less the same way—the more so as its methods became more accurate and more refined.

In Britain, the first major literary landmark of the nineteenth century in this area was perhaps Sir Walter Scott's *Minstrelsy of the Scottish Border*; but Scott's collection was confined to the *genre* of ballad, and it was left to lesser men in later years to collect humbler folktales and to observe quainter practices. In Germany, the movement was inseparable from the names of Jakob and Wilhelm Grimm in the 1830s, and in the later part of the century, from the work of Wilhelm Mannhardt.

Wilhelm Mannhardt (1831–1880) was not an academic in the strictest sense; a little misshapen librarian and archivist suspected by some of being one of the trolls he was investigating, he spent his life in obscurity. In his early years he had concentrated on the aristocratic mythology of the Germanic peoples, and had written two books, *Germanische Mythen* (Teutonic myths, 1858) and *Die Götterwelt der deutschen und nordischen Völker* (The gods of the Teutonic and Scandinavian peoples, 1860). But after long enquiries, not least among Austrian, Danish and French prisoners-of-war he had interviewed in his home town of Danzig, he turned his attention from 'higher' to 'lower' forms of myth—those involving the fairies and the spirits of wood, field and corn. These he held to be, on the one hand, genuine survivals of archaic belief, and on the other, products of that primitive mentality which had given rise to the great legends found within the higher and more developed cycles of myth. Three important books resulted from this study: *Die Korndämonen* (Spirits of the corn, 1868), *Der Baumkultus der Germanen* (Tree-worship among the Teutons, 1875), and most famous of all, *Antike Wald- und Feldkulte* (The ancient worship of forest and field, 1875–7). In these works Mannhardt was in effect building a bridge between mythological studies of the philological type and the nascent science of anthropology. His sympathies certainly lay with the anthropological, rather than the philological

---

[5] Gomme, 'Folklore', in *ERE* VI (1913), p. 57a.

school, and he attached little significance to the work of Max Müller.[6] Mannhardt's own work was to be of lasting importance. In the field of comparative anthropology he was one of the most important precursors of Frazer's *The Golden Bough*, and in the general study of Teutonic religion his work established significant precedents.

Otherwise it is perhaps true to say that in its early years folklore suffered to some extent from the attentions of the enthusiastic but indiscreet amateur. There was, unfortunately, some justification in Jordan's remark made in 1905 that too much of what had hitherto passed for folklore study had been little save 'solemn trifling', since too often 'guess-work and gossip and imperfect observation and hasty generalisation' had 'usurped the place of dispassionate and scientific accuracy'.[7] In all fairness it should be admitted, though, that comparative religion has seldom been altogether immune from the same criticism.

The link between anthropology and folklore was, however, a fairly obvious one. The men whom Dorson has called 'The Great Team' of Folklorists—Andrew Lang, G. L. Gomme, Alfred Nutt, E. S. Hartland, Edward Clodd and W. A. Clouston—were all in some sense anthropologists as well as folklorists.[8] The difference between an archaic belief held by a materially backward people and an ancient belief held within a materially advanced society was one of degree, not of kind. In either case it might be, and was, claimed that here were pointers to very early stages in the evolution of religion.

* * *

The first two writers in Britain, with the exception of Herbert Spencer, in whose work we find a significant combination of anthropological data and religious speculation were Sir John Lubbock (subsequently Lord Avebury, 1834–1913) and Edward Burnett Tylor (1832–1917). There is little point in arguing priority for the one over against the other. Their fields of interest were not identical: Lubbock was more concerned with prehistory, and his first major work, *Pre-historic Times* (1865) was largely responsible for familiar-

---

[6] 'Ich vermag dem von M. Müller angestellten Principe, wenn überhaupt eine, so doch nur eine sehr beschränkte Geltung zuzugestehen.' Mannhardt, *Wald- und Feldkulte* (1875), p. xx.

[7] Jordan, *Comparative Religion, its Genesis and Growth* (1905), p. xx.

[8] Dorson, *The British Folklorists* (1966), pp. 202ff.

ising the English-speaking public with the idea of prehistory. It was, incidentally, in this book that the terms 'Palaeolithic' and 'Neolithic' first appeared. Tylor was more concerned with surviving primitive peoples, and his first book, *Anahuac* (1861) had been on the ethnology of Mexico. Their major works, however, appeared within a year of each other: Lubbock's *The Origin of Civilisation and the Primitive Condition of Man* in 1870, Tylor's *Primitive Culture* in 1871. Lubbock was the more versatile of the two. He had never studied in a university, was professionally a banker and politician, and wrote widely on subjects unconnected in any way with anthropology or comparative religion.

In Lubbock's work we find the first example in Britain of the trend of which we spoke at the end of Chapter One—the combination of a broadly Comtean philosophy of history with the scientific data of Darwinist evolutionism in such a way as to produce a theory of the *religious* evolution of mankind. His conviction was that common among evolutionists, that 'races in a similar state of mental development, however distinct their origins may be, and however distinct the regions they inhabit, have very similar religious concepts'. Here we have, in a nutshell, the theory of *unilinear evolution* as applied to religion.

On this basis Lubbock worked out a hypothetical sequence in which he believed religion to have developed. His evolutionary ladder had six rungs. First and lowest came *atheism*, a state in which mankind had no regular system of mythology and no received and defined mode of belief. There followed the stages of *fetishism* (from de Brosses), nature-worship or *totemism* (from J. F. M'Lennan), *shamanism*, idolatory or *anthropomorphism*, and finally *ethical monotheism*. This is in effect an expanded and refined form of the first two stages in Comte's three-stage theory of the evolution of culture.

The scheme as a whole has little to recommend it, in the light of more accurate knowledge. Its first element, based on the belief, not uncommon among nineteenth-century anthropologists and travellers, that certain primitive races have nothing whatever that can be called religion, was summarily rejected by Tylor, and has never again been seriously maintained. The best one can say is that if one is working with an unsatisfactory definition of 'religion', then certain types of archaic belief and practice may appear not to belong within that category at all. The subsequent steps on the evolutionary ladder are all, it is true, elements of religion; but that they stand in an evolutionary, as opposed to a functional, relationship to one another, is simply incapable of proof. Lubbock's final assumption, that the link between religion and morals appears only at the highest point of religious belief, continued to be held, in one form or another, for many years. It has still not been altogether abandoned, despite all the evidence to the contrary that has accumulated since Lubbock's day.

* * *

The work of Lubbock's near-contemporary Edward Burnett Tylor normally commands a good deal of space in histories of anthropological and ethnological theory, and this is entirely proper, since his position among the founders of these twin sciences is unquestioned. He is equally important in the history of comparative religion, both as the major British representative of what tends to be called 'the anthropological school' in the study of religion, and as the begetter of the theory of 'animism'.[9] In neither respect was Tylor an absolute innovator, however. In anthropology, he was a systematiser; in the matter of animism, a refurbisher of a term coined in the eighteenth century. The word 'animism' had been used by the German chemist Georg Ernst Stahl (1660–1734), the *homo acris et metaphysicus* and originator of the 'Phlogiston' theory, to label the hypothesis that all living things derive from *anima*, 'soul' or 'mind'.[10] Tylor borrowed the term and gave it a meaning of his own, and it was in Tylor's sense that the word was to pass into the common vocabulary of the early twentieth century; Jung was in time to apply the words *animus* and *anima* to something quite different, but that development need not concern us for the moment.

Tylor came of Quaker stock, and hence was never closely concerned with that type of Christian orthodoxy which was so illdisposed towards the comparative study of religion in its early stages. Leaving school at sixteen, he went into the family firm of brassfounders, but his health proved unequal to the demands of the industrial world, and in 1835 he was dispatched to Mexico on a journey of recuperation and study, in the company of a fellow-Quaker, Henry Christy, one of the leading pre-historic archaeologists of his day. This friendship, and this journey, deprived industry of a brassfounder and gave the world an anthropologist. On his return to England, he began the systematic study that, reinforced by his Mexican experiences, was to result in the books *Anahuac*

[9] Marett, *Tylor*, passim.
[10] *Biogr. Lex. der hervorragender Aerzte* (1887), p. 502f. For Jung's treatment of these terms, see Wilhelm and Jung, *The Secret of the Golden Flower* (Eng. tr. 1962), pp. 115ff. cf. below, pp. 203–9.

(1861), *Researches into the Early History of Mankind* (1865) and *Primitive Culture* (1871).[11] In 1884 Tylor was appointed Reader in Anthropology in the University of Oxford, the first such post to be established anywhere in the world; and in 1896 he was granted a personal professorship in the subject. He never succeeded in making anthropology popular, and he had few pupils, but his personal distinction was marked by a knighthood in 1912—by which time Oxford anthropology had taken on an entirely new lease of life under the urbane R. R. Marett.

Tylor was made, as a theoretician in the field of religion, by Darwin and by Boucher de Perthes, by the German anthropologists Bastian and Waitz, by Comte and Herbert Spencer, and above all by the prevailing climate of opinion of his day. He was an evolutionist in regarding the culture of mankind as proceeding from lower to higher forms in (for the most part) unbroken sequence, though he was more flexible than many of his contemporaries in weighing the arguments for and against the rival theories of diffusion and unilinear evolution. He made the usual assumptions concerning the possibility of deducing the development of spiritual culture by analogy from the development of material culture. And he was one of the first to state formally the aforementioned theory of 'survivals' (indeed, the term is Tylor's), which made it possible—or appeared to make it possible—to study modern 'primitives' and see in them the essential conditions of prehistory. Since this is such an important point, a few more words in elaboration may be appropriate.

Survivals, wrote Tylor in the first volume of *Primitive Culture*,

> . . . are processes, customs, opinions, and so forth, which have been carried on by force of habit into a new state of society different from that in which they had their original home, and they thus remain as proofs and examples of an older condition of culture out of which the newer has been evolved.[12]

A survival, in other words, is any element of culture or society (or, for our purposes, religion) which the stream of evolution has left behind. Thus if a 'religious' concept be found among an otherwise undeveloped people, it is a fair deduction that the concept in question belongs to a correspondingly earlier stage in the evolution

---

[11] Too much must not be made of his field experiences. Marett noted that despite them, 'he must on the whole be classed as an anthropologist of the study, a circumnavigator of the world of books' (*Tylor*, 1936, p. 41f). Lowie, on the other hand, calls him 'the very opposite of an armchair anthropologist' (*The History of Ethnological Theory*, 1937, p. 69).

[12] Tylor, *Primitive Culture* I, (6th ed. 1929), p. 16.

of mankind, and hence of religion. When a series of such deductions has been made, it is possible to construct an elaborate sequence, on the principles set out some years later by Henry Balfour as follows :

> . . . the absence of historical and archaeological evidence of the *actual* continuity of development from simple to complex does not preclude investigation into the early history of any product of human ingenuity, nor prevent the formation of a suggestive and plausible if largely hypothetical series, illustrating the probable chain of sequences along which some highly specialised form may be traced back link by link to its rudimentary prototypes, or even to its absolute origin. . . Where an actual chronological series is not forthcoming, a comparative study of such types as are available, even though they be *modern* examples, reveals the fact that, if classified according to their apparent morphological affinities, these types show a tendency to fall into line; the gap between the extreme forms—that is, the most simple and the most advanced—being filled by a succession of intermediate forms. . . We are thus, at any rate, in possession of *a* sequence. Is it unreasonable for us to conclude that this reflects, in great measure, *the actual chronological sequence* of variations through which in past times the evolutionary history . . . was effected, from the earliest rudimentary forms?[13]

This is the theory on which the evolutionary anthropologists rested so much weight, not only in the study of 'products of human ingenuity', but also in the study of religion. That it was a dangerous theory goes without saying.

It is for the animistic theory of the origin of religion, however, that Tylor is chiefly remembered today. We shall look at this in a moment, but first we must note, by way of a *caveat*, something which he had written in the first chapter of *Primitive Culture*. Observing that the intelligent view of 'savage religion' is far different from that of 'some missionary journals' (an understandable sentiment), he goes on :

> Few who will give their minds to master the general principles of savage religion will ever again think it ridiculous, or the knowledge of it superfluous to the rest of mankind. Far from its beliefs and practices being a rubbish-heap of miscellaneous folly, they are consistent and logical in so high a degree as to begin, as soon as

[13] Balfour, Introduction to Pitt-Rivers, *The Evolution of Culture* (1906), p. xii.

even roughly classified, to display the principles of their formation and development; and *these principles prove to be essentially rational* [my italics], though working in a mental condition of intense and inveterate ignorance.[14]

The unavoidable question now is whether the phenomena of 'primitive' religion were always as consistent, logical and rational as Tylor would make them, or whether Tylor was not imposing upon his data an *a priori* rationality of his own. Spontaneity and the irrational in religion he had already devalued, claiming that culture's most spontaneous phenomena '. . . will be shown to come within the range of distinct cause and effect as certainly as the facts of mechanics'.[15] But there was, and is, a vast area of spiritual culture among pre-literate (and indeed other) peoples which an attitude of this order could only distort. It is doubly strange that Tylor, while so concerned with animism, should have been so bent on rationalising the shaman and all his works. The non-rational in fact receives such short shrift in Tylor's writings that his whole analysis suffers.

However, with this *caveat* we may proceed to Tylor's argument. He begins by defining religion in a celebrated phrase as 'the belief in Spiritual Beings'. Perhaps he ought to have used the phrase 'the mistaken belief in non-existent Spiritual Beings', though this may be unfair. He goes on to assert that 'the belief in spiritual beings appears among all low races with whom we have attained to thoroughly intimate acquaintance'. This belief he calls, with apologies to Stahl, 'animism'.[16]

The theory of animism divides into two parts :

. . . first, concerning souls of individual creatures, capable of continued existence after death or destruction of the body; second, concerning other spirits, upward to the rank of powerful deities.[17]

The origin of the doctrine of souls Tylor explains as follows : primitive man is struck by the difference between a living body and a dead one, and wonders what has caused the difference between them. At the same time he wonders what might have caused the apparitions which come to him in dreams and ecstatic visions. Putting the two together, primitive man postulates the existence of an

[14] *Primitive Culture* I, p. 22f.
[15] ibid.
[16] ibid., p. 424f. This was not the first time Tylor had used this word in this way. It appears in a number of earlier articles, beginning with 'The Religion of Savages', in *The Fortnightly Review* (1866), pp. 71ff.
[17] *Primitive Culture* I, p. 426.

'apparitional soul' or 'ghost-soul', which leaves the body temporarily in sleep or trance, and permanently in death, and which may wander far and wide in either condition. Tylor observes, correctly, the connection between words for 'soul' and words for 'breath' in many languages, and that in many cultures, man is believed to possess a plurality of souls.

From the souls of men Tylor passes on to the souls of animals and other beings, pointing out that in his view,

> the sense of an absolute psychical distinction between man and beast, so prevalent in the civilised world, is hardly to be found among the lower races . . . The lower psychology cannot but recognise in beasts the very characteristics which it attributes to the human soul, namely, the phenomena of life and death, will and judgment, and the phantom seen in vision or in dream.[18]

Hence 'in the primitive psychology' animals have souls like human beings; so too have plants and other natural objects. And the notion, though mistaken, is far from absurd, says Tylor. Any one can prove it merely by an effort of memory; for do not children attribute personality to 'posts and sticks, chairs and toys'? It is interesting in this connection to observe how often phrases like 'lower psychology', 'primitive psychology' and 'infant psychology' occur in his book. In reality, Tylor is writing about the mental processes of human beings already classified, to all intents and purposes, as children, and locating the origins of religion in a childish aberration (or at least inadequacy) of thought. When mankind was a child, evidently he thought and spoke and behaved as a child; evidently, too, by the end of the nineteenth century the time had come for him to put away childish things.

And yet the child-man could think, after his fashion. In a revealing sentence, Tylor writes :

> The savage thinker, though occupying himself so much with the phenomena of life, sleep, disease, and death, seems to have taken for granted, as a matter of course, the ordinary operations of his own mind.[19]

Tylor, too, was taking a great deal for granted. As Andrew Lang was shortly to point out, '. . . when we remember that Mr. Tylor is theorising about savages in the dim background of human evolution . . . we must admit that he credits them with great ingenuity, and

---

[18] ibid., p. 469.
[19] ibid., p. 426: 'Animism is, in fact, the groundwork of the Philosophy of Religion.'

strong powers of abstract reasoning'.[20] He does indeed. But there is another objection which can be levelled against Tylor's construction.

A great deal depended on the validity of the theory of survivals, and this theory led Tylor to illegitimate conclusions about the place of animism in the religious history of the world. Animism, he maintains in the second volume of *Primitive Culture*, is 'the direct product of natural religion'; animism is a characteristic of lower forms of culture; and therefore, 'Savage life, carrying on into our own day the life of the Stone Age, may be legitimately claimed as representing remotely ancient conditions of mankind, intellectual and moral as well as material'.[21] Thus Tylor believed simply that animism was 'Stone Age Religion', and that the problem of the origin of religion had thereby been solved. He was wrong. He had made a vast assumption, namely that levels of material culture *must* correspond exactly to levels of intellectual, moral and religious culture, and that survivals in one of these areas must inevitably correspond to survivals in another. He had assumed that just as man had (so it was being claimed) evolved from something other and lower than man, so religion must have evolved out of something other and lower than religion. He had assumed that the bridge of survivals stretched in any case back beyond homo sapiens. None of these assumptions was warranted. And hence, what Tylor has to say about animism as a theory of the origin of religion is simply incapable of either proof or disproof.[22]

What Tylor had done in his *magnum opus* was to give the world a first-rate compendium of some of the religious beliefs and practices of pre-literate peoples.[23] The term itself is eminently usable as a descriptive term. And it is here that Tylor's lasting contribution to comparative religion must be seen.

*   *   *

Among the immediate circle of Tylor's disciples the most para-

[20] Lang, *The Making of Religion* (2nd ed. 1900), p. 51.
[21] ibid., pp. 58ff.
[22] 'The ideas of soul and spirit could have arisen in the way Tylor supposed, but there is no evidence that they did.' Evans-Pritchard, *Theories of Primitive Religion* (1965), p. 25.
[23] His great antagonist Max Müller had reason to observe caustically that animism tells us nothing about the actual origins of religion, since 'these so-called savages are, so far as we know, not a day older or younger on the surface of the earth than the present inhabitants of India, China, or even of England.' This point was answered, though not very convincingly, by Andrew Lang, in *Myth, Ritual and Religion* II (2nd ed. 1899), p. 345f.

doxical, and in many ways the most interesting was the 'divine amateur', the Scottish man of letters Andrew Lang (1844-1912).[24] Lang's contemporaries hardly knew what to make of him. He certainly did not seem to fit into any of the accepted categories of scholarship. He was not a professional anthropologist, though given the opportunity he might well have become one; he was not a theologian; not a historian. Perhaps he is best thought of as a gifted amateur, or a dilettante (in the original sense of those much-maligned terms): poet, journalist, translator, classicist, novelist, writer of fairy-tales—the most brilliant and mercurial of characters. His very brilliance was such as to make him suspect in the eyes of the staid and the nervously academic: after all, how could one possibly take seriously the anthropological and religious theories of a man who wrote books about fairies and Bonnie Prince Charlie, and was as likely to express his views in a poem, in the pages of a novel or in a tongue-in-cheek 'letter' to Eusebius of Caesarea or Herodotus, as in a learned journal. Further, his essentially combative nature, though it seldom led him into polemics for its own sake, was not calculated to endear him to those who felt the sharp point of his pen.

And yet reading Lang on the subject of religion—or any other subject, for that matter—can still be a stimulating experience. His literary quality was uniformly high: as his only biographer has written, 'practically none of his voluminous writings can be considered hack-work'.[25] His pages are illuminated by the telling phrase, by an unusual sense of humour, and by a healthy disrespect for the unlikely or far-fetched theories of established authorities. Lang was in fact responsible for opening up many avenues of religious study, even when he was unable to follow those avenues to their conclusion. This is particularly true of his work on primitive 'high gods', with which his name is particularly associated in the history of comparative religion.

Lang's work on the history of religion and mythology can be conveniently divided into two parts, each of which was characterised by a main theme, a main focus of interest, and a main polemical object. From about 1873 to 1887 Lang was the faithful disciple of Tylor, and the chief spokesman of the 'anthropological school' in its running battle with the philologists and nature-mythologists led by Max Müller. From 1887 to 1897 he left the study of mythology

[24] See Roger Lancelyn Green, *Andrew Lang: a Critical Biography* (1946). Green does not however deal in detail with Lang's work on anthropology and religion. See on this subject Marett, *The Raw Material of Religion* (1929); and Rose, *Andrew Lang: His Place in Anthropology* (1951).
[25] Green, op. cit., p. 53.

and religion largely alone, although a number of important works appeared from the pens of Frazer, Farnell, Jevons and others during that time. Lang's second period of activity lasted from 1897 to practically the end of his life. The nature-mythologists having been eliminated, Lang's attention turned to the data of the anthropologists themselves, and to the problem of 'high gods'. His polemics now were directed against colleagues like Tylor, Hartland and Marett—though without personal acrimony.

Lang's training was, in the formal sense, classical; as a Fellow of Merton College, Oxford, he had done much work of lasting value on Homer. But he was also a son of the Scottish Border—that area which Sir Walter Scott had shown, rather more than fifty years before, to be an unusually rich repository of folk-traditions and ballads. It was this latter aspect which came to fascinate him more and more as he began in the early 1870s to trace and compare popular tales preserved in various oral traditions, with those he knew so well from Greece and Rome. This was a task similar to that carried out, with such important results, earlier in the century by Grimm in Germany.

Andrew Lang's interest was aroused in the first place by the fact of the diffusion of mythological material far beyond the boundaries that might conceivably be assigned to the Indo-European languages discussed by Max Müller. Was mythology, then, he wondered, 'a kind of linguistic measles'?[26] Or might mythology, particularly in its less attractive aspects, really be a survival from earlier ages of mankind, a form of fossilised thought? The problem of the nature and origin of myths, first broached in an essay in the *Fortnightly Review* (1873), was to provide a focus for Lang's anthropological work for some years—and often a target for his polemics. Of these early works it was perhaps his article, 'Mythology' in the ninth edition of the *Encyclopaedia Britannica* (1884), which dealt the hardest, because the most widely read and acknowledged, blow to the nature mythologists.

Myths, Lang pointed out, are part rational, part irrational, and it is the irrational, moving in a half-world of man and animal, cruelty and bestiality, that is in need of explanation. And so, 'The first objection to Mr. Müller's system is that it does not explain, but usually keeps clear of, the very horrors that need explanation.'[27]

[26] Lang, *Modern Mythology* (1898), p. 4. W. P. Ker wrote that the philologists '. . . may well have refused to believe that they were killed by a trifling sword of sharpness which they could not see. But their heads were off for all that . . .' *Commemorative Address* (1913), p. 12.

[27] Lang, 'Mythology', in *EB* 9 (1890), xvii, pp. 135-58. The quotation is from p. 139.

Müller's system is based explicitly on an analysis of Indo-European languages;

> But myths precisely similar in irrational and repulsive character to those of the Aryan races exist among Australians, South Sea Islanders, Eskimo, Bushmen in Africa, among Solomon Islanders, Iroquois, and so forth. The facts being identical, an identical explanation should be sought, and, as the languages in which the myths exist are essentially different, an explanation founded on the Aryan language is likely to prove too narrow.[28]

It had been claimed that in the earliest period of language, men possessed no myths, because myths were the product of a later linguistic aberration. This Lang was unable to accept, and instead reshaped the question. Is there, he asked, any stage in the development of human society in which the 'monstrous' and 'irrational' is simply accepted as commonplace?

> Our answer is that everything in the civilised mythologies which we regard as irrational seems only part of the accepted and rational order of things to contemporary savages, and in the past seemed equally rational and natural to savages concerning whom we have historical information.[29]

Myths, then, are a product of the childhood of the human race, arising out of the mind of a creature that has not yet learned to think in terms of strict cause and effect. In matters of religion, too, Lang is still thinking basically in Tylorian terms; though with the difference that he was much less willing to speak with confidence on matters of conjecture.

In his later book *Modern Mythology* (1898), written largely as a final anti-Müller manifesto, Lang stressed that he was simply not prepared to theorise in public about the ultimate origins of religion. 'I . . . persistently proclaim,' he wrote, 'that the beginning of religion is an inscrutable mystery.'[30] This reticence Lang was to preserve to the end of his days. In private, he certainly had opinions; but in public, he seldom went farther than to say that historical inquiry leads back, not to an emergent or evolving belief in spirits or gods, but to 'an unanalysable *sensus numinis*'.[31] How many scholars, one wonders, writing about Rudolf Otto, have observed this passage in Lang?

[28] ibid., p. 140.
[29] ibid., p. 142.
[30] *Modern Mythology*, p. 120.
[31] *The Making of Religion* (2nd ed. 1900), p. 46.

The second period of Lang's anthropological writing (and leaving aside much intermediate work by which this development might be illustrated) was characterised by a new focus of interest. Engaged in the study of totemism in Australia, Lang was struck by references in the Australian reports to a deity who could only be called a Supreme Being—a moral, spiritual, undying Creator who seemed to be in no way related to other, lesser gods and spirits. On further examination, similar evidence was forthcoming from other 'primitive' peoples. Why, he wondered, had so little account been taken of this material? Was it possible to do what most observers had hitherto done, and explain away these accounts as either the reflection of Christian missionary work (whether or not Christian missionaries had ever been in the areas in question), or of imperfect observation? Lang was not easily convinced that either could have been possible. Perhaps, he surmised, the evolutionists had committed a fundamental error. Bent on explaining the origin of religion out of that which was not religion, they had simply chosen to ignore evidence which did not square with their theories.

At the same time Lang had begun to show more than a casual interest in 'psychical' phenomena generally; extra-sensory perception, precognition, visions and hauntings he considered too prevalent in human experience to be explained away in every case as fraud or simple gullibility—though in this, as in so much else, Lang was a thoroughgoing sceptic who accepted only what he could not avoid accepting.

Thus during the last years of his active life, Lang's work had the twin foci of 'high gods' and psychical research. What is perhaps his most important book, *The Making of Religion* (1898), is devoted to both subjects. This may incidentally be one reason why his contemporaries refused to take him too seriously. Tylor, for instance, held that 'the modern spiritualism is pure and simple savagery both in its theory and the tricks by which it is supported',[32] and looked with disfavour on Lang for even suggesting that it might be more than that, and for pointing out that there may be '. . . a faculty for acquiring information not accessible by the known channels of sense, a faculty attributed by savage philosophers to the wandering soul'.[33] Animism was an excellent theory, apparently; but it might not be suggested to correspond to any actual condition of human life!

Leaving aside the aspect of psychical research (where the scholar must still tread delicately), a chapter of *The Making of Religion* was entitled 'High Gods of Low Races'. In it, Lang pointed out that

---

[32] Quoted by Marett, *Tylor*, p. 102f.
[33] *The Making of Religion*, p. 64.

observers have often noted that even the most primitive races have some kind of conception—alongside their belief in miscellaneous supernatural forces—of a Supreme Being, a divine ruler and creator, and that this idea can scarcely have come into their thought-world from any outside source. Usually the Supreme Being is undying, moral and above all creative; he may have nothing whatever to do with the doctrine of spirit, and still less to do with departed ancestors. He is not a spirit; not a ghost. Where, then, does he come from?

I do not pretend to know how the lowest savages evolved the theory of a God who reads the heart and 'makes for righteousness'. It is as easy, almost, for me to believe that they 'were not left without a witness', as to believe that this God of theirs was evolved out of the maleficent ghost of a dirty mischievous medicine-man.[34]

Might this, then, mean that primitive man was, as Father Schmidt was later so enthusiastically to announce, a monotheist? It might, though Lang was disinclined to say so in public. Here and there in his writings, though, he approaches a direct confession of belief in a kind of monotheism. In the revised edition of *Myth, Ritual and Religion* (1899), for instance, he goes so far as to say that

. . . man's earliest religious ideas may well have consisted, in a sense, of dependence on a supreme moral being who, when attempts were made by savages to describe the *modus* of his working, became involved in the fancies of mythology.[35]

In a letter to Grant Allen, Lang elaborates somewhat. Investigating the origin of the idea of God, he was surprised to find how little we know :

I did not expect this : still less to border on a primitive monotheist, of a kind : but the primitive monotheists, being mostly asses, have no idea what strong cards they hold. Not that there is really enough to do more than raise a presumption anyhow. To put it shortly, alongside of their magic, ghosts, totems, worshipful stones, κ.τ.λ. most of the very most backward races have a very much better God than many races a good deal higher in civilisation. We can't get behind those beggars, and know how this happened, we can only guess. As far as I guess the rudimentariest (*sic*) idea of a

[34] ibid., p. 170.
[35] *Myth, Ritual and Religion* I (1899), p. 305.

deity is fatherhood : a man can't have more than one father, so he becomes more or less monotheistic.[36]

In practice, therefore, Lang distinguished between higher and lower religion in antiquity, the lower being the province of mythology, the higher being centred on the high god. But he was not prepared to maintain that the one grew out of, or even preceded, the other :

> The worse side of religion is the less sacred, and therefore the more conspicuous. Both elements are found co-existing, in almost all our races, and nobody, in our total lack of historical information about the beginnings, can say which, if either element is the earlier, or which, if either, is derived from the other.[37]

Assuming, however, this degree of co-existence, it was not difficult to account for the comparative decline of the high god :

> That god thrives best who is most suited to his environment. Whether an easy-going, hungry ghost-god with a liking for his family, or a moral Creator not to be bribed, is better suited to an environment of not especially scrupulous savages, any man can decide.[38]

Space forbids further discussion of this, one of the most important contributions made by the anthropological school to the study of religion. Lang was forced to defend himself against many attacks— which he did with energy and enthusiasm. Most of his contemporaries chose to ignore him, however. Of the few who took him seriously, two in particular may be mentioned. In Austria, Father Wilhelm Schmidt published in 1908-10 in his periodical *Anthropos* a series of articles under the general title of *L'Origine de l'idée de*

---

[36] The letter is undated. It is one of a collection housed in the Lockwood Memorial Library of the State University of New York at Buffalo, and is reproduced here by permission of the Curator of the Poetry Collection. I am indebted to Mr. Roger Lancelyn Green for bringing this source to my attention.

[37] *The Making of Religion*, p. 183. Lang's general attitude of caution over disputed territory, and his unwillingness to make wild claims about such matters, may be further illustrated by a statement contained in a *Morning Post* article from 1909: '. . . The common mistake is to suppose that there is a "science" of religion. We have only collections of disputable facts : not knowledge but opinions. There can be no short and cheap cuts to reasonable familiarity with a subject of this nature. A man must work hard at first hand to know how little can be known.' 'Scientific Short Cuts', in *The Morning Post*, 1 October, 1909.

[38] *The Making of Religion*, p. 206.

Dieu (though with a Catholic apologetical purpose which Lang did not appreciate), in which Lang's theories were taken very seriously indeed.[39] In 1912, the year of Lang's death, Schmidt published the first volume of his monumental work *Der Ursprung der Gottesidee*. But even before this, in Sweden Nathan Söderblom, newly appointed Professor in the University of Uppsala, had written in 1902 :

> The science of religion shares with every other science the fate of being forced constantly to revise itself. It is not improbable that Lang's discoveries will bring about a considerable upheaval in certain branches of the history of religion.[40]

We now know these words to have been prophetic.

Now we are able to see that this talented amateur, his weaknesses notwithstanding, was able to accomplish more of permanent value than many of his professional colleagues. We may still, if we wish, dismiss Lang's attachment to ghosts and other occult phenomena as so much romantic wishful thinking. But we cannot dismiss his 'high gods' so easily. He saw what a too-rigid attachment to evolutionary theory had prevented his contemporaries from seeing—that the high gods of low races are facts of human experience, explain them how we will.

*　*　*

A third 'Oxford anthropologist' to call for consideration here is Tylor's disciple and successor Robert Ranulph Marett (1866-1943), concerning whom Lowie has written that '. . . in post-Tylorian England for poise in the judgment of values or for a sympathetic grasp of primitive values there is no superior to this philosophical humanist'.[41] The epithet 'philosophical humanist' is an apt one, and reflects something of the quality of British anthropology around the turn of the century. Marett, like Lang, was schooled in a far different tradition than that which is today called anthropology—social or otherwise. His work owed as much to the tradition of Oxford philosophical idealism as to currents of thought in emergent anthropology.

[39] These articles were reviewed by Lang in *Folk-Lore* (1910), pp. 516-23.
[40] Söderblom, 'Andrew Lang och Bäjämi', in *Ur religionens historia* (1915), p. 95. The article in question was first published in 1902. cf. Lowie, *The History of Ethnological Theory* (1937), p. 83.
[41] Lowie, op. cit., p. 111. Evans-Pritchard calls him 'this genial and ebullient classical philosopher' (*Theories of Primitive Religion*, p. 35). Marett's autobiography, *A Jerseyman at Oxford* (1941), gives many invaluable personal insights.

It was the reading of Andrew Lang's early book *Custom and Myth* (1884), which fired the imagination of the undergraduate Marett, and made him, as he put it, 'an enthusiastic, if extremely ignorant, disciple of the school of Tylor'.[42] His formal field of study was, however, philosophy, and it was as a philosopher that he was elected Fellow of Exeter College, Oxford. Until 1899 he taught philosophy, his only real excursion into anthropological theory being the writing of a prize essay on *The Ethics of Savage Races*.

The 1890s in Oxford were years during which Edward Caird was Master of Balliol, teaching there a form of personal idealism which emphasised the Platonic ideal of the unity of all human experience, and the summing up of all partial, incomplete truths in one all-embracing Reality. Caird, it has been said,

. . . sought the truth that lay hid in the doctrines he deemed erroneous, and treated the errors themselves as truths in the making, abstract statements summoning forth their opposites and pointing towards a unity beneath the opposition.[43]

Caird's final statement of this conviction, in its application to the world of religion, was contained in a two-volume book *The Evolution of Religion* (1902)—a work of philosophy rather than of the history of religion, but a work which has had significance in both fields. For Caird, as for all idealists, the underlying conviction was that the real is the rational, and that any approach to the phenomenon of religion (basically a unitary phenomenon, despite its varieties of expression) must be made along the lines of rational inquiry.

It is not, then, surprising that Marett the philosopher, when he turns to the problems of primitive religion, should choose to follow back into the remote past a line of rational reasoning. The circumstances in which Marett's theories first came to public attention are not without interest.

By the end of the century, Marett was an enthusiastic amateur anthropologist, with some practical training in prehistoric studies. In 1899 the British Association, meeting at Dover, invited him to enliven what promised to be a dull gathering with 'something startling' (the description is Marett's own).[44] He accepted the invitation, and produced a paper on what he called 'Preanimistic Religion'. We must remember that the Tylorian 'animism' theory of the origin of religion had been widely accepted for thirty years. In the previous year Lang had called part of the theory in question in his book *The Making of Religion*. Now it was Marett's turn.

[42] *Jerseyman*, p. 84.
[43] Jones and Muirhead, *The Life of Edward Caird* (1921), p. 35f.
[44] *Jerseyman*, p. 156f.

In his paper he began by saying that religion 'stands for a certain composite or concrete state of mind wherein various emotions and ideas are directly provocative of action'.[45] In this state of mind, animism (in Tylor's sense) is certainly very important indeed. But might there perhaps be something 'behind' animism—for instance a religious sense or instinct, made up of fear, awe, wonder and admiration in face of what is considered to be the supernatural? Marett could not accept that the concept of spirit was the *beginning* of the religious sense. Instead he suggested that primitive man began by venerating an impersonal power or force which he felt to be present in virtually any unusual object or striking natural phenomenon, such as the thunderstorm. He listed a number of terms— *Andriamanitra* (Madagascar), *Ngai* (Masai), *Wakan* (N. American Indian) and *Mana* (Melanesian) among them—which field anthropologists had said expressed similar concepts of supernatural power, and pointed out that although ghosts and spirits are powers, not all powers are ghosts and spirits 'even if they tend to become so'. The meaning of the various terms, or rather the state of mind which lies behind them, may perhaps be summed up in the word 'uncanny'. That which appears 'uncanny' to the primitive mind calls forth a sense or sensation distinct from other sensations. Religion, therefore, begins with the sense of the uncanny, the sense of an impersonal, inexplicable power attaching to virtually any object, and to many persons. Of the above-mentioned terms Marett chose the Melanesian *mana* as the focus of his theory. Faced with the awesome and the imponderable, primitive man is represented as saying, 'this has *mana*'; *mana*, then, is a possession.

The theory as such was not altogether new. For instance, in 1892 an American anthropologist, J. H. King, had published a book entitled *The Supernatural: its Origin, Nature and Evolution*, in which he had claimed that the ideas of 'ghost' and 'spirit' were too sophisticated for primitive man, and that there must therefore have been an earlier stage of thought in which the relatively simple ideas of 'luck' and 'power' were determinative. But King also held that religion is never anything save an illusion, and that it is always a brake on progress—views which Marett certainly did not share. Marett does not appear to have read King's book, which was entirely forgotten until resurrected and given an honourable mention by Wilhelm Schmidt in *Der Ursprung der Gottesidee*.[46] Schmidt, incidentally, was prepared to acknowledge King's priority in the matter of 'preanimism', but he was not prepared to call him the

[45] Marett, *The Threshold of Religion* (1902), p. 3f.
[46] Schmidt, *Der Ursprung der Gottesidee* 1 (2nd ed. 1920), pp. 493ff.

'founding father', since he had no offspring. It may be that the reason why King's book was so soon forgotten has something to do with its title, which suggested occultism rather than serious anthropology. King's rationalism, too, is of an insensitive kind.

Returning to Marett, following his Dover address he soon found himself, rather to his amusement, the head of a 'school'. In Britain his views were accepted by such outstanding men as E. S. Hartland; while in Germany, the illustrious Wilhelm Wundt, as Marett put it,

> even turned my adjective [preanimistic] into a noun and spoke of '*der Marettische Präanimismus*'; so that my mild protest against the all-sufficiency of the Tylorian animism must henceforth rank as a rival '-ism', the least of all that vast horde of pretentious abstractions.[47]

The idea was also accepted enthusiastically by another noted German anthropologist, K. T. Preuss, though with a twist that Marett had certainly never envisaged, since in Preuss' view, religion had originated in what can only be translated as 'primordial stupidity' (*Urdummheit*)—a somewhat clearer example than most of the place of value-judgements in anthropological theory.

A similar view also appeared in the work of some of the French sociologists, notably Hubert and Mauss, whose important work on the nature of magic appeared in Volume VII of the periodical *L'Année sociologique* (1905). There may have been some degree of indebtedness here; although Marett, with characteristic modesty, wrote in his autobiography that he had not read the French work, and that Hubert and Mauss had probably never heard of him. 'Both of us undoubtedly hit the same bird, and theirs was the heavier shot; but I fired first.'[48]

As it is the *mana* theory of the origin of religion which is always linked especially closely with the name of Marett, we must say a little more about it.[49]

Marett chose to apply the Melanesian term *mana* to the phenomenon of 'impersonal power', supposedly experienced by primitive man, and claimed this to be a source of belief in spirits, gods, and ultimately, God. The deduction is a psychological one—first, that the modern Melanesian term *mana* has reference to a state of mind, and secondly, *via* the 'survival equation', that this is an identical

---

[47] *Jerseyman*, p. 159.
[48] ibid., p. 161.
[49] The term *mana* has passed into the common vocabulary of comparative religion, and references to it are to be found in virtually all the handbooks. See e.g. Eliade, *Patterns in Comparative Religion* (Eng. tr. 1958), pp. 19ff.

state of mind to that which both preceded and gave rise to religion.
Clearly there are a number of separate assumptions being made
here. There is an assumption about religion originating in a state
of mind; an assumption about the actual meaning of *mana*; and an
assumption about the transferability of the modern term to a pre-
historic (in the fullest sense) situation. All three indeed can be
questioned. The first is simply incapable of either proof or disproof;
the third involves the validity of the 'survival equation', which we
have already seen to be at least questionable; and subsequent
research has cast grave doubts on the actual meaning of *mana* in
its Melanesian context. Here we cannot discuss all the implications
of Marett's theory; but some reference must be made to the alleged
'impersonality' of *mana*.

Recent research into Melanesian religion, and particularly the
work of F. R. Lehmann,[50] suggests that *mana* is scarcely to be
thought of as impersonal. Even R. H. Codrington, who was Marett's
chief source of information, though he claimed *mana* to be impersonal, also pointed out that it was always connected with some
person who directs it; all spirits have it, so do ghosts generally, and
some men.[51] The connection is important. It seems indeed that
mana should be thought of rather as a *quality* appertaining to the
supernormal or the supernatural—in short, to the 'parallel' and
unseen world of gods, spirits and ghosts, belief in the existence of
which is an *Urdatum* of religion. It is simply inconceivable to fear,
admire, or worship *mana* as such, though it is quite possible to fear,
admire or worship a being possessed of this quality. Again, Codrington recognised this :

> All success and all advantage proceed from the favourable exer-
> cise of this *mana*; whatever evil happens has been caused by the
> direction of this power to harmful ends, whether by spirits, or
> ghosts, or men. *In no case, however, does this power operate,
> except under the direction and control of a person—a living man,
> a ghost, or a spirit* [my italics].[52]

This seems clear enough, and one can only conclude that the use
of the abstract word 'power' in this connection led a generation
somewhat given to the reification of abstractions to suppose that

[50] Lehmann, *Mana* (1922); 'Die gegenwärtige Lage der Manaforschung,'
in *Festschrift Reche* (1939).
[51] Codrington, 'Melanesians', in *ERE* VIII (1915), p. 530a: 'This power is
impersonal, and not physical in itself, although it is always put in motion by
a person; and all remarkable effects in nature were thought to be produced
by it.'
[52] ibid.

the abstraction somehow or other once was self-existent. Of this there is no evidence; indeed, whatever evidence there is points in another direction, towards a belief in gods and spirits arranged in something of a divine hierarchy. One of the qualities of this hierarchy happened to be called by the Melanesians *mana*. (Genius is a similarly abstract quality, inconceivable apart from a person who embodies it.) Although we cannot proceed further along this line, much the same could be demonstrated of other 'impersonal' power-words, and particularly those produced from among the half-understood vocabularies of North American Indians—*wakan, orenda*, and the rest. Leaving aside the question of the modern observer's right to make such tendentious use of ethnographical parallels, none of these words can ultimately be separated from the spirit-beings of which they are qualities.

As well as postulating a prior stage in the development of religion to the Tylorian animism, Marett also criticised the views on the relationship between religion and magic that had been put forward by J. G. Frazer in the second edition of *The Golden Bough* (1900)— a work which we shall discuss more fully in the next chapter. Marett's objection was that Tylor and Frazer had each in his respective way failed to give sufficient weight to emotional states of mind, and had unwittingly regarded primitive man as a reasoning being primarily, and an emotional being only secondarily, instead of *vice versa*.

Another implicit criticism of current anthropology which gradually emerged in Marett's writing, partly under the influence of the French sociological school, concerned the individualism of the typically British interpretation of religion. Tylor and his followers tended to regard religion as having developed in the depths of the individual mind as a result of a peculiar reflective process, in which 'experiences' had played a large part. This interpretation was particularly congenial to the late-nineteenth-century liberal mind in Britain (and possibly still more in America, as we shall see); and it certainly needed a corrective. Perhaps Marett himself was too much of an idealist to provide it, and Durkheim and his followers did more to redress the balance. Nevertheless, Marett had seen at a fairly early stage that it is at least as important to observe what people actually *do* as to speculate about their inmost thoughts. In his autobiography he wrote that in his later work, '. . . I preferred, in dealing with very primitive folk, to lay less stress on what they thought, or were supposed to think, than on what they did.'[53]

---

[53] *Jerseyman*, p. 157f.

But he did not abandon the attempt to enter the mind of primitive man. Of his later publications we may content ourselves with mentioning his two series of Gifford Lectures, delivered in St. Andrews in 1931–2 and 1932–3. The first is called *Faith, Hope and Charity in Primitive Religion* (1932), and deals with such topics as hope, fear, lust, cruelty, faith, conscience, curiosity, admiration and charity; it is impelled by the conviction that '. . . the emotional quality of primitive religion is all-in-all',[54] though it also recognises that 'religion according to the savage is essentially something that you do.'[55] This latter aspect is more fully treated in the second series, published as *Sacraments of Simple Folk* (1933), which deals with eating, fighting, mating, educating, ruling, judging, covenanting, healing and dying. Emotion, then, is hidden deep within a mesh of customary practices; and 'Custom is king, nay tyrant, in primitive society.' To sum up,

> The religion of a savage is part of his custom, nay, rather, it is his whole custom insofar as it appears sacred—so far as it coerces him by way of his imagination. Between him and the unknown stands nothing but his custom. . . We may say that any and every custom, insofar as it is regarded as lucky, is a religious rite.[56]

This was potentially a very fruitful approach, not only to primitive religion, but to all religion. Probably it is true to say that the imagination of the 'savage' always was, and always will be, more or less a closed book to the latter-day Western observer. But there is a great deal of his life which can be observed, and which may well lead to a more fruitful understanding of his religion than all the psychologising in the world.

---

[54] Marett, *Faith, Hope and Charity in Primitive Religion* (1932), p. 7.
[55] ibid., p. 11.
[56] Marett, *Anthropology* (1911), p. 213.

IV

Totemism and Magic

Max Müller and his followers interpreted religion and its origins
mainly on a basis of the parallel data provided by the science of
language, and on the basis of material drawn from myths (tales
told in words); the first generation of Darwinian anthropologists
saw the origin of religion as being linked with the emergence of
belief in supernatural beings, perhaps out of a sense of an impersonal 'uncanny'. But these were not the only questions having a
bearing on religion; the genetic alternative was not the only
approach which the anthropologists might adopt. States of mind,
and their verbal expressions, are tenuous things, and in reality
hardly accessible to later investigators. Further, since religion is
clearly, as Marett knew so well, just as much a matter of 'things
done' and 'companies of the faithful (or the initiated)' as it is a
matter of 'things believed' or 'tales told', it was at least feasible that
close study of the ritual and other practices of mankind would prove
valuable. For the time being, it was not to be expected that scholarship would cease to concern itself with the question of origins : the
time of the functionalists was not yet. But in turning to the observables of religion, it is arguable that scholarship had taken a very
important step for the better.

The importance of ritual and other collective expressions of
religion is so much taken for granted by modern scholarship that it
is difficult fully to envisage a time when this was not fully recognised. And certainly, the West had for many years been interested
in 'savage rites'. Our earliest anthropological records are by no
means lacking in descriptions of social forms of religion. Nor was
there any shortage of travellers' tales from various parts of the
world, describing religion in its spectacular, bizarre and horrific
aspects. That ritual practices had a role in primitive religion no one
could reasonably doubt, but the consensus was that this role was
secondary and in a measure accidental. This judgement can be
directly related to the conviction common in the late nineteenth
century that religion becomes 'genuine' and 'spiritual' only insofar
as it is able to shake itself more or less free from such externals. Perhaps religion would always need a body, if only as a carrier for its
immortal soul; but often in the late nineteenth century this body
was something of an embarrassment.

Gradually, however, it came to be realised that religion could not be dealt with simply and straightforwardly in terms of the instinctive beliefs of 'primitive philosophers' concerning the fate of man after death, the nature of the human soul, and the character of deity. Religious belief and belonging involves much more than the mental processes of the individual—which are in any case often incoherent. It involves the collective notions of a tribe or other community concerning its own identity, its relationship to the unseen world of the supernaturals, and its convictions about the implications of that relationship to its members, old and young, male and female, living and dead. It involves all those practical measures which van Gennep was shortly to characterise for all time as 'rites of passage'—the rituals governing the transition of every human being from non-being to being, from childhood to maturity, from life to death.[1]

We cannot in this context examine all the ways in which students of religion attempted to uncover this aspect of the human condition. Instead we shall look at the work of a group of scholars who studied some aspects of the common experience of mankind, and particularly what came to be called 'totemism' and 'magic'. In the phenomenon of totemism it was thought that the scholar could isolate a stage in the religious evolution of mankind in which men collectively 'worshipped' animals, birds and other creatures, and identified themselves, their families and their tribes as being descended from such ancestors. The idea of magic, too, was eventually taken to represent a stage in the evolution of religion prior to the emergence of religion proper—corporately significant in that the worker of magic was able to assume a position of importance in the tribe, to act as a cohesive influence among a group of people, and to be the forerunner of the sacral king.

In writing about M'Lennan, Robertson Smith, Durkheim and Frazer in this context, I am of course selecting only four significant figures from among the mass of writers for whom the concepts of totemism and magic were important. On totemism, it would have been quite feasible to write once more about Andrew Lang, for whom the concept was of great importance; and other writers will no doubt suggest themselves to the reader.

*　　*　　*

---

[1] A. van Gennep, *Les Rites de passage* (1909). It is odd, in view of the importance of this book, that it was not translated into English until 1960. cf. also Goblet d'Alviella, 'Initiation (Introductory and Primitive)', in ERE vii (1914), pp. 314a-319b.

The term 'totemism' is now agreed to have been coined towards the end of the eighteenth century by a certain John Long, in a book called *Voyages and Travels of an Indian Interpreter and Trader* (1791).[2] As in the case of 'animism', the word which eventually came to rest in Tylor's system of thought, 'totemism' came to be used in many ways having little to do with Long's intentions. The celebrated passage in which the notion first appears reads as follows :

> One part of the religious superstitions of the Savages, consists in each of them having his *totam*, or favourite spirit, which he believes watches over him. This *totam* they conceive assumes the shape of some beast or other, and therefore, they never kill, hunt or eat the animal whose form they think this *totam* bears.[3]

There is no doubt that as far as it went, this is a valid description of a by now well-known phenomenon—that of the guardian spirit— among some tribes of North American Indians. But Long goes on to describe an episode in which a man killed his *totam* animal in error, and was stricken with the direst forebodings concerning his future success (or most probably, lack of it) in hunting. And he concludes :

> This idea of destiny, or, if I may be allowed the phrase, '*totamism*', however strange, is not confined to the Savages; many instances might be adduced from history, to prove how strong these impressions have been on minds above the vulgar or unlearned.[4]

In 1809, Alexander Henry the Elder, another fur-trader, described in his book *Travels and Adventures in Canada and the Indian Territories* the totem as a 'badge' or 'armorial bearing', without speculating further as to its possible or probable meaning.

Thus while it soon became recognised that some Indian tribes conceived of themselves as standing singly or collectively in a special relationship to certain plants, animals or birds, little was at first known about the implications of this fact, and no attempt was made to elevate the concept of totemism into a universal principle of religious development.

The first stage in such an elevation may be said to have been reached when it gradually came to be realised that the Australian aborigines possessed a family clan structure corresponding in many ways to that of the North American Indians, particularly in respect

---

[2] Reprinted in Thwaites (ed.), *Early Western Travels, 1748–1846* II (1904).
[3] ibid., p. 123.
[4] ibid., p. 124f.

of the place of animals, birds and the like within the family network. But beyond the pointing out of the resemblance, little could be done. The phenomenon might be 'religious', or it might not. If it were, of course, the fact of its having occurred within the survival-category of 'stone age man' would double its value. But there in fact the matter rested until the end of the 1860s, when the problem was taken up by the Scottish lawyer and amateur anthropologist J. F. M'Lennan.

* * *

The legal profession has always enjoyed vast esteem in Scotland, a fact which is worth bearing in mind when it is recalled that John Ferguson M'Lennan (1827–1881) contributed the article on 'Law' to what was still at that time a Scottish publication, the eighth edition of the *Encyclopaedia Britannica* (1857), in the same year in which he was called to the Bar. This was an unusual mark of distinction. For the rest of his life he adorned the legal profession, serving from 1872 to 1875 as Parliamentary Draftsman for Scotland.[5]

M'Lennan's researches into the subject of totemism arose quite incidentally out of his work on the purely legal problems connected with kinship and marriage in ancient societies. His maiden work, which has rightly been called epoch-making, but which need not concern us very closely, was *Primitive Marriage* (1865), in which he considered the bearing of symbolical forms of capture in primitive marriage ceremonies. He concluded that at some stage in the past there must have been rules to inhibit the taking of wives from within one's own social group or clan.[6] In so doing, he introduced two new technical terms, *endogamy* (marriage within the group) and *exogamy* (marriage outside the group) into the anthropological vocabulary.

Continuing to work along these same lines, in the following year, 1866, M'Lennan published in the *Fortnightly Review* two articles on 'Kinship in Ancient Greece', in which the topic of familial relationship with plants and animals is broached. But as far as totemism is concerned, he arrived at a definite position with a series of articles on 'The Worship of Animals and Plants', again in the *Fortnightly Review* for 1869–70. Here, abruptly, totemism ceases to be an entertaining curiosity of primitive life, and becomes a full-

---

[5] *Dictionary of National Biography* xxxv (1893), p. 210f. See also Lowie, *History of Ethnological Theory* (1937), pp. 44ff., for a sharp criticism.

[6] M'Lennan was here working, though independently, on similar lines to the Swiss jurist J. J. Bachofen (1815–1887), who had published a study of *Das Mutterrecht* (Matriarchy) in 1861.

blown theory of the origin of religion.[7] First, wrote M'Lennan,

> . . . we shall explain with some detail what totems are, and what
> are their usual concomitants; showing how far they have, or have
> recently had, a place among existing tribes of men; and we shall
> throw what light we can on the intellectual condition of men in
> what we might call the totem stage of development. Next we shall
> examine the evidence which goes to show that the ancient nations
> came, in prehistoric times, through the totem stage, having animals
> and plants, and the heavenly bodies conceived as animals, for gods
> before the anthropomorphic gods appeared, and shall consider
> the explanations that have been offered of that evidence. The
> conclusion we shall reach is that the hypothesis that the ancient
> nations came through the totem stage, satisfies all the conditions
> of a sound hypothesis.[8]

We need not recapitulate M'Lennan's argument in detail, but one
or two points may be noted. First, there is no very clear difference
in M'Lennan's argument between what had for a century—since
de Brosses—been called 'fetishism', what Tylor called 'animism',
and what M'Lennan himself called 'totemism' :

> Some explanation of the phenomena of life a man *must* feign for
> himself; and to judge from the universality of it, the simplest
> hypothesis, and the first to occur to men, seems to have been that
> natural phenomena are ascribable to the presence in animals,
> plants, and things, and in the forces of nature, of such spirits
> prompting to action as men are conscious they themselves pos-
> sess . . . This animation hypothesis, held as a faith, is at the root
> of all the mythologies. It has been called Fetichism; which, accord-
> ing to the common accounts of it, ascribes a life and personality
> resembling our own, not only to animals and plants, but to rocks,
> mountains, streams, winds, the heavenly bodies, the earth itself,
> and even the heavens. Fetichism thus resembles totemism; which,
> indeed, is Fetichism *plus* certain peculiarities. These peculiarities
> are, (1) the appropriation of a special fetich to the tribe, (2) its
> hereditary transmission through mothers, and (3) its connection
> with the *jus connubii*.[9]

Accordingly, in a good deal of what M'Lennan has to say, it is hard
to avoid the impression that Tylor would have accepted his descrip-

---

[7] The apparent parallel between the North American Indians and the
Australian Aborigines, on which so much of this theory was to depend, had
been pointed out in the 1850s by J. C. Prichard.

[8] M'Lennan, *Studies in Ancient History* II (1896), p. 493. cf. W. Robertson
Smith, *Kinship and Marriage* (1885), p. 258f.

[9] M'Lennan, II, p. 512.

tion happily as a description of animism, though modified by theories of matriarchy and exogamy. But when M'Lennan takes his American and Australian evidence, and postulates that all 'animal gods' must therefore be older than anthropomorphic deities (including the heavenly deities in the former category, these at some stage or other having been 'transferred' on high), the evolutionary character of his argument becomes apparent. However, in fairness to M'Lennan it must be noted that at the end of his essay he expressly disclaims having attempted to demonstrate the *origins* of totemism; his hypothesis, he says,

> . . . is not an hypothesis explanatory of the origin of *totemism*, be it remembered, but an hypothesis explanatory of the animal and plant worship of the ancient nations. It is quite intelligible that animal worship growing from the religious regard for the totem or kobong [the Australian equivalent]—the friend and protector—should, irrespective of the nature of the animal, be a religion of love. What we say is, our hypothesis explains the facts.[10]

Possibly. But it is not therefore a correct hypothesis, since it depends for its value upon a much greater hypothesis, that of unilinear evolution of the development of religious beliefs and expressions from lower forms to higher. On the face of it, a hypothesis of degeneration would suit the facts equally well—though we do not need to pursue that point here. We may merely note that the last words of M'Lennan's article— '. . . totemism was the foundation of their [the ancient nations'] mythologies'—was soon to be interpreted by Andrew Lang precisely as evidence of religious degeneration. For mythologies are not identical with religions.

At all events, M'Lennan had started a hare, which was not finally caught until Claude Lévi-Strauss published his book *Le Totémisme aujourd'hui* in 1962. But in the years before and after the turn of the century there were some uncommonly well-equipped and energetic hunters, none more so than M'Lennan's friend and fellow-Scot William Robertson Smith.

* * *

Robertson Smith (1846–1894), perhaps more than most of the scholars we have been considering thus far, had enemies, one of whom paid him the somewhat oblique compliment of saying that

> his mind is like a shop with a big cellar behind it, and having good shelves and windows. . . But he doesn't grow his own wool,

[10] ibid., p. 567.

nor does he spin the thread, nor weave the webs that are in his cellar or on his shelves. All his goods come in paper parcels from Germany . . .[11]

The reason for this was a fairly simple one, that he came from the intensely orthodox Free Church of Scotland, and never repudiated his churchmanship. Unlike other philologists and anthropologists, who stood almost without exception at a distance from the Christian churches, Smith was a man in the middle. Caught in the crossfire between liberal and evangelical, he was a convenient target, and in the event, he became a scapegoat.

A son of the manse, his father being Free Church minister at Keig, Aberdeenshire, Smith was educated at Aberdeen University (1861–6) and New College, Edinburgh (1866–70). He was no narrow scholar, excelling in 'natural philosophy' as well as the more conventional classics and theology. For two years he taught mathematics and physics at Edinburgh University, and he had many friends outside theological circles (R. L. Stevenson was one of his pupils). He visited Germany on a number of occasions, and there he cultivated the friendship of scientists and theologians alike. Among the latter, the most outstanding, and, in the eyes of the faithful, the most dangerous by far, was Albrecht Ritschl.

And yet it was a friendship formed at home in Scotland that was to lead him into his distinctive area of study. That friendship was with J. F. M'Lennan, who stimulated him into taking an interest in the subjects of kinship and totemism. In 1879, Smith paid his first visit to North Africa, where he was struck by what seemed to him clear evidence of totemism among the Bedawin of Sinai. By this time, Smith had become a convinced liberal theologian, though bound by strong ties of loyalty to his Church; in the academic world he was developing into an outstanding Semitic philologist. It was as a result of this visit that he produced his first important monograph, on 'Animal Worship and Animal Tribes among the Arabs and in the Old Testament' (1880), followed in 1885 by the book, *Kinship and Marriage in Early Arabia*. In 1886 he contributed the article 'Sacrifice' to the ninth edition of the *Encylopaedia Britannica* and in 1889 came his major work, *Lectures on the Religion of the Semites: the Fundamental Institutions* (2nd ed. 1894; 3rd ed., revised by S. A. Cook, 1927). But before we go on to say something about the content of Smith's work and its relevance to comparative religion, a word is necessary about the controversies surrounding him as a man. This may perhaps seem to be a needless raking up of old

---

[11] Black and Chrystal, *The Life of W. Robertson Smith* (1912), p. 401.

antipathies, but 'the Robertson Smith case' was part of the history of comparative religion (though in a sense an indirect part), and as such deserves to be remembered.

Smith had been appointed in 1870 to the Chair of Old Testament Studies at the Free Church College in Aberdeen, and held the post without trouble until 1875. In that year, however, he published in the *Encyclopaedia Britannica* an article, 'Bible', in which he called in question some generally held beliefs of his day, particularly that which ascribed to Moses in person the authorship of the entire Pentateuch. There were stirrings in high places, first in the popular press, and then in the Free Church courts. A committee was appointed to investigate, which published its findings in 1877. Despite Smith's assurances that he still believed in the inspiration of Scripture, his opponents, who by this time were both numerous and powerful, insisted that he could not possibly do so. He was suspended by his Church from his professorial duties, not, so the story went, because he was being personally censured, but in order to protect the susceptibilities of his students. At this point the furore might have subsided, had not Smith's article on 'Animal Worship' appeared in the *Journal of Philology* in 1880. Fresh fuel was fed to the dying fires of controversy; the article was promptly condemned, because it seemed to be saying that the Old Testament did not give an accurate account of certain facts, and might even contain something disreputable. Smith's work was called 'unscriptural and pernicious', and he himself was dismissed his post.[12] The 'Robertson Smith case' passed into ecclesiastical history. After an interval working as Editor of the 9th edition of the *Encyclopaedia Britannica*, Smith was appointed in 1883 to the Chair of Arabic at Cambridge, and three years later to the post of University Librarian. He died in 1894.

In Smith's struggles with ecclesiastical authority we see epitomised the struggle which accompanied the comparative study of religion throughout its first decades. The point at issue was a relatively simple one : were the Holy Scriptures of Christianity to be studied on genetic and historical principles, or were they forever exempt from such treatment? And following from this, was the individual scholar to be free to interpret his own faith, not in relation to an unquestioned principle of authority, but in relation to a personal quest for light and truth along the lines of free inquiry? This question was fought over again and again in the late nineteenth and

---

[12] As a *cause célèbre*, the Robertson Smith case is discussed in every history of the period. But see H. F. Henderson, *The Religious Controversies of Scotland* (1905), chapter XI, and Glover, *Evangelical Nonconformists and Higher Criticism in the 19th Century* (1954), pp. 117ff. It is perhaps worth noting that the final voting in favour of his dismissal was 491 to 113 (*Life*, p. 234).

early twentieth centuries; we shall meet it again. Many students of comparative religion sat sufficiently loose to ecclesiastical authority to enable them to move freely in these matters; Robertson Smith's misfortune was that he attempted to follow the path of comparative religion and to claim allegiance to an evangelical confession at one and the same time.

Turning now briefly to the scholarly aspect of Robertson Smith's work, he differed from most of the anthropologists we have so far been considering, first, in concentrating on a relatively narrow field of study in which he had thorough philological competence, and secondly, in dealing with his material from a social, rather than from a purely individual point of view.[18] Of course he had a great deal in common with the school of Tylor. He was interested in the problem of origins, and made a certain use of non-Semitic material for comparative purposes, particularly in his investigations into the question of totemism. But he was always careful in his comparisons, and *The Religion of the Semites* in particular stands out as one of the finest examples in the early history of comparative religion of constructive, original and independent scholarship.

The focal point of this book is the concept of sacrifice, and its underlying conviction is that the act of sacrifice is always fundamentally an attempt to establish communion with deity. The act is of far greater importance than any attempt to theorise about its significance, or about the 'beliefs' which underly it. In the beginning, in effect, was the act, the drama, the practical commerce of man and God. In Smith's own words,

> . . . it is of the first importance to realise clearly from the outset that ritual and practical usage were, strictly speaking, the sum-total of ancient religions. Religion in primitive times was not a system of belief with practical applications : it was a body of fixed traditional practices, to which every member of society conformed as a matter of course. . . . The rules of society were based on precedent, and the continued existence of the society was sufficient reason why a precedent set should continue to be followed.[14]

This concentration on the primacy of ritual, and on the role of ritual within primitive society, was something relatively new in anthro-

---

[13] cf. Malinowski, *Magic, Science and Religion* (1948), p. 37, who draws attention to Robertson Smith's view that primitive religion is the concern of the community rather than the individual, but continues : 'Robertson Smith did not do much more in this matter, in fact, than set forth the important problem : why is it that primitive man performs his ceremonies in public? What is the relation between society and the truth revealed by religion and worshipped in it?'

[14] *The Religion of the Semites* (3rd ed. 1927), p. 20.

pology, and in comparative religion. Here we have a bridge to the later discipline of the sociology of religion, and to later social anthropology. Durkheim in particular was to derive many fruitful impulses from Robertson Smith, while later social anthropologists frequently cite him (almost alone among nineteenth-century British anthropologists) with evident approval.[15]

In investigating the religious institutions of the Semites, Smith concentrated on social patterns, and particularly on the pattern of 'totemism', i.e. the worship of sacred animals. Between man and the animal in question there is a bond of kinship; but there is more than this, for the animal is sacred. By virtue of its blood, it is the property of Deity. Thus it is that when the animal is sacrificed, a bond of mediation is established between man and God. According to Smith,

> . . . throughout the Semitic field, the fundamental idea of sacrifice is not that of a sacred tribute, but of communication between the god and his worshippers by joint participation in the flesh and blood of a sacred victim.[16]

He was not, however, prepared to assert that behind every Semitic conception of deity there must of necessity lie a barely-hidden totemism; merely that the Semites, like every other race, had passed through a 'totemistic stage' in their religious evolution, and that something of this stage was still to be discerned by way of survivals. 'It is one thing,' he wrote, 'to say that the phenomena of Semitic religion carry us back to totemism, and another to say that they are all to be explained from totemism.'[17]

We cannot proceed to a more detailed examination of Robertson Smith's arguments on this and other subjects. But there is one other point which may be mentioned. On taking up his appointment at Cambridge, Smith had been brought into contact with another expatriate Scotsman, James George Frazer, who had just been appointed Fellow of Trinity College. Smith's interest in the problem of totemism communicated itself to Frazer, and when the time came for the articles 'Totem' and 'Taboo' to be written for the *Encyclopaedia Britannica*, Smith entrusted them to Frazer. He wrote to a friend :

---

[15] cf. Mary Douglas, *Purity and Danger* (1970), pp. 20ff. She writes: 'Whereas Tylor was interested in what quaint relics can tell us of the past, Robertson Smith was interested in the common elements in modern and primitive experience. Tylor founded folk-lore: Robertson Smith founded social anthropology.' (p. 24f.) Tylor, of course, did not found folk-lore!

[16] *The Religion of the Semites*, p. 345.

[17] ibid., p. 139.

D

Totemism is a subject of growing importance, daily mentioned in the magazines and papers, but of which there is no good account anywhere—precisely one of those cases where we have an opportunity of getting ahead of every one and getting some reputation. There is no article in the volume for which I am more solicitous. I have taken much personal pains with it, guiding Frazer carefully in his treatment . . .[18]

We shall move on shortly to consider some aspects of Frazer's work; but before we do so, it will be necessary to inquire briefly into parallel developments in France, where the heirs of Auguste Comte, and particularly Émile Durkheim, were producing—partly on the basis of the work of M'Lennan and Robertson Smith—strikingly similar results.

*   *   *

We have previously touched upon the influence of the Comtean philosophy of history in creating an intellectual climate in nineteenth-century Europe. Comte had many followers, among them Jean-Marie Guyeau (1854-1888), whose book *L'Irréligion de l'avenir* (1887) had confidently predicted the demise of all religion, and the creation of a more or less anarchic and utopian state.

Although this type of sociological prophecy appealed to some, greater influence on the future of religious study was exercised by the less extreme Émile Durkheim (1858-1917).[19] An atheist of Jewish extraction, he studied law, philosophy, social science and *Völkerpsychologie* (the influence of Wundt is clear) and spent his academic career at the universities of Bordeaux and Paris, where he occupied a chair at the Sorbonne from 1892. Among his published works may be mentioned *De la division du travail social* (1893), *Les Règles de la méthode sociologique* (1895), *Le Suicide* (1897) and—a classic in the sociology of religion—*Les Formes élémentaires de la vie réligieuse* (1912).

Comment on a thinker and writer of Durkheim's stature is difficult in a survey of this kind, not only because of the far-ranging character of his work, but also because of the vast secondary literature which has grown up around his name since his death. As far as comparative religion is concerned, however, there are certain themes

[18] *Life*, p. 494f.
[19] Among the mass of writings on Durkheim, mention may be made of Nisbet, *Émile Durkheim* (1965) and Wolff (ed.), *Émile Durkheim 1858–1917* (1960). See also Rex, 'Émile Durkheim', in Raison (ed.), *The Founding Fathers of Social Science* (1969), pp. 128ff.

which recur frequently in Durkheim's writing and which were to
place the entire study, in some quarters at least, on a new footing. It
is on these—notably his interest in totemism, his consequent interpretation of religion as a social fact *par excellence*, and his parallel
conviction that religion can be treated adequately only in terms of
its social function—that we must now focus.

First of all it should be noted that Durkheim's work was conceived
in sharp reaction against the psychologically-oriented individualism
of much of the ostensibly 'social' thought of the late nineteenth
century (precisely that kind of thought under the influence of which
comparative religion and anthropology first developed). The way to
an understanding of the forms in which humans band themselves
together is, he held, not through a piecemeal analysis of the minds
of the individuals concerned, but through a close study of the groups
themselves. There are, in other words, 'social facts', which exercise
compelling power over the individual, and which appear to be the
product of a collective consciousness, above and beyond the minds
of the individuals who make up the collective. Only these 'social
facts' can be scientifically investigated. On this general foundation
Durkheim built a considerable edifice of theory concerning the
development of social life, and such elements within that life as the
division of labour, suicide, morals and religion. He attempted to
describe the division of larger social units into smaller, more homogeneous units, and then to demonstrate how each separate group
possesses what might be called a mind of its own, distinguishable
from the sum of the minds of its members. There are thus collective
states of mind, the nature of which cannot be reduced to the sum of
the opinions of individuals.

To Durkheim, religion is the most characteristic product of the
collective mind. Its attitudes, values and sanctions are imposed upon
the individual by the group of which he is a part; this is indeed the
condition on which he becomes (by initiation) and remains a member
of the group. Further, each of its constitutive elements, such as cult,
rite and symbol, fulfils an integrative function within the group. In
this, Durkheim was to some extent recapitulating the thesis expressed by one of his most influential teachers, Numa-Denys Fustel
de Coulanges (1830-1889), whose book *La Cité ancienne* (1864) had
analysed the city-state in terms of its religious beliefs and traditions.
But Durkheim carried de Coulanges' theories into a much wider
area of principle.

Durkheim's mature views on the subject of religion are to be
found in two works in particular, *De la définition des phénomènes
religieux*, an essay of twenty-eight pages published in the second
volume of his periodical *L'Année sociologique* (1899), and the cele-

brated *Les Formes élémentaires* (1912). In a way, the former is methodologically the more important of the two, since it discusses matters which are presuppositions for the later work.

In the preface to the second volume of *L'Année sociologique*, Durkheim stressed that 'facts' in the spheres of religion, law, morals and economics should all be treated in conformity to their own nature, i.e., as *social facts*, attached to a definite social milieu. The science of religion, he points out, had hitherto spoken of religious beliefs and practices as though they belonged to no social system at all. The criticism was not unjustified; nevertheless it is important to realise that the reason for this particular point being raised was largely that of safeguarding the possibility of dealing with religion on scientific lines, and to guard against undue subjectivity in treatment. 'Scientific', it may be added, was a term used in antithesis to attitudes involving commitment and belief; popularly it was supposed to guarantee a state of freedom from distorting presuppositions. Durkheim's desire was to establish principles, patterns and laws : so far so good. But it is soon evident that in rejecting one set of presuppositions, he is merely accepting an alternative set, involving the thesis of the non-existence of any supernatural order whatsoever.

It was in line with this conviction that Durkheim maintained that the concept of deity, so far from being fundamental to religious life, is only 'a secondary episode'—a product of a special process by virtue of which various 'religious' characteristics are hypostasised. What is genuinely fundamental is the basic separation of all things into the two categories of *sacred* and *profane*, a distinction which is, he asserts, 'very often independent of every idea of god'—which idea was formed subsequently 'in order to introduce the beginnings of organisation into the confused mass of sacred things'.[20]

The picture thus emerges of the primitive group behaving in certain ways, asserting certain obligations incumbent on every single member of the group. In reality, these obligations have no other sanction than that provided by the need to perpetuate the life of the group; but they are given a further absolute sanction by being referred to supernatural originating agencies, which are in effect products of the collective imagination.

'Religious phenomena,' according to Durkheim, 'consist in obligatory beliefs, connected with definite practices which refer to objects given in these beliefs.' It is precisely the quality of *obligation* which characterises them.[21] But obligation presupposes an authority : and to Durkheim, the only conceivable authority is that of the group of

[20] *L'Année sociologique* II (1899), p. 15.
[21] ibid., p. 21.

which the individual is part. It follows that 'society' prescribes to the faithful the dogmas which he must believe and the rites which he must observe; religion, then, originates in collective states of mind (*états de l'âme collective*).

> The force before which the believer bows are not simple physical energies, such as are presented to the senses and the imagination; they are social forces.[22]

In this perspective, religion becomes comprehensible. If it emanates from the individual, it remains a mystery :

> For since, by definition, it expresses things otherwise than they are, it appears as a sort of vast hallucination and phantasmagoria of which humanity has been the dupe and the *raison d'être* of which is impenetrable.[23]

Admit that religion is a social phenomenon, and the mystery is dispersed. Whatever residual mystery may remain is a product only of ignorance, and will inevitably vanish in the clear light of science, given time.

We have said that it is in the distinction between sacred and profane that Durkheim sees the germ of all religion. This is the achievement of the collective mind : to establish such a distinction, and to specify in each separate instance to which category a phenomenon belongs. All else is derivative and secondary. Thus in a celebrated formulation Durkheim defines a religion as

> . . . a unified system of beliefs and practices relative to sacred things, that is to say, things set apart and forbidden—beliefs and practices which unite into one single moral community called a church, all those who adhere to them.[24]

Religion involves the formation of communities bound together by a common attitude to certain 'sacred' objects, places and persons. The individual can only accept this common attitude; nothing more is expected of him, and nothing more is acceptable.

Durkheim's indebtedness to the Scottish anthropologists is most clearly seen in the argument which he uses in support of this general theory. He holds in fact that it is precisely in the social institution of totemism that a collective representation, involving a clear and socially motivated distinction between sacred and profane, is most evident in human history. Hence there is much totemism in Durk-

[22] ibid., p. 21.
[23] loc. cit.
[24] *The Elementary Forms of the Religious Life* (Eng. tr. 1915), p. 47.

heim's work. He makes use of the customary turn-of-the-century theory of survivals to justify reference to the Australian aborigines as an example of the earliest human social system. There he finds totemism, and in totemism he sees the beginning of religion. In the totem there lies a mysterious power (*mana*), by which means transgressions against *tabu* might be punished; *tabu* is of course 'the sacred' in its simplest form. The totem itself is both a symbol of the tribal deity or deities and a symbol around which the tribe might gather, and by which it might identify itself. It follows that if the same symbol can serve two such functions, then *a priori* there must be more than merely a casual relationship between these functions. Such is Durkheim's conclusion : to all intents and purposes the god *is* the tribe or clan; god and totem are simply alternative expressions of 'society', the collective. To be sure, there have been developments out of this originally homogeneous form of religion; but they constantly betray their collective origin, since

. . . the great tribal god is only an ancestral spirit who finally won a pre-eminent place. The ancestral spirits are only entities forged in the image of the individual souls whose origin they are destined to explain. The souls, in their turn, are only the form taken by the impersonal forces which we found at the basis of totemism, as they individualise themselves in the human body. The unity of the system is as great as its complexity.[25]

Although widely read, Durkheim was so dominated by the desire to explain away the phenomenon of religion that his theories about the origins of religion are of little consequence. His failure to accept mankind's belief in the actual existence of an unseen supernatural order—a failure in which he was to have many followers—led him into serious errors of interpretation. In addition, many of the anthropological theories and assumptions on which he built have since been shown to have been unreliable.[26] The student of comparative religion will, perhaps, read him less in order to acquire a knowledge of either the nature of religion or the thorny problem of the origins of religion, than to learn something of the standing of these theories in turn-of-the-century France.

*　　*　　*

[25] ibid., p. 295.

[26] We shall not enter here into the question of the long-term validity of Durkheim's theories, save to point out that much of the anthropological data on which they are based has since been shown to be unreliable : the theories of totemism and *mana* in particular have been challenged. Sociologists often remain unaware of such criticisms, and continue to write as though these turn-of-the-century positions remained entirely unchallenged.

Returning now across the Channel, we may observe that the hundred years of comparative religion which we are considering have not produced very many literary classics, or even works of literary quality. Writers on problems of comparative religion are not as a rule noted for their elegance and lucidity. One exception would of course be William James' *The Varieties of Religious Experience*; another—and perhaps a more widely-known contender—J. G. Frazer's *The Golden Bough*. Unfortunately, like most classics, *The Golden Bough* is seldom read today. Its sheer size and the complexity of its publishing history have made abridgment more than usually necessary, and those who know it other than as a yard of green bookcloth on the library shelves usually know it only in its abridged form. But Frazer's writing was a model of classical English prose : the English of the scholar, fastidious, balanced and sane. He was never obscure, even when dealing with matters obscure enough in themselves. Therein lay his strength—and perhaps also his weakness.

James George Frazer (1854-1951)[27] was born in Glasgow, and was brought up, like his close friend William Robertson Smith, as an orthodox son of the Kirk. Robertson Smith's work and example was one of the great formative influences upon his scholarly career—the other being the example of E. B. Tylor. But unlike Robertson Smith, Frazer's attachment to Christianity remained implicit, rather than explicit. His allegiance was early given to science, and he frequently applied the Comtean philosophy of human history to the world as he saw it; in this cosmic vision, mankind was seen to be moving into a new stage of development, characterised not by religion, still less by magic, but by science. And yet he admitted that he cherished

> . . . the blind conviction, or the trembling hope, that somewhere, beyond these earthly shadows, there is a world of light eternal, where the obstinate questionings of the mind will be answered and the heart find rest.[28]

Frazer was in fact conventionally Christian all his life, and in no way wanted to see his work applied to the dismissal of religion. In all probability, he gave little thought to the possibility of any 'application' whatsoever of his work; his biographer has drawn attention to his utter simplicity and even naïvety in the ways of the world. He worked in the area of anthropology simply because he

---

[27] There is no adequate critical biography of Frazer. See however Downie, *James George Frazer: The Portrait of a Scholar* (1940) and *Frazer and the Golden Bough* (1970). A recent critical study is J. Z. Smith, 'When the Bough Breaks', in *History of Religions* 12/4 (1973), pp. 342–71.

[28] Quoted by Downie, *James George Frazer*, p. 54f.

was intrigued by the problems presented by primitive religion and mythology, magic and ritual. But in himself he was a man of reason, 'essentially an eighteenth-century person' who 'lived and died in a rational, three-dimensional Newtonian world', and whose favourite authors were Cowper and Gibbon.[29] Personally, too, he was a man of painful shyness and extraordinary tenderness of scholarly conscience. The latter-day *Besserwisser* who accuses Frazer of carelessness in the use of source material would do well to recall that Frazer once tendered his resignation from his Trinity Fellowship over a trifling error in his translation of Ovid. In later years, when Freud and T. S. Eliot paid him tribute for his influence on their work, he confessed that he did not understand either of them in the slightest!

Frazer was trained in classics and law, and was called to the Bar in 1881, but never practised. Two years previously, in 1879, he had been elected a Fellow of Trinity College, Cambridge, and never moved from there, although in 1904 he gave serious attention to the possibility of becoming the first Professor of Comparative Religion in the University of Manchester, and for a short time held a post in the University of Liverpool. His first love was, and remained, the world of classical scholarship; he published an edition and translation of Pausanias in 1898,[30] an edition of Apollodorus in 1921 and an edition of the *Fasti* of Ovid in 1929, and brought his classically trained mind to the study of anthropology, which he took up seriously in the early 1880s.

We have already seen that following his dismissal from his Aberdeen chair in 1881, Robertson Smith had become Editor of the *Encyclopaedia Britannica*; we have seen, too, that he looked upon the problem of totemism as of the first importance. Frazer was asked to contribute the 'Totemism' and 'Taboo' articles to the ninth edition, and thereafter, in a manner of speaking, his scholarly fate was sealed. In 1887 he published in Edinburgh a little book on *Totemism* (the *EB* article did not appear until three years later) which was in effect the first of Frazer's anthropological compendia.

He could see that in the then current state of affairs, the gathering of material was of the utmost importance. The 'science of man', if carried out thoroughly, would necessitate the recruiting of every possible helper in every possible part of the world. Accordingly there

---

[29] ibid., p. 16.

[30] The most recent translator of Pausanias into English has noted that Frazer resembled him (the words are applied to Pausanias but would have suited either) '. . . in that all his scholarship and topography and encyclopedic curiosity were a burden undertaken in an attempt to satisfy a deeper anxiety which had once been apprehended in religious terms.' Peter Levi (ed.) *Pausanias: Guide to Greece* 1 (1971), p. 2f.

appeared in 1887 a little pamphlet entitled *Questions on the Manners, Customs, Religion, Superstitions, etc., of Uncivilised or Semi-civilised Peoples*, which was distributed throughout the world, and the answers to which laid the foundations of Frazer's immense collection of anthropological data.

In recent years, Frazer has been much criticised for being an 'armchair anthropologist', that is, for attempting to understand the primitive mind from the safety and comfort of a Cambridge study. E. E. Evans-Pritchard has written, for instance, that

> . . . men like Avebury, Frazer and Marett had little idea how the ordinary English working man felt and thought, and it is not surprising that they had even less idea how primitives, whom they had never met, feel and think.[31]

This is very probably true; but given the conditions and presuppositions of the time, it is very difficult to imagine how it could have been otherwise. It is a barren and pointless exercise to criticise a scholar for having been born fifty or sixty years too soon. By the 1890s evolution, from being a theory, had become an atmosphere; and its value as a principle of classification was hardly questioned. Clearly there had to be facts to classify, and leaving aside the question of the accuracy of the facts thus produced (another sore point with modern anthropologists), clearly the conditions of a university provided the best possible nerve-centre for what was essentially an intellectual process. An 'armchair anthropologist' he may have been; but he took great pains to make his hypotheses agree with the facts available to him. The conditions, then, produced Frazer, and he fulfilled his role with great dignity and even greater industry, as the successive volumes and editions of *The Golden Bough* testify.

From a modest two-volume beginning in 1890 *The Golden Bough* expanded to three volumes in the second edition of 1900; thereafter it was further expanded to include a host of more or less separate studies. Among these were *Adonis, Attis, Osiris; The Magic Art and the Evolution of Kings; Taboo and the Perils of the Soul; The Dying God; Spirits of the Corn and of the Wild; The Scapegoat;* and *Balder the Beautiful.* These and others—not to mention books not included in the literary monolith—went to make up the third edition of 1911-15. The abridged edition appeared in 1922.

The Golden Bough was in intention an explanation of a legend

---

[31] Evans-Pritchard, *Theories of Primitive Religion* (1965), p. 108f.

recorded by Servius in his commentary on Virgil.[82] In the sacred grove of Diana at Aricia (Nemi), so the legend went, there grew a 'golden bough'; the priesthood of Diana was held by the person who was able to break off the bough and slay the incumbent priest in single combat. In Frazer's analysis, the priest represented Virbius, the god of the grove, and his slaughter was a symbolic representation of the death of the god. But this was only the beginning. From Aricia Frazer moved on to consider the whole question of the killing of men and animals regarded as divine (the area of totemism, of course). The 'golden bough' itself he identified as the mistletoe, which led him into the further, dangerous, area of the Druids and their worship, and into a consideration of the Norse legend of the death of Balder. From this relatively simple beginning, he followed one promising trail after another, and left his original purpose farther and farther behind, until it was almost entirely lost sight of. The final result was a vast compendium of data concerning religious belief and practice, a compendium which it is quite impossible to summarise. However, it may be of value to have Frazer's own statement of the way in which he was *proposing* to use the comparative method in his book, whether or not he actually did so:

> Recent researches into the early history of man have revealed the essential similarity with which, under many superficial differences, the human mind has elaborated its first crude philosophy of life. Accordingly, if we can shew that a barbarous custom, like that of the priesthood of Nemi, has existed elsewhere; if we can detect the motives which led to its institution; if we can prove that these motives have operated widely, perhaps universally, in human society . . . then we may fairly infer that at a remote age the same motives gave birth to the priesthood of Nemi.[83]

From *The Golden Bough* later scholarship derived three things: first, a working definition of magic; secondly, an interest in the question of divine kingship; and thirdly, the concept of the dying and rising god or goddess of vegetation. We may consider these three themes briefly, beginning with magic.

If we analyse the principles of thought on which magic is based, they will probably be found to resolve themselves into two: first,

---

[82] How far Frazer's original intention was carried out is discussed by J. Z. Smith, in his article. He writes: 'He [Frazer] was not successful in establishing any connection between the golden bough and the priesthood at Nemi. The bulk of his description was imaginative reconstruction without textual warrant' (ibid., p. 353).

[83] Frazer, *The Magic Art* I (1932), p. 10.

that like produces like, or that an effect resembles its cause; and,
second, that things which have once been in contact with each
other continue to act on each other at a distance after the physical
contact has been severed. The former principle may be called the
Law of Similarity, the latter the Law of Contact or Contagion . . .
Charms based on the Law of Similarity may be called Homoeo-
pathic or Imitative Magic. Charms based on the Law of Contact
or Contagion may be called Contagious Magic.[34]

In this celebrated statement, Frazer set up, one is almost tempted
to say for all time, the two pillars of his theory of 'sympathetic
magic'. This definition (quite different, of course, from the currently
vague assumption that magic means 'things that just can't happen,
but do') has done sterling service as a descriptive basis of magic. To
expand slightly, when a person imitates an event in the belief that
his mime will bring about the event in question, this is homoeo-
pathic or imitative magic; examples would be the pouring of water
on parched ground in order to induce rain, or the piercing of an
effigy of a person in order to harm that person. In the latter case,
should the effigy be equipped with nail clippings, a tuft of hair, or
a scrap of garment that had once belonged to the person in question,
this would be in effect contagious magic. When the ultimate object
is to harm, this is 'black magic'; when the desire is to help and heal,
this is 'white magic', as in the work of countless generations of folk
healers and 'wise women' the world over.

In Frazer's view—and here he passes from descriptive to evaluation—both principles are misapplications of the association of ideas;
and magic as an art and craft is a spurious system of natural law as
well as a fallacious guide of conduct; '. . . it is a false science as well
as an abortive art'. Nevertheless magic is an attempt at science,
since it is an attempt to establish and use laws of cause and effect.

Wherever sympathetic magic occurs in its pure unadulterated
form, it assumes that in nature one event follows another necessarily and invariably without the intervention of any spiritual or
personal agency. Thus its fundamental conception is identical
with that of modern science; underlying the whole system is a
faith, implicit but *real and firm*, in the order and uniformity of
nature.[35]

According to Frazer, the practice of magic assumes that man is
capable of exercising direct control over the circumstances. But this

[34] ibid., p. 52.
[35] ibid., p. 220.

assumption of Frazer's is open to serious question. It is true that in magic man appears to influence the course of events by deliberate means; but it does not follow that there is a direct cause-and-effect relationship between the action and the desired effect, without any intervention from outside. On the contrary, magic involves the harnessing and the manipulation of powers coming from 'beyond', from the 'parallel world' of gods, ghosts and spirits. Magic does not assume that effect follows cause 'without the intervention of any spiritual or personal agency'. On the contrary, it sees such agencies everywhere, and does its best to use them, either with or without acknowledgment.

Frazer also theorised about the relationship between magic and religion. Religion he defined as 'a propitiation or conciliation of powers superior to man which are believed to direct and control the course of nature and of human life'.[36] Roughly speaking, he believed that man began by attempting to manipulate his environment by magical means, and then turned to 'religion' once he discovered that such manipulation was impossible. Religion differs from magic in that magic bases its case on immutable laws, religion on a belief in controlling forces. Frazer allowed, correctly, that the two are often tightly interwoven in a tangled web of precept and practice, faith and fear. But, says Frazer, we may assume that 'magic is older than religion in the history of humanity', both since logic seems to demand it, and since among the Australian Aborigines,

. . . the rudest savages as to whom we possess accurate information, magic is universally practised, whereas religion in the sense of a propitiation or conciliation of the higher powers seems to be nearly unknown.[37]

Hence 'an Age of Religion' has everywhere been preceded by an 'Age of Magic'.

Unfortunately, this thesis has since been shown to be quite wrong. Not only do the Aborigines possess a highly developed religion (on any definition); not only is Frazer's definition of religion unnecessarily arbitrary; but there is absolutely no evidence of an age of magic having everywhere preceded an age of religion in human history. It is often desperately difficult to draw an adequate line of demarcation between two such abstractions as 'magic' and 'religion'. If the two are to be distinguished at all, it seems that the difference between them is a matter of little more than a subtle shift of personal emphasis, from manipulation to reverence for higher powers.

[36] ibid., p. 222.
[37] ibid., p. 233f.

In the history of religion the two are always closely related, but it should be emphasised that there is no question of magic 'developing into' religion; if anything, the movement is in the opposite direction, since religion has very often been observed degenerating into magic.

As so often in the writing of this period, in Frazer's work on magic one has the feeling of many acute and genuine observations being made, and yet somehow being distorted by being put together in an inappropriate framework. As it is, 'magic' is certainly an attempt at manipulating man's environment, and Frazer illustrated many of its aspects very well. But the all-pervasive evolutionary theory was an unsafe guide to historical priorities.

The 'King of the Wood' at Nemi was endowed with more than human powers, and in *The Magic Art and the Evolution of Kings* Frazer advanced many cases from many parts of the world of the institution of divine or sacral kingship. It is very much open to question, though, whether he was right in tracing the descent of the king back to the worker of magic. In time the whole question of divine kingship was to be taken up by another generation of scholars, and shown to be of outstanding importance in the history of religion. Here, as in so many other areas, Frazer was a layer of foundations, even though the final result was not precisely what he himself would have envisaged.

The dying and rising vegetation-deity—a deity whose life and death and subsequent resurrection follows closely the changing pattern of the seasons—is dealt with in detail by Frazer in *The Dying God* and in *Spirits of the Corn and of the Wild*. Strictly speaking, Frazer was not breaking new ground here, but following a path which had been traced a quarter of a century earlier by Wilhelm Mannhardt. Again, the details of his argument need not concern us, but it is perhaps worth noting that the extreme familiarity of this idea to students of comparative religion in the English-speaking world is due in large measure to Frazer. Although too much use may be made of the idea, it is scarcely possible to explain the Hellenistic mystery religions and certain popular beliefs of northern Europe (to take only two examples at random) on any other grounds.

Perhaps, finally, we may return briefly to two questions. First, that since Frazer's entire work in anthropology was dominated by the hypothesis of a three-stage evolution of human thought, its ultimate value as an 'epic of humanity' (Frazer's own words) is dependent on the validity of that hypothesis. This is undoubtedly one of the reasons why today the throwing of brickbats at Frazer and his contemporaries is such a popular pastime. But even if this should be admitted (as it must be) this falls far short of invalidating the whole of his work. A period of synthesis, such as that provided by Frazer and his contemporaries, was inevitable in the history of comparative religion; and without it, much subsequent detailed work would have been immeasurably more difficult than it has in fact proved. But secondly, it must be emphasised that Frazer was under no illusions as to the permanence of his own theories, which he expected to be superseded. In the 1932 edition of *The Magic Art* he admitted candidly that the investigation of the early history and institutions of mankind had been prone to 'an attractive but fallacious simplicity' of interpretation, and that many theories had had only a short life as a result. He expected no other fate for his own theories than that they should in time be 'consigned to the same peaceful limbo of forgotten absurdities'. But he hoped that things might be different :

> It is not for the anthropologist himself [he wrote] to anticipate the verdict of posterity on his labours; still it is his humble hope that the facts which he has patiently amassed will be found sufficiently numerous and solid to bear the weight of some at least of the conclusions which he rests upon them, so that these can never again be lightly tossed aside as the fantastic dreams of a mere bookish student.[38]

Perhaps the time is now approaching when fashionable impatience with Frazer will give place to a sober estimate of his contribution to comparative religion in its anthropological aspect. He may then prove to have been greater, rather than smaller, than we thought.

* * *

We have now come to the end of our survey of a very few of the outstanding anthropologists whose sights were set on the problem of the origins of religion. Clearly other names might have been included. But before we pass on to another aspect of our study, it is necessary to say a brief word about the potential scope of the anthropologists' solution to the problem of religion.

The period between the 1870s and the 1920s in the comparative study of religion was to all intents and purposes dominated by the anthropologists and their theories. But this is not to say that studies in other areas of religion were at a standstill during these years. On the contrary, if we had time to trace the study of any specific religious tradition, we should find there a growing bibliography of scholarly works, and a steady increase in solid factual knowledge.

[38] ibid., p. 334.

Probably it would be true to say that scholarly emphasis rested to a great extent (possibly to an unhealthy extent) on the religious traditions of the ancient world, particularly the Semitic peoples, classical antiquity and India. But everywhere the combination of literary and archaeological evidence was opening fresh fields and providing wider and wider perspectives. And yet it was the anthropological approach which dominated *comparative* (as opposed to straightforward, one-thing-at-a-time historical) studies. Virtually every philologist, every historian, every archaeologist would at this time have been able to subscribe to what Jane Harrison had written in 1885 in her *Introductory Studies in Greek Art*, that

> The historical instinct is wide awake among us now. We seek with a new-won earnestness to know the genesis, the *origines* of whatever we study . . .[39]

And again, the evolutionary method as applied by the anthropologists, whether 'unilinearists' or 'diffusionists', seemed to provide the only possibility of sure knowledge of origins, the only feasible key to the understanding of stages of development.

So while comparative religion was never solely a matter of anthropology, and always implied the individual scholar's right to work in any field, the student of comparative religion would be accustomed to following the anthropologists in what they were doing, as a prolegomena to his own specialist studies. Thus when in 1913 J. Estlin Carpenter published his popular handbook *Comparative Religion*, he had these words to say about a basic assumption of the entire study:

> It is on this great idea [evolution] that the whole study of the history of religion is now firmly established. At the foundation of all endeavours to classify the multitudinous facts which it embraces, lies the conviction that whatever may be the occasional instances of degeneration or decline, the general movement of human things advances from the cruder and less complex to the more refined and developed.[40]

In the working out of this 'great idea' the European anthropologists had played a notable part. In the forty-odd years which separate Max Müller's *Chips from a German Workshop* and Tylor's *Primitive Culture* from Carpenter's *Comparative Religion*, the ancient world and the world of primitive survivals had been scoured; lines,

[39] Jane Harrison, *Introductory Studies in Greek Art* (1885), p. 2.
[40] Carpenter, *Comparative Religion* (1913), p. 33.

both real and hypothetical, had been drawn; a subject and its vocabulary had been created, and teaching posts had been set up. But before we go on to consider the practical consolidation of the subject, it will be necessary to cross the Atlantic, in order to consider certain parallel developments in the area of the psychology of religion.

V

Some Varieties of Religious Experience

The origins of comparative religion, as we have examined them thus far, have been bound up very closely indeed with the intellectual history, or *Geistesgeschichte*, of nineteenth- and early-twentieth-century Europe. Historical philology and evolutionary anthropology were, after all, disciplines which had been shaped in or around European universities, where the Christian theology against which both were busily operating still enjoyed a privileged position. During this same period the United States of America (still, following the Civil War of the 1860s, an emergent nation) was scarcely in a position to make a similarly large-scale contribution to the development of the subject. The important word here is 'large-scale', for certainly there had been individual scholars and men of letters here and there in America who had done more—much more—than simply re-think European thoughts. It is still worth remembering that Max Müller's *Introduction to the Science of Religion* had been dedicated to Ralph Waldo Emerson; and Emerson and his associates among the Transcendentalists (almost all of whom were enthusiastic, although tendentious, amateur Orientalists) had helped by the third quarter of the nineteenth century to create in America a climate in which comparative religion of a kind could, and did, flourish. Before the end of the nineteenth century it was to have one of its most startling manifestations in the Chicago 'World's Parliament of Religions'; but we shall return to that in a later context. A few elite universities and colleges were able by the end of the century to employ scholars of the very highest calibre to work in various areas of the historical and philological study of religion.

Men of the scholarly status of W. D. Whitney, James Freeman Clarke and George Foot Moore were the equals of their European counterparts, but nevertheless there was very little they could do to make a *distinctively American* contribution to the comparative study of religion.

It would have been very strange, however, had the dynamic and cosmopolitan New World been in the long run content to remain just a cultural extension of Europe. Some distinctively American area of study had to be created sooner or later; and in the event, that area was the psychology of religion, the opening up of which took place in the years around the turn of the century.[1]

There are still those for whom the psychology of religion has always been, and remains, a typical 'auxiliary science', somewhere on the fringe of the study of religion. In part this is doubtless due to the daunting difficulties which confront the newcomer to the field, and the greatly specialised techniques in which the professional psychologist has always delighted. Today there are few comparative religionists who are able to cope with these techniques, while most psychologists are prevented by their behavioural presuppositions from treating religion as anything in any way distinctive. Thus what once appeared to be a highly promising, and tolerably accessible, field of study has fallen on evil days. For a time there was a fair number of university posts in the psychology of religion in Western universities; now almost all of these have disappeared. The explanation of this is perhaps to be found in the way in which behavioural psychology has developed since about the second decade of the present century, toward belief in subconscious motivation on the one hand, and toward a refined form of mental engineering on the other. In this development, religion has been occasionally nodded to, but seldom taken seriously. We shall, however, return to this subject later.

In understanding the original status of the psychology of religion, clearly a great deal is going to depend on the precise shade of meaning given to the word 'psychology'. Modern psychology concerns itself for the most part with the minutiae of human behaviour, and hence the description and mapping out of the various ways in which the human organism experiences and reacts to its environment. Human experience can be understood, on this view, only to the extent to which it expresses itself in measurable patterns of behaviour.

But this is a 'modern' view; and the nascent psychology of the late nineteenth century did not believe itself limited in this way. The writers with whom we shall be concerned in this chapter were all men who believed that as psychologists they were studying the rational human *psyche*—that non-material part of the individual (which might be called the soul, mind, feeling, consciousness, Transcendental Ego, or whatever) through which the individual as such operates. On such broad terms as these, it was unlikely that there

---

[1] E. R. Goodenough has written that in the earlier years of the century, 'While all the leaders of thinking in the history of religion were European or English (*sic*), and Americans were eagerly reading their books, all Europe and England were reading William James, Starbuck, Leuba, and Pratt.' 'Religionswissenschaft,' in *Numen* vi (1959), p. 80.

would be any very precise agreement as to methods or goals; and indeed, they approached their task in a variety of ways. But common to all—and to very many more who cannot be discussed or even named here—was the conviction that the study of religion was a very fruitful field for the student of the human psyche.

Those who believed this to be so were not always professional psychologists; and broadly 'psychological' methods tended to be part of the common currency of the age around the turn of the century. For instance, we find Louis Jordan writing in 1905 that 'the study of Animism, in Sir Edward Tylor's hands, was often simply a study of Psychology, i.e. he deliberately analysed the psychological impulse of the individual savage.'[2] A few years later, J. Estlin Carpenter recorded that the origin of religion '. . . can never be determined archaeologically; it must be sought *conjecturally* through psychology.'[3]

Nineteenth-century psychology might, then, appear to have been made up of a process of random observation and conjecture, virtually anything serving as grist to its mill, and to have differed from evolutionary anthropology (or, for that matter, from comparative religion) only in emphasis, and not in essential method. At all events, the evolutionary study of the conscious human *psyche* could not well ignore religion, and the evolutionary study of religion could not but involve the psychological attempt at understanding. This being so, it is easy to see why the comparative religionist and the psychologist of religion could be regarded in some circles as being tarred with the same brush. To the question of what the comparative study of religion had to gain from this psychological approach, then, the answer might well have been that the two were merely alternative approaches to more or less the same material, and that although their language might differ, their presuppositions and methods differed hardly at all. Both were attempting to account for the origin and the nature of religion as an important aspect of the workings of the human mind; and there was absolutely no reason why the psychologist and the comparative religionist should not be the closest of colleagues.

Some methodological difference there had to be, however. Whereas the comparative religionist was limited entirely to what he could observe to be happening, or to the historical study of past events, the psychologist began to discover that he could in a sense *cause* things to happen, and observe by implication (this came to be called 'pulling habits out of rats'). In 1879, Wilhelm Wundt had started

---

[2] Jordan, *Comparative Religion, its Genesis and Growth* (1905), p. 40.
[3] *Encyclopaedia Britannica* (11th ed.) 23, p. 62.

his famous laboratory of experimental psychology at Leipzig—a centre which soon became a Mecca to the aspiring psychologists of the Old and New Worlds alike (in 1873-4 he had published 'the bible of experimental psychologists', *Grundzüge der physiologischen Psychologie*). Wundt's work had the effect of reducing the random quality of psychological observation, establishing pragmatic, and repeatable, tests by which psychological qualities and characteristics could be measured. Further, in emphasising the *physiological* basis of psychology, he had taken the first important step toward making a somewhat disorganised approximate field of study into an organised and independent science. It was, however, only a first step. In 1890 we find another experimental psychologist, the celebrated William James, writing : 'It seems to me that psychology is like physics before Galileo's time—not a single elementary law yet caught a glimpse of.'[4]

Be that as it may, it was for one or other form of the *experimental* approach that the 'American school' of psychology of religion became known. This was partly a matter of impulses derived directly from Leipzig, and Wundt, though it ought to be obvious that there cannot, properly speaking, be a 'laboratory approach' to religion (the idea of a laboratory type performance of an initiatory ritual, or even of a simple prayer, is a manifest absurdity). More important, it was also, and increasingly, a matter of allowing *homo religiosus* to speak for himself, particularly by means of standard questionnaires—the implication being that the individual in question is *capable* of speaking for himself (i.e., that all religion is an aspect of the consciousness of the individual concerned), and that what he has to say is worth taking seriously, particularly in respect of his 'religious experiences'—conversion, prayer, experience of the transcendent, and so on.

I do not here propose to inquire too closely into the reasons why this particular approach should have proved so attractive and acceptable in the American setting. Doubtless it was due in part to the influence in America of various forms of 'personal religion', with its characteristic emphasis on individual experience. Individualism was, of course, a thoroughgoing characteristic of the American intellectual life of the period. As Robert Nisbet has said, 'Individualism, as an analytical perspective, was common enough in the Europe of the nineteenth century; in America it was part of the very air men breathed.'[5] Significantly, too, the typical American philosophy of the period (or rather, as Daniel Boorstin has called

---

[4] Quoted by Matthiessen, *The James Family* (1961), p. 371.
[5] Nisbet, *Durkheim* (1965), p. 4.

it, 'an American substitute for a philosophy'[6]) was 'pragmatism'—
the method which sought to interpret each separate notion by
tracing out its practical consequences. Thus it proved possible to
say, in effect, 'religion is what religion does', with the important
corollary that religion is what the individual *believes* that it does.
Further, the America of the turn of the century was, thanks to two
centuries and more of often religiously motivated immigration,
virtually a laboratory of living religions—a community in which
every individual had his own distinctive views and experiences.
These—and particularly the experiences—the psychologist was
able to set himself to investigate.

That there was a certain degree of short-range religious utilitar-
ianism in this process cannot well be denied. In 1910 we find E. S.
Ames drawing attention to the fact that in his day, interest in the
psychological processes of religion was often closely connected with
the practical problems of Christian apologetics. The first publications in the area were, he noted, concerned 'chiefly, almost exclusively, with conversion, taking that term in its broadest sense.' This
he took, not unjustifiably, to be a reflection of Protestant insistence
on the centrality of the conversion experience in the life of the
individual Christian :

> The work of the Church has been conceived to be that of making
> converts. Therefore the understanding of this process with a view
> to controlling it successfully among all classes attains first import-
> ance.[7]

In the overall history of the comparative study of religion there
would appear to be a world of difference between this type of
material and that with which the philologists and anthropologists
were concerned. But comparative religion cannot accept the arbitrary exclusion of *any* area of the religious life of mankind from its
potential material, on any grounds whatsoever. Otherwise its claim
to be concerned with religion as an identifiable and universal
phenomenon would be patently false. Before Ames and Pratt, the
American psychologists of religion did in fact tend to work in the
somewhat narrow field of Christian and semi-Christian religious
movements; but in time, and in other parts of the world as well as
the United States, their work came to merge with that of workers
in other fields, to help form the broad river of comparative religion.
Eventually, as E. R. Goodenough was to say many years later,

---

[6] Boorstin, *The Americans* II: *The National Experience* (1969), p. 61.
See also Thayer (ed.), *Pragmatism: the Classic Writings* (1970).
[7] Ames, *The Psychology of Religious Experience* (1910), p. 5.

'Through practically inventing new approaches to the psychology of religion, [the] American spirit made its idiomatic contribution to the scientific study of religion.'[8]

Leaving aside further questions of background, we may turn now to a brief consideration of the work of some of the pioneer American psychologists of religion, and in particular Starbuck, Leuba and James. In this company there is no question that William James occupies the pre-eminent place, both as a psychologist and as an international celebrity. But the others are not for that reason without interest. Each had his own distinctive approach, Starbuck's being that of the theist and Leuba's that of the positivist. Later, in the work of J. B. Pratt, we shall see the beginnings of a coalition between psychology and some other branches of the comparative study of religion.

There is, however, one other name which is deserving of honourable mention at the threshold of this new scientific departure. We have already drawn attention to the formative role of Wilhelm Wundt's laboratory in Leipzig as a meeting-ground and training-ground for psychologists of religion. It happens that the first American student to enrol in Wundt's laboratory was Granville Stanley Hall (1844–1924).

Hall is not now regarded as a seminal figure, or even a very important figure, in the psychology of religion, since he possessed little originality. Nevertheless he was to exercise a far-reaching indirect influence through the opportunities he afterwards provided for other scholars in the field. Hall strikes the latter-day European as in many ways the archetypical American—the first Ph.D. in philosophy of Harvard; the founder of the first journal of psychology in the English language (*The American Journal of Psychology*, begun in 1887); the first President of Clark University; the first President of the American Psychological Association; and a man who could sum up his own career by writing that

> in the views I have attained of man, his place in nature, his origin and destiny, I believe I have become a riper product of the present stage of civilisation than most of my contemporaries, have out-grown more superstitions, attained clearer insights, and have a deeper sense of peace with myself.[9]

On his death, however, a contemporary (also a psychologist) called him 'the most intricate, dominant, involved and self-contradictory personality that has come upon the psychological horizon'.[10]

---

[8] Goodenough, op. cit., p. 80.
[9] Hall, *Life and Confessions of a Psychologist* (1923), p. 596.
[10] Starbuck, in *The Psychological Review* (March 1925), p. 104.

Hall's contribution to the psychology of religion might well be summed up as that of the impresario, not the soloist. In his journals (to the above-mentioned *American Journal of Psychology* he added in 1904 the short-lived *Journal of Religious Psychology*) he gave room to many an aspiring writer on the subject. But most spectacularly of all (in the clear vision of hindsight), it was Hall who was responsible, as early as 1909, for bringing to America both Freud and Jung, to lecture (in German) on the as yet novel techniques and intentions of psychoanalysis. It is perhaps doubtful whether even Hall, who was later shrewdly characterised by Freud as possessing 'a touch of the king-maker',[11] quite realised the consequences for American psychology of the revolution which was to result from this innocuous visit. His role here was perhaps not unlike that of the unknown person who introduced Antony to Cleopatra!

This episode aside, Hall was not an innovator. Nevertheless his contribution was a real one, since he provided a forum and to some extent a workshop in which first-hand psychological research could be carried out. But he was no great theorist, and as a later historian was to sum up, 'he made no pretense at evolving a system of psychology, quite content to set a few bricks here and there'.[12]

*　　*　　*

Among the more prominent American psychologists of religion of the early decade of the century, the practical influence of Hall can be seen most clearly in the work of James H. Leuba (1868–1946).[13] The theoretical background of both men was that of a form of what in Europe was called 'Positivism'—materialistic and functional, explaining religion in order to try to supersede it.

Leuba was born and brought up in Switzerland, at Neuchâtel, where he received his early education and where he conceived an intense dislike of orthodox Calvinism (without, however, attempting to understand it). His early life was not without religious influence; in the setting of the Salvation Army he passed through a form of 'conversion experience', which he later rationalised in ethico-religious terms. He was to call this experience 'perhaps the most beneficial one of my life; it was certainly the most violent one'— though it was to leave few traces on his mature thinking. Continued study drew him more and more away from the accepted categories

[11] Freud, *An Autobiographical Study* (1935), p. 93f.
[12] Roback, *History of American Psychology* (1952), p. 162.
[13] cf. de Vries, *The Study of Religion* (Eng. tr. 1967), pp. 151ff.

of religion, and more and more toward the adoption of an evolutionary world-view: 'With regard to the "truths" preached by the Churches, which appeared to me in direct contradiction with Darwinism and science in general, I found myself siding without hesitation with science.'[14]

On arrival in the United States, Leuba entered the department of psychology at Clark University to study for his doctorate under Stanley Hall. Partly as a result of his Salvation Army experience, he chose to write on the problem of conversion; and his dissertation was published in 1896 in the *American Journal of Psychology* as 'Studies in the Psychology of Religious Phenomena—Conversion', antedating the work of Starbuck and James by a few years, but a parallel effort to Starbuck's *The Psychology of Religion* (1899) and James' *The Varieties of Religious Experience* (1902). Parallel, and yet different. Starbuck and James were both prepared to accept the genuineness of the transcendental reference in religious experience, at least as a hypothesis; Leuba would make no such admission. He was by this time a thoroughgoing scientific rationalist. His methods were somewhat similar to those of Starbuck and James, it is true; but his general conclusion, that the religious consciousness is no different in kind from normal human consciousness, was quite strikingly different. Leuba refused to regard religion as anything but a natural phenomenon, having no reference to any 'beyond' or any transcendent reality. The supernatural he dismissed abruptly. 'The general fact of man's entering into relations with certain hyperhuman agents,' he later wrote, 'needs no other explanation than is afforded by the lust for life.'[15]

These convictions animated all his later studies. In 1912 he published *A Psychological Study of Religion* (reprinted as recently as 1969); and in 1916 *The Belief in God and Immortality*—the first of these tracing out the origins of human conceptions of deity, and the second dealing with human beliefs in immortality. Both sets of conceptions he interprets as projections. Beliefs in deity, for instance, are essentially causal explanations, supplemented by the desire to obtain help in the difficult circumstances of human existence. Oddly enough, the effort is not altogether in vain, since

. . . by objectifying his ideals in gods, originally due to an effort

---

[14] Leuba, 'The Making of a Psychologist of Religion,' in Ferm (ed.), *Religion in Transition* (1937), p. 179f.

[15] Leuba, *A Psychological Study of Religion* (1912), p. 111f. William James, in a letter to Leuba, once characterised his [Leuba's] position as 'dogmatic atheistic naturalism'. *The Letters of William James* II (1920), p. 211f.

to explain striking experiences, and in entering into social relations with them, man actually accomplishes the miracle of lifting himself up by his bootstraps : he gets from his relation with gods something at least of the wealth with which he has endowed them.[16]

The belief in immortality is similarly explained away as originating in 'an unavoidable explanation of certain pseudo-perceptions', such as dream-visions of the dead, and being maintained by the intense desire for the preservation of deeply-held values. It is not surprising, in view of Leuba's habits of mind, that when he later turned his attention to the phenomena associated with mysticism—following a path blazed largely in Europe by Inge, von Hügel, Evelyn Underhill and others—he should summarily dismiss the mystic's claims :

> His assurance of the presence of God has the same kind of origin as that of the assurance of the non-civilised who, when he hears the thunder, thinks he is aware of the thunder-god. What he really hears is a particular sound, and from it he *infers* the existence of a great being who produces the sound. Similarly, the mystic experiences a mass of more or less unusual sensations, feelings, emotions, and concludes that they are a divine manifestation.[17]

Leuba is here basing his argument on the *a priori* assumption of the non-existence of the supernatural, and consequently one cannot altogether avoid the impression that a fundamental antagonism toward the outward forms of religion, as presented to him in his younger days, prevented him from ever taking the 'religious case' seriously. Certainly he was interested in the emotional states of mind connected with religion. He had been through some of them himself, and seems to have been deeply ashamed of his weakness. But he refused to interpret them other than as aberrations—a criticism which can be levelled at far too many subsequent psychologists, not least among them Freud. Nevertheless he, and others like him, provided a pattern of work which was to dominate one side of the psychological treatment of religion for years to come.

*   *   *

At the time when Leuba, prompted by Hall, was producing his

---

[16] *Religion in Transition*, p. 187.
[17] ibid., p. 193.

first essays in the psychology of religion, similar work was being done at Harvard by two men of far different presuppositions and character, the Quaker Edwin Diller Starbuck (1866–1947) and the unorthodox theist William James. James was the master, Starbuck the pupil; nevertheless Starbuck can justifiably be counted among the pioneers of the psychology of religion, if only because he appears to have made the first successful use of the questionnaire method of research.

Starbuck had emerged from University (where he had read philosophy) a Hegelian and a firm believer in evolution, although this position was eventually modified into something approaching personal idealism. In his younger days he was an enthusiastic adherent of what tended to be called the 'New Humanism', but this did not alter his fundamental, though unclear, religious commitment. It should be borne in mind that unlike Leuba, Starbuck was a 'religious' man, and that his psychological researches were in no sense intended to undermine religion or even to offer a rationalistic explaining-away of religious experience. Equally, he was far from orthodox, even in the liberal Quaker sense, though it seems that he was no stranger to the kind of personal *religious* experience sometimes called 'mystical'.

As a student, Starbuck was introduced to the comparative study of religion by reading, first, James Freeman Clarke's *Ten Great Religions* ('A flash that cleared the skies and precipitated afresh the sense of the Universal Soul of religion . . .')[18] followed by Max Müller's *Lectures on the Science of Religion*, which impelled him to write and deliver a paper on the science of religion and its place in education. After an interlude, teaching mathematics, he decided to pursue the study of religion further, and chose to do so at Harvard University, because 'Harvard almost alone offered courses that seemed dispassionate and that promised assistance . . .'[19]

During his two academic years (1893–5) at Harvard, Starbuck began the serious study of psychology under Münsterberg and William James. He was already convinced that it was necessary to discover and apply some kind of scientific method to the study of religion; he was neither a linguist nor a historian, and his acquaintance with the religions of the world was scarcely profound, but the psychological methods being elaborated by Hall and James seemed to him to offer the opening he was looking for. Again in his own words :

The central guiding principle was that the study must deal

---

[18] Starbuck, 'Religion's Use of Me,' in Ferm (ed.), *Religion in Transition* (1937), p. 219f.
[19] ibid., p. 221.

primarily with the first-hand religious experience of individuals, not so much with their *theories* about religion as with their actual *experiences. . .* One must catch at first hand the feelings of spirituality.[20]

American Protestantism provided an ideal field for this kind of enquiry. It was highly individualistic, laid great stress on the necessity of first-hand spiritual experience, particularly the experience of conversion, and was far from reticent in speaking of such experiences (indeed, the refusal to speak might well be interpreted as a confession that there was no experience worth speaking about). Accordingly, in the winter of 1893-4 Starbuck began to circulate his questionnaires, one on conversion, one on the breaking of habits (!) and a third, more elaborate, on the lines of religious development not attended by conversion.

The venture was bold, naive and immature (Starbuck was still only a research student); nevertheless it worked. Replies poured in, and formed the foundation of a number of books. First William James borrowed them when preparing his Gifford Lectures on *The Varieties of Religious Experience*; in the meantime Starbuck himself had contributed 'A Study of Conversion' to the *American Journal of Psychology* (1897), later elaborated into his first book, *The Psychology of Religion* (1899).

Opposition there was, of course. Although Starbuck had the full support of James, his other teacher of psychology, Münsterberg, was '. . . antagonistic, and finally explosive', declaring that 'his problems were those of psychology, while mine belonged to theology, and that they had absolutely nothing to do with each other'.[21] This was understandable. For the psychologist whose view of his subject is restricted to an examination, under experimental conditions, of the workings of the human mind, Starbuck's method must have seemed like the worst form of dilettantism. And then Starbuck was 'religious', and therefore unlikely to be a dispassionate observer.

Similar reactions were forthcoming when the subject of the psychology of religion was introduced cautiously into the Harvard curriculum in the winter of 1894-5. The first seminar at which Starbuck's results were discussed he called '. . . a sort of christening ceremony for the babe newly born into the family of academic subjects', adding wryly that 'some quite hot water was poured into the baptismal font'.[22] On this occasion, however, the water was

[20] ibid., p. 222f.
[21] ibid., p. 225.
[22] ibid., p. 226.

heated by orthodox Christians, to whom it seemed that an attempt was being made to profane the sanctuary. In fact, like comparative religion, the psychology of religion was scorned by Christians as being too scientific, and scorned by other psychologists as being not scientific enough—a situation which on the whole persisted throughout its brief and stormy history.

* * *

The outstanding figure among the first generation of American psychologists of religion was, however, unquestionably William James (1842–1910), though it must be recognised that his popularity stems more from his work as a philosopher than for his purely psychological theories and insights. His most famous work, *The Varieties of Religious Experience* (1902) is psychological in the sense that it approaches the phenomenon of religion through the feelings of 'religious' individuals; but in breadth of treatment and in speculative energy it passes far beyond the limits of even an ill-defined new science. Psychology to James was largely a matter of approach; in the treatment of the data which it provided it would be wrong to think of him as other than a speculative philosopher.

It is necessary to bear in mind that James carried within him a heritage stretching back into the eighteenth century, and to the enigmatic and extraordinary figure of the Swedish visionary Emanuel Swedenborg. His father, Henry James, Sr. (1811–1882) (the novelist Henry James was William's younger brother), was a Swedenborgian and a critical associate of the group of New England Transcendentalists which gathered around Ralph Waldo Emerson. His criticism of the Transcendentalists was sometimes bitter—as when he castigated them for their 'puerile Pantheistic gabble' (the very charge which F. D. Maurice had once levelled against Thomas Carlyle). One of the circle, Ellery Channing, called him '. . . a little fat, rosy Swedenborgian amateur, with the look of a broker, and the brains and heart of a Pascal'.[23]

Henry James, Sr. wrote in 1869 *The Secret of Swedenborg*, and was a bitter opponent of orthodox Calvinism (as were all the New England group). The God of orthodoxy he once called a 'lurid power—half pedagogue, half-policeman, but wholly imbecile in both aspects'.[24] However, he was opposed to the extreme individualism of Emerson and Thoreau, and indeed preferred Thomas Carlyle to Emerson, who he called an 'obdurate naturalist' and a 'man with-

[23] Quoted in Matthiessen, *The James Family*, p. 15.
[24] ibid., p. 14.

out a handle'. There is no evidence that Henry James, Sr. shared the self-confessed plagiarism and amateur orientalism of the other Transcendentalists; but he certainly shared their basic philosophical and theological outlook—open, undogmatic and impressionistic. Although equally an idealist, he was more of a socialist than any of the others of the group.

William James' early life gave little indication of the paths he was later to follow. He attempted to study art, and failed. He obtained a medical degree, but never practised. He lived for years in constant and totally unproductive neurosis. He was appointed in 1872 to teach physiology at Harvard and, his difficulties notwithstanding, succeeded in 1876 in introducing courses in physiological psychology—three years before Wundt had opened his famous Leipzig laboratory. For the next fourteen years James was concerned with the production of his biggest and in a sense his only book, *The Principles of Psychology* (1890)—the first thorough attempt in the English language to treat the functions of mind from the biological and functional point of view, and a work which has been described as both definitive and innovating in its field.

This was James' last work of pure psychology. From the time of its publication, he virtually abandoned laboratory psychology, which he appears to have disliked, and turned his attention more and more to the problems of the borderland between philosophy and religion; all his subsequent published work originated either as courses of lectures or as series of articles. During the 1880s James' mind had been occupied almost entirely with the problems of refining his own psychological method; in the 1890s he became far more widely known as a popular philosopher, and in the series of works which culminated in *The Varieties of Religious Experience* he was never far away from the problem of belief with which he was continually wrestling.

On the face of it, this has little enough to do with *comparative* religion. James' material was drawn entirely from his own culture, and from that part of it with which he felt the closest affinity. Of non-Christian religions he knew little or nothing. Nevertheless the stimulus which his work provided for the continued study of the phenomena of the individual religious life cannot be overestimated, and this is its justification.

In his book *The Will to Believe* (1896) James had defined his attitude as being one of 'radical empiricism' : empiricism because every conclusion regarding matters of fact is a hypothesis; radical because of its rejection of the Transcendental heritage of monism. 'If religious hypotheses about the universe be in order at all,' he wrote, 'then the active faiths of individuals in them, freely expressing themselves in life, are the experimental tests by which they are verified, and the only means by which their truth and falsehood can be wrought out.'[25] This concern with problems of truth and falsehood is of course outside the province of psychology, and for that matter of comparative religion, but it is interesting to see that James' approach to these problems is by way of experimental estimate of the consciously expressed beliefs of individuals—a point on which subsequent schools of psychology were to move far away from him, as we shall in due course see.

Approaching the 1900 Gifford Lectures, James seemed at times to revert to positions very close to those of his Swedenborgian father, or rather of the tradition which his father represented. A note for these lectures reads, 'Remember that the whole point lies in really *believing* that through a certain point or part in you you coalesce and are identical with the Eternal.'[26] Perhaps he did not so believe, but he was prepared to allow the validity of others' beliefs on this point, to probe beyond the limits of the rational, so far as this was possible to him, and to accept first-hand testimonies in so doing. Much of this material had in fact been gathered by his friend and former colleague Starbuck; but the conclusions were in every case his own.

The working methods of *The Varieties of Religious Experience* (1902), his published Gifford Lectures, were very simple. James adopted three subjective criteria for estimating the value of religious experience. These he called 'immediate harmoniousness', 'philosophical reasonableness', and 'moral helpfulness'. More problematical was his concentration on cases of religious pathology or near-pathology, and his justification for this course of action :

> If there were such a thing as inspiration from a higher realm, it might well be that the neurotic temperament would furnish the chief condition of the requisite receptivity.[27]

This cautious judgement gave rise in later years to not a little criticism from those who accused him of writing not about religious man as such, but about psychopaths as such. But there is a great deal hidden behind this simple statement, as may be seen by reference to his later lectures on *Human Immortality* (1908).

In cases of leading, providence, conversion and the like, he there wrote, it seems to the subjects concerned that they are entered by some 'external' power, as though their life

---

[25] Quoted in ibid., p. 229.
[26] ibid., p. 232.
[27] *The Varieties of Religious Experience*, p. 25.

. . . suddenly opened into that greater life in which it had its source. The word 'influx', used in Swedenborgian circles, well describes this impression of new insight, or new willingness, sweeping over us like a tide.[28]

He also suggested, in terms remarkably reminiscent of the Transcendentalists, that the brain might have a *permissive* or *transmissive* function, rather than merely a *productive* function, and that the lowering of the threshold of consciousness in various states might be conducive to contact with an external Reality.[29] But this was disputed territory.

Another area of dispute concerns his definition in *Varieties* of religion itself :

. . . the feelings, acts, and experiences of individual men in their solitude, so far as they apprehend themselves to stand in relation to whatever they consider the divine.[30]

To be sure, he observed that much controversial matter was bypassed by this definition; exactly how much he seems hardly to have realised, however. It was left to Durkheim and his fellow-sociologists to make the point, by adopting precisely the opposite point of view, and perhaps also by falling into a diametrically opposite error. To James, the 'body' as opposed to the 'soul' of religion—such matters as theologies, organisations and institutions—was in every case secondary and derived. This particular value judgement makes the overall study of the phenomena of religion virtually an impossibility. However, James' presuppositions being what they were, it could scarcely have been otherwise.

It is not possible in this context for us to penetrate deeply into the argument of *The Varieties of Religious Experience*, but some attention must be paid to the most important pair of 'varieties', viz., the distinction between the optimistic and the pessimistic view of religion, or as James called them, 'the religion of healthy-mindedness' and 'the religion of the sick soul'. At the back of his mind—another heritage from the past—was certainly the conflict which his father's generation had passed through when attempting to come to terms with Calvinistic orthodoxy and its overmastering sense of sin.

It is, then, not surprising to find Emerson put forward as an outstanding personal representative of the religion of healthy-minded-

---

[28] *Human Immortality* (1908), p. 37f.
[29] ibid., p. 30.
[30] *Varieties*, p. 31.

ness :[31] optimistic, incapable of feeling deeply the problem of evil (a point on which Henry James, Sr. had attacked Emerson), liberal and tolerant. Other examples were the 'mind-cure' movements, of which Christian Science is the outstanding surviving example and Ralph Waldo Trine's little book *In Tune with the Infinite* (first published in 1897) was the most widely-read manifesto. To the healthy-minded, sin, disease, failure, suffering and death are all avoidable; or unreal, or both. The theory of evolution, noted James, '. . . fits the religious needs of the healthy-minded so well that it seems almost as if it might have been created for their use'.[32]

The sick soul, on the other hand, is well acquainted with the bitterness of failure to live up to ideals, and with the guilt that arises when one's own standards of judgement (irrespective of their source) are perpetually present as accusers. Here it seems that James is writing out of his own experience; and it is worth noting that the rejection of an oppressive orthodoxy does little or nothing to help such a soul.

> Let sanguine healthy-mindedness do its best with its strange power of living in the moment and ignoring and forgetting, still the evil background is really there to be thought of, and the skull will grin in at the banquet.[33]

James set out to deliver a series of lectures on the psychology of religious experience, and succeeded in writing one of the few religious classics of the twentieth century. He applied a highly individual—not to say individualistic—view of religion to the data of religious experience, as obtained by reasonably straight-forward methods. Although scarcely an orthodox believer, he seems to have wanted to leave all the options open—including the theistic option which he could not personally accept. His methods—at least as they appear in *Varieties*—are open to criticism; however, it is not here that his importance lies, but in the way in which he canonised the individual approach to the problems of religion, and left others a ready-made source of fruitful impulses.

* * *

With *The Varieties of Religious Experience* the psychology of

---

[31] ibid., p. 81.
[32] ibid., p. 91. It is interesting that James himself called the 'mind-cure' movement the Americans' '. . . only decidedly original contribution to the systematic philosophy of life' (*Varieties*, p. 96). It is not clear how far James is here being ironical.
[33] *Varieties*, p. 140f.

religion in America might perhaps be said to have emerged from its infancy, and in the first three decades of the twentieth century it became an increasingly popular approach to the problem of religion. Naturally it continued to have its critics. The English philosopher R. G. Collingwood, for instance, called psychology 'the fashionable scientific fraud of the age', and remarked sourly that William James' *Varieties* '. . . professed to throw light on a certain subject, and threw on it no light whatever'. The fault lay in its method, and it failed to be illuminating 'not because the book was a bad example of psychology, but because it was a good example of psychology'.[34] The cynicism was perhaps understandable, and perhaps not altogether unjustified; but it did little justice to the early psychologists themselves, who were nothing if not conscious of their own lack of competence in what was practically unexplored territory.

Such consensus as there was, began to emerge in the first couple of decades of the twentieth century in popular and semi-popular textbooks and summaries. Some of these were good; others less so. Although selection is not easy, mention may be made of C. C. Everett, *The Psychological Elements of Religious Faith* (1902), E. S. Ames, *The Psychology of Religious Experience* (1910), G. M. Stratton, *Psychology of the Religious Life* (1911) and G. A. Coe, *The Psychology of Religion* (1916). Of these, the most controversial approach was perhaps that of Edward Scribner Ames (1870-1958), who argued strongly that religion should be understand as social righteousness, and as the consciousness and preservation of the highest social values.[35] Similarly, he maintained that the idea of God is nothing but a crystallisation and concentration of all the worshipper's social values, a thoroughgoing pragmatism expressed in the language of religion and metaphysics. Ames, like Leuba, with whom he had many affinities, was criticised both for his method and for his conclusions. J. B. Pratt, for instance, found his pragmatic approach

> . . . both bad psychology and bad epistemology. Bad psychology, because it neglects altogether certain real elements in the religious consciousness, whether found in philosopher, priest, or humble worshipper—men who through all the ages have truly meant by 'God' something more than the idea of God, something genuinely transcendent. Bad epistemology because based ultimately upon a viciously subjective view of *meaning*, a view which would iden-

[34] Collingwood, *An Autobiography* (1939), pp. 93ff.
[35] See V. M. Ames (ed.), *Beyond Theology: The Autobiography of Edward Scribner Ames* (1959).

E

tify our objects with our ideas of our objects, and which, carried to its logical conclusion, would result in solipsism.[36]

* * *

The writer of these words, James Bissett Pratt (1875–1944), is himself worthy of more than merely a passing mention. As we have seen, in the beginning the connection between the psychology of religion and comparative religion was often a tenuous one, if indeed it existed at all. In Pratt's work, however, we find an energetic attempt to combine these areas of inquiry by extending the psychologist's field of investigation beyond the boundaries of the dominant Protestant Christianity. Pratt was trained and employed (at Williams College) as a philosopher; but his interests led him beyond the confines of Western philosophy. He travelled in the East, in India, China and Japan, and as well as publishing such books as *The Psychology of Religious Belief* (1907), *What is Pragmatism?* (1909) and *Democracy and Peace* (1916), he wrote *India and its Faiths* (1915), and *The Pilgrimage of Buddhism* (1928). It is worth noting that even the first of these, *The Psychology of Religious Belief*, contains treatment of historical forms of religion other than Christianity; primal religion, Indian and Jewish material are all introduced for the purpose of illustration. Pratt's most important and influential work was, however, undoubtedly his comprehensive study *The Religious Consciousness*, first published in 1920.

The Religious Consciousness is characterised by synoptic clarity and by balanced judgement.[37] Never other than scrupulously fair, it attempts to sum up the findings and possibilities of the psychology of religion, and to strike a necessary balance between excessive individualism and an equally excessive social emphasis in the study of religion. Both elements are interestingly combined in Pratt's definition of religion as

> . . . the serious and social attitude of individuals or communities toward the power or powers which they conceive as having ultimate control over their interests and destinies.[38]

Other useful coinings include the term 'Determiner of Destiny' (to be compared, though not equated, with Söderblom's *Frambringare*) to describe the wielder of the 'power or powers' hinted at in the

[36]Pratt, *The Religious Consciousness* (1920), p. 209.
[37]R. H. Thouless, writing in *Theology* (May 1921), p. 267, said that 'this is a great work, probably the greatest that has yet appeared on the subject',
[38]Pratt, op. cit., p. 2.

definition. For Pratt, the task of the psychology of religion was 'to describe the workings of the human mind so far as these are influenced by its attitude toward the Determiner of Destiny'.[39] This is cautious, but justifiably so, and it is encouraging to find how firmly he insists on the psychology of religion remaining a descriptive, and never a normative, science : the psychology of religion, he wrote,

. . . must content itself with a description of human experience, while recognising that there may well be spheres of reality to which these experiences refer and with which they are possibly connected, which yet cannot be investigated by science.[40]

The Religious Consciousness contains, from this point on, consideration of most of the normal problems of psychology as applied to religion in East and West, culminating in an extensive treatment of the phenomena of prayer, ecstasy and mysticism. There were weaknesses in the book, however. Perhaps, as R. H. Thouless suggested, Pratt had not quite done justice to the Freudian revolution in psychology; his chapter on 'Religion and the Sub-conscious' is admittedly less than enthusiastic in this regard : but such criticisms are made largely in the light of psychoanalytic hindsight, and may not be serious in the perspective of 1921.

There is one further point about Pratt's work which is worth raising in conclusion. Whenever he dealt with matters having to do with a religious tradition other than his own, he endeavoured to reach a point of emphatic understanding such that the believer in that tradition would recognise his own faith in what was being said by the investigator. Whether he succeeded in this virtually impossible task it is not possible to say. But it is significant that he should have found the attempt worth making, and in such words as these he points forward to the coming 'dialogue of religions' with which we shall be concerned later :

It would be possible [writes Pratt] to write a learned book on Buddhism which should recite the various facts with scholarly exactness, yet leave the reader at the end wondering how intelligent and spiritual men and women of our day could really be Buddhists. I have sought to avoid this effect and have tried to enable the reader to understand a little *how it feels to be a Buddhist.* To give the feelings of an alien religion it is necessary to do more than expound its concepts and describe its history. One must catch its emotional undertone, enter sympathetically

39 ibid., p. 30.
40 ibid., p. 42.

into its sentiment, feel one's way into its symbols, its cult, its art, and then seek to impart these not merely by scientific exposition but in all sorts of indirect ways.[41]

*   *   *

This first, predominantly American, phase in the history of the psychology of religion was, perhaps, of fairly brief duration. Nevertheless the very novelty of the approach which it represented was such as to attract to itself a good deal of attention, not least from the side of those who felt their own position to be in some way or other threatened by its presence. For the most part, as we have seen, its approach was individualistic, and it certainly concentrated to a very great extent on questions of 'religious experience'—experience on the conscious level, tied up with the overt functions of the mind of man. This was, we can now see, its Achilles' heel. Even in its heyday it was in process of being undermined, and shortly it was to be virtually replaced, by the new 'depth-psychology' coming out of Vienna and Zürich, and by the sociology of Paris (itself a type of psychology, perhaps). But before we leave this first phase, there is one related trend which must be mentioned briefly.

The first decades of the twentieth century saw the writing, mainly though not exclusively in the English-speaking world, of a large number of books on the phenomenon, or group of phenomena, labelled 'mysticism'. Mysticism is, as Evelyn Underhill noted in 1910, 'one of the most abused words in the English language . . .', and one which has been 'claimed as an excuse for every kind of occultism, for dilute transcendentalism, vapid symbolism, religious or aesthetic sentimentality, and bad metaphysics'.[42] This being so, and recalling the breadth of her own definition of the word as 'the science and art of the spiritual life',[43] it is perhaps not surprising that the study of mysticism has not yet found its historian.

However, the study of 'the science and art of the spiritual life' was naturally closely allied to the study of the psychological foundations of that same life. Most of the psychological studies so far mentioned in this chapter have taken up the problem of mysticism at some point. But this development was not a simple one. Although pragmatists, positivists, Quakers, Roman Catholics and miscellaneous transcendentalists could unite in a field of study, it was hardly to be expected that their conclusions would show a very high degree

[41] Quoted in C. F. Andrews, *Mahatma Gandhi's Ideas* (1929), p. 353.
[42] Underhill, *Mysticism* (1910), p. xiv.
[43] ibid.

of unanimity. Additionally, at that time in Europe a complex development was taking place, influenced partly by James and by comparative religion, as well as by the idealistic tradition in philosophy, in which one feature was a wave of 'mystical' devotion (*die Neumystik*) outside the Christian churches. In short, the historicism which had dominated so much of the intellectual life of the nineteenth century was being very seriously questioned. In Protestantism, Ritschl was losing ground to the newly rediscovered Schleiermacher; the element of immediacy and spontaneity in religion was being recognised afresh; orthodoxy was suffering one of its periodic eclipses. Hence it would probably be true to say, with George A. Coe, that on both sides of the Atlantic, 'mysticism was becoming a refuge from the disintegrating structure of modern theology'.[44] Here and there, this trend, recognisable from other periods of religious history, resulted in the reawakening of classical mysticism (or what was taken to be such) as a way of life; but in reality the whole gamut of intuitive religious experience was involved, from seances, tabletapping and occultism generally to Vedantic Hinduism (Swami Vivekānanda spent the years from 1893 to 1897 in the West) and its second cousin, Theosophy. Generally speaking, however, the 'mystical revival' of the turn of the century and after was, as the Quaker Rufus Jones somewhat sadly put it, '. . . in the main confined to the historical and psychological interpretation of mysticism as revealed in the autobiographies and expositions of dead prophets'.[45]

Among the more outstanding studies of mysticism during these years, pride of place should probably go to Baron Friedrich von Hügel's *The Mystical Element of Religion* (1908), which, although centred on the life of St. Catherine of Genoa, explores a vast range of mystical experience in all the major religious traditions. Also worthy of honourable mention are W. R. Inge's *Christian Mysticism* (1899)—the first of a number of works in this area from an Anglican Platonist—Evelyn Underhill's *Mysticism* (1911), and Rufus Jones' *Studies in Mystical Religion* (1908). In America, Leuba gave a Positivist interpretation of mysticism in several works, culminating in *The Psychology of Religious Mysticism* (1925), James a Pragmatist interpretation and the philosopher W. E. Hocking a liberal theological interpretation in the book *The Meaning of God in Human Experience* (1912). This list might be prolonged almost indefinitely.

We cannot however pursue this line further in this context,

---

[44] Coe, in *Religion in Transition* (1937), p. 102.
[45] ERE IX (1907), p. 103a.

though we shall return later to the problem of Nathan Söderblom's treatment of the concept of mysticism.

Perhaps this first flourish of interest in the problems of the spiritual life in general, and the problems of the virtuosi of the spiritual life in particular, was too closely bound up with a particular *Zeitgeist* to survive indefinitely, at least in its first form. Perhaps in the exclusive emphasis of the psychologists on personal testimony, and in its relative neglect of so much else that lies within the spectrum of religion, it was too open to counter-attack from sociologists and historians. Certainly the coming of depth-psychology (to be considered separately in a later chapter) made it too easy to dismiss the intensified personal dimension of the spiritual life as the pathology of neurosis. At all events, though for a time the psychology of religion continued to flourish, and became, particularly when centred on mysticism, an essential item in every comparative religionist's equipment, eventually the subject as originally conceived subsided for want of a coherent and convincing method. Soon, all the talk was to be of repressions, neuroses, symbols and archetypes.

VI

The Quest for Academic Recognition

An academic subject, it might be argued, comes of age when it first attains the dignity of a University Chair, and the comparable privileges of scholarly journals, lectureships and congresses. The early years of comparative religion, as we have seen, were noteworthy not for any very unified pattern of study, though there was general allegiance to the evolutionary method, but for the intensity with which comparative religious studies were pursued by a variety of individual scholars in a number of widely-scattered institutions. Some of these scholars were entirely without institutional backing, and regarded themselves, not without justification, as scientific voices crying in a theological or materialist wilderness. But the last quarter of the nineteenth century and the first few years of the twentieth century saw a gradual, if local, change in the climate of university opinion, as a number of universities and colleges in the West (Europe and America) made some effort to provide for the teaching of the new subject. It would be gratifying to be able to record that once launched into the scholarly world, comparative religion was accepted without question into the curricula of every responsible seat of learning; such was, however, very far from being the case. Usually its introduction came as a result of the advocacy of some influential scholar, not infrequently in the teeth of opposition. In those places where traditional theological studies were strong, the impression was usually current that comparative religion was out to corrupt the faithful by relativising a rightful absolute; some secular universities, on the other hand, were concerned to preserve their theological innocence. In both these cases—the former commoner in Europe, the latter in America—it was difficult to introduce comparative religion on a par with other academic subjects. A review of the teaching posts established during the late nineteenth and early twentieth centuries in Europe and America is therefore a useful and interesting guide to the status of the subject in academic circles. Often the establishment of a chair or lectureship was accomplished only after much debate, in which latent tensions came into the open.

Regrettably, a review of this nature cannot hope to be comprehensive, but the examples we shall give will show how difficult it was in practice to delimit the subject, and how many non-academic as well as academic factors played their part in winning—

and in some cases denying—a foothold for comparative religion in the world of the universities.[1]

*   *   *

The honour of establishing the first professorial chair in the subject of *Allgemeine Religionsgeschichte* (the general history of religions) belongs to Switzerland, and the University of Geneva, although the first recorded teaching in the subject seems to have been at the University of Basel, where from 1834 to 1875 J. G. Müller lectured on 'The History of Polytheistic Religions' in the Faculty of Theology. The Geneva Faculty of Theology began the teaching of *Allgemeine Religionsgeschichte* in 1868, and the chair was created in 1873. Its first occupant was Theophile Droz (to 1880), followed by Ernest Stroehlin (1880–93). Although in both Faculties the subject was taught merely by way of background to the study of the Old and New Testaments, it appears that the theological authorities at Geneva were uneasy at the alien presence in their midst, and on the retirement of Stroehlin in 1894 the chair was summarily suppressed. In the following year it was, however, re-established in the Faculty of Arts, where its presence was less controversial. One must admire this early enterprise on the part of the Swiss, but one's admiration is somewhat tempered by the fact that the next chair to be created (by endowment) in the University of Zürich was given the bizarre title of 'History of Religions and Biblical Geography'. In later years, the main centre for the teaching of comparative religion in Switzerland was to be in the University of Basel, which counted among its outstanding professors Conrad von Orelli, Bernhard Duhm and Alfred Bertholet, and served as host for the second International Congress for the History of Religions (1904).

*   *   *

Shortly after the Swiss initiative, in 1877, a comparable, though much more broadly-based, development took place in Holland.[2] Before 1877, the Dutch theological faculties fulfilled, like other con-

---

[1] In this chapter we shall be concerned only with the first steps toward the establishment of comparative religion in the various countries. A review of the *total* history of the discipline in any country, or even in any university, would be a vast undertaking, as can be seen from such a book as K. Rudolph, *Die Religionsgeschichte an der Leipziger Universität* (1962).

[2] Van Hamel, 'L'Enseignement des religions en Hollande', in *Revue d'Historie des Religions* 1 (1880), pp. 379ff.

fessional faculties, a double function, being on the one hand centres of scholarship and on the other training centres for the ministry of the Dutch Reformed Church. Other denominations had seminaries for their ministerial training. At one of these, the Remonstrant Seminary at Leiden, C. P. Tiele had been teaching the history of religions since 1873. The Dutch Universities Act, passed on 1 October 1877, separated the theological faculties at the four state universities (Amsterdam, Groningen, Leiden, Utrecht) from the Dutch Reformed Church; the original draft of the Bill had referred to the establishment of 'Faculties of Religious Sciences', but in the event, the title 'Faculties of Theology' was retained. However, dogmatics and practical theology were were removed from the curricula (though the subjects were taught elsewhere by church-appointed professors), their place being taken by the history of religions, which was assumed to be neutral and scientific. Tiele became professor at Leiden, P. D. Chantepie de la Saussaye at Amsterdam; at Groningen and Utrecht, the new subject was added to the curricula of existing chairs.

There were powerful secularising influences at work in this development, and in this sense the Dutch university served as a paradigm for the kind of situation which was to arise in other countries. The reformers' ideal was to provide a form of religious instruction which was as far removed from narrow confessional concerns as possible. Comparative religion, or the history of religions, seemed a very suitable subject indeed to be taught in this setting. Theologians might not have agreed; but in a state educational system they do not have to agree! It is perhaps also worth noting at this point that the theologian and phenomenologist Gerardus van der Leeuw, who was appointed in 1918 to the Groningen chair, eventually became Dutch Minister of Education.

The high reputation of Dutch comparative religion in the earlier professors, Tiele and Chantepie de la Saussaye. Cornelius Petrus Tiele (1830-1902) was perhaps the continental equivalent of Friedrich Max Müller in England—and this despite the vast differences in temperament and interest which characterised the two men. Both years was due entirely to the work of the Leiden and Amsterdam spoke with authority, but whereas Max Müller's field of interest was language, and Indo-European languages in particular, Tiele's first large book had been on the religion of Zoroaster, and his second on Egypt and Mesopotamia. But he was the first scholar in any country to attempt to sum up comparative religion as a whole, and as his compendia show, he aimed at encyclopaedic knowledge within the scope of evolutionary historical method. He was a careful and exact scholar, and as such became an indispensable guide to generations of historians of religion, particularly since he was, within due limits, a model of impartiality.[3] Chantepie de la Saussaye, too, achieved a world-wide reputation, not least as the originator of the concept of 'the phenomenology of religion', in which connection we shall consider him separately in due course.

*   *   *

The secularisation of higher education also contributed to the impressive developments which took place in this field in France during the 1880s—though it should be recorded that the radically secular and anti-clerical element in French public life was as apt to deny all value to descriptive religious instruction as it was to despise normative, dogmatic religious teaching. It was in the teeth of secular opposition that there was established, in December 1879, a chair of the history of religions in the Collège de France, with Albert Réville as its first incumbent. Also in 1879 there was founded at Lyons the Musée Guimet, the world's first museum and library devoted expressly to the history of religions.

But the most spectacular innovation was connected with the Sorbonne, and with the Ecole Pratique des Hautes Etudes, which had been inaugurated in 1868 in four sections—mathematics; physics and chemistry; natural history and physiology; and historical and philological sciences. In 1885 the Catholic faculties of theology were suppressed, but there were those who felt that the study of religion ought not to be abandoned altogether. One stipulation only was made : in the words of René Goblet, Minister of Public Instruction, 'We do not wish to see the cultivation of polemics, but of critical research; we wish to see the examination of texts, and not the discussion of dogmas.'[4] Accordingly in 1886 there was created a fifth 'section', the Section of Religious Sciences, which was installed in the buildings of the old Catholic faculty of theology.

At first the Section was divided into ten separate departments of historical study (India, the Far East, Egypt, Semitics, Greece-Rome, Christian Origins, the History of Doctrine, Church History, Christian Literature and Canon Law). In time this original division of the field was diversified considerably Among the first professors were Albert Réville (President of the Section), Jean Réville, Auguste

[3] Jordan wrote of him that 'he had the power, when framing slowly his ultimate conclusions, to hold himself quite aloof from everything like partisanship and special pleading'. *Comparative Religion: its Genesis and Growth* (1905), p. 184 n. 2.
[4] See *Problèmes et méthodes d'histoire des religions* (1968), pp. vii ff., 283ff.

Sabatier, Maurice Vernes (joint founder in 1880 of the *Revue d'Histoire des Religions*) and Sylvain Lévi. No teaching in comparative religion as such was offered. Emphasis was laid on the close and detailed study of texts, monuments and ethnological data in well-defined areas, and no attempt was made to create the grand synthesis. The Section was in short devoted to advanced historical scholarship, and within a very few years became the Mecca of the subject. The importance of Paris as a centre of religio-historical scholarship was further enhanced when in 1888 the Musée Guimet was transferred from Lyon to Paris, and in 1900 the first International Congress of the History of Religions (of which more later) was held in Paris, on the initiative of the Section of Religious Sciences, and under the Presidency of Albert Réville. Honorary presidents (neither of whom was actually present) were Max Müller and C. P. Tiele.

As far as the French academic world was concerned, then, the study of religion could only be carried out under conditions of the strictest scientific stringency, and although *oeuvres de vulgarisation* were written, France produced nothing to compare with Tiele and Chantepie in the way of compendia until the classical scholar and archaeologist Salomon Reinach wrote his *Orpheus: a History of Religions* in 1908.[5] The popularity of this work (and perhaps its lack of competition) can be judged from the fact that when a new English edition appeared in 1930, *Orpheus* had seen no less than thirty-eight French editions—eloquent testimony to the appeal of a book whose chief claim to fame is that it contains the most tendentious definition of religion ever seriously put forward.[6]

*   *   *

Another well-known name in the early history of comparative religion in the French-speaking academic world was that of the aristocratic rationalist Count Goblet d'Alviella (1846-1925), a lawyer and member of the Belgian Senate who in 1884 was responsible for introducing comparative religion (*histoire des religions*) into the curriculum of the Free University of Brussels. At the turn of the century this course was compulsory for all candidates for the doctorate in philosophy, and formed part of the general social studies curriculum. D'Alviella himself was a prolific, though unoriginal, writer, the author of several books, including *Introduction à l'histoire générale des religions* (1887) and a series of Hibbert Lectures, *The*

---

[5] Also author of *Cultes, mythes et religions* (5 vols., 1908–23).
[6] 'A sum of scruples which impede the free exercise of our faculties.' *Orpheus* (Eng. tr. 1942 ed.), p. 3.

Origin and Growth of the Conception of God (1891). His position was broadly speaking that of the evolutionary anthropological school.

The 1880s also saw the modest beginnings of comparative religion in Italy, as Baldassare Labanca was appointed in 1886 to a chair of the history of religion in the University of Rome. However, two years later the chair was renamed—on the express wish of the incumbent—the chair of the history of Christianity, and it was some considerable time before an independent school of comparative religion began to flourish in Italy, with the appointment in 1924 of Raffaele Pettazzoni to a Rome chair.[7]

* * *

Moving now further north, to Sweden, in 1877 a new chair was created in the Theological Faculty of the University of Uppsala with the elaborate name of Theological Propaedeutics and Theological Encyclopaedia. Although the objectives of the new chair, as was only to be expected in a confessional Lutheran faculty, were clearly theological in scope, it was understood that the history of religion was to be taught under its auspices.[8] The first two professors to occupy this chair were K. H. G. von Schéele and J. A. Ekman; both indeed held courses in the history of religion, but entirely from the point of view of Christian apologetics (as their appointment demanded). Von Schéele eventually found his true *métier* in the ecclesiastical, rather than the academic world; his academic work is of little importance. Ekman became Archbishop of Uppsala, but not before he had published a large-scale work on the religion of primitive peoples—a book which took no note of advancing work in anthropology, and was consequently out of date before it was even finished.

From 1877 to 1901 (the year of Ekman's elevation to the Archbishopric) the Uppsala chair functioned largely as a tool of Lutheran apologetics. Its establishment was in no way symptomatic

---

[7] See Jordan and Labanca, *The Study of Religion in the Italian Universities* (1909).

[8] See Sharpe, 'Nathan Söderblom and the Study of Religion', in *Religious Studies* 4 (1968), pp. 259ff. Edsman, 'Theology or Religious Studies', in *Religion* IV/I (1974), pp. 59ff. The word 'propaedeutics' is defined by Tor Andrae as follows (in *Nathan Söderblom in Memoriam*, 1931, p. 45): 'By propaedeutics (Sw. *prenotioner*) is meant, that by way of scientific introduction to the study of theology the distinctive nature of the Christian religion and its difference from other forms of religion are to be expounded; the importance of theology as a science is also to be examined, together with its relationship to other spheres of human knowledge.'

of that new attitude to the religions of the world which the term comparative religion' epitomises, but rather represented the attitudes of the earlier part of the nineteenth century. The turning point came in 1901, with the appointment to the chair of a liberal, Nathan Söderblom, in theology a Ritschlian, in comparative religion an Iranist, who had just become the first (and last) foreigner ever to gain a Doctorate at the Protestant Faculty of the Sorbonne in Paris. Söderblom's first steps in comparative religion had been taken under Ekman, but the two stood on either side of a boundary—the boundary of comparative historical method—and under Söderblom the chair became what it had not previously been : a chair of comparative religion. We must consider Söderblom's contribution to his subject more closely in a later chapter; here it will suffice to say that it was during his professorship that the study of comparative religion in Sweden became an accepted and for the most part respectable part of the university curriculum. Söderblom's studies in Paris, and his close spiritual affinities with Germany, enabled him to break free from the narrow provincialism of his predecessors.

As in other countries, the provision of texts and handbooks (not contemplated by either of Söderblom's predecessors) was an important element in the establishment in Sweden of the study of religion along comparative lines. For these Söderblom was almost entirely responsible.

*　　*　　*

For two years, from 1912 to 1914, Söderblom held simultaneously the chair at Uppsala and a chair of *Allgemeine Religionsgeschichte* in the University of Leipzig. It may seem strange that a leading German university needed to call an already employed non-German to such a chair, and still more stranger that the parallel chair in Berlin was at the same time filled by a Dane, Edvard Lehmann (who had never been really happy in Germany, and was shortly to return to Scandinavia, when in 1913 a duplicate of the Uppsala chair of Propaedeutics and Encyclopaedia was set up at the University of Lund). In reality, the circumstances surrounding these appointments provide a remarkable example of the tension between theology and science, and between the approaches to the study of religion to which each gave rise.

At the turn of the century, most of the constituent elements of comparative religion were more than adequately represented in the German universities : classics, Biblical studies, Germanic studies, Oriental studies, comparative philology—all had their accepted places in the academic curriculum. By 1905, for instance, there were more than fifty chairs of Oriental studies in Germany—but there was no chair of comparative religion (under any name). Before the First World War, when a German wished to familiarise himself with the general history of religion, he had to read a compendium produced in Holland by Tiele or Chantepie de la Saussaye, in the former case as revised by a Swede (Söderblom). When the time came to provide a review of work in the field in *Theologisches Jahresbericht*, this was done in turn by a Swiss (Fürrer), a Dutchman (Tiele) and a Dane (Lehmann). And the first two chairs in *Allgemeine Religionsgeschichte*, when these were finally set up in Berlin in 1910 and in Leipzig in 1912, were both filled by Scandinavians.

The reason for this extraordinary situation is to be seen partly in the fact that the university faculties of theology, established on firmly confessional lines, regarded *Religionsgeschichte* with a good deal of suspicion as the enemy of all true religion. There was, of course, some reason for this. *Religionsgeschichte* had already by the turn of the century become the watchword of a type of study which, as we have seen, was attempting to break free from the confines of theology, and especially of confessional theology. Some of its German representatives (particularly those who were later to achieve a certain notoriety as the *Religionsgeschichtliche Schule*) felt that what they were doing was to affirm the essential freedom of the Church from its dogmatic shackles; the influence of Albrecht Ritschl was considerable, especially among his younger Göttingen colleagues. Others may have felt that they were knocking nails into the Church's coffin. At all events, it was virtually axiomatic that a man could not be a *Religionsgeschichtler* and a respectable theologian at one and the same time. It was equally open to doubt, in the eyes of some, whether a man could be a *Religionsgeschichtler* of the wider variety and a scholar at the same time. Perhaps lessons might have been learned, had the German faculties been more willing to look dispassionately at what had already been achieved in Holland and France. But the essential insularity of the German approach to scholarship at this time made this difficult. During the formative decades of comparative religion elsewhere, then, the German universities were regarding the subject either with studied aloofness, or with downright hostility. Neither attitude was calculated to appeal to those who were attempting to place the subject on a firm scholarly footing in other countries—nor was that tradition which had in Germany made use of some of the facts of religious history for philosophical purposes. 'The German investigator collects most diligently the facts of the religious consciousness,' wrote L. H. Jordan in 1905, 'but he is willing to face and accomplish this task, not that he may afterwards busy himself in making scientific *comparison* of these facts, but that he may proceed (with the least possible delay) to introduce them into the foundations of a religious philosophy.'[9] This was not altogether fair; but neither was it altogether false. During the first decade of the twentieth century, it was the possibility of the setting up of a chair of *Allgemeine Religionsgeschichte* at Berlin that seemed likely to set the trend, one way or the other, for German universities as a whole. The debate surrounding this proposal was heated, a prominent part being played by the historian and New Testament scholar Adolf von Harnack.

In 1901, when the debate was at its height, Harnack, as Dean of the Faculty of Theology in Berlin, delivered an address on *Der Aufgabe der theologischen Fakultäten und die allgemeine Religionsgeschichte* (The task of the theological faculties and the general history of religion).[10] In it he asked whether the founders of the Faculty were right in restricting its studies to Christianity, or whether it would be justifiable to broaden its scope so as to include the study of religions other than Christianity. In terms of abstract theory, he allowed that a case might be made out for the latter course of action; nevertheless he had fundamental methodological objections to make. Briefly, his contention was that unless such a general study could be carried on under the same conditions of scientific stringency as were now accepted in the case of Christianity—and this did not appear to him to be even remotely possible—then it would be better not to make the attempt. Harnack warned his hearers that the study of religion on any but the strictest scientific principles would inevitably land the would-be student in 'unhealthy dilettantism'. But the student should not despair : he is far better equipped to study religion through Christianity than through a menagerie of religions : 'Anyone who does not know this religion [Christianity], knows no religion, and anyone who knows Christianity, together with its history, knows all religion.'[11] And after all, 'What is the importance of Homer, of the Vedas, of the Koran, beside the Bible?'[12] The theological student—and we must remember that these words were spoken in the context of a faculty of theology—therefore has more than enough in the Christian heritage; if he does his best with it, he will have absolutely all he ever needs. Christianity is *die Religion*— the absolute religion, in which all others find their fulfilment— anyway, and so further discussion is superfluous.

These views were received with a certain scepticism among students of comparative religion elsewhere. Among the most pointed

[9] Jordan, *Comparative Religion* (1905), p. 513.
[10] Harnack, *Reden und Aufsätze* II (1906), pp. 159–87.
[11] ibid., p. 168.
[12] ibid.

of replies was that of Jean Réville, who wrote in the *Revue d'histoire des religions* that it is not necessary to specialise in every conceivable subject in order to avoid the charge of dilettantism, that Biblical religion is seen more clearly in comparison with other religions, and that if the views of Harnack represented the true situation of the German universities, then he was glad to be a Frenchman![13]

The second German university to establish a chair of *Religionsgeschichte* was Leipzig, which in the first decade of the present century was actually much more conservative and confessional than was Berlin. This confessionalism was in a sense the cause of the establishment of the chair, since one of the objects which it was believed would be served by such an innovation was the discrediting of the 'liberal' extravagances of the *Religionsgeschichtliche Schule*, and of the *Religionsgeschichtliche Volksbücher* in which their results had been popularised. The intention was a sound one : a question of scholarship can never be served by mere polemics or apologetics, but by bringing every possible scholarly influence to bear upon it.

As the influence of Harnack had been decisive in postponing for a decade the introduction of the subject into the University of Berlin, so the Leipzig situation was shaped above all by one man, Rudolf Kittel. This is not the place to review Kittel's vast contribution to Old Testament scholarship, save to say that he was utterly opposed to the then current pan-Babylonism of A. Jeremias and others. Kittel's theological respectability in fact did much to encourage the more conservative members of the Leipzig faculty to accept *Religionsgeschichte* as a legitimate subject for theological study, and to pave the way, in 1912, for the appointment of Nathan Söderblom as the first professor.[14] Others who helped to create a favourable climate of opinion were Wilhelm Wundt, who in the summer of 1911 had held a series of lectures on collective psychology (later published as the famous *Elemente der Völkerpsychologie*), in which he considered religion, entirely sympathetically, in the total context of human culture, and Karl Lamprecht, whose *Institut für Kultur- und Universalgeschichte* already possessed a fine collection of the literature of comparative religion.

But the problem remained : assuming that a chair might profitably be set up, who could be expected to fill it? In 1910 Berlin had solved a similar problem by appointing a Dane, Edvard Lehmann. In 1911 a General Evangelical Lutheran Conference met in Sweden,

---

[13]*RHR* xliv (1901), pp. 423ff. It is sometimes overlooked that it was on Harnack's initiative that Edvard Lehmann was called to Berlin in 1910, to teach in the Faculty of Arts.

[14]Gerhard Kittel, 'Kring Söderbloms Leipzigtid', in Thulin (ed). *Hägkomster och Livsintryck* xiv (1933), pp. 110ff.

and one of the German delegates was Professor Albert Hauck of Leipzig, who met the Uppsala professors during the course of his visit. On his return to Leipzig he went straight to Rudolf Kittel, announcing that the search was over, and that the Uppsala Professor of Theological Propaedeutics and Theological Encyclopaedia, Nathan Söderblom, was obviously the man they were looking for.[15] It was something of a drawback that Söderblom was unwilling to move permanently to Leipzig; and in the event, for the two years before his election as Archbishop of Uppsala he held the Uppsala and Leipzig posts simultaneously. But a beginning was made nevertheless. The subject was established.

It is perhaps superfluous to emphasise that the coming of war in 1914 made the question of a successor to Söderblom difficult, particularly since Söderblom himself was not in Leipzig long enough to train his own successor. But it is not generally known that on Söderblom's retirement, it was agreed that the post should be offered to the Belgian classical scholar Franz Cumont. Now Cumont was a Roman Catholic, and the extraordinary situation arose of a Lutheran faculty of theology being prepared to offer a chair to a Roman Catholic scholar. In the circumstances, it was doubly unfortunate that the outbreak of the First World War prevented this bold ecumenical venture from materialising.[16]

*   *   *

Great Britain was for many years in a somewhat anomalous position with regard to the establishment of teaching posts in comparative religion. For while on the one hand many of its earliest pioneers—particularly among the philologists and anthropologists—had been British, before 1904 not one of these occupied a university post devoted to the subject, and some occupied no university post at all. It is doubly interesting, then, to note that the first two comparative religionists in Britain to devote regular courses of lectures to the subject under that name did so within Christian theological colleges. No one would claim that these two—Joseph Estlin Carpenter and Andrew Martin Fairbairn—were other than exceptional men, and their simultaneous presence in Oxford alongside Max Müller and E. B. Tylor was no doubt fortuitous. The debt which the study of comparative religion in Britain owes them is consider-

[15] ibid., p. 113.
[16] Gerhard Kittel wrote that the Leipzig faculty were agreed that Cumont was the only possible candidate, and expressed his regret both that nothing came of the proposal, and that the events of the war years even caused the proposal to remain virtually unknown. ibid., p. 116.

able, and their position is a salutary reminder to an often hyper-critical posterity that the Churches were by no means always united in implacable opposition to this new thing.

Joseph Estlin Carpenter (1844-1927) was a Unitarian—a group which, by reason of its undogmatic stance, was always more hospitable to the exotic than some other Christian denominations. The son of a distinguished physiologist, he was early introduced to the theory of evolution, which he embraced wholeheartedly. He was appointed to the staff of Manchester College (then, despite its name, in London) in 1876, having already begun to establish a reputation in Biblical studies, and it seems to have been in that year—only three years after the appearance of Max Müller's *Introduction to the Science of Religion*—that he began to offer courses of lectures in comparative religion. Also in 1876 he began the study of Pali under the guidance of T. W. Rhys Davids, and to the end of his life he had these two strings to his scholarly bow.[17]

Carpenter was thus no dilettante in comparative religion. In 1877 he published the English translation of C. P. Tiele's *Outlines of the History of Religion*. Between 1886 and 1911 he edited, together with Rhys Davids, four volumes in the *Pali Text Society* series (the *Sumangala-Vilāsinī* and the *Digha Nikāya*), and in later years several further volumes of essays in the general area of Buddhism and Christianity, as well as a considerable volume of work on the Old and New Testaments. In 1913 he published a highly appreciated handbook entitled simply *Comparative Religion*—evolutionary in emphasis, but written with grace and clarity. In the meantime Manchester College had moved to Oxford (this was in 1889), and under Carpenter's guidance became a notable centre for comparative religious studies. Of course there was more than one reason why the academic establishment tended to look askance at this strange manifestation in its midst. The evolutionary science of religion was bad enough; coupled with Unitarianism it called forth a double measure of suspicion! And so, although comparative religion came to be taught at Oxford in the 1880s (Max Müller had never taught it), it was not taught in the university.

Carpenter's teaching had begun in London in 1876. In the same year a minister of an orthodox Scottish denomination, the Evangelical Union, had published his first book, which was entitled *Studies in the Philosophy of Religion and History*, and in which the influence of the fathers of comparative religion—Tiele, Chantepie

---

[17] Herford (ed.), *Joseph Estlin Carpenter: A Memorial Volume* (1929), contains, as well as a memoir of Carpenter, a chapter by L. H. Farnell on 'Comparative Religion: Pali, and the Religions of India' (pp. 162ff.).

and Max Müller—was apparent. Its author, Andrew Martin Fairbairn (1838-1912) was later to become the first Principal of the Congregational Mansfield College, Oxford, where teaching in comparative religion was introduced in 1886. But in 1876 the subject was very new, and Fairbairn deserves the greatest credit (which by and large he has not received) for his openness and enterprise.[18]

Fairbairn's interests, like Carpenter's, were mainly theological; unlike Carpenter, Fairbairn had no major non-Christian field to call his own. But he did exercise a wide influence among generations of Congregational ministers and laymen. He inspired the introduction of courses in comparative religion into the curricula of other theological colleges, not all of them Congregational; and when in 1904 a British University—the University of Manchester—finally established a chair of comparative religion, one of the men mainly responsible was A. S. Peake, who had been a friend and colleague of Fairbairn's at Mansfield College.[19]

The University of Manchester, along with the Universities of Wales and London, differed from Oxford and Cambridge in being totally free from every denominational restriction, and in imposing no confessional tests on staff or students. After 1904, it differed from Wales and London in being prepared to teach and examine (Wales and London examined, but did not teach) the full range of theological subjects, with one exception, systematic theology, or the history of doctrine. It was rightly pointed out that the establishment in 1904 of the Manchester Faculty of Theology was '. . . the first occasion in this country on which theology, unfettered by tests, has been accepted as an integral part of the University organisation and has been treated like any other subject.'[20] This was important enough in itself. But still more important was the fact that the Faculty insisted that every theological student should take a course in comparative religion—apparently the first time that the subject had been placed on a compulsory basis in any European university. This was a radical departure from the accepted patterns of what

[18] I see no reason to disagree with Fairbairn's biographer, who wrote: 'If many of its conclusions have now become commonplaces, and others have been altogether abandoned, there is still due to the writer the credit of having stated them when and how he did.' Selbie, *The Life of Andrew Martin Fairbairn* (1914), p. 76.

[19] Fairbairn, like other early comparative religionists, was regarded with a fair measure of suspicion by his more orthodox colleagues: '. . . he was known to be a student of German theology, a proof in itself that he was dangerous. He was suspected of knowing something of Hindu philosophy, and it was even whispered that he had quoted in his pulpit passages from the Vedas. Plainly a man to avoid.' Selbie, op. cit., p. 52.

[20] Tout, in Peake (ed.), *Manchester Inaugural Lectures* (1904), p. 20.

was generally taken to be the function of a faculty of theology; that it could have taken place was due almost entirely to the presence in Manchester of two outstanding Methodist scholars, Arthur Samuel Peake (1865–1929) and James Hope Moulton (1863–1917)— both primarily biblical scholars, but the latter in addition an outstanding Iranist.[21]

The Victoria University, comprising colleges in Manchester, Leeds and Liverpool, had been in existence since 1880, and during its first twenty years a number of abortive attempts had been made, on Manchester initiative, to start a theological faculty. These had all foundered on the opposition of secularists in Leeds and Liverpool. But in 1903 the three constituent colleges separated, and by December of 1903 the University Court in Manchester had sanctioned the setting up of a faculty of theology, having its own professors, but working in the closest conjunction with the various denominational theological colleges in the city.

At that time Peake was Principal of Hartley Primitive Methodist College. He became the first Dean of the new faculty, and the first Rylands Professor of Biblical Criticism and Exegesis. Moulton was Tutor at Didsbury Wesleyan Methodist College, and after 1908 Greenwood Professor of Hellenistic Greek and Comparative Indo-European Philology in the University. The two together embodied a remarkable conspectus of the strands that had gone to make up comparative religion. Peake, as we have said, was a former colleague and associate of Fairbairn in Oxford, and a lifelong friend of Farquhar in India (he came to Manchester in 1923). Moulton, more of a comparative religionist, described himself, in a letter to Peake written in 1904, as

. . . a comparative philologist at Cambridge, a classic mostly for teaching purposes, a N. T. student from the grammar side . . ., and a Zendist as a philologue originally, finally a disciple of Frazer from the growing taste for comparative religion.[22]

As a comparative philologist, he drew from the tradition of Indo-European studies; as a papyrologist, he was in a sense part of the British equivalent of the *Religionsgeschichtliche Schule*, and as a close personal friend of Frazer, he inherited the general approach of the British anthropologists.

In fact it was Frazer who was first approached to fill the new chair at Manchester, but he rejected the offer on the grounds that

---

[21] See Wilkinson, *Arthur Samuel Peake* (1958); and *James Hope Moulton, by his Brother* (1919).

[22] *James Hope Moulton*, p. 75.

his views on 'religion in general and Christianity in particular' would make it difficult for him to teach men preparing for the Christian ministry.[28] In the event, the first occupant of the chair was the Pali scholar T. W. Rhys Davids, who had been Estlin Carpenter's tutor in London. After Rhys Davids' retirement, and a longish interregnum, he was succeeded by another Indologist, J. N. Farquhar.[24]

The significance of the Manchester chair was that for the first time in Europe comparative religion had found its rightful place alongside the other theological disciplines in a faculty dedicated to the pursuit of knowledge along strictly historical lines, and without recourse to doctrinal considerations. In time, other teaching posts were established in comparative religion at other British universities; but in no other case were the underlying principles so clearly stated, or the historical position so clearly held, as at Manchester. At the same time, the older-established faculties of theology, with their clearly Anglican position, held themselves formally aloof from comparative religion, other than as a sideline—a situation which has for the most part persisted to this day.

* * *

In the four Scottish Universities of Edinburgh, Glasgow, Aberdeen and St. Andrews, comparative religion has never been held to be of sufficient importance to warrant the setting up of specialist chairs, though some comparative religion has long been taught as an aspect of Christian apologetics. However, on the death of Lord Gifford in 1887, a bequest of £80,000 was set aside for the provision of a lectureship in 'Natural Theology' in all four universities. Under the auspices of the Gifford Lectureship, by the beginning of the twentieth century a number of outstanding series of lectures had been held, by such men as Max Müller, C. P. Tiele, Edward Caird, E. B. Tylor, A. M. Fairbairn and Andrew Lang.[25]

This pattern—of 'endowed comparative religion' in an officially sceptical milieu—was in the late nineteenth century not dissimilar to that obtaining at the older universities in England. The Scottish universities, and particularly their faculties of divinity, were, by virtue of their close links with the Established Church, unsympathetic to the notion of providing concentrated teaching in non-

---

[28] Letter from Frazer to Moulton, quoted in ibid., pp. 164ff.

[24] On Farquhar, see below, pp. 151-4. It is perhaps worth noting that Farquhar's appointment was due in large measure to Peake. See Sharpe, *J. N. Farquhar: A Memoir* (1962), pp. 89ff.

[25] A complete list of the early lectures will be found in Jordan, *Comparative Religion*, p. 570f.

Christian forms of religion, and such moves as there were took place on the initiative of private persons. Individual initiative in fact far outstripped official action, not only in the provision of lectureships, but also in the provision of handbooks and works of reference. It would, therefore, be entirely wrong to suggest that Scottish scholars were devoid of interest in the problems raised by comparative religion, although they did tend to place them within the framework of Christian orthodoxy. For instance, Robert Flint of Edinburgh had dealt with a variety of non-Christian systems in his two books *Theism* (1876) and *Anti-Theistic Theories* (1879). A contemporary, John Robson, compared Hinduism and Christianity in a volume of that name (3rd ed. 1905), having previously published a pamphlet on *The Science of Religion and Christian Missions* (1876), in which he had gone a long way towards accepting the position of Max Müller. And among the anthropologists, Andrew Lang was a son of the Scottish Border, and J. G. Frazer was a Scot, though both worked for the most part in England. A. M. Fairbairn and J. N. Farquhar were both representatives of another Scottish tradition, that of the Evangelical Union.

The first genuinely Scottish handbook of comparative religion, Allan Menzies' *History of Religion*, was published in 1895 (though there had been an earlier encyclopaedia of the religious systems of the world, published in Edinburgh in 1867). Menzies was Professor of Biblical Criticism in the University of St. Andrews, but his intention in writing his handbook was not narrowly apologetical. 'It is obvious,' he wrote in his preface, 'that in a work claiming to be scientific, and appealing to men of every faith, all religions must be treated impartially, and that the same method must be applied to each of them.'[26] His position was that of the liberals, i.e. a consistent theological evolutionism; thus while stressing that the science of comparative religion 'is seeking to grasp the religions of the world as manifestations of the religion of the world',[27] he held that Christianity was the highest evolutionary form of the religion of the world, being a form of religion particularly suited to the more evolved nations :

> Christianity has a message to which men become always more willing to respond as they rise in the scale of civilisation . . . [Christianity] is surely the desire of the nations, and is destined to be the faith of all mankind.[28]

Simplistic as these words now appear, the book itself has many solid

[26] Menzies, *History of Religion*, p. v.
[27] ibid., p. 5.
[28] ibid., p. 425.

virtues—clarity, comprehensiveness and accuracy among them—and it fully deserves its popularity; it was still in print in the 1920s.

Menzies, although not a professional comparative religionist, was at least a professor in a Scottish university. But the crowning Scottish achievement was brought about by a man whose position could scarcely have been more modest, by the Free Church minister of Kinneff, a village on the Kincardineshire coast, twenty miles south of Aberdeen. The minister's name, James Hastings (1852–1922); his achievement, the indispensable twelve volumes of the *Encyclopaedia of Religion and Ethics*.

It is difficult to speak of Hastings' work other than in superlatives. As well as the *Encyclopaedia* (by which time he had left Kinneff for wider fields of service; he ultimately resigned his pastoral charge to be able to devote himself wholly to his editorial work) he had already edited a *Dictionary of the Bible*, a *Dictionary of Christ and the Gospels* and a *Dictionary of the Apostolic Church*; he had founded the influential journal of Biblical exegesis *The Expository Times* in 1889, and edited it until his death. It was in fact in the *E.T.* for May 1908 that Hastings first wrote of his plans for a vast encyclopaedia of comparative religion, though the preliminary work had already been under way for some six years. In his own words :

The aim of the ENCYCLOPAEDIA will be to give an account of Religion and Ethics in all ages and in all countries of the world. If it is found impossible to attain so high a purpose, that is no reason why the purpose should not be entertained. . . It is true that the attempt has never been made before. For never before have Religion and Ethics held the place which they now hold in men's thoughts and interests. There was not encouragement before. Here and there a man has, single-handed, attempted an explanation of each of the great religions of the world. And once or twice each of the great religions has been put into the hands of a special student of it. But never before has every separate religious belief and practice, and every separate philosophical and ethical idea or custom, been treated in separate articles, and each of them by a man who has made that particular custom or idea his special study. . . There has been no difficulty in fixing the scope of the ENCYCLOPAEDIA OF RELIGION AND ETHICS, but there has been great difficulty in estimating its probable extent. What is wanted is thoroughness. Every line will be watched to see that it is not wasted, but in the present temper of the students of Religion and Ethics the book that is content with colourless epitomising is doomed to failure.[29]

29 *The Expository Times* XIX/8 (May 1908), pp. 337ff.

There may have been some 'colourless epitomising' in the *ERE*, but the wonder is that there was so little. In its twelve volumes (1908–21; the Index Volume was added after Hastings' death), there is quite remarkable breadth and depth of treatment, and a no less remarkable coherence of approach, bearing in mind that there were almost 900 scholars involved in its production. In fact it would not be too much of an exaggeration to say that the *ERE* represented in its day the epitome of European (and, to a lesser extent, American) scholarship at its best. Its only serious competitor, the Göttingen-inspired *Die Religion in Geschichte und Gegenwart*, is tendentious in comparison, though successive revisions have enabled it to keep up with the times more successfully than the *ERE*, which has never been revised, and probably never could be without being entirely rewritten. All in all, this Scottish venture (which, incidentally, could never have been realised without the initial generosity of the Edinburgh publishers T. and T. Clark) has given far more to the world of scholarship than many a university teaching post.

* * *

Joseph M. Kitagawa has noted that in the United States of America the discipline of the history of religions (the common American equivalent of comparative religion) did not develop until a fairly late date, partly due to the complex religious background of America.[80] The main feature of this religious background was religious pluralism, but a pluralism in which that type of Protestantism which W. W. Sweet has characterised as 'left-wing' (not, however, in the modern sense) was dominant. Nor should it be forgotten that from 1861 to 1865 America—whose universities were mainly in the Eastern seaboard states—had been ravaged by civil war.

> In this situation the religious problems which were relevant to Americans centred around the relations among different ecclesiastical groups. . . Tales were told of other religions in far-off lands, but religions other than Judaeo-Christian traditions presented no real alternative and thus did not concern the citizens of the new republic.[81]

But although popular American religion in the late nineteenth century was a relatively narrow affair, here and there were to be

---

[80] Kitagawa, 'The History of Religions in America,' in id. (ed.), *The History of Religions: Essays in Methodology* (1959), pp. 1ff.
[81] ibid., p. 2.

found individuals and groups, for the most part influenced by contemporary currents of thought in Europe, where interests were far
wider. Mention has already been made of the New England Transcendentalists—Emerson, Thoreau, Alcott and the rest—and their
enthusiastic, albeit uncritical, reverence for literary Orientalia. A
more scholarly approach was typified by such men as James Freeman Clarke (1810–1888), who had begun the study of comparative
religion in the early 1840s, and who published in 1871 *Ten Great
Religions: An Essay in Comparative Theology*, a two-volume work
dealing partly with individual histories of religious traditions and
partly with the origin and development of religious doctrines.
Clarke's work was genuinely comparative, and written as it was
within a year of the programmatic statement of Max Müller concerning the possible scope of the science of religion, must be reckoned to be one of the early milestones of the subject.[32]

Four years before, in 1867, Clarke had been appointed Professor
of Natural Religion and Christian Doctrine at the Harvard Divinity
School—not, it is true, a chair of comparative religion pure and
simple (the apologetical inference is clear, and invites comparison
with the Scandinavian concept of 'Theological Propaedeutics'), but
nevertheless an important new departure. Similar appointments
were made by Boston University in 1873 (William Fairfield
Warren), by Princeton in 1881 and by Cornell in 1891. Also in
1891 Harvard appointed George Foot Moore to the chair of the
history of religions. The University of Chicago established a department of comparative religion in 1892, and in the same year a
number of universities and colleges joined forces to set up 'The
American Lectures on the History of Religions'—'for the purpose
of encouraging the intelligent study of religions'. The first holder of
this lectureship, which was similar in scope to the Hibbert Lectureship in England or the Gifford Lectureship in Scotland, was the
Buddhist scholar T. W. Rhys Davids (later Professor of Comparative
Religion at Manchester, England), and subsequent lecturers included
the ethnologist D. G. Brinton and the Near Eastern scholars T. K.
Cheyne, Karl Budde and G. Steindorff.

It is also worth noting that during this formative period there
were a number of American scholars who made important contributions to the development of one or another branch of comparative
religious study. The psychologists of religion—Hall, Starbuck,
Leuba and James—we have already met; we might add, more or
less at random, the Indologists Hopkins and Whitney (one of Max

---

[32] The popularity of this work may be judged from the fact that up to
1893 it had passed through no less than 30 editions.

Müller's bitterest opponents, incidentally), the missionary scholars Hume and Griswold, and the Assyriologists Goodspeed and Morris Jastrow Jr., whose little book *The Study of Religion* (1901) contains an excellent *apologia* for the comparative study of religion as a necessary element in a liberal education.

In effect, the situation of comparative religion in America at the turn of the century, modifying factors notwithstanding, did not differ fundamentally from that obtaining in many parts of Europe at the same time. The same elements—motive, material and method—were in evidence. Liberalism, both theological and political, provided the ground in which it was able to flourish. Perhaps there was less liberalism in America than in Europe; and anti-liberal forces were undoubtedly stronger. Eventually, comparative religion was to suffer something of an eclipse, despite its promising beginnings, under the pressures of conservatism and orthodoxy. But before this had happened, the United States was able to mount one of the most spectacular manifestations of the 'new' spirit in religion—the World's Parliament of Religions, held at Chicago in 1893. It is, however, necessary that this remarkable gathering should be seen in context—the context of that most Western of Western phenomena, the tradition of scientific congresses.

*   *   *

The first genuinely scientific congress of comparative religion was held in 1900, in Paris. Previously, however, there had been two congresses which are deserving of mention in this context.

The first was the celebrated (some would say notorious) World's Parliament of Religions, convened in Chicago in 1893, as part of the World's Columbian Exposition of that year. From May to October no less than 200 separate congresses were held, covering such diverse subjects as women's progress, the public press, medicine and surgery, temperance, moral and social reform, commerce and finance, music, literature, education, engineering, art and architecture, government and law reform, science and philosophy, labour, social and economic science, religion, Sunday rest, public health, and agriculture. Under the heading of 'religion' there were in fact forty-one separate denominational and inter-denominational congresses. The actual Parliament of Religions was meant as a demonstration of world brotherhood, and in the eyes of its organisers at least, succeeded in its aim. As one commentator wrote, 'The great triumph of the parliament has been the frank statements, clearly defining, in every possible shade of human thought, the various faiths now holding up appealing hands to the Father of all !'[33]

Regrettably no modern scholar has been bold enough to attempt to analyse this extraordinary gathering from the point of view of the religious thought of late-nineteenth-century America. Nor can we attempt such an assessment here. But it is worth noting nevertheless that the humanitarian unity toward which the parliament strove probably existed only in the minds of its organisers, and in a few of the delegates. It was bitterly attacked by many orthodox Christian agencies as, in the words of one of them, the Church Missionary Society, a 'menagerie of religions . . . the most profane and the most unpardonable outrage upon Christianity that the world has known'.[34] The motives of the participants were very diverse. Some accepted the programme of the organisers, others carried out straightforward propaganda, occasionally disguised, occasionally not. But some scholarly addresses were given, and amid the welter of sentimental euphoria and the incredible prolixity of the proceedings, some wise words were being spoken.

The parliament was an encouragement, and a danger, to the emerging science of religion. An encouragement, because it showed the extent to which earlier impatience and intolerance was being overcome. A danger, because it tended to associate at least some comparative religionists (those who dared to associate themselves with it) with an idealistic programme of world peace and understanding. Observers were right when they pointed out that this meeting could only have been held in brash, sentimental, pluralistic America. But the ideals which were so desirable in the Chicago of the 1890s were not necessarily those of, for instance, the European universities, where the science of religion was slowly finding its feet. It was perhaps permissible for Max Müller to associate himself *in absentia* with the parliament; his reputation could bear it. Others held themselves firmly aloof—and have continued to hold themselves aloof from any further such gatherings simply on the grounds that whatever the need for inter-religious understanding, the scientific study of religion, committed to the quest of truth for truth's own sake, ought not to be saddled with such an onerous and subjective incidental. This is not to say that there have been no scholars who in later years have embraced a refined form of the Chicago programme. There have been many, not least in America. But an

---

[33] Houghton (ed.), *Neely's History of the Parliament of Religions* (3rd ed. 1893), p. 30. This is one of two unofficial accounts of the Parliament. The official report is the two-volume account edited by J. S. Barrows.
[34] Quoted in Sharpe, *Not to Destroy but to Fulfil* (1965), p. 155 n. 4.

incipient conflict was apparent in 1893, and it still exists, as the proceedings of much later congresses show.

At the second 'preliminary' congress, held in Stockholm in 1897, the tension between possible approaches was more evident than it had been at Chicago.[35] Entitled the Congress of the Science of Religion (*Religionsvetenskapliga Kongressen*), it was organised in connection with King Oscar II's Silver Jubilee by three men—a Swedenborgian pastor, a Jewish Rabbi and a Lutheran Old Testament scholar (S. A. Fries). At first conceived by the Swedenborgian Albert Björck on the lines of Chicago, it was turned by Fries into 'scientific' channels, and the original invitation stressed its scholarly aspect; however, the echoes of Chicago had not subsided, and although some notable scholars were present—including P. D. Chantepie de la Saussaye, W. Brede Kristensen and Nathan Söderblom—many more stayed away, fearing a repetition of Chicago. In the event a third force, that of Lutheran orthodoxy, did more than the Chicago spirit to obscure the spirit of scholarship. The list of lectures and discussions reveals an almost exclusive concern with the problems of Protestant Christianity in a new age. Apart from Rabbi Klein, there were no non-Christian speakers, and the whole subject of non-Christian religions was treated with the utmost caution, and largely in relation to Christianity. There was evidently a great deal of suspicion among delegates of 'liberal' trends—comparative religion being one of them—in Christianity. Symptomatic of the divided loyalties of the conference as a whole was the fact that although it opened with a message of greeting from Max Müller (who was not able to be present), it also included an attack on Müller from the conference chairman, Bishop von Schéele of Visby.

Probably it would be true to say that northern Europe was not yet ready for such a congress, since the science of religion was not yet sufficiently well established as an independent entity, being still viewed largely in the perspective of Christian apologetics.

In France, however, a vastly different situation obtained. We have already taken note of the setting up of the 'Section of Religious Sciences' at the Sorbonne, and it was as a result of the initiative of this Section that *Le Premier Congrès International d'Histoire des Religions* was called in connection with *l'Exposition Universelle* in 1900. On the whole the organisers were justified in calling it the *first* congress of the history of religions, since it was the first such

---

[35] Fries (ed.), *Religionsvetenskapliga Kongressen i Stockholm 1897* (1898). It is perhaps to be regretted that the subsequent series of international congresses organised by the IAHR should be regarded as having begun with the Paris congress of 1900, rather than with this pioneer assembly.

meeting devoted exclusively to the scientific study of religions. In fact it reflected very accurately the methods and concerns of the Sorbonne, being organised in eight sections, each devoted to a particular historical area.

The proceedings of this congress sum up, in effect, the position of comparative religion at the turn of the century.[36] Its officials and vice-presidents comprised practically all the leading scholars of the period. Papers were read which attempted to evaluate the present position of the discipline, and to look to the future. A report was delivered on the aims and successes of Chicago 1893; a greeting was received from S. A. Fries on behalf of Stockholm 1897—it is pleasing to record that neither earlier conference was condemned as 'unscientific'. The spirit in which the congress was undertaken can perhaps be judged by this extract from the opening address by Albert Réville :

> The History of Religions, like all histories, is possible only through the collective labour of all those who devote their strength to it, and it will never be possible to say that it has been done completely, definitively, and without the possibility of revision. But what can be said is that its broad outlines have been traced, that the area of the mine has been sounded, divided, deepened, and that it is now up to each miner to excavate to the best of his ability the seam which has been allocated to him. We neither exaggerate nor do we depreciate the place which we occupy in the field of general scientific progress. We are for the most part modest and obscure artisans, but we are extracting precious metal from the soil. Our Congress will probably not create a great stir among all those philanthropic, economic, industrial, scientific and artistic meetings, whose programmes speak more directly to the preoccupations of the multitude. But he would indeed be deaf who did not hear the voices energetically demanding, in the field which we have chosen, light, more light, still more light. . . In spite of all that still separates us from the ideal goal which draws us, the nineteenth century will have the honour of bequeathing to the twentieth, in respect of the History of Religions, a capital which cannot but grow. If we are sincere lovers of truth, this must be a sufficient ambition for us.[37]

With Paris 1900 and subsequent congresses in Basel 1904 and Oxford 1908 began that series of scholarly conferences which was to continue, with interruptions due to two wars, until the present

[36] *Actes du premier congrès international d'Histoire des Religions* (1901).
[37] ibid., p. 48f.

day. The general pattern was that each congress planned for its successor by appointing a committee; it was not until 1950 that the International Association for the History of Religions was set up as a continuing professional body, with its own journal.

Space does not permit a congress-by-congress report of subsequent developments. We shall, though, return to some of the questions of principle raised at later congresses in a subsequent chapter.

* * *

With this sketchy and incomplete review of the position of comparative religion in the scholarly world of the late nineteenth and early twentieth centuries, we may perhaps claim to have reached the end of the formative period of the subject, a landmark established externally by the publication in 1905 of Louis H. Jordan's rambling book *Comparative Religion: its Genesis and Growth*. The fact that Jordan found it constantly necessary, in writing the first history of the subject, to be defending its right to be regarded as an independent field of study, is not without significance. Whether he succeeded is another matter entirely. With enormous stamina, he conducted his readers through the confused and confusing world of comparative religious study, from book to book, from theme to theme, from country to country—all with a view to demonstrating that there was indeed a new force abroad in the world of scholarship. He rested his case squarely on evolutionary historical study; and he was right to do so. Throughout this period, virtually the only thing binding together the heterogeneous material that we have—like Jordan—tried to pass in review, was the implicit belief that in the theory of evolution the scholar has the key which can interpret religion to his own day and age. Thus all the writers, from Max Müller onward, that we have considered were at bottom inspired by the same historical ideal—that of tracing the stages by which religion has evolved in human consciousness. All were convinced likewise that in studying 'religions' they were studying species of the genus 'religion', whether in the remote history of mankind, in the beliefs and practices of surviving 'primitives', in the emotions and aspirations of present-day Europeans and Americans, or in the great scriptures of the great traditions. Within the evolutionary synthesis, all had its place.

The evolutionary ideal continued to dominate Western thought for some decades; nevertheless, from this point on, it becomes less proper to speak of a synthesis. For one thing, there was opposition, at first hesitant, and cautious, but soon to attack the evolutionists at their roots. There were a variety of sharp reactions, then, against the over-optimistic synthesis. Some involved a better awareness of the limitations of history over against undue theorising. Some involved a bitter rejection of the positivist thesis (inherited from Comte) that evolution must mean an evolution *out of* religion into science. Some insisted on more first-hand knowledge, particularly of 'primitive' peoples, as opposed to the practices of armchair anthropologists in piling hypothesis on hypothesis when they knew nothing directly of the people about whom they were writing. All in all, the years after the First World War saw a methodological revolution within comparative religion, and it is to the processes of reaction and consolidation which this involved to which we must now turn.

VII

Religion, Comparative and Absolute

We have had frequent occasion to be reminded, in the course of this book, that the comparative study of religion was capable of making an appeal to two types of mind, the 'scientific' and the 'religious'. The 'scientific' mind was concerned to apply a particular method to a body of data—data taken as a rule to refer only to the workings of the human mind, and not to any type of transcendent reality. The 'religious' mind, on the other hand, had as its essential point of departure a stance of faith in the actual existence of a transcendent order of being; and although the emergent data of comparative religion might well come into conflict (or appear to do so) with certain traditional answers to questions of religious authority, these could not contradict the basic stance of faith itself. There might be false gods, or inadequate beliefs about God, but there was no *a priori* reason to question all religious belief, at least not on these grounds.

Christian theologians were, as we have noted, at first extremely wary of the whole subject of comparative religion. Some, indeed, still are. Committed as they were to the acceptance of a highly detailed doctrine of revelation, contained either in the words of the Bible alone or in the Bible as interpreted by the cumulative life and witness of the Church, it seemed to some of them as though comparative religionists were bent on undermining the very foundations of Christian belief. The scientist did indeed hold up to examination the authorities on which the Christian case had always rested, and often rejected them. The doctrine of evolution in its late-nineteenth-century form was clearly and irrevocably in conflict with a literal interpretation of certain parts of Scripture, particularly, of course, the first chapters of Genesis; and anyone making use of the evolutionary method was apt to be regarded as the enemy of revealed truth, however much he might protest that such was not his intention at all.

Another factor contributing to the general 'attack and defence' situation was the manifest interest shown by comparative religionists in religious traditions which had traditionally been regarded as at best worthless, at worst the work of the devil. This particular conflict of principle has cropped up at intervals throughout the history of the Christian Church. To take only one example, one of the first Protestant missionaries to India, Bartholomew Ziegenbalg, sent early in the eighteenth century the result of his researches into South Indian Hinduism home to Europe, only to be informed that 'his business was to root out Hinduism in India, and not to propagate heathen superstition in Europe'.[1]

Ziegenbalg would in all likelihood have agreed; but he would certainly have disagreed with the assumption that the enemy of Hinduism is not required to have an accurate, and within due limits a sympathetic knowledge of Hinduism. Many other Christian missionaries well before the modern period proved, despite their irrevocable commitment to the truth of the Christian position, capable of acquiring detailed and accurate knowledge of a variety of non-Christian traditions, thereby helping to lay the foundations of comparative religion.

Roman Catholic missionaries in particular had played a large part in communicating information to the West. The Jesuit missionaries in China—among them Matteo Ricci, Trigautius, Varen and Athanasius Kircher—not only brought China to the notice of Europe, but helped create an intellectual fashion.[2] Our earliest reliable knowledge of the religions of Central and North America also comes from Jesuit sources. In India, Abbé Jean-Antoine Dubois (1765–1848), whose best-known work, *Hindu Manners, Customs and Ceremonies,* was first published at the instigation of the East India Company in 1816,[3] may serve as an example of a missionary who was a scrupulously accurate observer and recorder, though fundamentally out of sympathy with the phenomena observed, and incapable of evaluating them other than on a Christian dogmatic basis. A Protestant parallel might perhaps be provided by the work of the Baptist Missionary William Carey (1761–1834) and his colleagues at Serampore, who were similarly keen observers of Hinduism, while remaining wholly uncompromising in their rejection of its theology.

While missionaries were thus often forced by the exigencies of their situation to learn a great deal about non-Christian religions, their orthodox counterparts in the West looked upon other religions in a thoroughly biblical manner as opponents to be overcome, and their defenders as dangerous heretics or perishing sinners. There were, of course, the exceptions which we have mentioned elsewhere,

---

[1] Neill, *A History of Christian Missions* (1964), p. 230. The document in question was finally published in 1867 as *Genealogie der Malabarischen Götter.*

[2] See above, pp. 15ff.

[3] Dubois, *Hindu Manners, Customs and Ceremonies* (translated and edited by Beauchamp, 3rd ed. 1906).

F

but by the third quarter of the nineteenth century, the liberal viewpoint had made little enough headway.

But Christian opinion in the West could not in the long run remain satisfied with such an over-simplification of the situation. The early comparative religionists were listened to far more widely and far more respectfully than we sometimes tend to imagine. But although they were listened to, and although the data they were providing was by the end of the century taken into account, Christian theology reserved the right to supply its own interpretation of the data—as it had every right to do.[4] In view of the far-reaching claims being made in the name of science, some theological rejoinder was imperative. A precipitate retreat into obscurantism took place here and there; witness for example the divine (whose name I have forgotten) who thundered from his pulpit : 'There may be comparative religions, but Christianity is not one of them !' On the whole, though, as soon as comparative religion had overcome its sillier phase—in which some wild theories were very properly ignored—some theologians began to take it very seriously indeed.[5]

The Christian theologians with whom we shall be mainly concerned in this chapter were for the most part active in the first three decades of the twentieth century; but they were thus not absolute innovators. In every case they were building on foundations laid much earlier. One might claim that they were all 'liberals', and that they were all reasserting, in various ways, a 'Hellenic' attitude to religion over against a dominantly Hebraic tradition, but at the same time claiming the right to make such a reassertion within the framework of the historic Christian community rather than from a position either outside the community or on its sidelines. This is not the place to trace the far ancestry of these men; even to trace this ancestry back through one century is difficult enough, though it may safely be said that behind them all stand the figures of Schleiermacher in Germany, Coleridge in England and perhaps also Emerson in America.

In England, an early representative of this general position was the Anglican theologian F. D. Maurice, whose Boyle Lectures of

---

[4] Chantepie de la Saussaye, *Lehrbuch der Religionsgeschichte* (1887), p. 7.

[5] Here and there one finds some extreme claims indeed. Thus according to W. E. Griffis, the science of comparative religion '. . . is Christianity's own child . . . the direct offspring of the religion of Jesus . . . Christian scholars began their investigations, formulated their principles, collected their materials and reared the already splendid fabric of the science of Comparative Religion, because the spirit of Christ which was in them did signify this.' Griffis, *The Religions of Japan* (1895), p. 4f.

1845–6, *The Religions of the World and their Relations to Christianity* (1st ed. 1846; 6th ed. 1886) exhibit a breadth of sympathy, together with a desire for accurate and up-to-date information, which were unusual at the time. The qualities of this influential book stand out clearly if we contrast it with another Anglican product, Charles Hardwick's *Christ and Other Masters* (1855–8; 3rd ed. 1874). Hardwick knew far more than Maurice, who could on occasion be dreadfully inaccurate, and yet it was Maurice who succeeded in presenting the non-Christian religions, not merely as tissues of falsehood, but as evidence of an unalienable aspect of human nature—the desire to worship. The *fulfilment* of the desire Maurice believed was to be found ultimately only in the Church; nevertheless he could speak of a 'wonderful testimony . . . borne from the ends of the earth' and of Christians as 'debtors' to Buddhism, Hinduism and Islam.[6]

The tone of Hardwick's book is far different. Not only did he criticise sharply the idea that religions generally are '. . . mere expressions of the fundamental beliefs inherent in our spiritual nature',[7] and pour scorn on the notion of the statues of the great religious founders being erected 'side by side in the Walhalla of spiritualism';[8] he took an utterly uncompromising position with regard to the claims of Christianity.

> Christianity will tolerate no rival [he wrote]. They who wish to raise a tabernacle to some other master, be it even for the greatest worthies of the old oeconomy,—a Moses or Elias,—must be warned that Christ, and Christ alone, is to be worshipped . . .[9]

This pattern, of orthodox warnings confronting liberal sympathies, was intensified greatly in the decades which followed, as evolutionary judgements became more and more common. In time, however, the liberal alternative became stronger. A Robertson Smith (like Maurice before him) could be dismissed his post; but he could not be silenced. Theological students could not be prevented from reading Max Müller, any more than they could be prevented

---

[6] 'We owe them [the three great religions and the "modern infidels"] the deepest gratitude if they have led us to ask ourselves whether there is any faith, and what kind of faith it is, which must belong, not to races or nations, but to mankind; still more, if they have forced us to the conclusion, that the real test, whether there be such a faith, and whether it has been made known to us, must be action, not argument; that if it exist, it must show that it exists; that if it have power, it must put forth its power.' Maurice, *The Religions of the World* (6th ed. 1886), p. 244.

[7] Hardwick, *Christ and Other Masters* (3rd ed. 1874), p. 15.

[8] ibid., p. 16.

[9] ibid., p. 28.

from reading Wellhausen, Ritschl or Henry Drummond. And gradually it became apparent that for a variety of reasons, not all of them connected with comparative religion (though mostly linked with the causes that had brought comparative religion to birth), the entire emphasis in Christian theology was in process of shifting, from belief in the authority of Book or Church, to belief in the authority of a God actually revealed in the processes of history. In short, the theological reorientation which brought into being both Liberal Protestantism and Catholic Modernism in Europe was one in which transcendent doctrines of God were being widely exchanged for immanentist doctrines. A view which saw Deity as essentially external to the historical process was being replaced by a doctrine of God 'at work', progressively revealing himself within the very process which evolutionary theory was engaged in tracing. It was all very well for some of the scientists to claim that there could never be a reconciliation between evolution and theology; but theology was not static in the way the scientists supposed, and a far-reaching reconciliation was in fact attempted.[10]

Often enough, the liberal theologians were not particularly interested in what was happening in the field of comparative religion, simply because they lacked the necessary specialist knowledge. For many of them, it was a sufficiently onerous task to attempt to come to terms with scientific thought in the West, without having to extend their horizons so as to embrace the entirety of man's religious experience, as the first comparative religionists had attempted to do. It must not be forgotten, however, that many of the founding fathers of comparative religion were liberal Christians. Max Müller had said as early as 1858 that 'the real history of man is the history of religion : the wonderful way by which the different families of the human race have advanced towards a truer knowledge and a deeper love of God.'[11] C. P. Tiele and P. D. Chantepie de la Saussaye would certainly have concurred. And by the end of the century, occasional Christian scholars had begun to publish books having a more popular appeal, in which the phenomena of religious evolution were given a confidently Christian interpretation. In the English-speaking world the best-known of these was probably F. B.

---

[10] cf. Drummond, 'The Contribution of Science to Christianity', in *The New Evangelism* (2nd ed. 1899): 'Religion is probably only learning for the first time how to approach science. Their former intercourse, from faults on both sides, and these mainly due to juvenility, is not a thing to remember' (p. 155). 'Certain it is that the Christian view and the scientific view together frame a conception of the object of worship, such as the world in its highest inspiration has never reached before.' (p. 187).

[11] Müller, *Chips from a German Workshop* I (1867), p. 21.

Jevons' *An Introduction to the History of Religion*, which first appeared in 1896, although it was run a close second in popularity by the Scottish biblical scholar Allan Menzies' *History of Religion* (1st ed. 1895); both view the religious quest of mankind as divinely inspired, and as finding its fulfilment in Christianity. A similar position, though in this case worked out with the help of a far more massive weight of learning, was maintained by another Scotsman, A. M. Fairbairn, in *The Philosophy of the Christian Religion* (1902). This book, part of which was based on a series of unpublished Gifford Lectures, in fact deals in some detail (despite its title) with Buddhist and Islamic material.[12]

At about the same time in Germany, and particularly in the University of Göttingen (where the school of Albrecht Ritschl and his disciples was firmly entrenched), there was emerging a group of theologians who were putting the data of comparative religion to a far different use. These were the members of the *Religionsgeschichtliche Schule*, or 'the history of religion school'. Despite their impressive collective title, however, they were to be of limited significance for the future development of comparative religious studies, though they did leave a profound mark on the study of the Old and New Testaments, and on other specialised historical disciplines, and they gave the scholarly world one of its outstanding encyclopaedias in *Die Religion in Geschichte und Gegenwart*.

Characteristic of this school was the attempt to trace historical connections between the Old and New Testaments and the surrounding cultures, though its most important contributions were made in relating the New Testament to Hellenism generally. Its main affirmation was that '. . . Christianity can be understood only if it is studied as one phenomenon among the many phenomena of religion in the decaying Roman empire and Levantine world'.[13] The members of the school were led by this means to concentrate on real or apparent parallels and analogies in first- and second-century thought—helped by the new discoveries that were constantly being made in such fields of study as Gnosticism and the mystery religions.

Often—although this is not a subject we can discuss in detail here—their parallels were justified; sometimes they were not. And the inevitable result followed, that resemblances in belief and practice were taken as incontrovertible proof of borrowing, and that such hypotheses quickly assumed the status of fact—a status which in some cases they have still not lost. This process was assisted materi-

---

[12] On Fairbairn, see Sharpe, *Not to Destroy but to Fulfil* (1965), pp. 126ff.
[13] Neill, *The Interpretation of the New Testament, 1861–1961* (1966), p. 158.

ally by the eagerness of the school to popularise its results in a series of small monographs, the *Religionsgeschichtliche Volksbücher*. The 'father' of the school was Otto Pfleiderer (1836–1908), whose main work, *Das Urchristentum* (1887), was translated into English as *Primitive Christianity* (1906–11). Of its other members, the best-known included in Old Testament studies H. Gunkel (*Genesis*, 1901) and in New Testament studies Wilhelm Bousset (*Kyrios Christos*, 1913), Eichhorn, Heitmüller, Wernle, Clemen and Reischle. The theorist of the school was Ernst Troeltsch (1865–1923).[14]

As *Privatdozent* at the University of Göttingen in the 1890s, Troeltsch came into close contact with the 'little theological faculty' of Wilhelm Bousset, William Wrede, Herman Gunkel and their colleagues, all of whom were strongly influenced by Albrecht Ritschl and by Paul de Lagarde. Troeltsch, the only systematic theologian among a company of biblical scholars and church historians, was led to consider the two important questions of the problem of the place of religion in the overall context of man's intellectual development, and the *historical* process by which religion as we know it has come into being. He insisted that every aspect of human history, including Christianity, has evolved and developed, and set himself to trace, in bold outline, the nature of that developmental process. The most important work in which these questions are considered was his monograph *Die Absolutheit des Christentums*, in which he argues that Christianity can have only 'a certain superiority' because of the universal appeal of its ethics—a conclusion typical enough of the 'history of religion school' of theologians. But of course Troeltsch was not himself a close student of the data of comparative religion, and his influence on subsequent developments in the field was at best indirect.

The school as a whole certainly established for all time the principle that Christian origins can only be understood against their contemporary background, and helped popularise the principle of critical historical study in the biblical area. But although its members were in a real sense historical theologians, their results were cold comfort to the orthodox; indeed, they seemed all too often to have sold the pass, wittingly or unwittingly, to the rationalists, by claiming that virtually every important and significant element in

---

[14] The members of this school did much of their most important work while still young men. It is interesting to note that in 1900, their relative ages were: Eichhorn, 44, Gunkel 38, Wrede 41, Weiss 37, Troeltsch and Bousset 35, Heitmüller 31 and Wernle 28. On Troeltsch, see e.g. Pauck, *Harnack and Troeltsch: Two Historical Theologians* (1968), and the Introduction by James Luther Adams to the English translation of *The Absoluteness of Christianity and the History of Religions* (1972), pp. 7ff.

early Christian history could be explained in terms of culture-contacts or direct imitation. Seen in this perspective, there was some justification in what might otherwise seem an absurd criticism first made in 1919 by an Anglican bishop, Frank Weston:

> The comparative study of religion is, like psychology, a new obsession of the liberal mind. We are supposed to set out in parallel columns the beliefs and customs of all known religions contemporary with, or antecedent to, Christianity, to note their similarities, and to account for them all by labelling them products of the human mind. The residue of Christianity that has no parallel . . . has been sadly overweighted by many doctrines and rites evidently stolen, in germ at least, from the parallel columns.[15]

However, the *Religionsgeschichtliche Schule* did not have things entirely its own way in the first couple of decades of this century; but before we go on to consider the alternative solutions to the problems of theology and comparative religion offered by such men as Söderblom, Otto, von Hügel and Baillie, we must take a little time to recall the special case of the missionary scholars.

* * *

The Göttingen (and other) scholars were theorists; missionaries were above all practical men, concerned with the living realities of non-Christian religions. To be sure, their Christian presuppositions were well defined, and clearly acknowledged. In the eyes of many this meant—and still seems to mean—that they were in no position to do other than distort and misrepresent the religious traditions they were professionally concerned to undermine. But the development of comparative religion, together with other factors (which I have discussed elsewhere),[16] as well as making public certain standards of observation, reporting and judgement against which missionary accounts could be measured, came in time to influence the work of the missionaries themselves.

Perhaps the most outstanding representative of the new school of missionary thought—and at the same time the only one we have space to consider in this connection—was a Scotsman, John Nicol Farquhar (1861–1929).[17] Although brought up in an intensely orthodox setting, as a student at Oxford he had come under the

---

[15] Weston, *The Christ and His Critics* (1919), p. 57.
[16] Sharpe, *Not to Destroy*, passim, but especially pp. 35ff.
[17] Sharpe, *J. N. Farquhar: a Memoir* (1963).

direct influence of A. M. Fairbairn, and indirectly under the influence of Max Müller and the Boden Professor of Sanskrit, Monier Monier-Williams. On his arrival in India in 1891, Farquhar had also, it seems, been introduced to the work of T. E. Slater, a liberal missionary of a slightly earlier generation who had in his turn been influenced by F. D. Maurice. Between 1902 and 1923 he served the Indian Y.M.C.A., from 1912 as its Literature Secretary. In 1923 he was appointed Professor of Comparative Religion in the University of Manchester, in succession to the Buddhist scholar T. W. Rhys Davids—a post which he held until his death in 1929. His first 'comparative' book, *Gita and Gospel*, appeared in 1903; thereafter *A Primer of Hinduism* (1911), *The Crown of Hinduism* (1913), *Modern Religious Movements in India* (1915) and *Outline of the Religious Literature of India* (1920). He also edited various series of scholarly works on the religious traditions of India.

The quality of Farquhar's own work was uniformly high, and fully in accordance with the findings of the leading scholars in his field. As early as 1901 he had written appreciatively of the science of religion, although he noted—and was perfectly justified in so doing—that the science had had 'rather more than a moderate share of the follies of youth'. In future, he wrote,

> There will be fewer attempts to answer such questions as 'What was the earliest form of religion?'; for it is better to deal with questions to answer which sufficient evidence exists, than to speculate wildly on the most important themes. The relation of religion to society, morality, law, art, and civilisation generally, the influence of environment and race character on the forms of religion, the psychological basis and the essential forms of religion, are problems which will not be finally solved for some time yet; but they will be constantly kept in view, and will help to guide workers in selecting materials. In the immediate future the strength of the best men will probably be almost exclusively given to the writings of monographs on individual religions. . .[18]

This was extremely perceptive, and in the event, proved to be a remarkably accurate forecast of the shape of things to come in comparative religion. In respect of Hinduism, Farquhar was particularly concerned to combat the tendency on the part of some missionaries to write inaccurately or unsympathetically about it. Justice to the material, he maintained, requires sympathy above all else :

[18] Farquhar, 'The Science of Religion as an Aid to Apologetics', in *The Harvest Field* (1901), pp. 369ff.

An unsympathetic student of the Gospels inevitably misinterprets them; and the same is true of an unsympathetic student of the Upanishads, the *Mahabharata* or the Puranas. The attitude of the great scholars of the West to Hindu literature ought to be the ideal of every Missionary. I do not mean that he will necessarily praise what they praise and condemn what they condemn : let him adopt their attitude of mind, their patience, their eagerness to understand even that which is furthest away from their own conceptions, and the penetrating sympathy which enables them to look at an ancient text with the eyes of those who first read it.[19]

The framework of Farquhar's theological thinking was given very largely by an evolutionary scheme interpreted in Christian terms. Thus in his view Christianity (in its 'simple' form as seen in the teaching of Jesus) was the evolutionary crown of Hinduism, both because it offered the fullest satisfaction of a universal religious need revealed by comparative religion, and because every element of religion appears in its highest form in Christianity. He could, then, speak of Christianity as the 'fulfilment' of all religion (taking his text from Matt. 5 : 17). Perhaps his conclusion is unimportant in this particular context; what is, on the other hand, of the greatest importance is that he was able as a missionary to combine close, accurate and sympathetic study of a particular non-Christian tradition with a distinctively Christian theological interpretation of it, without losing his grip on either. He was also responsible for encouraging other writers to follow substantially the same path, and for neutralising the earlier attitude of impatient criticism which had been so prominent a feature of evangelical missions in the nineteenth century.

Among the many statements of principle which Farquhar made during his career, this, from 1909, will serve as well as any. His method, he said,

. . . consists in setting forth Christianity as the fulfilment of all that is aimed at in Hinduism, as the satisfaction of the spiritual yearnings of her people, as the crown and climax of the crudest forms of her worship as well as of those lofty spiritual movements which have so often appeared in Hinduism but have always ended in weakness. . . The theory [of fulfilment] thus satisfied the science of religion to the uttermost, while conserving the supremacy of Christ.[20]

[19] Sharpe, *J. N. Farquhar*, p. 127f.
[20] id., *Not to Destroy*, p. 255f.

It is no part of our present purpose to decide whether this view did, indeed, 'satisfy the science of religion to the uttermost'; it is sufficient to know that Christian missionaries early this century were concerned that it should. An entire missionary generation learned by this means to take comparative religion seriously. In India alone, important works produced by missionaries as a result of Farquhar's initiative included Nicol Macnicol, *Indian Theism* (1915) and *Psalms of Maratha Saints* (1920); Margaret Stevenson, *The Heart of Jainism* (1915) and *The Rites of the Twice-Born* (1920); J. M. McPhail, *Asoka* (1917); H. A. Popley, *The Music of India* (1921) and H. Whitehead, *The Village Gods of India* (1916). Not directly influenced by the 'fulfilment school', but expressive of similar ideals of accurate historical scholarship were certain works of German missionaries, among which H. W. Schomerus, *Der Çaiva-Siddhānta* (1912) is in every way outstanding.[21]

Nor was this movement restricted to India; missionaries to Islam and in China often shared the same qualities. In the former category come the works of the German-American Samuel Zwemer, and in the latter the books written by the Norwegian Karl Ludwig Reichelt, in which is to be found a *logos* theology similar to that applied by some of the Church Fathers.[22]

One form of 'theological reaction' was, then, to be found among Christian missionaries, who were able to embrace many of the methods of comparative religion without the rationalist interpretation which was so common in the West. Another type was found among Western theologians, this time addressed more specifically to the academic debate in Europe and America, and it is to this type of reaction, as exemplified by the work of the Swede Nathan Söderblom and the German Rudolf Otto, that we must now turn.

* * *

The brilliant and ubiquitous Swede Nathan Söderblom

---

[21] Schomerus was in fact sharply critical of the 'fulfilment' idea. He was a missionary of the Leipzig Mission, a body which ever since the 1850s had been involved in a theological feud with 'Anglo-Saxon' missions, chiefly over the question of caste, but involving deeper principles of acculturation. He was also for a time Söderblom's assistant at the University of Leipzig. For his mature views on the problem as a whole, see *Indien und das Christentum* I-III (1931–3).

[22] To the best of my knowledge, there is no adequate study of Reichelt in English, though several of his books were translated. Of the Norwegian works, see Thelle, *Karl Ludvig Reichelt* (1954), a volume which contains an assessment of his work in the history of religion by Carl-Martin Edsman (pp. 119ff.). But see Eilert, *Boundlessness: Studies in Karl Ludvig Reichelt's Missionary Thinking* (1974).

(1866–1931) compassed a world of scholarship and culture in his own person.[23] As Professor in Uppsala and Leipzig he was responsible for creating an atmosphere in which comparative religion and theology were reconciled as never before or since; as Archbishop of Uppsala from 1914 to 1931 he is justly regarded as one of the fathers of the ecumenical movement. His versatile genius spanned the fields of Iranian studies, church history (one of his most outstanding books was on humour and melancholy in Luther), music and the arts in a manner otherwise found only in the Dutch phenomenologist Gerardus van der Leeuw. Although it would be tempting to discourse at length on this remarkable man, we shall confine ourselves here to a summary account of his work on the boundaries of theology and comparative religion.

On 24 September 1901, Nathan Söderblom, who was then thirty-five years old, was installed as Professor of Theological Propaedeutics and Theological Encyclopaedia in the University of Uppsala. His inaugural lecture is still reckoned as a milestone in the history of Swedish theological and religious thought; though less because of the actual academic content of the lecture than because of a postscript, in which the young professor addressed the theological students in his audience :

Gentlemen, in these days you have to listen to many words of commiseration. I must congratulate you.

People commiserate with you because you serve a supposedly anachronistic cause, that of Christianity, or at least—and the distinction should be borne clearly in mind—because you serve an anachronistic Church. Some commiserate with you because you have to take upon you the yoke of the Church's confession. Others because you live in an age when accepted opinion, particularly as regards the origin of certain books of the Bible and certain details in the sacred account of the dealings of God with men, has been shaken and changed . . .

Now, gentlemen, I take this opportunity of offering my most sincere congratulations on your present course of study. . .[24]

Söderblom's words reflected an optimism the like of which had not

---

[23] See most recently Sundkler, *Nathan Söderblom* (1968), a work which concentrates mainly on his career as a churchman and ecumenist. On his scholarship, see van Veen, *Nathan Söderblom, Leven en Denken van een Godsdiensthistoricus* (1940, in Dutch), and Sharpe, 'Nathan Söderblom and the Study of Religion', in *Religious Studies* 4 (1968), pp. 259ff. See also Andrae, *Nathan Söderblom* (1931, in Swedish), still the best biography. What follows is taken very largely from my 1968 article.

[24] Söderblom, *Om studiet av religionen* (1951), p. 44.

been heard in a Swedish theological faculty for many a year. For three decades or more theological studies in Sweden had been under a cloud; to be a theological student was tantamount, in the eyes of the radical intelligentsia, to being a naïve obscurantist. The watchword of the radicals was 'science'—a quality in which theologians were considered to be completely deficient. And yet Söderblom was able to rally his students with the very same watchword : '. . . not less science, but more science, a deeper sense of reality, for this will lead to new clarity, new humility, and with it, new strength.'[25]

The inaugural lecture itself was on the subject of 'The General History of Religion and the Theology of the Church'—which we might perhaps paraphrase as 'Comparative Religion and Theology'. Its object was in the first place to reassure those who were uneasy at the thought of introducing a professor of comparative religion into a conservative confessional faculty (Söderblom's two predecessors in the chair, K. H. Gezelius von Schéele and J. A. Ekman, were theologians who had lectured on comparative religion more or less as a sideline; both had become bishops); and secondly, to outline the kind of religious study which he believed ought to be carried on in a modern faculty. His contention was that the tension between the theologian and the student of comparative religion was all a mistake : an understandable mistake, but one which had arisen due to a profound misunderstanding of the nature of theology on the one hand and the nature of comparative religion on the other. 'They [the protagonists in the quarrel] have a view of churchmanship which is in conflict with the fundamental tenets of Evangelical Christianity. They have a view of scholarship which is drawn from the realm of abstraction, not from the real world.'[26]

For Söderblom, following Ritschl and Sabatier, the religious ideal and the scientific ideal were one : 'Every scientific study of religion, provided that it is carried out with competence and directed toward a worthy object, must—with or against the will of the scholar, consciously or unconsciously—serve the cause of religion.'[27]

The grounds on which this judgement was made were, of course, those of Liberal Protestantism : that the course of human history is the record, not of man's gradual emancipation from the need for religion, but of God's gradual self-revelation of himself to man; and that science, bent on elucidating the processes of historical development, cannot conceivably come into conflict with this new

[25] ibid., p. 46.
[26] ibid., p. 19.
[27] ibid., p. 24.

Christian idea.[28] At certain points in the past, however, man's knowledge of God has reached new high points, seen most clearly in
the work of the Jewish prophets. But also in the great Prophet
of Iran, Zoroaster, for Söderblom was appointed Professor on the
strength of his reputation as a specialist in the religion of ancient
Iran.

Why should he have chosen just this field? It was far from
being an obvious field for a beginner in the comparative discipline.
It was scarcely represented at Uppsala, and the impulse is unlikely
to have been derived from any member of the Uppsala faculty. H.
S. Nyberg has investigated this question, and finds that Söderblom
was turned to Iran by three independent circumstances. First, by
his reading of Nietzsche, whose *Also sprach Zarathustra* appeared
in 1883 and 1884. Secondly, by his reading of the novelist, Christian
Platonist and scholar Viktor Rydberg, whose influence on Uppsala
students was then at its peak. Rydberg was treated with almost un-
qualified reverence by Söderblom, Fries and their circle of friends;
his monumental *Undersökningar i germansk mytologi*, with all its
many comparisons between ancient Scandinavian and ancient
Iranian ideas, was published between 1886 and 1889, and is quoted
frequently in Söderblom's doctoral thesis. The third circumstance is
pure chance : on a visit to Stockholm, Söderblom was loaned a copy
of a periodical, *The Thinker*, which contained an article on Mazda-
ism by James Hope Moulton. This, on Söderblom's own evidence,
was enough to convince him that he had found his speciality. Leaving aside—temporarily—some of his other concerns, he began in
the autumn of 1893 to study Avestan.[29]

By the following year he was ready to start printing a thesis on
Persian eschatology! However, it was never completed, and in May
1894 Söderblom was on his way to Paris to take up a post as pastor
to the Swedish legation, and to continue his Avestan studies under
Meillet. There he remained until his appointment to the Uppsala
chair in 1901.

In the meantime, Söderblom had made his reputation as a historian of religion with two works in the Iranian field : the monograph
Les Fravashis (1899) and the dissertation *La Vie future d'après le
Mazdéisme* (1901), which earned him the only doctorate ever
awarded by the Protestant faculty of the Sorbonne to a foreigner,

---

[28] The influence of the Scottish scientist-evangelist Henry Drummond is
worth bearing in mind. Both were involved in the student movement, and
Drummond's works enjoyed a great vogue in precisely the circles in which
Söderblom moved as a student.

[29] Nyberg, 'Nathan Söderbloms insats i utforskandet av den iranska
religionshistorien', in *Religion och Bibel* II (1943), pp. 1–13.

and caused him to be nominated, without application, to Tiele's chair of the history of religion at Leiden.

La Vie future is an essay in the comparative method—but an essay with a difference, as Söderblom uses the method, not to stress resemblances between religions, but to emphasise their *sui generis* character. Already it is clear in what direction his thought is moving. The nature of prophecy and the nature and significance of religious experience were two problems which were to occupy more and more of his time in later years, together with the kindred notions of revelation and mysticism. There is no doubt that the foundations were laid in Paris.

From 1901 to 1914 Söderblom was Professor in Uppsala, and during the last two of these years he was simultaneously Professor of the History of Religion at the University of Leipzig. In 1914 he was appointed Archbishop of Uppsala, a position he held with the greatest distinction until his death in 1931. In 1903 he revised Tiele's *Kompendium der Religionsgeschichte*, and published the first of his three important monographs on the problem of revelation, *Uppenbarelsereligion* (the other two parts, *Uppenbarelse* and *Ett bidrag till uppenbarelsens tolkning*, appeared in 1910 and 1911 respectively, and were gathered together in one volume in 1930; this volume was reprinted in 1963). In 1907 came his three-volume collection of texts, *Främmande religionsurkunder*, and in the following year a companion volume, *Studiet av religionen*. 1910 saw the publication of his study of Catholic Modernism, *Religionsproblemet inom katolicism och protestantism*, in which important questions of principle are discussed, and the article 'Communion with Deity' in Hastings' *ERE*. In 1913 he published his *Natürliche Theologie und allgemeine Religionsgeschichte*, and the best-known of his English-language articles, that on 'Holiness' in the *ERE*; in 1914 his best-known work (apart from *The Living God*) in this field, *Gudstrons uppkomst*, translated into German two years later as *Das Werden des Gottesglaubens*; and in 1915 a collection of occasional essays, *Ur religionens historia*. From this time onward, he was so closely concerned with other, more specifically Christian, matters that his work as a historian of religion came virtually to an end. It was revived only at the eleventh hour, in his famous Gifford Lectures of 1931, published two years later in English as *The Living God*. It must be emphasised, however, that *The Living God* contains little that is not to be found in his work of twenty years earlier. In a sense it is to be seen as a recapitulation, a summing-up, and (in the event) as a last testimony. A month after the delivery of the lectures, Söderblom was on his death-bed, saying to his family and friends, 'I know that God lives; I can prove it by the history of religion.'[30]

In 1920, Söderblom, in the course of an address to Danish students, said : 'Most of my spiritual strength has been spent in the study of religion. No part of my far too diverse, and yet, perhaps, basically concordant work has given me a purer sense of satisfaction.' As far as Sweden is concerned, there can be no doubt that he was personally responsible for placing the subject of comparative religion on an entirely new footing, and for giving a new impetus to Iranian studies. But after 1901 he devoted very little time to the religions of ancient Iran, and it is generally agreed that his specific contribution is not to be sought there. Nor is it to be sought in the propounding of any special theory of the origins of religion : his book *Gudstrons uppkomst* contains detailed accounts and criticisms of practically all the current theories of the origins of religion, but he never settled finally for any one of them. In fact he distrusted theories. 'Very many recognised works,' he wrote in 1920, 'are nothing more than the forcing of a given material into a temporarily fashionable pattern.'[31]

Söderblom's distinctive contribution to comparative religion is perhaps to be seen in the *attitude* with which he approached his material : taking all religions seriously, not merely as objects of scientific study, but *as religions*. His Swedish predecessors and many of his Swedish contemporaries had been more inclined to treat them from the point of view of Christian dogmatic theology, as anti-religions or false religions; and many of his contemporaries in the field of religious study had tended, explicitly or implicitly, to regard them as exotic curiosities. In his concern for the *sui generis* character, not only of religion as such, but also of separate religions, he anticipated the attitude which we know today as the phenomeno-logical approach.

But the study of religion was for Söderblom a theological study. To be sure, not theological in the spirit of post-Reformation scholasticism, but theological—so Söderblom believed—in the spirit of the Reformation, of Luther, and of Ritschl, who had pointed the way to Luther. Believing with Ritschl that God reveals himself in and through the historical process, the high point of which was reached, once and for all, in Christ, every dispassionate historical study must, he felt, necessarily lead, if it be carried out in a spirit of reverence for truth, nearer the absolute Truth.

A further aspect of Söderblom's contribution to the study of

30 Andrae, *Nathan Söderblom* (1931), p. 328.
31 Söderblom, *Tre livsformer* (1922), p. 117.

religion concerns his use of the terms 'holy' and 'holiness'. Rudolf Otto's famous work *Das Heilige*, which is commonly regarded as the pioneer work in its area, appeared in 1917, and was translated into English as *The Idea of the Holy* in 1923. But Söderblom had written these words in 1913 :

> Holiness is the great word in religion; it is even more essential than the notion of God. Real religion may exist without a definite conception of deity, but there is no real religion without a distinction between holy and profane.[32]

In fact, Söderblom's definition of religion, if it can be called a definition, went : 'Religious is the man to whom something is holy.'[33]

Although the chronological priority of Söderblom's work is thus clearly established, this does not necessarily mean that Otto derived his theories from Söderblom. In fact the two were working on parallel lines, and each welcomed the support of the other.[34] Both were influenced by Schleiermacher, and they had met in 1896 and 1897. Their common purpose was to demonstrate, in Otto's words, that

> . . . all ostensible explanations of the origins of religion in terms of animism or magic or folk-psychology are doomed from the outset to wander astray and miss the real goal of their inquiry, unless they recognise this fact of our nature [the capacity to feel religious awe]—primary, unique, underivable from anything else—to be the basic factor and the basic impulse underlying the entire process of religious evolution.[35]

We have already spoken of Söderblom's view of religious experience as an experience *sui generis*. Holiness, *tabu*, possessed of *mana*, were in his opinion the qualities of that in face of which religious experience is formed. But again, he was not disposed to over-systematise, warning his readers in 1913 that '. . . a supposed uniformity must not be allowed to obscure the peculiar features of holiness in particular societies at the lower stages of civilisation.'[36] It would, therefore, be wrong to suppose that Söderblom was setting up a new theory of religion against existing theories. What he was doing was

---

[32] id., 'Holiness', in *ERE* vi (1914), p. 731.
[33] ibid.
[34] Edsman, 'Ur Nathan Söderbloms arbetsverkstad', in *Religion och Bibel* xxv (1966), pp. 18–44, esp. p. 24f. cf. Otto, *The Idea of the Holy* (Eng. tr. 1959 ed.), p. 29n.
[35] Otto, op. cit., p. 29.
[36] *ERE* vi, p. 732.

attempting to establish a category under which religious experience could be viewed in its own right, as a first step in the *religious* interpretation of history which was always his overriding concern.

* * *

In touching upon Söderblom's work on the categories of 'holiness' and 'the holy', we have been brought into an area which tends to be associated less with Söderblom himself than with his German contemporary, fellow-theologian and friend Rudolf Otto (1869–1937).[37] Otto's book *Das Heilige* (1917; Eng. tr. *The Idea of the Holy*, 1923) attained a degree of popularity which no work of Söderblom's ever achieved. No book of the field and the period (save perhaps Reinach's *Orpheus*) has been reprinted so frequently, or read so widely. The reasons are not far to seek. *The Idea of the Holy* appeals (or seems to appeal) to the intuitive and the non-rational in man as the fundamental fact of religion, and in recurring periods of doubt and disillusion with accepted orthodoxies, it has seemed to offer a defence of individualism, spontaneity and immediate experience over against creeds, dogmas and institutions. The book, in other words, aroused an immediate and lasting response in the mind of the twentieth century, and now holds near-canonical status as one of the books which every student of comparative religion imagines himself or herself to have read.

One suspects, however, that Rudolf Otto himself would have been less than happy with this development. He certainly did not want to be judged solely on the merits (solid though they be) of this one work; still less did he wish to be regarded as an 'irrationalist' in religion. As it is, *The Idea of the Holy* has by its very success obscured the personality of its author, and has thoroughly eclipsed his other works.

The Idea of the Holy was written during the First World War, while its author was Professor of Systematic Theology at Breslau, and published in the year of his appointment to a similar chair at Marburg (the Introduction to the English edition is wrong on this point). Otto never held a chair of *Allgemeine Religionsgeschichte* or *Vergleichende Religionswissenschaft*; he was, and wished to be regarded as, a systematic theologian. His early studies took place at Erlangen and Göttingen, where he was especially influenced by Häring, and after a short period as Vicar of the German Church

[37] On Otto's life and work, see Lemaitre, *Le pensée religieuse de R. Otto* (1924); Davidson, *Rudolf Otto's Interpretation of Religion* (1947); R. Boeke, 'Rudolf Otto, Leben und Werk', in *Numen* XIX (1967), pp. 130ff.; Schütte, *Religion und Christentum in der Theologie Rudolf Ottos* (1969).

at Cannes, he was appointed to his first teaching post at Göttingen in 1904. At the time, the *Religionsgeschichtliche Schule* was in its heyday, and Göttingen was, of course, its major stronghold. Others of his colleagues included the phenomenologist Edmund Husserl, though Otto does not appear to have attached himself to the phenomenological school. From 1914 to 1917 he taught at Breslau, and in 1917 was appointed to the University of Marburg, where he remained until his retirement in 1929.

Otto's work falls into two categories, and into two largely distinct periods. After having presented, in 1898, a doctoral dissertation on *Geist und Wort nach Luther* (Spirit and Word in Luther), he published, almost simultaneously, a book of Luther's doctrine of the Holy Spirit—Luther studies were, one need scarcely add, a common ingress to systematic theology in the German faculties of the period. In the same year he betrayed his theological affinities by publishing a new edition of Schleiermacher's *Über die Religion: Reden an die Gebildeten unter ihren Verächtern* (On religion : speeches to its cultured despisers; Eng. tr. 1893, 1958 etc.). In the Introduction which now forms part of the standard English edition of this seminal work, Otto wrote that in it, Schleiermacher

. . . aimed to recapture the position religion had lost in the intellectual world where it was now threatened with total oblivion. It aimed to lead religion out of the remote corner into which it had been cast, to prove that religion was not just a concern of the 'uncultured' and old-fashioned people who found in it an emergency substitute for the higher things of life, but something that belonged to truly cultured, authentic, and well-rounded human beings; moreover, that without religion the intellectual life of mankind would deprive itself of its noblest ingredient.[88]

In addressing himself in this way to a work of apologetics, Otto was undertaking what he felt to be an important task, that of restating the Christian message in an essentially materialistic world. One of the main ingredients in turn-of-the-century materialism was, of course, 'Darwinism', and this formed a further focus of Otto's interest, *inter alia* in the book *Darwinismus und Religion* (1909). In the meantime, however, he had been working steadily on the problem of developing a rational statement of the Christian faith, against the background of that philosophical tradition stemming from Kant, and expounded above all by Jakob Friedrich Fries. This resulted in a major book, *Kantisch-Fries'sche Religionsphilosophie* (1909; Eng. tr. *The Philosophy of Religion*, 1931). Already in this

---

[88] Schleiermacher, *On Religion* (Harper Torchbook ed. 1958), p. ix.

book one can see the extent to which Otto's theological position is being formulated in contrast to the overly rationalistic theology of the Ritschlian school, but there is as yet no hint of an interest in the problems of comparative religion, or of the concern with the 'non-rational' which was to come to the fore in *The Idea of the Holy*.

In 1910, however, Otto published an article in *Theologische Rundschau* on the *Völkerpsychologie* of Wilhelm Wundt, in which he considered the question of the *sensus numinis* as the historical origin of religion (a suggestion previously made by Andrew Lang). This was the seed of which *Das Heilige*, seven years later, was to be the fruit.

In 1911–12 Otto paid his first visit to India, began the serious study of Sanskrit, and entered an entirely new phase in his academic career. For a variety of reasons, these were years in which the problem of the relationship of Christianity to the great non-Christian religions of the world was becoming the most prominent theological problem of the period. The Liberal Protestant interpretation of this relationship as one of promise and fulfilment had been advocated for two decades or more, not least among Indologists and missionaries in India, but the holding of the World Missionary Conference at Edinburgh in 1910 had given the 'fulfilment doctrine' an official *imprimatur*, and the most outstanding work of the school, J. N. Farquhar's *The Crown of Hinduism*, was shortly to appear, in 1913.

In 1916 Otto published his first Indological work, *Dīpikā des Nivāsa: eine indische Heilslehre*, followed ultimately by two further comparative works, *West-Östliche Mystik* (1926; Eng. tr. *Mysticism East and West*, 1932), and *Indiens Gnadenreligion und das Christentum* (1930; Eng. tr. *India's Religion of Grace*, 1930). Thus there began the second period of Otto's career, in which he was still concerned with apologetics, but this time with Christian apologetics *vis-à-vis* the non-Christian world, and particularly Hinduism. In this period he fully accepted the aims and methods of comparative religion, while reserving the right, like Söderblom and Farquhar, to interpret his findings in a Christian sense.

Das Heilige was written, then, at the outset of this second period, as an attempt to formulate a series of categories in which all religion is to be understood. The argument of the book is well known, and may be recapitulated rapidly.

'Holiness' is a category peculiar to religion. It does not mean 'completely good'; it is rather a mental state, '. . . perfectly *sui generis* and irreducible to any other',[39] and while it may be dis-

---

[39] Otto, *The Idea of the Holy* (Pelican ed. 1959), p. 21.

cussed, it cannot be defined. For this state Otto coined the word 'numinous' (*das Numinose*), derived from the Latin *numen*, a supernatural entity. To experience the numinous is to experience the presence of a *numen*, to sense one's own 'creature-consciousness'; the numinous manifests itself as a *mysterium tremendum*, communicating senses of 'otherness' (the *numen* is 'wholly other'), awefulness, majesty and energy. But the mystery, while it is 'uncanny', also attracts; as well as being *tremendum*, the mystery is also *fascinans*, 'fascinating'.

Ordinary language does not have the means with which to speak comprehensibly of the qualities and attributes of the *numen*. It is therefore necessary constantly to resort to figurative language, images to which Otto gave the name of 'ideograms'. An ideogram is 'a sort of illustrative substitute for a concept',[40] 'an analogical notion taken from the natural sphere, illustrating, but incapable of exhaustively rendering, our real meaning'[41]—an illustration would be 'the wrath of God'. Another term used by Otto to describe 'the faculty, of whatever sort it may be, of *genuinely* cognising and recognising the holy in its appearances' is 'divination'—normally used in the more specific sense of receiving communications from the supernatural world.[42] This Otto specifically describes as a 'theological discovery', and refers back to the classical Christian doctrine of the witness of the Holy Spirit (the subject of his doctoral dissertation), the theology of Schleiermacher, and the doctrine of *Ahnung* as found in J. F. Fries. From this—and from other points in his book—it is clear that Otto is in many ways engaged in a summing-up of his theological work hitherto. The line from Luther passes through the Pietists to Schleiermacher and Fries, bypassing Ritschl and Troeltsch, and the attitude common to all—that of the essence of religion as consisting in a type of immediate, almost intuitive apprehension of Deity—is applied to the concept of holiness, as previously expounded by Söderblom and Lehmann, and later taken up by many other scholars.

The numinous is, however, not to be inferred from man's contemplation of sense-data :

> It issues from the deepest foundation of cognitive apprehension that the soul possesses, and, though it of course comes into being in and amid the sensory data and empirical material of the natural world and cannot anticipate or dispense with those, yet it does not arise *out of* them, but only *by their means*. They are

[40] ibid., p. 33.
[41] ibid., p. 40.
[42] ibid., p. 161.

the incitement, the stimulus, and the 'occasion' for the numinous experience to become astir, and, in so doing, to begin—at first with a naïve immediacy of reaction—to be interfused and interwoven with the present world of sensuous experience, until, becoming gradually purer, it disengages itself from this and takes its stand in absolute contrast to it.[43]

There is clearly a great deal of common ground between this view and the 'animatism' theory of R. R. Marett, which Otto indeed regarded as coming 'within a hair's breadth of what I take to be truth about the matter'.[44] And it suffers from the same defects. If put forward as a *historical* argument for the origin of religion, it admits of neither proof or disproof, since the earliest data are totally inaccessible to the researcher. We do not know how early man felt—and the 'numinous' can be expressed only in terms of states of mind and feelings. And then it is terribly difficult to take the step from the observation (supposing this to be possible) of a state of mind to the inference of an objectively-existing 'wholly other' or *numen* which has called forth the state of mind in question. Marett does not really consider this question; Otto simply asserts that the *numen* must be there, for what else could produce these sensations? The 'mental state' (Otto's own expression) is 'perfectly *sui generis* and irreducible to any other'; 'creature-feeling' is an effect of another feeling-element, 'which in itself indubitably has immediate and primary reference to an object outside the self'.[45] But these are assertions, or rather faith-judgements, and however much one may be inclined to agree with him, it is necessary to recognise that Otto does not—indeed, he cannot—adduce solid evidence to prove his case. Evans-Pritchard puts his finger on the weakness of Otto's case (though he is here not writing about Otto), when he asks:

What is this awe which some of the writers I have cited say is characteristic of the sacred? Some say it is the specific religious emotion; others that there is no specific religious emotion. Either way, how does one know whether a person experiences awe or thrill or whatever it may be? How does one recognise it and how does one measure it?[46]

In the last resort, however, Otto is making his appeal to the individual reader to compare what he has to say with such experiences in his own life, and at the beginning of Chapter III goes so far as to request the reader who has had no such experience 'to read no

[43] ibid., p. 130.
[44] ibid., p. 29n.
[45] ibid., p. 24.
[46] Evans-Pritchard, *Theories of Primitive Religion* (1965), p. 44.

further'. Surely an odd request to make in a work of comparative religion ! But *The Idea of the Holy*, despite its profound influence in the field of comparative religion, is a work of theology and of the psychology of religion. Its primary datum is a faith-judgement, not a rational demonstration; but this once accepted, Otto's treatment is as rational as one could wish.

In the author's foreword to the first English edition of *The Idea of the Holy*, Otto stated that he felt that 'no one ought to concern himself with the *Numen ineffabile* who has not already devoted assiduous and serious study to the *Ratio aeterna*'.[47] Eight years later, in 1931, fearful (not without reason) of being misunderstood, he wrote :

> *On no account* do I wish to be considered a 'non-rationalist'. In all religion, and in my own religion, I indeed recognise the profundity of the non-rational factor; but this deepens my conviction that it is the duty of serious theology to win as much ground as it can for *Ratio* in this realm, and even at the point where our rational concepts desert us, to satisfy the demands of judicious theological teaching by framing 'ideograms' as accurately as possible, where dogmatic concepts are impossible.[48]

In Otto's case one senses something of the difficulty experienced by a scholar employing 'rational' methods to demonstrate a point which, if valid, must remain forever inaccessible to the very methods he is using. His 'ideograms' do not really bridge the gap, since imagery cannot by its very nature be as universal as the *numen* to which they refer. But his book, its weaknesses notwithstanding (one German scholar accused it of 'staggering from one superficiality to another'), aroused the attention of scholars—and other readers—the world over. Perhaps, as Harnack said, it was not altogether a good sign that it had so unerringly caught the spirit of the age.[49] But that it drew attention to the fact that religion is not merely a matter of doctrines, dogmas, scriptures and societies cannot well be doubted.

The very popularity of *The Idea of the Holy* has contributed materially to the neglect of Otto's other books, as we have already suggested. This is unfortunate, but in this present survey we can do little to redress the balance. Otto's philosophical works fall alto-

---

[47] *The Idea of the Holy*, p. 13.

[48] Quoted by Schütte, *Religion und Christentum in der Theologie Rudolf Ottos* (1969), p. 123f.

[49] 'Selten ist ein theologisches Werk der Stimmung der Zeit so entgegenkommen und so rastlos eingesogen worden wie dieses. Das ist nicht nur ein günstiges Zeichen.' Q. in Schütte, op. cit., p. 6.

gether outside our scope, and his Indology arouses questions of a specialist nature, which it would be impertinent to dismiss in a phrase. But his studies of Śankara Eckhart (in *Mysticism East and West*) and Rāmānuja and the *bhakti* tradition (in *India's Religion of Grace*) demonstrate a remarkable mastery of the Indian material, together with a careful attempt to relate that material to the data of the Christian tradition.[50]

We shall have one further occasion to return to Otto, in connection with his work in the 1920s on behalf of international understanding through religion. It was perhaps partly because of this initiative on his part that Otto's work was subsequently to suffer a more than usually severe vilification after his death, from scholars who were for a variety of reasons ill-disposed toward the eirenic internationalism that Rudolf Otto so strongly represented.[51]

* * *

A disciple of Söderblom and Otto in whom the theological reaction was equally embodied was Friedrich Heiler (1892–1967), though in this case a purely scholarly evaluation is complicated by an extraordinarily complex personal ecclesiastical development. Heiler's two best-known works were *Das Gebet* (1920; Eng. tr. *Prayer*, 1932)—a typical example, inspired by Söderblom,[52] of what one might call selective descriptive phenomenology—and *Erscheinungsformen und Wesen der Religion* (1949), a comprehensive work of phenomenology which we shall deal with briefly later. Heiler's basic position echoed both Söderblom and Otto, in that the various manifestations of religion he held to point beyond themselves, to the objective existence of 'the Holy', called by Christians 'God'. There is, however, little in his writings that is not to be found in

[50] A different type of meeting of East and West is seen in Otto's critical edition of the *Bhagavad Gītā, The Original Gītā* (Eng. tr. 1939), in which he attempts to do what most Western scholars are tempted to do, and which few Hindus will permit, namely to separate the various strands that have gone to make up the most widely-read of all Hindu scriptures. The methods are those of the European 'higher criticism'—criteria of language and structure, form and content—and under this treatment, the *Gītā* separates out into its component parts and teachings. It has found little support from Western Indologists, and none at all from Hindu scholars.

[51] See below, pp. 256ff.

[52] Heiler's scholarly career began with a reading of Söderblom's revision of Tiele's *Kompendium*. 'That book became my text book in the history of religion, which I almost knew by heart.' As a medical orderly during the First World War, Heiler read it while on night duty. He travelled to Sweden to meet Söderblom in 1919, and remained a faithful disciple of his. See Heiler, 'En härold för de heligas samfund', in Thulin (ed.), *Hågkomster och livsintryck: till minnet av Nathan Söderblom.* XIV (1933), pp. 209ff.

principle in the work of his mentors (he joined Otto at Marburg in 1922).

Heiler occupied an uneasy position on the frontiers of Catholicism and Protestantism, but his troubles were of an ecclesiastical, rather than a purely theological, nature. Another prominent Catholic scholar was Alfred Loisy (1857–1940), who was appointed Professor of the History of Religions in the Collège de France in 1909.[53] Previously a liberal biblical scholar, he came more and more to attempt to create a version of the Comtean religion of humanity, while still remaining a Catholic (a view set out most concisely in his book *La Religion*, 1917). But previously he had been identified with the school of thought known vaguely as 'Catholic Modernism', which formed an equivalent to Liberal Protestantism, but which suffered a serious blow by being made the object of official Papal disapproval (*Dominici pascendi gregis*, 1907). Most of the Catholic modernists were in close contact with leading Protestant scholars, Söderblom in particular serving as a centre of communication; and most were to a greater or lesser extent followers of developments in comparative religion.[54] Loisy was one who became an independent scholar in his own right—though abandoning in the process most of the distinctly Catholic position.

Of the others, the most influential was certainly Baron Friedrich von Hügel (1852–1925), who remained throughout his life a devoted son of the Church, and in a productive theological career (though as an amateur; he never held an academic post) attempted to keep fully abreast of the changing world of the comparative study of religion.[55] His *magnum opus*, *The Mystical Element in Religion*, we have already mentioned; otherwise his *Essays and Addresses* show at a number of points how seriously he took this science, an impression strengthened by his correspondence with scholars working in the field.

All the names we have so far mentioned in this chapter were, one

---

[53] See Petre, *Alfred Loisy: his Religious Significance* (1944); Poulat (ed.), *Alfred Loisy: sa vie—son oeuvre* (1960). In the late 1890s Loisy had written: 'A science of religion is taking shape outside Catholicism and in opposition to it. To neutralise the dangerous influences of this science . . . we need a religious science in and for the Church.' Q. by Petre, p. 43.

[54] Söderblom wrote an important book on the Catholic (and other) Modernists: *Religionsproblemet inom katolicism och protestantism* (1910)—regrettably never translated.

[55] See de la Bedoyère, *The Life of Baron von Hügel* (1951). In 1904 he was instrumental in founding the London Society for the Study of Religion, which brought together scholars of many different persuasions. 'It was a power for good in the work of constructive personal relations between men of religion.' op. cit. p. 170.

might say, believers in 'progressive revelation'—i.e., the evolutionary hypothesis in its theological guise. In making this assertion, they were declaring their right to offer a theological alternative to the positivist thesis that the process of evolution must inevitably lead mankind *out of* religion. But there is one last criticism to consider, before passing on : that offered by the Scottish philosopher and theologian John Baillie (1886–1960), not only of positivist evolution, but of the methods and presuppositions of the science of religion as a whole.

* * *

Baillie's book *The Interpretation of Religion* (1928), subtitled 'An Introductory Study of Theological Principles', was written with the ambitious purpose of presenting 'a true theory of religion', and at the same time of providing a guide through 'the winding labyrinths both of historical opinion and of contemporary literature on the subject'. Although its author outgrew it, partly under the influence of Karl Barth, and refused either to revise it or to have it reprinted (a paperback reprint edition finally appeared in the U.S.A. in 1956, only four years before Baillie's death) it remains an impressive achievement.

For our purposes it is interesting as an example of the way in which a Christian theologian of the Calvinist tradition was attempting, in presenting a theory of religion, to take account of all the available evidence, non-Christian as well as Christian. He also criticises the presuppositions and methods of a number of earlier scholars working within the field of comparative religion, and it is this aspect of his work which is of most interest in this context.

Baillie's main contention is that it is impossible to apply external criteria to the evaluation of religion. Religion, he maintains, can be justly estimated only from within—a point also made by Söderblom. The science of religion he holds to be defective simply because it has tried to be a *natural* science,

> . . . and has essayed to treat the faiths of mankind as so much *dead matter*, to be understood not by introspective insight but by internal inspection and comparison. But the truth is that, regarded from this point of view, the religious experience of mankind is the merest chaos of kaleidoscopic forms; and that only by regarding it from within, and through the glass of the experience itself, can either meaning or order be discerned in it.[56]

---

[56] Baillie, *The Interpretation of Religion* (1956), p. 122.

Those who advocate the comparison of religions, in the attempt both to evaluate particular religions and to discern the nature of religion-as-such (and here he is thinking mainly of the earliest representatives of the science of religion, with their evolutionary basis of judgement) without religious experience, he compares, again like Söderblom, to the unmusical person attempting to construct a theory of the development of music. The enterprise is an impossible one. So, too, is the attempt to lay aside one's own religious convictions when judging religions other than one's own.

> But religious judgments being what they are, and making claim to objective truth as they undoubtedly do, it is psychologically an impossible feat, as well as logically a self-contradictory desire, *not* to make one's own fundamental religious convictions the criterion of religious truth. If we believe them to be true (as we must do, if they are really convictions), then we are, *ipso facto*, making them the criterion. And, once again, what *other* criterion is at all conceivable?[57]

Actually, Baillie points out, this ideal is seldom fully adhered to : most scholars do have convictions; '*Voraussetzungslose Wissenschaft* has usually meant only a science that has been blind to its presuppositions, not a science that has had none';[58] and all scholars express their presuppositions :

> Yet it is remarkable how seldom in such writings we are able completely to escape the impression that we are here having religion described to us by one who either lacks a religious experience of his own or has left that side of his spiritual equipment behind him at home when he came to this workshop.[59]

Baillie is more sympathetically inclined towards those who would restrict the field of comparative religion to the area of pure historical description, leaving questions of interpretation to be settled by philosophers and theologians. But he still allows himself to be sceptical about the possibility of writing history divorced from inspiration, of reproducing on paper *was eigentlich geschehen, wie es eigentlich gewesen*. History involves interpretation; and as such it differs only in degree, and not in kind, from philosophy. The history of religions and the philosophy of religion (or for that matter theology) differ only in scope. Both try to tell the truth about the religious experience of man; but whereas philosophy and theology attempt to

---

[57] ibid., p. 123.
[58] ibid., p. 127.
[59] ibid., p. 124.

see the area as a whole, the historian abstracts, and studies, a part only. Sections may be drawn in various ways (which is just another way of saying that the field may be considered by means of a variety of methods), of which the chronological or ethnographical sections are only alternative examples.

Not even of the history of the temporal development of human religion 'from the earliest times to the present day' is it true that its subject-matter is religious experience as a whole, because it has in mind only the chronological seriation of experience, which is but one aspect of its general significance.[60]

And most handbooks of the history of religion (he mentions specifically de la Saussaye, Menzies, Tiele-Söderblom and Moore)

. . . are so far from being anything that could properly be called 'universal history' of religion (and so be indistinguishable from theology) that they are hardly more than a series of separate and largely unrelated essays on the religious systems of the various races—bound together in one volume for convenience's sake.[61]

Baillie sums up—and we may bring this examination to an end at this point—by saying that theology and the historiography of religion should work hand in hand, since they grow together and each has much to learn from the other :

It is from a sound theological outlook that the historiography of religion must take its cue, but when, having done so, and having completed its work, it brings home its finished results, then it is theology's turn to make what use of them it can.[62]

[60] ibid., p. 130.
[61] ibid., p. 131.
[62] ibid., p. 131f.

VIII

Culture and History

Comparative religion began, and for many years flourished, on the basis of an explicit or implicit belief in the monogenesis of the human race. Henry Balfour, writing in 1906, pointed out that those who accepted this theory—'as most of us undoubtedly do'—are forced to admit '. . . that there prevails a condition of unity in the tendencies of the human mind to respond in a similar manner to similar stimuli'; there is in other words '. . . a tendency of the human intelligence to evolve independently identical ideas where the conditions are themselves identical'.[1] Animistic, pre-animistic, totemistic and other theories of religion were able to flourish against the background of such intellectual assumptions; and it was not felt necessary to inquire too closely into the historical evidence on which they were based.

The early years of the century, though they saw this theory pass from strength to strength, also saw a serious challenge aimed at its very foundations. Its normal corollary, belief in the inevitability of progress, suffered a body-blow at the time of the First World War. This is common knowledge, and it is customary to blame the war for putting an end, at a stroke, to the pre-war atmosphere of optimism which had carried the evolutionary theory to its more notable triumphs. But the war was not the only cause of this shaking of the evolutionary foundations. The impact of the world tragedy, severe as it was, was only part of a more complicated intellectual upheaval. At least two other factors must be taken into account.

The first of these concerned the *diffusion* of culture.[2] The theory of unilinear evolution was originally no more than an alternative solution of a problem which might be equally seriously, and perhaps equally successfully, dealt with in terms of the diffusion of cultural elements. An anthropologist like Tylor, though in the end a convinced believer in evolution, took diffusion very seriously indeed.[3] Others were out-and-out diffusionists, not least because they believed the evolutionists to have allowed dominant theory to outstrip available fact. Others again turned firmly aside from such synthetic

---

[1] Introduction to Pitt-Rivers, *The Evolution of Culture* (1906), p. xix.
[2] Daniel, *The Idea of Prehistory* (1964), pp. 63, 99f., 106f.
[3] ibid., p. 90.

theories, preferring to concentrate on more immediately demonstrable relations between cultures in a well-defined geographical area. The second factor is more important, but much harder to characterise briefly. It concerns the impact of nationalism on the intellectual climate of the early part of the century. Writing in 1919, Franz Boas pointed to two sources of nationalism in Italy and Germany : '. . . the memory of times in which the nation had great political power and the desire to bring back these (*sic*) times, and the consciousness that a certain literature and art is the common property of all those who constitute the nation.'[4] The social and ethical standards of nationalism, he noted, are considered in this situation to be 'more fundamental than those that are general and human'.[5] Nationalism was of course closely associated historically with imperial expansion, particularly into Africa and Asia, and thus helped to provide the conditions in which some at least of the raw material of comparative religion was assembled. But while on the one hand it thus served the immediate needs of evolutionists, on the other it carried with it a quite opposite trend. For if justice were to be done to the total national character, or *Kultur*, of Germany, Italy or Great Britain, there could be no reason to deny that other nations, too, had their own cultural heritages, each of which was utterly unique, being the product of factors which were never wholly duplicated in any two areas of the world. To speak of German *Kultur* made it logically necessary to speak, for instance, of Indian *Kultur*; to isolate the constituent elements of the one in such a way as to emphasise its uniqueness was implicitly to admit that the other was also unique, though conceivably less developed.

It is necessary to point out also that the period around the turn of the century, as well as witnessing a powerful surge of national feeling in the West, saw a no less important rise in nationalism in non-Western countries. India in particular passed, between the 1880s and the 1920s, from the state of being a subject colony to the state of being a totally self-conscious nation, concerned passionately with the preservation and maintenance of its own cultural heritage. But as Rabindranath Tagore saw, and lamented, nationalism had come to India from the West, and had set itself up in direct opposition to the wider ideals of humanity.[6]

[4] Boas, *Race and Democratic Society* (1945), p. 118.
[5] ibid., p. 121.
[6] Tagore, *Nationalism* (1917), passim. That nationalism could, and did, lead to the most horrific distortions in the area of religion may be seen from the emphases of the Nazis. See e.g. Beck, *Deutsche Vollendung* (2nd ed. 1944), pp. 435ff. What is especially interesting here is the emphasis placed upon the concept of *das Heilige*, though in an entirely this-worldly sense.

As far as comparative religion was concerned, this general shift in the climate of opinion which had begun before the turn of the century and reached its first climax in the years around the First World War, meant two things : first, that immeasurably more attention came to be paid to questions concerning individual religious traditions, each in its uniqueness, than to questions of 'religion-as-such'; and secondly, that theories of unilinear evolution, which had ruled almost undisputed since the 1870s, came to fall into a certain disrepute—materially aided, of course, by the mental consequences of the war itself. Evolutionary optimism did not immediately disappear; but it captured fewer imaginations. Instead, the newer tendency among scholars in the field of the study of religion was to specialise, engaging in close and detailed studies in a limited area rather than in vast comparisons and synthetic pattern-making.

As we have said, this tendency was not created by the First World War, but was left in more or less total control of the field when the war removed much of its opposition. Now we must examine briefly this emphasis, dating from the later nineteenth century, on ethnological theories of cultures and culture history.

*   *   *

We have seen that the dominant personalities in the early years of comparative religion were often anthropologists, concerned with the primary question of the origin of religion, and that they were almost without exception adherents of the theory of unilinear evolution. In the study of religion in the ancient civilisations (Greece, Rome, Egypt, the Ancient Near East), there was less reason for scholars to hold strongly to this theory, since culture contacts could be demonstrated with considerable accuracy, once the observer had passed beyond the curtain of prehistory. But the ease with which historical links could occasionally be demonstrated was an open invitation to certain enthusiastic scholars to extend these chains of evidence by means of free hypothesis, and to suggest, on inadequate evidence, that all civilisation—or in this case, religion— had originated in some temporarily fashionable corner of the world. This appeared to be history, of a sort. But as with the eighteenth-century hyperboreans, it rapidly discredited itself. Two examples will suffice.

'The Holy' in effect becomes 'the Nation' and even 'the Party', while 'Ein jenseitiges Heilige kann kein Lebenswert sein . . .' (p. 438) Rudolf Otto's reputation suffered at the hands of those who believed in ideologies such as this.

Around the turn of the century a school of German scholars, led by Hugo Winckler, E. Stucken and (to a lesser extent) A. Jeremias, were attempting to demonstrate the Babylonian origin of all Near Eastern religion, mythology, and especially astrology.[7] Some twenty years later, two British writers, Grafton Elliot Smith and W. J. Perry, were making very similar (and equally extravagant) claims for the primacy of Egyptian civilisation[8]—claims which have recently aroused unexpected echoes in the work of the Norwegian explorer Thor Heyerdahl.

But the problem was if anything still more pressing with regard to prehistoric cultures. Were the advances in ethnology and pre-historic archaeology capable of shedding any light on ancient culture contacts? Or would such problems as those attending the origin and early forms of religion still have to be solved by means of *a priori* hypotheses?

The question of ultimate origins will probably always be inaccess-ible to the historical investigator. But in the early years of the present century a growing feeling of disenchantment with the simplistic theory of unilinear evolution set in, particularly among scholars in Germany and Austria. They were not all students of religion (in some cases, the study of religion played a very minor part indeed in their investigations); but their cumulative effect was to create a new, and vital, link between anthropology—or ethnology—and his-torical method. As F. W. Maitland put it, 'My own belief is that by and by anthropology will have the choice between being history and being nothing.'[9]

The choice which in fact faced anthropologists and ethnologists in the inter-war years was not exactly between being history and being nothing; but there did develop two major schools of thought, one of which paid relatively more attention to historical questions than did the other.

Of more importance in the English-speaking world was the school of thought associated with the names of Bronislaw Malinowski (1884–1942) and A. R. Radcliffe-Brown (1881–1955). Malinowski,

---

[7] Jeremias, *Die Panbabylonisten* (2nd ed. 1907).

[8] See Daniel, op. cit., pp. 88ff. Perry's works were *The Children of the Sun* (1923), *The Origin of Magic and Religion* (1923) and *The Growth of Civilisation* (1924). In the latter he wrote (p. 109): '. . . all the evidence is to the effect that the outlying civilisations were founded by men wandering about the world seeking for gold, pearls, and other desired substances, who found fresh lands either uninhabited by men or tenanted by wandering bands of food-gatherers. Out of the combination of these two elements, physical and cultural, grew the great civilisations of the earth.'

[9] Fisher (ed.), *The Collected Papers of Frederic William Maitland* III (1911), p. 295.

born in Poland, always considered himself a disciple of Frazer, describing himself in 1925 as 'bound to the service of Frazerian anthropology'.[10] Yet he passed beyond Frazer at one vital point, the point of 'fieldwork' or 'participant observation'. He dealt in large measure with the same topics as Frazer had done—religion, magic, totemism—and reached not altogether dissimilar results. But he did so having spent a considerable period of time among the Trobriand Islanders, and virtually everything he wrote was grounded in his own first-hand Melanesian observations. His books included *Argonauts of the Western Pacific* (1922), *Myth in Primitive Psychology* (1926), *Crime and Custom in Savage Society* (1926), *Sex and Repression in Savage Society* (1927) and the posthumous compilation *Magic, Science and Religion and Other Essays* (1948). In them one may observe a mind deeply rooted in traditional anthropology, and yet bent on extending the frontiers of that science by direct observation over an extended period of time. In so doing he was clearly concerned less with theorising about remote origins than with the actual, day-to-day lives of living human beings. In this perspective history is of little direct importance (though 'tradition' may be all-important). Similarly Radcliffe-Brown, though concerned with somewhat different problems, and though not agreeing with Malinowski on a number of issues, relegated history to the background of his studies, concentrating instead on problems of function. John Beattie writes that

> As Radcliffe-Brown conceived it, social anthropology was 'ahistorical' rather than anti-historical; where historical evidence was available he quite explicitly admitted it, but in most of the societies studied by anthropologists up to that time there just wasn't any.[11]

Together Malinowski and Radcliffe-Brown, with Boas and his followers in America, inaugurated a new era in social anthropology—the era of field worker and participant observer. The two former also did much in the English-speaking world to discourage the anthropologist from thinking in terms of history (Boas' emphasis was different). But in the German-speaking world, a quite different tendency was noticeable.

*   *   *

We have been mainly concerned in this chapter with develop-

---

[10] Malinowski, *Magic, Science and Religion* (1948), p. 72. Firth (ed.), *Man and Culture* (1957).
[11] Raison (ed.), *The Founding Fathers of Social Science* (1969), p. 182.

ments in the field of ethnology, and have previously indicated that parallel developments in sociology lie outside our present objectives; a very brief word must nevertheless be said at this point about the greatest of the German sociologists of religion, Max Weber (1864–1920).[12] Brevity and Max Weber are of course incompatibles. His work was of an astonishing breadth and penetration, and has inspired an army of commentators, not least since the 1950s. Much of his writing is of only indirect significance for the comparative study of religion. But Weber, of all the social theorists of the period before 1920, took the greatest pains to support his theses on the subject of the interplay of religion and *Kultur* with material drawn from a plurality of religious traditions; and although the tendency he represents is often taken to lie to one side of the mainstream of *Religionswissenschaft*, he made extensive use of the findings of that science.

For instance, on the subject of the origin of religion, Weber produces, in *The Sociology of Religion*, what is in effect a compendium of anthropological comparative religion, bound together by the conviction that

. . . gods and demons, like vocabularies of languages, have been directly influenced primarily by the economic situations and the historic doctrines of different peoples.[13]

Other manifestations of the religious life are similarly conditioned by the changing economic circumstances of specific human communities, each of which has its own character and ethos. Each, in short, is a *Kultur*, a totality within which religious elements form a highly specific and individual pattern.

Weber's most notable work, from our point of view, emerged from his extended studies in the Hindu, Jewish and Chinese religious traditions—studies aimed at determining why specific cultures had evolved specific economic and social systems, and the role of religion in that process. He began by tracing, in *The Protestant Ethic*, the historical and ideological relationship between Western Protestantism and capitalism; his comparative studies in the Indian and Chinese fields were intended, it seems, to provide further evidence of this relationship by drawing on cultural situations in which quite different circumstances existed, not productive of capitalist systems. The greater part of this comparative work was done during the

---

[12] Bendix, *Max Weber, an Intellectual Portrait* (1959), Parsons, Introduction to Weber, *The Sociology of Religion* (Eng. tr. 1963), pp. xix–lxvii.
[13] Weber, *The Sociology of Religion*, p. 13.

G

period of the first world war, but was published only after his death, and translated piecemeal, after many years' delay.

Rapid judgement on Weber's comparative studies is simply an impossibility; but a couple of very general points may be made. First, that he made the fullest possible use of all the best material available to the comparativist in the pursuit of his studies. Much of it, and particularly the Indian material, we now know to have contained manifest imperfections, leading him to what have since been shown to have been false evaluations and mistaken conclusions.[14] But these were the errors of the Western scholarship of the period, and Weber can scarcely be faulted for not outstripping specialists in their own specialisation. And secondly, it may once more be emphasised that Weber's work, though concerned with the great developed civilisations rather than with the pre-literates, maintains to the full the important tendency of the period, to treat each culture as an autonomous entity shaped by its own deepest traditions.

It is no doubt true, as Talcott Parsons has said, that

> Weber would have altered many of his opinions and generalisations, if he had had access to the subsequent fifty years' anthropological research into primitive religion and historical scholarship relevant to advanced religions.[15]

And Trevor Ling calls his work 'in one very important sense a paradigm for the modern comparative study of religion, in that he approached religion with other than theological questions in mind'.[16] This being so, it is perhaps not without some significance that in the English-speaking world, where theology continued to be closely related to comparative religion, the 'discovery' of Weber did not take place until the 1950s—by which time the question of *Kultur* had in any case taken on new aspects.

*   *   *

Returning now to the ethnological tradition, we have seen that the evolutionary comparative religionists regarded it as axiomatic that religion had developed out of modest beginnings, in animism, animatism, magic, totemism or whatever, and that a genuine belief in personal deity had emerged only gradually, as the end product

[14] Ling, 'Max Weber in India', in *The University of Leeds Review* (May 1973), pp. 42–65.
[15] Weber, *The Sociology of Religion*, p. xxxvi.
[16] Ling, op. cit., p. 43.

of an inordinately long and slow process. Only Andrew Lang among the first generation of anthropologists had dared to take at face value the observations of some field-workers in Australia, that there is evidence of belief in a Supreme Being among otherwise undeveloped peoples, and to suggest that the evolutionary scheme might not be the inflexible thing which so many of his colleagues had attempted to make it.

It is perhaps worth pointing out once more that Lang was emphatically not suggesting that the origin of all religion is to be sought in some form of primitive monotheism. The origin of religion he consistently held to be an impenetrable mystery. What he did was to point to the evidence, to suggest that belief in high gods is at least as old as belief in ghosts and spirits, and to leave his readers to make up their own minds on the cogency or otherwise of his arguments. It is a matter of history that at the time few scholars were prepared even to give him a respectful hearing.

Andrew Lang died in 1912, and in that same year there appeared the first volume of what was to be a monumental work (not completed until the appearance of its twelfth volume in 1955) by an Austrian Roman Catholic priest, Father Wilhelm Schmidt, S.V.D. : *Der Ursprung der Gottesidee.* Four years previously Schmidt had begun to publish in his periodical *Anthropos* a series of articles in French of the same subject, which Lang, in fact, read. Schmidt was not the first to treat Lang's theories with the seriousness they deserved. Nathan Söderblom of Uppsala had given them a respectful mention in an article first published in 1902. The Indo-European scholar Leopold von Schröder of Vienna had taken them up to consideration at the 1904 Congress in Basel, in a paper entitled *Über den Glauben eines höchstes gutes Wesen bei den Ariern*, and in his book *Wesen and Ursprung der Religion* (1906). But it was Schmidt's book which convinced at least part of the scholarly world that here was something to be taken with the utmost seriousness.

It would be gratifying to be able to record that the discussion about the origin and evolution of religion was thereby placed, once and for all, on a purely academic plane, above personalities and polemics. Certainly the issues were serious enough to warrant this, for if belief in high gods were once demonstrated among culturally primitive peoples, then one cornerstone of the theory of religious evolution would have been removed. Regrettably, from the point of view of objective scholarship, Schmidt suffered from a disability even greater, if anything, than Lang's 'spiritualism' : he was a Roman Catholic priest. Hence, in the eyes of his critics, he had a vested interest in demonstrating the chronological priority of monotheism over polytheism and animism, and his testimony, its weight of learning notwithstanding, was not to be trusted. Of course, Schmidt *did* believe the emergent data of historical ethnology to be fundamentally in accord with the biblical revelation—a point which he made in a book entitled *Die Uroffenbarung als Anfang der Offenbarung Gottes* (1913)[17]—but this personal stance of faith (to which he was perfectly entitled) served only too easily as an excuse on others' part for not listening to what he had to say. At all events, Schmidt's views can be characterised, as Lang's could not, as an affirmation that primitive monotheism was the origin of all religion.

This being so, it was far from clear at first whether Schmidt would make any more impression on scholarly opinion than Lang had done. The Protestant scholar E. W. Mayer of Strasbourg, writing in 1913, noted (somewhat sadly, one feels) that Lang's intuitive thesis had simply not been listened to, and went on : 'Whether Father Schmidt will make more impression, especially on ethnologists, than his predecessor Lang, I do not pretend to decide. That must be left to the seer who knows the past and can prophesy after the event; but it is not likely.'[18] At the same time, he pointed out, not unnecessarily, that dogmatism cannot be met by dogmatism, and that no one who had denied the theory had as yet troubled to examine the facts on which it rested.

In the event one aspect of Schmidt's theories—that concerning the legitimacy of talking about high gods—came to be more and more widely accepted by historians of religion during the 1920s and 1930s; ethnologists remained for the most part unconvinced, less by the theory of high gods than by the 'culture-historical method' on which Schmidt and his colleagues were working.

*   *   *

The originator of the 'culture-historical' movement in ethnology is recognised to have been Friedrich Ratzel (1844–1904), a geographer by profession, who approached the problem of geography in terms of the distribution of peoples and cultures (his own term for this was anthropo-geography). It is interesting to note that he was bitterly opposed to the methods of Adolf Bastian, 'the out-and-out evolutionist who would not believe in diffusion'.[19] For Bastian

---

[17] A revised and augmented version of this apologetical monograph was published in an English translation as *Primitive Revelation* (1939).
[18] Quoted in Schmidt, *The Origin and Growth of Religion* (Eng. tr. 1931), p. 18f.
[19] Daniel, *The Idea of Prehistory*, p. 90.

the occurrence of similar ideas among apparently differing peoples was to be explained by recourse to the theory of *Elementargedanken*, 'fundamental ideas', which, given the premises of unilinear evolution, must be identical in every human setting. To Ratzel, this was a wholly unhistorical solution of a historical problem. All peoples without exception have a history, he pointed out, and it is necessary to trace that history, particularly when it involves migrations and culture-contacts. He went on from there to postulate that when a form of material culture having any kind of specialist function agrees with any other such form (his own primary investigations began with the history of the bow in Africa), then it is necessary to postulate a historical and genetic connection. The 'criterion of form' must judge.

Ratzel's theory was enlarged and elaborated by one of his pupils, Leo Frobenius (1873–1938) into the doctrine of culture-circles (*Kulturkreise*)—a culture-circle being an area of human civilisation within which a uniform material culture can be demonstrated to have existed. This implies a further criterion over and above Ratzel's criterion of form, viz., a criterion of quantity. Frobenius also investigated the relations between culture-circles, for instance between West Africa and Melanesia, and believed that connections existed between cultures as entireties.

Frobenius' work was followed closely by two assistants at the Berlin *Museum für Völkerkunde*, F. Gräbner and B. Ankermann, who each delivered, in 1905, a lecture applying the Frobenius method to a specific area—Gräbner to Oceania and Ankermann to Africa. As yet no particular conclusions had been drawn from this method for the problem of the study of religion. But in the next two decades, the emergent culture-historical school turned its attentions more and more to the problem of religion, and in particular to the problem of 'high gods'. This development was materially helped by the creation in 1906 of the new periodical *Anthropos*.

Leaving aside the contributions of other adherents to the school, such as W. Foy, director of the Rautenstrauch-Joest Museum in Cologne, and concentrating on Gräbner, we see in him yet another case of the 'remote-control anthropologist', who had little first-hand knowledge of his material. He entered ethnology through a narrow door, as Pinard de la Boullaye points out, being concerned in his early days almost entirely with the Australian evidence.[20] But his *Methode der Ethnologie* (1911) shows him to have been a considerable theorist, with great respect for historical method; in fact this

---

[20] Schmidt, *Origin and Growth*, pp. 228ff, Pinard de la Boullaye, *L'étude comparée des religions* I, p. 432f.

book is based on Bernheim's *Lehrbuch der historischen Methode* (1899, 6th ed. 1908). In his later book *Das Weltbild der Primitiven* (1924) he builds up a historical pattern on the basis of the theory that in the (now extinct) Tasmanian tribes of Australia, and in certain African peoples, notably the Kalahari Bushmen, we see the earliest known forms of human culture. He discusses the economic, familial and social conditions under which these people live, and stresses their closeness to, and dependence upon, the natural world— shown, for instance, in their reliance on hunting and on the gathering of plants for food. He has much to say about the modes of thought of these peoples—matters which cannot concern us here. But it is worth noting that he recognises in the case of the Tasmanians the propensity to think in two categories, one of which gives rise, by way of association, to myth, and the other to belief in some form of Supreme Being. The Tasmanians, according to Gräbner, were in fact dualists, believing in a good and an evil power, the former ruling the day and the latter the night. The relationship between these powers is, however, a subject which Gräbner does not fully consider.

Writing on the subject of the Aboriginal tribes of south-east Australia, Gräbner expresses himself far more clearly. He is convinced that these tribes know of a Great God, a Supreme Being, to which they give a variety of names—Mungan Ngaua, Bunjil, Baiame, Nurrundere—and who is considered to be the creator and maker of all things. But more importantly, he is also believed to be the guardian of the morality of the tribe, the originator of those rites and practices by which man is enabled to govern part of the natural world, and the preserver of both the physical and the social existence of man.

Ratzel, Frobenius, Gräbner and Ankermann were ethnologists, and concerned with the problems of religion only incidentally, as elements within the larger problem of the diffusion of culture. In Wilhelm Schmidt these priorities were reversed. To him, ethnological theory was a tool to be used in the elucidation of the development of religion. He had been a missionary and a linguist, and turned to the serious study of ethnology as a result of hearing Leopold von Schröder's lectures on Andrew Lang and the problem of high gods, and as a result of studying the theories of Gräbner, of which he remained a constant (though occasionally critical) interpreter. In 1906 he started the periodical *Anthropos* as a vehicle for his ideas and those of his disciples—for he gradually accumulated a not inconsiderable following, largely, though not exclusively, from within the ranks of Roman Catholic scholars. He had also been early attracted by the work of the French scholars J. L. A. de

Quatrefages and A. le Roy on the Pygmies, and adopted the theory that the pygmies of Central Africa, the Andaman Islands, the Malacca peninsula and parts of the Philippines represent the oldest stratum of humanity known to us. His earliest large-scale work, *Die Stellung der Pygmäenvölker in der Entwicklungsgeschichte der Menschen* (The place of the pygmy peoples in the history of human development, 1910) deals with this subject. Schmidt's other great field of interest was Australia, and in the same year he published a paper entitled *Grundlinien einer Vergleichung der Religionen und Mythologien der austronesischen Völker* (Outlines of a comparison of the religions and mythologies of the Austronesian peoples). The first volume of his *magnum opus*, *Der Ursprung der Gottesidee* (The origin of the idea of God), appeared in 1912; in the following years this volume was entirely rewritten, and a second edition appeared in 1926, followed thereafter at intervals by eleven further volumes, each devoted to the detailed consideration of the religious beliefs of some 'primitive' people. In the meantime, however, Schmidt, recognising that these massive tomes would be of interest to only a limited readership, published a smaller work, translated into English as *The Origin and Growth of Religion: Facts and Theories* (1931, 2nd ed. 1935), in which he gave an epitome of his position, and a review of the theories which had led up to it.

Although Schmidt was a constant critic of 'evolutionism', his criticisms are in fact directed against a particular form of evolutionism, viz., the unilinear evolutionism of the late nineteenth century. Accordingly, in his attempts to outline the origins and growth of religion, he is in reality advancing an alternative pattern of evolution, albeit one which he believes to be better supported by the facts of historical ethnology. He was undoubtedly right to object to the naïve assurance with which some of the early anthropologists treated the whole problem of 'primitivity'; but this was no guarantee that his scheme of historical development was any better founded.

Schmidt's overriding concern was to demonstrate that the older a stratum of human culture, the more clearly can one discern in it clear evidence of the worship of a Supreme Being. He did not, it is true, mean to suggest that what we find there is a complete survival of the earliest form of man's religion :

It cannot but be that in this period religions, like other things, underwent very considerable changes. We may therefore be certain that the religious forms of the primitive cultures now available do not immediately and without more ado show us the primitive form of religion. However, we do come a long step nearer this ultimate form if we work out the common element in these primitive religions and put the results together into a living synthesis.[21]

This is precisely what Schmidt does, arriving at the conclusion that the earlier the people, the more clearly is evidence of the Supreme Being identified with, or living in, the sky to be found—'. . . not indeed everywhere in the same form or the same vigour, but still everywhere prominent enough to make his dominant position indubitable'[22]—and that this points to such a belief 'at the very dawn of time, before the individual groups had separated from one another'.[23] This belief Schmidt held to be a true monotheism, the Supreme Being having the attributes of eternity, omniscience, beneficence, morality, omnipotence and creative power. In time, the figure of the Supreme Being came to be overlaid by lesser gods, ghosts, spirits and demons; but its original power cannot be gainsaid. Thus far Schmidt.

For one who is not himself an ethnologist to evaluate the purely ethnological parts of Schmidt's argument is not easy, but it seems that his colleagues and successors in this area, while admiring the sheer weight of material he produced in support of his case, were never really convinced by it. Much the same may be said of his theory of primitive monotheism, though with this difference, that although few were prepared to accept his thesis that *all* religion originated in a belief in one Supreme Being, many scholars came to realise that 'high gods' were undeniably a feature of primitive religion, explain them how we will.

The strongest support for Schmidt's theory of the origin of religion came, not altogether surprisingly, from other Roman Catholic scholars, notably Pinard de la Boullaye, in volume two of his monumental *L'Étude comparée des religions* (3rd ed. 1929), and K. L. Bellon of Holland, in *Inleiding tot de vergelijkende Godsdienstwetenschap* (1932), both of whom accepted Schmidt's method, as well as his conclusions.

More typical of the reaction of European scholarship generally was, however, the judgement of the outstanding Italian scholar Raffaele Pettazzoni (1883–1959), that 'monotheism' is a historically conditioned term, implying some form of *Auseinandersetzung* with polytheism, and that it is therefore historically illegitimate to speak of monotheism in connection with the origins of religion. Pettazzoni dealt in full with this question in his most important books *Dio*

---

[21] Schmidt, *Origin and Growth*, p. 255.
[22] ibid., p. 257.
[23] ibid., p. 261.

(1922) and *The All-Knowing God* (Eng. tr. 1956), and in several other contexts. In a later article he wrote that 'what we find among uncivilised peoples is not monotheism in its historically literal sense, but the idea of a Supreme Being, and the erroneous identification, the misleading assimilation, of this idea to true monotheism can give rise only to misunderstandings.'[24] This was, of course, not to say that 'high gods' should be dismissed from the argument : merely that Schmidt was, despite himself, wrestling with an insoluble problem—insoluble, that is, in terms of historical evidence—and simply replacing one hypothesis with another. Pettazzoni, and some years later, E. O. James and Geo Widengren, were to prove the point about 'high gods' with caution and objectivity, that they are certainly *there* in the 'primitive' and ancient religions, but that it is wise not to speculate unduly as to how they came to be there.[25]

Subsequent support for the culture-historical school among comparative religionists has tended to be sharply localised. In the English-speaking world it has been of little real significance, few scholars having had either the ability or the desire to penetrate the methods of the school. It is true that some American ethnologists, most of them followers of Boas, have approximated to the culture-historical method in their work, without, however, sharing the school's implicit theological concern, or its methodological emphases. Although the American school of ethnology of the 1920s and after did most of its best work in its own back yard, so to speak, on the cultures of the North American Indians, its more outstanding representatives, Lowie and Radin, each produced a valuable book on the subject of primitive religion as a whole.

As is only to be expected, the later history of the movement

[24] Pettazzoni, *Essays on the History of Religion* (1954), p. 9. On Pettazzoni, see Schmidt, *Origin and Growth*, pp. 209ff., and cf. Eliade, *The Quest* (1969), p. 29 : 'His learning was vast and exact, and he wrote with clarity, poise and elegance. Brought up under the pervasive influence of Croce's historicism, Pettazzoni viewed religion as a purely historical phenomenon.' Eliade also calls him the last of the encyclopaedists. In 1954 Pettazzoni himself defined his science in these words: 'La nature particulière et la caractère même des faits religieux en tant que tels confèrent le droit de constituer l'objet d'une science spéciale. Cette science est la science des religions au sens propre du terme; le caractère essentiel des faits religieux en est la raison d'être, nécessaire et suffisante.' *Numen* 1 (1954), p. 2. Among Italian scholars influenced by Pettazzoni—exponents of exact scholarship and the strictest historical method—may be mentioned Angelo Brelich, Alessandro Bausani and Ugo Bianchi, author of *Problemi di storia delle religioni*, translated into German as *Probleme der Religionsgeschichte* (1964) and into Swedish as *Religionshistoriska problem* (1966).

[25] Widengren, *Hochgottglaube im alten Iran* (1938); *Religionsphänomenologie* (1969), pp. 46ff. cf. James, *The Worship of the Sky-God* (1963).

launched by Leo Frobenius has moved along essentially German lines, in the process becoming increasingly refined and specialised in its aims. The greater part of this development lies outside our scope to discuss, but one late facet is certainly worth mentioning. Adolf E. Jensen, in his book *Mythos und Kult bei Naturvölkern* (1951, Eng. tr. *Myth and Cult among Primitive Peoples*, 1963), stands squarely in the Frobenius tradition and yet very largely bypasses Gräbner and Schmidt (though he treats both with respect). The theory of high gods, in Schmidt's form, he does not accept, since it presupposes a degree of unity in the oldest history of mankind which cannot be demonstrated by historical or ethnological evidence. His own method he characterises as 'culture-morphological'; this involves the analysis of the forms in which the religion of pre-literate peoples presents itself, with due attention paid to factors of environment.this view of the scope and task of the ethnological approach to religion has had an important following among Scandinavian scholars; in the work of, for instance, Åke Hultkrantz of Stockholm one notices that 'a usable morphology of religion' is stated to be one of the main *desiderata* of comparative religion.[26]

For a summing up of the position of the culture-historical school of comparative religion we must return to Vienna, and to the three-volume compendium *Christus und die Religionen der Erde* (Christ and the religions of the world, 1951), edited by F. König, then professor in the University of Salzburg and subsequently Roman Catholic Archbishop of Vienna. Written for the most part by disciples of Schmidt, and entirely by Roman Catholics—W. Koppers, P. Schebesta, T. Corbishley, H. C. Puech, C. Regamey, J. Bonsirven, *et al.*—this work exhibits a vast depth and breadth of exact scholarship. Although its final position is openly apologetical, its various chapters, dealing with separate culture-circles, contain much of which any student or scholar might make use. There is, perhaps, an exaggerated tendency for some of the contributors to defer to the towering figure of Schmidt; in spite of this—or perhaps because of this—it is one of the most consistent of handbooks. From Schmidt's own *Foreword* we may gather that in the forty years of scholarly investigation which had followed the publication of his first book on the pygmies, he had seen no reason to change his mind on any important question of principle—and this despite the waves and the billows that had washed over him in the meantime. More material there certainly was, to be greeted with satisfaction

[26] Hultkrantz, 'The Phenomenology of Religion: Aims and Methods', in *Temenos* 6 (1970), p. 86.

as illustrating an age-old thesis, nothing more. And in the final reckoning, Jesus Christ '. . . breaks through all the categories of the history of religions and the history of human culture'.[27] There is no way from religion to revelation, from Trimurti to Trinity. Scholarship is fulfilled in faith—a position which the Vienna school had, of course, held all along.

* * *

On the other side of the Atlantic, during these same years a profound reappraisal of the relationship between history and culture, and particularly archaic culture, was taking place under the guidance of the anthropologist Franz Boas (1858–1942).[28] Probably it is true to say that religion did not hold the central place in Boas' work that it did in, for example, Schmidt's; nevertheless, the cumulative effect was in some ways similar, and a great deal of incidental work was done on the problems of primitive religion in the process of re-evaluation which Boas started, and which his many disciples carried on.

Boas, a German by birth, began his anthropological work in Baffin Land, among the Central Eskimo, in 1883–4. He returned to Berlin for some four years, and was then recommended by E. B. Tylor to concentrate on the Indian tribes of the west coast of Canada. Thus it was that he came back to America in 1888; and there he stayed, making the southern Kwakiutl his special field of study. In 1895 he was appointed to a chair at Columbia University, which he occupied for the remainder of his active life, making him, in Lowie's words, '. . . the first anthropologist who combined ample field experience with an unrivalled opportunity to train investigators'.[29]

Boas was an anti-evolutionist even during the heyday of evolutionism. Siding rather with the diffusionists (though without subscribing to their extreme aberrations), he always held that although in the case of primitive peoples, the history of a phenomenon may be hard enough to discern, the phenomenon can nevertheless be understood only through its history. He always showed an extreme distrust of theories—his own, as well as other people's—and preferred to work quietly along empirical lines, theorising as little as possible along the way. His overall aim was to investigate tribal customs in relation

---

[27] *Christus und die Religionen der Erde* I, p. xi.
[28] Herskovits, *Franz Boas: The Science of Man in the Making* (1953); Kroeber and others, 'Franz Boas 1858–1942', in *American Anthropologist* 45 (1943).
[29] Lowie, *A History of Ethnological Theory* (1938), p. 129.

to the totality of tribal cultures, and particularly to outline the processes by which those cultures have developed; this inevitably involved him in the consideration of the dissemination of cultural elements from tribe to tribe. Among such cultural elements myth took an important place—not least because of its being expressed in words. Boas was always profoundly interested in verbal elements, though he held that ritual was prior to myth, and that myths themselves frequently serve merely to sanction rituals. The study of religion, therefore, was only one element of his work, and although myth and religion cannot readily be separated, there are methodological difficulties involved when an attempt is made to approach religion from this angle. In seeking to decide in what ways mythology reflects culture, he showed clearly enough where his sympathies lay—and what were his limitations.[30]

It is not for the content of his theories about religion that Boas is significant in this context, but rather because his great influence helped to move the climate of opinion still further away from theories of unilinear evolution, and towards a separate appreciation of human cultures as self-contained, though interdependent, totalities, each of which needs to be evaluated in its own terms and against its own individual background. Like Malinowski and Radcliffe-Brown, he stood for a type of functionalism. Like them, too, he insisted on the absolute necessity of field-work for the anthropologist. His method was that of careful and precise observation and recording in a very specific area, and of drawing no conclusions which were not substantiated by first-hand observation and evidence. In this he set the tone for a whole generation of American anthropologists.

Among Boas' disciples were numbered practically all the anthropologists of significance in America between the wars; a couple of dozen of them produced work of lasting significance, very largely from within the field of the North American Indians. Clearly, not all would claim (or want) a place in the history of comparative religion, but among the many, four names may be mentioned in all brevity.

Robert H. Lowie, who had done 'intense and sober' field-work among the Crow Indians of Montana, and was always fascinated by the problem of religion,[31] published in 1924 a book, *Primitive Religion*, in which he applied the critical methods of Boas to a much larger field than any in which Boas himself was ever involved. The

---

[30] Hultkrantz, 'North American Indian Religions in the History of Research', in *History of Religions* 6/3 (1967), p. 185.
[31] ibid., p. 191.

result was inevitably somewhat negative; but much dead wood was cleared away in the process. A less critical spirit was demonstrated by Paul Radin, who also wrote a book on *Primitive Religion* (1937). Radin's field-work had been among the Winnebago, and out of this emerged a number of outstanding works, including *The Trickster* (1956), a study of the paradoxical demiurge of the Woodlands Indians. It was part of Radin's story that he, almost alone among working anthropologists, had connections with the Eranos group around C. G. Jung, and his 'Trickster' idea was in fact taken up and applied in these circles to phenomena having little enough to do with Indians. Although his brilliance was not questioned, his judgement sometimes was; and as Hultkrantz remarks, rather primly, 'His ambitions were certainly laudable, but his canons of procedure did not safeguard a correct interpretation.'[32] Presumably Boas would not have approved of some of the company he kept.

More clearly in the genuine Boas line was A. A. Goldenweiser, who staked out a claim for himself in one important area of anthropological and religious theory, viz., the theory of totemism.[33] Since M'Lennan and Robertson Smith, totemism had been a happy hunting ground for other than North American Indians, and the French sociologists in particular had regarded it with a good deal of affection as a peg on which to hang ever heavier and heavier burdens of social theory. Boas himself had expressed serious doubts whether it was ever the unitary phenomenon which the evolutionists had wanted to make it, and in a long series of articles, stretching over a period of some twenty years, Goldenweiser confirmed these suspicions. He did not, it is true, analyse totemic phenomena in the precise manner of the later structural anthropologists, but he did relocate the discussion in a most valuable way.

Last among the disciples of Boas we may mention Ruth Underhill, whose specialist area was the south-west (notably the Papago), and who published as recently as 1965 a monograph on the subject of North American Indian religion, under the title *Red Man's Religion*. Her particular contribution to the general discussion lies perhaps in the role which she accords archaeology as a primary source of information, alongside the more traditional sources. The historical perspective, in this light, speaks for itself, although *Red Man's*

---

[32] ibid., p. 196.
[33] Goldenweiser, 'Totemism, an Analytical Study', in *Journal of American Folklore* xxiii (1910), 'Form and Content in Totemism', in *American Anthropologist* 20 (1918). R. C. Poole, in his introduction to Lévi-Strauss, *Totemism* (1969), writes: '. . . in the end Goldenweiser's 110 pages were to exercise a more lasting theoretical influence than the 2,200 pages in Frazer's four volumes.' The reference is to the 1910 article.

Religion does in fact contain echoes of earlier evolutionary views.

Europe's foremost expert on North American Indian religion has paid tribute to the Boas era in American anthropology by saying that '. . . nowhere on earth may the student of religion find as many thorough field reports on primitive religions as in this American corpus of works, published and unpublished'.[34] The era as such perhaps ended in the 1930s, since when American anthropology has been less concerned with the problems of religion than was formerly the case. But during its heyday, much was achieved which has been entirely beneficial to the study of primitive religion, and indeed to the overall methodology of comparative religion. In a word, it helped create an empirical, practical and historical science out of a second-hand speculative philosophy.

It would be wrong, of course, to conclude from this type of ethnological and cultural theory that anthropology had abandoned all further pretence to speculation on subjects connected with religion. That this was emphatically not the case can be seen if we examine briefly the work of the French anthropologist-philosopher Lucien Lévy-Bruhl (1857–1939).[35] The contrast between Lévy-Bruhl and the respective schools of cultural and social anthropologists is very marked; yet he brought his own distinctive contribution to the comparative study of religion, and complemented the German and American schools at a number of points. The fundamental concept is still that of culture; but Lévy-Bruhl's answer is bolder, and more controversial, than that ventured by most of his contemporaries.

Between 1910 and 1938, Lévy-Bruhl wrote six books on the problem of 'primitive mentality', the concept with which his name is particularly associated. The first of these, *Les Fonctions mentales dans les sociétés inférieures*, appeared in 1910, and was translated into English under the unfortunate title of *How Natives Think* in 1926. Twelve years later, in 1922, there appeared his best-known work *La Mentalité primitive* (Eng. tr. *Primitive Mentality*, 1923); there followed *L'Âme primitive* (1927, Eng. tr. *The 'Soul' of the Primitive*, 1929), *Le Surnaturel et la nature dans la mentalité primitive* (1931), *La Mythologie primitive* (1935) and *L'Expérience mystique et les symboles chez les primitives* (1935).

Lévy-Bruhl's interest in anthropology was created and stimulated by contact with the Durkheim school, and to a certain extent he

---

[34] Hultkrantz, op. cit., p. 190.
[35] Trained, like R. R. Marett, in philosophy, for many years Lévy-Bruhl was Professor of the History of Modern Philosophy at the Sorbonne, lecturing especially on Descartes, Hume and Schopenhauer. cf. Evans-Pritchard, *Theories of Primitive Religion*, pp. 78ff.

shared their concern with those problems which he considered inexplicable in terms of individual psychology. But only to a certain extent—and after 1927 he went his own way. In his early years as an anthropologist he was, however, concerned with what he called 'collective representations' within cultures, ideas and conceptions which

> . . . are common to members of a given social group; they are transmitted from one generation to another; they impress themselves upon its individual members, and awaken in them sentiments of respect, fear, adoration, and so on, according to the circumstances of the case.[36]

The question he set himself to answer was whether such collective representations—determinative of the character of each culture—arise out of higher mental functions identical with our own, or whether they have to be referred to an entirely different type of mental habit. His answer was that there is indeed a type of 'primitive mentality', which he characterised as 'prelogical' and 'mystical'—both of these, incidentally, terms calculated to cause difficulties—and which, although it still to some extent exists in developed societies, is found in all primitive cultures. Collective representations, which embody the fruits of primitive mentality, he wrote,

> . . . force themselves upon the individual; that is, they are to him an article of faith, not the product of his reason. And since the collective representations, as a rule, predominate most where the races are least advanced, the mind of the 'primitive' has hardly any room for such questions as 'how?' and 'why?' The ensemble of collective representations which master him and excite in him an intensity of feeling which we cannot even imagine, is hardly compatible with that disinterested contemplation of a matter which a purely intellectual desire to probe into its cause would demand.[37]

In this mentality, nothing is what it appears to be to our minds; everything may serve as a symbol of something beyond the world, and in fact does so. Images, names, shadows, dreams—all point to another order of reality, which is to the 'primitive' part of his total order of being, and to which he cannot but react, not as a result of conscious processes, but because he is part of a culture, a collective in which the 'law of participation' obtains. This law consists in the conviction that

---

[36] Lévy-Bruhl, *How Natives Think* (1926), p. 3.
[37] ibid., p. 15.

. . . objects, beings, phenomena can be, though in a way incomprehensible to us, both themselves and something other than themselves. In a fashion which is no less incomprehensible, they give forth and they receive mystic powers, virtues, qualities, influences, which make themselves felt outside, without ceasing to remain where they are.[38]

We have seen that Lévy-Bruhl called this mode of thought 'prelogical' and 'mystical', and although he stressed that he was using neither word in its strict etymological sense—'prelogical' implying not an antecedent stage in the evolution of thought but a type of thought indifferent to logical contradiction; 'mystical' meaning belief in forces and influences imperceptible to the normal senses—he was in this way leaving himself open to a great deal of misunderstanding.

The lack of enthusiasm with which Lévy-Bruhl's theories were received by other anthropologists and comparative religionists (at least outside France) was due only in part to his somewhat erratic terminology. The crux lay in the fact that he was stressing, not the resemblances between primitive and modern thought, but their profound differences—a direct contradiction of, for instance, the Tylorian vision of primitive man as a 'primitive philosopher'. The influence of Comte and of positivism is certainly to be seen here, since on this view the mental processes involved in the various 'stages' of human evolution are more or less mutually exclusive. The scientific stage in particular involves the total abandonment of the mentality of the previous mythological and religious stages. This was not to say that survivals could not occur; on the contrary, they were to be observed to a greater or lesser extent everywhere. But a process of evolution is always, in the history of human thought, viewed from what is taken to be the highest point reached by the process thus far—a rather crude rule to which Lévy-Bruhl was no exception.

There were two latent drawbacks to this procedure. On the one hand it could lead to the assumption that 'civilised' man is always 'logical'; and on the other, it might suggest that 'primitive' man is never other than 'prelogical' and 'mystical'. Lévy-Bruhl held to neither position : his view was simply that primitive cultures exhibit a *greater* dependence on the law of participation than do civilised societies. The primitive, in other words, can be logical when 'collective representations' are not involved in his thinking; the civilised European can be prelogical when they are. Again it must be stressed

[38] ibid., p. 61.

that Lévy-Bruhl was judging civilised society from the vantage-point of the Sorbonne, and civilised thought from the angle of the Chair of Modern Philosophy. Needless to say, this was not representative of the entirety of Western civilisation! Also he was judging primitive cultures from the same eminence.[39] The contrast appeared to be vast; but it was soon pointed out that examples of primitive mentality are to be found everywhere, among the peasantry, and among apparently civilised peoples. In time, anthropologists were to point out equally strongly that primitive peoples are in no wise strangers to logical thought. And so, as Evans-Pritchard puts it,

. . . When Lévy-Bruhl contrasts us with primitives, who are we, and who are the primitives? He does not distinguish between the different sorts of us, the different social and occupational strata of our society, more pronounced fifty years ago than today. In his sense of the word, did the philosophers of the Sorbonne, and the Breton peasantry, or the fishermen of Normandy, have the same mentality? And, since the modern European developed from barbarism, from a type of society characterised by primitive mentality, how and why did our ancestors pass from the one to the other?[40]

Examples of 'primitive mentality' can be discovered without much trouble at any level of human thought—not least in religion—by any observer. It is a matter of common observation that there are vast areas of religion which are controlled, not by the independent exercise of logic and reason, but by the transmission of inherited traditions, presuppositions, attitudes and beliefs. These may be capable of rational motivation, but in many cases they are not, since they exist alongside, or interwoven with, elements of rationality. It is perhaps not out of the question to call these 'collective representations'; but they might also be called stereotypes or unconscious presuppositions. At all events, their nature seems to correspond to what Lévy-Bruhl would have ascribed to the primitive mentality, though they have, strictly speaking, nothing whatever to do with 'primitivity' in any evolutionary sense. To this extent, Lévy-Bruhl is claiming to do one thing, and achieving another : claiming to distinguish between levels of developing or evolving culture, and in reality describing what appears to be a universal characteristic

[39] This identical point was made by Murray, *Personal Experience and the Historic Faith* (1939), p. 290.

[40] Evans-Pritchard, *Theories of Primitive Religion*, p. 87. See also Allier, *Le Psychologie de la conversion chez les peuples non-civilisés* (1925), *Les Non-civilisés et nous* (1935), *Magie et religion* (1935). cf. Webb, *Group Theories of Religion and the Individual* (1916).

of the human mind at all times and in all places. Symbolism is the element in which these stereotypes and presuppositions move; nothing is quite what it seems, and anything can suggest an infinite range of associations and interpretations having little or nothing to do with scientific causality—though symbolism involves a causality of its own.

So although Lévy-Bruhl's theories are commonly taken to centre, to quote one recent commentator, on

> the theory of a special kind of 'primitive mentality', replete with strange magical associations and random imagistic concepts and utterly devoid of anything we should recognise as reason or logic,[41]

—it can, I think, be shown that this kind of judgement totters on the edge of a very serious misrepresentation. It is not a matter of 'strange magical associations' and 'random imagistic concepts' (which are in any case extraordinarily vague collections of words, for which we have no need to blame Lévy-Bruhl). At worst it is a matter of semantic obscurity within the framework of a too-rigid Comtean theory of development which vitiates Lévy-Bruhl's argument.

Among more recent commentators, it is Gerardus van der Leeuw who has seen the worth of Lévy-Bruhl's analysis most clearly. 'Primitivity', he maintains, is to be found everywhere; it is not a difference between two men, but a difference within men, which is involved. Alongside the civilised qualities there are the qualities of intuition and instinct, and between the two there may be a deep discord. He suggests that in this discord it may well be that the mind of Western man has taken a disastrous turn somewhere along the road : that 'logical thought', so far from being a norm by which all else is to be judged, may possibly itself be an aberration or a deviation from intuitive values and standards.

---

[41] Kirk, *Myth : its Meaning and Functions in Ancient and Other Cultures* (1970), p. 246.

IX

Religion and the Unconscious

It will be remembered that at an earlier stage of this study we considered the contribution made to the comparative study of religion by the earliest 'psychologists of religion', Starbuck, Leuba, William James, J. B. Pratt and others. Their main characteristic was their belief that in matters of religion, the believer must whenever possible be permitted to speak for himself; religion, in other words, rests in the *conscious* mind, and can be produced for examination by a straightforward effort of will. All the psychologist needs to do in order to acquire the material on which to base his studies is to learn to ask the right questions. A further general characteristic of this first group of psychologists of religion was their understanding of, and sympathy for, the data of religion, particularly as concentrated in the individual's 'religious experience' (a term which gained in strength and popularity partly due to their efforts).

Not surprisingly, in view of this emphasis on experience, one of the most tangible results of this first wave of scholarly effort had been a series of studies of the virtuosi of the spiritual life, the 'mystics'.[1] Here, too, scholarship had taken with the utmost seriousness what the mystics had had to say about their own experiences—visions, trances, auditions and the rest. The movement had begun by concentrating very largely on Christian data; but material was shortly brought in from other religious traditions, and particularly from the Hindu and Buddhist traditions, to support conclusions which became more and more far-reaching. We may recall, however, that since the study of religion was not then—around and shortly after the turn of the century—as compartmentalised as it was later to become, 'psychological' presuppositions, data and methods were used almost universally by scholars involved in the interpretation of religion. Thus the findings of the psychologists could be, and were, made use of by anthropologists, theologians, sociologists and historians alike. Tylor, Marett, Lévy-Bruhl, Wundt, Söderblom, Otto, and many others were all to some extent psychologists of religion in the 'old' sense, in that they were all concerned to elucidate the role of religion in the heart and mind of the individual believer, and to ask him more or less direct questions, inviting

[1] See above, pp. 116-18.

him to speak for himself on those matters which concerned him most intimately. Probably it would be true to say that for the first three decades of the new century, no student of comparative religion was able entirely too ignore this approach.

But was it psychology? At least one school of psychologists (and it goes without saying that psychology has been no more free from sectarianism than have other scholarly pursuits) maintained that it was not. Psychology was first of all a branch of medical science, resting on a more or less exact knowledge of the workings of the human brain and nervous system, and the behaviourists among the professional psychologists were rather liable to maintain this to be the be-all and end-all of the subject. Psychology could so easily be interpreted on these premises as a subtle and refined form of human engineering, concerned only with the functioning of these parts of the human anatomy. From this angle, the psychology of religion seemed a complicated and abstruse waste of time, and the psychologists of religion dabblers who had never taken the trouble even to learn elementary anatomy and physiology. Starbuck and James encountered this criticism from their Harvard colleagues; and the subsequent history of 'pure' psychology has been in large measure the story of a progressive alienation from even an interest in the religious data.

A second problem was contained in the early psychologists' insistence on dealing with their data almost entirely on an individual basis. The rise of sociology as an independent discipline meant, among other things, that the integrity of the individual's experience, whether of religion or any other serious matter, was called seriously in question. At all events, the structure and function of religion in the life of the nation, caste, tribe or family could not, it seemed, be investigated by means of a simple questionnaire. Actually, few of the sociologists proved capable of dealing satisfactorily with the inwardness, as opposed to the outward machinery, of religion; but that is another story.

Most serious of all was, however, the assumption of the early psychologists of religion that ultimate understanding of the nature and meaning of religion was to be reached by a process of examination of the overt contents of the individual's conscious mind. Shortly after the turn of the century, it was beginning to be asked whether this was really so : whether, in fact, the conscious mind was even the most important part of man's mental equipment. By the late 1920s, after almost three decades of persistent and serious questioning in this area, the writer of a popular handbook of psychology was able to describe the conflict in these drastic terms :

We have a body of newer psychologists who are out on the war-path against the very foundational principles of their seniors. It is not, of course, a matter of age, but of point of view, and these belligerent new psychologists are not in the least doubt about what they believe and what they deny. They know exactly what they want and are quite clear about the way they propose to attain it. There is a lion in their path; they want that lion killed and decently buried. This lion is Consciousness, and they have the grave all nicely arranged for him.[2]

Now this is certainly not the place to enter into a detailed description of the war against 'Consciousness' to which Sir John Adams is here alluding. Some of its features will in any case emerge in what follows. It will be enough to point to the names of Sigmund Freud and Carl Gustav Jung, and to recall that both were physicians, seeking to cure mental illness (and of course in many cases its physical consequences) in the atmosphere of the consulting room. Both concluded that consciousness was merely as it were the tip of a mental iceberg, and that beneath the conscious mind there is a subconscious or unconscious mind, commonly inaccessible to direct investigation, but capable of being conjured up by the skilled investigator. A primary—indeed, practically the only—gap in the curtain of consciousness is however to be found in the patient's dreams; and it is with dreams and their interpretation that the work of analysis begins.

Had the work of the psychoanalysts remained a medical technique it would scarcely have called for comment here. But of course it did not. Both Freud and Jung, and their disciples, beginning at this point, started to theorise in universal terms about the workings of the human mind as such. In that process of theorising, religion played a prominent part; indeed, religious terms, categories and symbols (particularly symbols) came in Jung's work to occupy a position of primary importance. Freud's attitude to religion was, as we shall see, less enthusiastic. Nevertheless the two together, and their followers, made a serious attempt to revolutionise the study (and perhaps also the experience) of religion. They were not altogether successful, as we shall see; but the terms in which the attempt was made demand serious attention.

*   *   *

Three years before the publication of the book which is popularly,

[2] Adams, *Everyman's Psychology* (1929), p. 17.

but mistakenly, supposed to have introduced the category of the irrational into the study of religion in the Western world, Rudolf Otto's *Das Heilige*, there appeared a book with similar pretensions, but with far different terms of reference. This was Sigmund Freud's *Totem and Taboo* (1915). On the surface, this book appeared to be an anthropological study. It was about the age-old problem of the origins of religion, it drew heavily on the work of such well-known men as Robertson Smith, Frazer and Wundt, and it moved in familiar categories. But it was not anthropology, and the anthropologists, almost to a man, dismissed it abruptly as fanciful nonsense.

By the time of its publication, Freud had been fighting for almost twenty years for recognition, in the face of what he took to be the compact and wrong-headed refusal of scholarly and scientific opinion to take him and his work seriously. His story has often been told.[3] It had begun with the conviction that behind mental illness in general there was inevitably to be found the same problem; in his own words, '. . . it was not *any* kind of emotional excitation that was in action behind the phenomena of the neurosis but habitually one of a sexual nature'.[4]

Thus far, despite a certain amount of support, from Switzerland and America mainly, Freud and his theories were still being treated with a certain caution by other practitioners in the field. It was not easy for a professional body brought up on other assumptions to accept, for instance, that everything mental must be regarded as 'in the first instance unconscious', the further quality of consciousness perhaps being present, perhaps not. The idealist philosophers, not surprisingly, had treated Freud and his theories with disdain—to his disappointment, but not his despair, since he was sure that this was no more than an 'idiosyncrasy' on their part, which 'could only be disregarded with a shrug'.[5] Subsequently, of course, the picture altered radically. 'Psychoanalysis' and 'depth-psychology' flourished in the desperate mental atmosphere of the inter-war years, and Freud and his followers (as well as representatives of other psycho-analytical sects) came to be treated in some quarters at least with emotional and uncritical adulation. Psychoanalysis, in a word, became fashionable, and Freud himself came to be regarded as an oracle, a twentieth-century shaman with compelling power over the spirits.

[3] Jones, *The Life and Work of Sigmund Freud* I-III (1953–5), Nelson (ed.) *Freud and the 20th Century* (1958), Sundén, *Religionen och rollerna* (2nd ed. 1960), pp. 267ff.
[4] Freud, *An Autobiographical Study* (1935), p. 41.
[5] ibid., p. 56.

Totem and Taboo was Freud's first book on the problem of religion; later there came other books and essays, notably *The Future of an Illusion* and *Moses and Monotheism*. But it was *Totem and Taboo* which first brought Freud's views on the subject before the public, and since it has later become, in Eliade's words, 'one of the minor gospels of three generations of the Western intelligentsia',[6] it is clearly worthy of attention.

We have seen at an earlier stage in this study that the evolutionary anthropologists often drew parallels between 'primitive' peoples and children, and often attempted to explain the behaviour of the former by means of a simple reference to the latter. Freud's starting-point in *Totem and Taboo* is methodologically similar, and yet different, in that he draws his parallel between the primitive man and the modern neurotic. Both, he maintains, exhibit forms of compulsive behaviour, and hence the parallel is justified. Thus it is possible to examine the origins of religion in precisely the same way as the psychiatrist examines the origins of a neurosis; and since all neuroses, in Freud's view, have their origin in repressed childhood experiences, entirely of a sexual nature, the origins of that strange form of compulsive behaviour called religion must be bound up with some repressed experience in the childhood of the human race. The chief of these experiences was, in Freud's view, that to which he gave the name of 'Oedipus complex'—repressed sexual desire of the mother on the part of a male child, and of the father in the case of the female child, with consequent rivalry and jealousy of the other parent's sexual rights and privileges. This mental pattern Freud set out, with the help of a number of entirely innocent anthropologists, to demonstrate as having been created in the childhood of the human race, and as having given birth to religion in consequence.

Totem and Taboo contains four essays. In the first Freud deals with '. . . the savage's dread of incest', which he calls '. . . a subtle infantile trait and . . . in striking agreement with the psychic life of the neurotic'.[7] The second essay considers the well-known ambivalence of the concept of *taboo* (*tabu*), as it is applied on the one hand to that which is held in the highest reverence, and on the other to that which is shunned as unclean. *Taboo* Freud explains as being any forbidden action for which there exists a strong inclination in the unconscious. The injunction 'Thou shalt not' excites in primitive man the response 'I want to, but I daren't'. The taboo on kings is

6 Eliade, 'Cultural Fashions and the History of Religions', in Kitagawa (ed.), *The History of Religions* (1967), p. 25.

7 Brill (ed.), *The Basic Writings of Sigmund Freud* (1938), p. 819.

therefore caused by everyman's wish to be a king. The taboo on the dead is connected with everyman's guilt at the possibility of his having brought about that death. Dangerous ghosts and demons are 'mere projections of hostile feelings which the survivor entertains toward the dead'. And human conscience, being 'the inner perception of objections to definite wish impulses that exist in us', is also a fruitful cause of taboos, since

> Taboo is a command of conscience, the violation of which causes a terrible sense of guilt which is as self-evident as its knowledge is unknown.[8]

The third essay, on 'Animism, Magic and the Omnipotence of Thought', sets forth a theory which Freud seems to have believed to be close to Marett's 'animatism' theory, viz., that man's early life is controlled by impersonal forces, born of his (usually repressed) wishes. But it is in the celebrated fourth essay, 'The Infantile Recurrence of Totemism', that Freud's fantasy takes wing.

Interestingly enough, Freud begins by disclaiming too wide validity for his theories, and acknowledges how difficult it is for the amateur to know when he is dealing justly with the anthropological material.[9] This is admirable. But he then goes on to throw all caution to the winds and create one of the wildest and most bizarre constructions in the history of modern thought. The bricks out of which it was built were respectable enough, however : the totemic studies of Frazer and Robertson Smith, and a vague hint in Darwin that mankind originally lived like the higher apes, in 'hordes' under the control of a 'father', a dominant male with unlimited sexual control over all the horde's females. This 'father' refused to allow any of his sons to approach any of the females, producing, in Freud's version, the following story :

> One day the expelled brothers joined forces, slew and ate the father, and thus put an end to the father horde. Together they dared and accomplished what would have remained impossible for them singly. Perhaps some advance in culture, like the use of a weapon, had given them the feeling of superiority. Of course these cannibalistic savages ate their victim. This violent primal father had surely been the envied and feared model for each of the brothers. Now they accomplished their identification with him by devouring him and each acquired a part of his strength. The

---

[8] ibid., p. 860.
[9] ibid., p. 884 : 'The reader need not fear that psychoanalysis . . . will be tempted to derive anything so complicated as religion from a single source.'

totem feast, which is perhaps mankind's first celebration [this element from Robertson Smith] would be the repetition and commemoration of this remarkable, criminal act with which so many things began, social organisation, moral restrictions and religion.[10]

Overcome by feelings of remorse for what they had done, the cannibal brothers transmuted their deed into a prohibition, and their dead father into a god; this had the effect of bringing about a reconciliation with the father :

> The totem religion had issued from the sense of guilt of the sons as an attempt to palliate this feeling and to conciliate the injured father through subsequent obedience. All later religions prove to be attempts to solve the same problem, varying only with the stage of culture in which they are attempted and according to the paths which they take; they are all, however, reactions aiming at the same great event with which culture began and which ever since has not let mankind come to rest.[11]

And Freud concludes 'that the beginnings of religion, ethics, society and art meet in the Oedipus complex', in a drama once played out on the stage of history. 'In the beginning was the deed'.[12]

Now what is the student of comparative religion to make of this primordial horror-story? It clearly deals with matters that concern him; it quotes authorities which he is accustomed to use—Frazer, Lang, Marett, Robertson Smith, Wundt; it breathes calm authority. And yet if he has any background knowledge or any sense of historical probabilities, to read *Totem and Taboo* is like entering a fairground hall of distorting mirrors. Everything is there, and yet everything is out of shape and out of proportion. The Swedish psychologist of religion and Islamicist Tor Andrae expressed the feelings of very many students of comparative religion confronted by Freud when he wrote :

> One . . . feels a little uncertain to what extent this ingenious author really wishes to be taken seriously. In this extraordinary manner of interpreting the data of the history of religion is one to see a pure naïvety, a complete lack of a sense of realism, or a deliberate playing about with facts purely for the sake of satisfying an unquenchable, creative desire to tell fables? Every single

[10] ibid., p. 915f.
[11] ibid., p. 918.
[12] ibid., p. 930.

ethnographical and religio-historical presupposition on which
Freud builds, is false . . .[13]

It seems undeniable that Freud *believed* he was interpreting
history, and that the value of religion lies only in the historical truth
which it expresses. But Andrae was right: *Totem and Taboo* expresses no historical truth whatsoever. There were no primal hordes;
even the higher apes do not live as Freud supposed them to live;
primitive men were not cannibals; most primitives have not passed
through a 'totemistic stage' of development. One may well wonder,
if one brick after another is removed from the house that Freud
built, what can remain of the edifice?

A similar contempt for history masquerading as history is seen in
his later book *Moses and Monotheism*, in which Moses is 'proved'
to have been an Egyptian, the spiritual heir of Akhenaten, murdered
by the ungrateful Israelites and subsequently elevated to the status
of a divinely-inspired lawgiver. Historically, this tortured theory is
sheer rubbish, and quite unworthy of serious consideration.

However, this is not to say that we must simply dismiss Freud as
being of no account. Certainly the historian of religion turns to his
theories, if at all, only for light relief. But two major facts remain
nevertheless. The first, and the more important, is that Freud
seriously located the religious impulse below the level of the conscious mind. We may or may not wish to speak of the Oedipus
complex in this connection; but we shall probably never again rely
to any great extent on the questionnaire method in the study of
religion. And secondly, there remains the undeniable impact made
by this neurotic, egocentric, intolerant, imaginative scientist on the
twentieth-century mind. Why, in a word, did anyone ever believe
him? On this question, I side with Mircea Eliade, who relates the
impact of *Totem and Taboo* to the psychology of the inter-war years
in the West.

Of course [he writes] the genius of Freud and the merits of psychoanalysis ought not to be judged by the horror-stories presented as
objective historical fact in *Totem and Taboo*. But it is highly
significant that such frantic hypotheses could be acclaimed as

[13] Andrae, *Mystikens psykologi* (1926), p. 513. cf. Malinowski, *Sex and
Repression in Savage Society* (1927), pp. 135ff. On p. 164f., Malinowski
writes: 'Freud in fact burdens his Cyclopean family with a number of tendencies, habits and mental attitudes which would constitute a lethal endowment for any animal species. . . It is easy to perceive that the primeval horde
has been equipped with all the bias, maladjustments and ill-tempers of a
middle-class European family, and then let loose in a prehistoric jungle to
run riot in a most attractive but fantastic hypothesis.'

sound scientific theory in spite of all the criticisms marshaled by the major anthropologists of the century. Because psychoanalysis won the battle against the older psychologies, and for many other reasons, it became a cultural fashion, and after 1920 the Freudian ideology was rather taken for granted in its entirety. A fascinating book could be written about the significance of the incredible success of this *roman noir frénétique*, *Totem and Taboo*. Using the very tools and methods of modern psychoanalysis, we can lay open some tragic secrets of the modern Western intellectual : for example, his profound dissatisfaction with the worn-out forms of historical Christianity and his desire violently to rid himself of his forefathers' faith, accompanied by a strange sense of guilt, as if he himself had killed a God in whom he could not believe but whose absence he could not bear.[14]

It must be recorded, finally, that apart from this initial impetus, the Freudian approach made sympathetic and accurate study of the phenomena of religion impossible. For a more fruitful approach, we must turn to Freud's *quondam* colleague Jung.

*   *   *

Ever since the earliest days of comparative religion, the general tendency among scholars was to stand well back from the material under review, ostensibly the better to view it in all its variety. The scholar's ideal commitment was to scientific objectivity, to consistent method and to cool appraisal of religion as an element in the lives of other people. Too close attachment to any particular religious tradition tended to be frowned upon as an inevitable source of distortion. Images, myths, symbols, rituals and the other 'observables' of religion were of course important as keys to understanding and as elements in the gigantic human jigsaw puzzle which scholarship was trying to piece together; but they were seldom regarded as living options, in which the observer himself might have some share.

This perhaps may serve in part to explain the vague suspicion with which many historians of religion have looked upon the work of Carl Gustav Jung (1875-1961).[15] As a psychiatrist, he was not

14 Eliade, op. cit., p. 25.
15 Works on Jung which are of significance for the comparative study of religion include Campbell (ed.), *The Portable Jung* (1971), which contains an introduction and a good selection of his writings; Sundén, *Religionen och rollerna* (2nd ed. 1960), pp. 304ff.; Fordham, *An Introduction to Jung's Psychology* (1956); Jaffé, *From the Life and Work of C. G. Jung* (Eng. tr. 1971); and Jung's own autobiography (edited by Jaffé), *Memories, Dreams, Reflections* (Eng. tr. 1961).

part of the appropriate scholarly profession, and it was always easy to dismiss him as an enthusiast or a dilettante, despite his obvious breadth of interest and remarkable competence. His general lack of a consistent system prompted the criticism that he had failed to digest in his own mind the material he poured out, year after year, in the attempt to interpret the innermost structures of the human mind. This, incidentally, is fully recognised by such a partisan interpreter as his former secretary Aniela Jaffé, who writes that his characteristic method '. . . did not mean following a straight line or some infrangible law of action, nor did he favor it. On the contrary, Jung was highly inconsistent and well aware of this fact.' But he believed, she maintains, that inconsistencies '. . . reflect psychic truth better than straightforward thinking.'[16] His terminology was sometimes confusing, and his presuppositions were hard for the philologist or the historian to disentangle. His theories were not 'objective' in the accepted sense (hence the historian's nervousness); but attempting as they do to penetrate the depths of the human mind and to interpret its workings, they fall in line with the earlier concerns of comparative religion—though with one important difference. Whereas for the early comparative religionists, religion was largely a phenomenon located in the past, a stage of human development which mankind had for the most part left behind, for Jung and his followers religion was, and is, located firmly in the present. To be sure, religion has a history; but that history serves to illuminate the present, not to act as a dark backdrop to modern illusions of progress. Myths and symbols for Jung were not mere curiosities, but keys to a vital understanding of mankind.

There is of course a world of difference between Freud's impatient dismissal of religion, and his fears of 'the black tide of mud'—of 'occultism', and Jung's generous and sympathetic attempt to understand the mystery.[17] Both, however, were motivated originally by the same professional concern for the physical and mental well-being of their patients. Jung became assistant at the Burghölzli Mental Hospital, Zürich, in 1900 at the age of twenty-five. By this same year he had read Freud's *The Interpretation of Dreams*, but was not convinced by Freud's thesis that neurosis is always rooted in sexual trauma. The two met in 1907, travelled to the United States, on the invitation of G. Stanley Hall, in the following year, and worked together for four more years, after which came Jung's

---

[16] Jaffé, *From the Life and Work of C. G. Jung*, p. 111.

[17] Jung's view of the relationship in *Memories*, pp. 146ff. 'I see him [Freud] as a tragic figure; for he was a great man, and what is more, a man in the grip of his daimon' (p. 153).

declaration of independence and his break with Freud. This story, and that of Jung's subsequent career, is well enough known, and we have no reason to retell it here. But some of the steps by which Jung's interest in religious symbolism and mythology developed may be borne in mind nevertheless.[18]

After his visit to the United States, in about 1909, Jung became interested in mythology. He read Creuzer's *Symbolik*, and from there branched out, in his customary grand style, in all directions. He later wrote that 'it was as if I were in an imaginary madhouse and were beginning to treat and analyse all the centaurs, nymphs, gods and goddesses in Creuzer's book as though they were my patients.'[19] From this point he developed many separate areas of study, though all were bound together by his desire to penetrate beneath the surface of the conscious mind to the regions below. He was, for instance, struck by the remarkable resemblances between the dream-categories of some of his patients and those of classical mythology, and came along these lines to speak of a 'collective unconscious' on which consciousness is superimposed, and which it is (ideally) designed to modify and control. It was the search for a fuller and more adequate understanding of the collective unconscious that led him to the study of the once officially disreputable world of Gnosticism, and subsequently to a study of its mediaeval equivalent, alchemy.[20] The alchemists talked in symbols, which Jung felt compelled to try to decipher.

> I had very soon seen that analytical psychology coincided in a most curious way with alchemy. The experiences of the alchemists were, in a sense, my experiences, and their world was my world. This was, of course, a momentous discovery : I had stumbled upon the historical counterpart of my psychology of the unconscious. The possibility of a comparison with alchemy, and the uninterrupted intellectual chain back to Gnosticism, gave substance to my psychology.[21]

Henceforth, for Jung alchemy came to be a necessary complement and compensation for the world of consciousness; in a sense, it was a historical prototype, replete with significant imagery, of the dream.

Thus in Jung's theory, the conscious and unconscious minds exist in a complementary relationship, and mental health consists in the maintenance of a balance between the two. The balance is, however, not a partnership. Rather it is a matter of the recognition, acknow-

18 *Memories*, passim; Fordham, op. cit., pp. 69ff.
19 *Memories*, p. 162.
20 On Jung's alchemical studies, see Jaffé, op. cit., pp. 46ff.
21 *Memories*, p. 205.

ledgment and control of the unconscious by the conscious. Without such a recognition, the unconscious is forever liable to burst into consciousness in unpredictable and uncontrollable ways. The process of recognition and acceptance Jung called 'individuation', '. . . the process by which a person becomes a psychological "in-dividual", that is, a separate, indivisible unity or "whole" ', the process of 'coming to selfhood'.[21a]

But by the nature of things, this conflict can express itself only in an obscure and enigmatic fashion, through an elaborate symbolism, traces of which Jung found scattered throughout human *Geistes-geschichte*. As well as the accepted images of light and darkness, East and West, *yin* and *yang*, Jung himself devised new images. Space precludes, however, more than a mention of the most important of these (not least in view of past intellectual history), the *animus* and the *anima*. In brief, *animus* and *anima* are the unconscious in woman and man respectively; both are deceptive as they stand; but they transmit images from the unconscious to the conscious mind, and when controlled, are indispensable for human individuation. When uncontrolled,

> . . . the insinuations of the anima, the mouthpiece of the unconscious, can utterly destroy a man. In the final analysis the decisive factor is always consciousness, which can understand the manifestations of the unconscious and take up a position toward them.[22]

It is also worth noting in this connection that Jung, despite his desire to incorporate the insights of Eastern cultures into his understanding of the situation of Western man, had serious misgivings about any attempt simply to imitate the East. Schematically, one might say that the 'wisdom of the East' (the unconscious) must be totally assimilated into and controlled by the mind of the West (the conscious); this is thus another aspect of the process of individuation.[23]

[21a] ibid., p. 395f.

[22] ibid., p. 187. There may be a point of comparison here with Otto's category of 'the numinous'. Although ostensibly a non-rational category, it has to be consciously understood, and placed under the microscope of the conscious intellect. There is no abandonment to irrationality in either case. cf. above, pp. 161-7.

[23] Wilhelm and Jung, *The Secret of the Golden Flower* (1962), p. 128: 'Denial of our own historical premises would be sheer folly and would be the best way to bring about another deracination. Only by standing firmly on our own soil can we assimilate the spirit of the East.' And on p. 144: 'Unfortunately, the spiritual beggars of our time are too inclined to accept the alms of the East in specie, that is, to appropriate unthinkingly the spiritual possessions of the East and to imitate its way blindly. That is the danger about which it is impossible to give too many warnings.'

By about 1920, Jung had conducted cautious experiments with the oracle system of the Chinese Taoist classic the *I Ching* (The book of changes). It was at this time he met the German missionary and Sinologist Richard Wilhelm, who had published an edition of this book, and found in him an intellectual ally. 'He had the gift,' wrote Jung later, 'of being able to listen without bias to the revelations of a foreign mentality, and to accomplish that miracle of empathy which enabled him to make the intellectual treasures of China accessible to Europe.'[24] Subsequently Jung and Wilhelm collaborated in the production of a version, with commentary, of a Chinese alchemical text, *Das Geheimnis der goldenen Blüte* (The secret of the golden flower, 1930). It was, incidentally, this collaboration which initiated Jung's later passion for alchemy, and the book itself and its contents have since been described as one of the cornerstones of the Jungian edifice. Later collaborations were with the Indologist Heinrich Zimmer (1890-1943) and the classicist Károly Kerényi (1897-1973). Out of this latter friendship emerged one of the most widely read statements of the mature Jungian position, *Einführung in das Wesen der Mythologie* (1941; Eng. tr. *Introduction to a Science of Mythology*, 1951).

Each of these areas produced an 'archetype'—a symbol of the unity of conscious and unconscious and a link between the individual and the cosmos of which he is part. Each is in effect a symbol of the self. From China came the symbol of the golden flower; from classical culture the symbol of the child; and from India the symbol of the *mandala*. A few brief words about the last of these may not be out of place here.

A *mandala* (or *yantra*) is a geometrical pattern found particularly in the Hindu and Buddhist traditions, made up of a combination of circles, squares and triangles arranged symmetrically around a central axis, and symbolising the universe, both macrocosmic (*Brahman*) and microcosmic (*ātman*) and its elements. Jung gives many examples of such patterns occurring spontaneously in the dreams and visions of his patients; usually they are not understood by them, but their manifestation is often, he maintains, accompanied by feelings of peace and harmony. The symbolism involved may be complex or relatively simple, but Jung interpreted it always as a striving after individuation and inward purpose.[25]

Important as these symbols are, it is in the world of myth that Jungian psychology and comparative religion approach each other most closely, though again with the difference that whereas the

[24] *Memories*, p. 375.
[25] Fordham, *An Introduction to Jung's Psychology* (1956), pp. 65ff.

typical comparative religion question has been about the role of myth in man's past history, Jung inquires into the role of myth in man's contemporary life. Myth, being the natural and indispensable intermediate stage between unconscious and conscious cognition, brings the great images and symbols, and the archetypes, into the realm of the conscious by verbalising them. (In dreams, on the other hand, they are less verbalised than acted out.) The archetypes are part of the stuff of dream and myth—great and powerful symbols emerging from the depths of the collective unconscious, and which are able to some extent to lead the individual out of time into timelessness. As Mircea Eliade has said :

> The world of the archetypes of Jung is like the Platonic world of Ideas, in that archetypes are impersonal and do not participate in the historical Time of the individual life, but in the Time of the species—even of organic Life itself.[26]

The archetypes, then, are patterns or symbols which belong to the collective unconscious, but which can cause further symbols or images to appear before the conscious mind. They are also productive, as we have said, of dreams and myths. Jung sums up :

> In the dreams, as in the products of psychoses, there are numbers of combinations to which one can find parallels only in mythological associations of ideas . . . Had thorough investigation shown that in the majority of such cases it was simply a matter of forgotten knowledge, the physician would not have gone to the trouble of making extensive researches into individual parallels . . . [But since such foreknowledge is often ruled out, it was necessary to assume] . . . that we must be dealing with 'autochthonous' revivals independent of all tradition, and, consequently, that 'myth-forming' structural elements must be present in the unconscious psyche . . . Myths are original revelations of the preconscious psyche, involuntary statements about unconscious psychic happenings . . . A tribe's mythology is its living religion, whose loss is always and everywhere, even among the civilised, a moral catastrophe. But religion is a vital link with psychic processes independent of and beyond consciousness, in the dark hinterland of the psyche.[27]

Scholarly reaction to the Jungian position has been very varied.

[26] Eliade, *Myths, Dreams and Mysteries* (1968), p. 54.
[27] Jung and Kerényi, *Introduction to a Science of Mythology* (1951), pp. 99, 101f.

Philologists and 'pure' historians have held themselves almost entirely aloof from his work, accusing him of 'Gnostic speculation' or worse. Sociologists have regarded his concerns as peripheral, though often they would have profited from closer knowledge of them. But whoever has experienced either the religious *Anlage* in any of its aspects, or the disintegration of personal integrity and even of personality itself that has resulted from the pressures of modern civilisation, cannot but meet at least the broad outline of Jung's theories with a sense of recognition. The scholar who is in search of a genuine inward understanding of religion will, it seems to me, always be more of a 'Jungian' than his *soi-disant* objective colleague is ever likely to be. And this is likely to hold good even though he recognises Jung's limitations in some of the scholarly areas in which he moves so freely. Jung was not, could not be, a specialist in every area into which he penetrated. But why do specialists write books if not to instruct those less gifted than themselves, and to open the way to wider appreciations than those which they themselves are prepared to undertake?

At the same time it must be granted that Jungian theory can, and does, exercise a fatal fascination for the crackpot and the dilettante. However, *abusus non tollit usum*, and a look at those scholars who have come to a greater or lesser extent under Jungian influence far outweighs the more dubious associations. We may agree, finally, with Jan de Vries, that 'what matters is that Jung's reasoning gives a greater significance to the unconscious and considers religion an affair of supreme importance. Religion is no longer regarded as a neurosis but rather as an age-old mysterious experience of life and work expressed in undying symbols.'[28] And for that recognition we cannot but be grateful.

* * *

It is possible that one reason for the hesitation felt by many professional scholars in the field of comparative religion in the face of the Jungian vision (or as some held, aberration) was due to the fact that in this area Jung himself appeared to be an amateur. He had in fact read and absorbed more than many professionals; but he did not hold a teaching post in the subject—and for many years, a few exceptions notwithstanding, the only road to academic recognition passed through the great European and American universities.

This reflection is prompted by the circumstance that we now have to consider one important exception to this rule—the one significant extra-professional forum of comparative religious study this century,

[28] De Vries, *The Study of Religion* (Eng. tr. 1967), p. 146.

H

the series of 'Eranos Conferences', held in Switzerland since 1933. These find their present place in our record mainly because they were virtually taken over by Jung and his followers, and became an important Jungian forum. But they were not conceived with this purpose in mind. They started in fact as the brainchild of a lonely and remarkable woman.[29]

Just after the First World War, at the time when depth-psychology was becoming a new obsession of the modern mind, a certain Frau Olga Froebe-Kapteyn, newly and prematurely widowed, had come to live at Ascona, on the shores of Lake Maggiore. She was both rich and idealistic, and wanted therefore to do something useful with her time and money. It may be coincidental that at this time she was being psychoanalysed. At all events, she had a dream-vision that she should devote her money and property to some useful cause, preferably connected with psychoanalysis. Above all she wanted to do something useful with her house. So she had a conference centre built on her land, the intention being that it should serve as a centre of research and fellowship. But for whom?

In the summer of 1933 she sent out invitations to a number of scholars to come and meet together in her house. Among those who accepted were C. G. Jung, the Indologist Heinrich Zimmer and the disciple of Söderblom, Friedrich Heiler. The following year Martin Buber joined the group, and from this time its name and fortune were made. Originally the conferences had no particular name, but Rudolf Otto later suggested the name *Eranos*—a banquet to which each participant brings his own contribution, elsewhere known as a 'pot-luck supper' or 'Jacob's join'. It was agreed that the goal of the meetings should be to bring the highest possible intellectual capacity and competence to bear on matters of spiritual importance. Of course there were to be no professional or confessional barriers.

The members of the conference took as their first task the establishing of a common ground on which Eastern and Western thought could meet, and it was in this connection that the first significant confrontation with depth-psychology took place, on Jung's initiative. He had spoken at the 1933 conference on the concept of individuation, but subsequently addressed himself first to questions of archetypal symbolism, and later to alchemical symbols. The *Eranos* conferences were not intended to become a Jungian conclave; however, they did in fact come to be dominated by his personality and his theories. This became still clearer after 1938, when the conferences began to deal with archetypal themes.

Eranos as a conference [wrote Ira Progoff] was in no sense committed to the specific constructs in Jung's theory of archetypes, but in a general sense the idea of archetypes had a central position in the conception of human life that projected itself in the Eranos meetings as a whole.[30]

Mircea Eliade has referred appreciatively in many contexts to Jung's seminal influence. He writes, for instance, that

when Jung revealed the existence of the collective unconscious, the exploration of those immemorial treasures, the myths, symbols, and images of archaic humanity, began to resemble the techniques of oceanography and speleology . . . Similarly, archaic modes of psychic life, 'living fossils' buried in the darkness of the unconscious, now became accessible to study, through the techniques developed by depth psychologists.[31]

This was, under Jung's guidance, precisely the aim of *Eranos*—what Progoff calls 'a cumulative movement into the depths'.

So the significance of *Eranos* lies primarily in the fact that the conferences could bring together all manners of expertise for a purpose. That purpose is however not merely the joy of discovery. Jung was a physician and a healer; and the aim of *Eranos* has always been ameliorative. Mankind is a complex human document, if you will; but the document has to be treated gently, since it tears so easily : detachment and objectivity, however well meant, are not enough.

We cannot here devote more space to the *Eranos* conferences, save to note that the annual publication of the year's proceedings in the *Eranos-Jahrbuch* (1933 ff.) has established itself as an outstanding source for the student of comparative religion, more particularly, as far as the English-speaking world is concerned, in the translated volumes of *Papers from the Eranos Yearbooks*, edited by Joseph Campbell (six volumes, 1954-69). And it may finally be worth noting that a list of *Eranos* participants takes on the appearance of a roll of honour of comparative religion, including as it does Martin Buber, Joseph Campbell, Jean Daniélou, Mircea Eliade, Erwin R. Goodenough, Friedrich Heiler, E. O. James, C. G. Jung, Károly Kerényi, Gerardus van der Leeuw, Erich Neumann, Raffaele Pettazzoni, Laurens van der Post, Paul Radin, C. A. F. Rhys Davids, Gershom

---

[30] Progoff, in *Eranos*, p. 15.
[31] Eliade, in *Eranos*, p. 4.

Scholem, D. T. Suzuki, Paul Tillich, Giuseppe Tucci, R. C. Zaehner and Heinrich Zimmer.

* * *

In a survey of this kind it is unfortunately impossible to estimate the contributions of each of these scholars separately, or even to reflect on their various degrees of dependence upon Jungian theory. A few, indeed, can have depended on Jung only slightly; but others we have already named as collaborators (Kerényi, Zimmer). From the remainder we may single out Erich Neumann, particularly on the strength of his monograph *The Great Mother* (1956); the South African novelist and explorer Laurens van der Post, whose many books, among them *Venture to the Interior* (1952) and the remarkable *The Dark Eye in Africa* (1955) present profoundly 'Jungian' themes; Joseph Campbell, and Mircea Eliade.

The American scholar Joseph Campbell (b. 1907) has for many years been the major representative among students of comparative religion of the heritage of Jung. His industry has been remarkable, and he has in fact attempted a total Jungian interpretation of world mythology, particularly in the four volumes of *The Masks of God* (1959-68): *Primitive Mythology, Oriental Mythology, Occidental Mythology* and *Creative Mythology*. In these books Campbell has assembled, rather after the manner of Frazer, material from every corner of the mythological meadow, weaving it all together into a pattern which some feel to be rather too neat, but the cumulative impact of which is undeniable. Although to extract quotations is particularly invidious in this case, we may add just two extracts, to give a taste both of Campbell's profound convictions, and of his style.

Campbell believes that the conditions of the modern world have rendered impossible the divisions and separations—and the partial understandings—of the past. And he writes :

> The four representatives, respectively, of human reason and the responsible individual, supernatural revelation and the one true community under God, yogic arrest in the immanent great void, and spontaneous accord with the way of earth and heaven— Prometheus, Job, the seated Buddha, eyes closed, and the wandering Sage, eyes open—from the four directions, have been brought together. And it is time, now, to regard each in its puerility, as well as in its majesty, quite coldly, with neither indulgence nor disdain.[32]

[32] Campbell, *Oriental Mythology* (1962), p. 33f.

Their coming together has brought about no less than the creation of a world culture and a world consciousness :

> . . . just as in the past each civilisation was the vehicle of its own mythology, developing in character as its myth became progressively interpreted, analysed, and elucidated by its leading minds, so in this modern world—where the application of science to the fields of practical life has now dissolved all cultural horizons, so that no separate civilisation can ever develop again—each individual is the center of a mythology of his own, of which his own intelligible character is the Incarnate God, so to say, whom his empirically questing consciousness is to find.[33]

This is a dangerous quest; but the rewards may be infinite :

> Out beyond those walls, in the uncharted forest night, where the terrible wind of God blows directly on the questing undefended soul, tangled ways may lead to madness. They may also lead, however, as one of the greatest poets of the Middle Ages tells, to 'all those things that go to make heaven and earth'.[34]

*   *   *

Mircea Eliade was born in Romania in 1907. His early studies were in philosophy, and it was as a philosopher that he went to India in 1928, to study under Dasgupta at the University of Calcutta. He spent four years in India, including six months at Rishikesh, learning the theory and practice of yoga. In 1933 he took his Ph.D., with a dissertation on yoga, and worked until 1940 at the University of Bucharest. The war years were spent in diplomatic service in Portugal and Great Britain, and in 1945 he became Visiting Professor at the Sorbonne. In 1957 he became a 'Distinguished Service Professor' at the University of Chicago, in which capacity he still serves.[35]

The publishing history of his books has a complexity all its own. Before the Second World War, he wrote mainly in Romanian, and subsequently mainly in French; most of his best-known works are indeed translations from the French. Of these we may mention *The Myth of the Eternal Return* (1955, subsequently reprinted as *Cosmos and History*, 1959), *Patterns in Comparative Religion* (1958), *Yoga: Immortality and Freedom* (1958), *The Sacred and the Pro-*

[33] id., *Creative Mythology* (1968), p. 36.
[34] ibid., p. 37. It is worth noting that Campbell has also written perceptively on James Joyce.
[35] A bibliography of Eliade's works is included in his *Festschrift (Myths and Symbols)*, pp. 417ff., and a list of works about him on pp. 432f.

fane (1959), *Myths, Dreams and Mysteries* (1960), *Images and Symbols* (1961), *The Forge and the Crucible* (1962), *Shamanism: Archaic Techniques of Ecstasy* (1964), *Mephistopheles and the Androgyne* (also published as *The Two and the One*, 1965), *The Quest* (1969), *Zalmoxis* (1972) and *Australian Religions: an Introduction* (1973). An important *Festschrift*, entitled *Myths and Symbols*, and edited by Joseph M. Kitagawa and Charles H. Long, was published in 1969; this includes, as well as the general essays customary in such volumes, some highly illuminating writing on the subject of Eliade's Romanian past, a subject which the language barrier otherwise makes difficult of access.

Eliade is another scholar who, like Frazer, ranges far and wide over the world of religion. His most specialised works are his studies on yoga, *Yoga: Immortality and Freedom* (1958) and *Patanjali and Yoga* (1969), and his far-reaching study *Shamanism: Archaic Techniques of Ecstasy* (1964); perhaps also the study in which he followed in Jung's footsteps into the obscure area of alchemy, *The Forge and the Crucible* (1962). Yoga and shamanism, however different they may appear, are not two worlds, but one. If the goal of the yogic exercises is the experience of *samādhi*, this is difficult to understand clinically as anything other than ecstatic 'trance'—whatever theological or metaphysical interpretation may subsequently be placed upon it. And similarly, the heart of the shaman's experience and function is a set of instruments and techniques by means of which the shaman (and occasionally others) may also enter into trance-states. In either case it is a matter of entering into a state in which time is annihilated, in which history becomes meaningless, save as *māyā or līlā*, in which eternity and the life of the spirit is as it were present to the individual.

For Eliade, the desire to understand and interpret these 'archaic' techniques was not undertaken merely out of curiosity. Rather it has been part of a personal confrontation with the Western intellectual heritage and its compulsive historicism, and parallels similar attempts made by Jung and Lévi-Strauss.

But again like Jung, he insists on an intellectual interpretation within the context of the Western intellectual tradition. An understanding of the 'archaic' traditions enriches; but one need not therefore oneself become archaic, or for that matter oriental. A commentator has written of him that among Romanian writers, Eliade is

. . . the first to have a direct experience of it [India] while knowing enough not to be dissolved in it. India did not overwhelm his work and his thoughts; it only nourished them. . .[36]

[36] *Myths and Symbols*, p. 345.

With this we may compare Eliade's own statement (one among many), that

> ... Western culture will be in danger of a decline into a sterilising provincialism if it despises or neglects the dialogue with the other cultures. Hermeneutics is Western man's response—the only intelligent response possible—to the solicitations of contemporary history, to the fact that the West is forced (one might also say : condemned) to this encounter and confrontation with the cultural values of 'the others'.[37]

It is certainly hazardous to attempt to find a single key concept in Eliade's work; but throughout his writing there is a depth of concern, almost at times amounting to an obsession, with *time* and *history*.[38] The historicism of the Western mind he appears always to have found intolerable, and in his researches into the values of the archaic mentality he has attempted to enter into a world dominated by the belief in timelessness, a belief resting on the one hand upon the trance-experience of yogin and shaman, and on the other upon those annually or seasonally repeated rituals and festivals by which archaic man has attempted to come to terms with the passage of time. Eliade's uneasy relationship with Western culture, obsessed as it is with ideas of progress, evolution, history and making the most of every moment, must be borne in mind, particularly in connection with his most celebrated theory, that of the 'eternal return'.

We may attempt to outline Eliade's theory as follows : in contrast to Judeo-Christian man, who feels himself to be placed within an ongoing process, to which he can either surrender or not, 'archaic man' localises himself by constantly attempting to return to 'the mythical time at the beginning of things'.[39] The New Year, for instance, is every year 'a resumption of time from the beginning, that is, a repetition of the cosmogony'; at the moment of transition, there is 'a repetition of the mythical moment of the passage from chaos'.[40] In Frazerian fashion, Eliade produces a mass of material in support of his statement; and he goes on :

> Differing in their formulas, all these instruments or regeneration [rituals, sacrifices, etc.] tend toward the same end : to annul past time, to abolish history by a continuous return *in illo tempore*, by the repetition of the cosmogonic act.[41]

[37] Eliade, *Myths, Dreams and Mysteries* (1968), p. 10.
[38] For a criticism of Eliade's theory of the Eternal Return, see Brandon, *History, Time and Deity* (1965), pp. 65ff.
[39] Eliade, *Cosmos and History* (1959), p. xi.
[40] ibid., p. 54.
[41] ibid., p. 81.

In this perspective, for archaic man everything is constantly beginning afresh at every moment, and he is therefore freed from the terror of the passage of time, since time itself is constantly being regenerated.

Within this pattern of constant repetition, a further, Jungian, pattern emerges :

> If all moments and all situations of the cosmos are repeated *ad infinitum*, their evanescence is, in the last analysis, patent; *sub specie infinitatis*, all moments and all situations remain stationary and thus acquire the ontological order of the archetype.[42]

It seems, then, that archaic man *lives* his archetypes, as it were; modern man, on the other hand, has fallen out with his. The results (looking at things now in Jungian perspective) are plain for all to see : empty and self-deluding theories of progress; a refusal, or at least an inability, to come to terms with either the problem or the manifestations of evil; fatuous optimism living alongside self-destructive pessimism, sometimes both nourished by the same image (science fiction being the best example). How, Eliade wonders, can man tolerate the terror of time and history? In part he has done so by interpreting it all—though this is perhaps an illegitimate intellectualism—in terms of archetypal repetitions :

> . . . by virtue of this view, tens of millions of men were able, for century after century, to endure great historical pressures without despairing, without commiting suicide or falling into that spiritual aridity that always brings with it a relativistic or nihilistic view of history.[43]

On the whole, then, 'archaic' and 'modern' man might well enter into some form of dialogue, fruitful to both, though more fruitful to a Western man in search of his lost soul. This is of course the *Eranos* theme. It is clinical depth-psychology writ large, the ultimate justification for the history of religions (or comparative religion) as a new humanism.

> Sooner or later [writes Eliade in another context] our dialogue with the 'others'—the representatives of the traditional, Asiatic, and 'primitive' cultures—must begin to take place not in today's empirical and utilitarian language (which can approach only

[42] ibid., p. 123.
[43] ibid., p. 52.

realities classifiable as social, economic, political, sanitary, etc.) but in a cultural language capable of expressing human realities and spiritual values.[44]

Perhaps it would not be too far-fetched to suggest that Jung gave Eliade at least part of the grammar of that language; the comparative study of religion provides the vocabulary; the syntax, however, is Eliade's own.

* * *

Before leaving the subject of the impact, direct or indirect, of 'depth-psychology' on the comparative study of religion, mention may finally be made of a related trend in anthropology, that of 'structuralism'.[45] I do not propose to attempt in this context to proceed beyond the barest mention of the method : the structuralists have so far shown little interest in religion as such; but they have characteristically paid a great deal of attention to myth, and have thus touched upon a subject long associated with comparative religion.[46]

The structuralist technique, roughly speaking, is to take a myth (or for that matter any other form of human communication) and analyse it in such a way as to reveal the workings of the human mind or minds which have produced the communication in question. Its chief exponent is Claude Lévi-Strauss (b. 1908) of the Collège de France. Like Eliade, he has been influenced by depth-psychology, at least to the extent of accepting fully that the human mind works most characteristically on a subconscious level. The goal of the anthropologist, he has written, is '. . . to grasp, beyond the conscious and always shifting images which men hold, the complete range of unconscious possibilities.'[47] He may begin by investigating the conscious mind of man, but he will gradually move more and more deeply into the dark hinterland of the subconscious, and in so doing will pass from the particular to the universal.

[44] Eliade, in *Eranos*, p. 8.
[45] Sharpe, 'Structural Anthropology', in Cox and Dyson (eds.), *The Twentieth Century Mind* III (1972), pp. 185ff.
[46] Recent works on myth—most of which come in the category of compilations—include Middleton (ed.), *Myth and Cosmos* (1967); Kirk, *Myth : its Meaning and Functions in Ancient and Other Cultures* (1970); Maranda (ed.), *Mythology* (1972), Sebeok (ed.), *Myth : a Symposium* (1972); and Feldman and Richardson (eds.), *The Rise of Modern Mythology* (1972).
[47] Lévi-Strauss, *Structural Anthropology* (1963), p. 23.

If, as we believe to be the case, the unconscious activity of the mind consists in imposing forms upon content, and if these forms are fundamentally the same for all minds—ancient and modern, primitive and civilised (as the study of symbolic function, expressed in language, so strikingly indicates)—it is necessary and sufficient to grasp the unconscious structure underlying each institution and each custom, in order to obtain a principle of interpretation valid for other institutions and other customs, provided of course that the analysis is carried far enough.[48]

Now the intention behind the structural quest and that which we have seen reflected in the work of Jung, Campbell, Eliade and the *Eranos* conferences is similar. There is an underlying criticism of modern Western culture; and there is an attempt to enter into a sympathetic relationship with the members of another, less spoiled, society, perhaps for the purpose of measuring the extent of Western man's loss. The Jungian objective, of course, reaches beyond this to attempt a work of recovery, restoration and reintegration; the structuralist seems for the most part only to wish to understand.

Apart from the work of Lévi-Strauss, the sheer complexity of which has made assimilation difficult, structuralist studies on 'religious' themes include E. R. Leach's *Genesis as Myth and other Essays* (1970), and G. S. Kirk's *Myth: its Meaning and Functions in Ancient and Other Cultures* (1970). So far, however, structuralism has made little overall impression upon comparative religion.[49]

* * *

In this chapter we have attempted to come to terms with the direct and indirect influence of 'depth-psychology' on the study of religion. The indirect influence has been considerable; the direct influence, on the other hand, has been seriously limited by the psychologists' difficulties in establishing their own professional credentials as students of religion, and by their technique of accepting second-hand material, usually unchecked, from a wide variety of sources. Their intentions, though, were highly honourable.

In moving now to a consideration of the phenomenology of religion, we enter a field, and a company of scholars, some of whom owed much to Jung. But whether or not they were prepared to

---

[48] ibid., p. 21.
[49] Leach has in fact been one of Eliade's most outspoken critics, especially in his review article 'Sermons by a Man on a Ladder', in *The New York Review of Books* vii/6 20 October, 1966). For an answer, see Ricketts, 'In Defence of Eliade', in *Religion* 3/1 (1973), pp. 13ff.

acknowledge a debt in this direction, their quest for an understanding of religion was profound, and went far beyond pure historicism. In this sense the phenomenologists were sharers in the *Eranos* banquet.

X

The Phenomenology of Religion

The pressures of the immediate post-war years in Europe and America led in many ways to a more careful and certainly more critical attitude to the materials of comparative religious study than had been usual, or perhaps even possible, in the first period of our study. But they also had the unfortunate effect of widening an already existing breach between scholars of different inclinations and temperaments. On the one side were the specialists—historians, philologists, archaeologists and others—who had little interest in creating a synthesis out of the material at their disposal. On the other were those who considered that the times required some fresh attempt to achieve an integral understanding of the overall nature and essence of religion, making use of the more refined and accurate methods and findings of historical scholarship in so doing. The recently-celebrated hypothesis of the unilinear evolution of religion was now felt, particularly following the trauma of the war years, to be a positive hindrance to the achievement of such an understanding, since it involved the imposition of so many alien value-judgements on the material. Instead, a method was sought which would eliminate such value-judgements, allow the believer to speak clearly for himself, and in this way arrive at an objective assessment of the role of religion in human life. So while the specialists, each in his individual field, continued to work intensively and fruitfully on their texts and editions, and went on producing indispensable monographs on all manner of subjects, a small company of scholars, mainly in Holland and Scandinavia, began to investigate the possibilities of a method already known as *Religionsphänomenologie*, or 'the phenomenology of religion'.

The method, as we shall see, was not new, having been known at least since the 1880s; nor was it in its original form especially remarkable, being little more than a thematic counterpart to the history of religion. But during the inter-war years certain claims came to be made on its behalf. The most significant of these was that it provided a path to the understanding (*Verstehen*) of religion, and to a grasp of its essence (*Wesen*), by means of an as far as possible value-free examination of its manifestations (*Erscheinungen*).

The first real milestone of the discipline in its newer form was

the publication in 1933 of the Dutch scholar Gerardus van der
Leeuw's book *Phänomenologie der Religion* (Eng. tr. *Religion in
Essence and Manifestation*, (1948). Since the appearance of this
book, the term 'the phenomenology of religion' has gradually
acquired a certain vogue, and indeed now occupies in a few quarters
the kind of position once held by the older term 'comparative
religion'. The label is, however, far from explanatory, and simply
to use this form of words without further definition would be
unwise, since even the scholars who use this term, and claim to
apply this method to their work, are not always sure as to its precise
definition. Moreover the general impression seems to have been
conveyed here and there that it means little more than 'the sympathetic study of religion'—an assumption which is not false, but
which is scarcely adequate. In fact a number of separate strands
have been woven together to create this new approach, and we shall
examine a few of these briefly before considering the work of some
of its more outstanding representatives.

*   *   *

We have mentioned the attempts made by scholars of the late
nineteenth century to understand the 'essence' or 'nature' of religion
along genetical lines. Even then, this was not the only possible
approach to this problem, though it was that which proved most
attractive to the 'scientific' mind, dominated as it was by one or
another form of the historical method. An alternative approach
was tested by the philosophers of the late eighteenth and early
nineteenth centuries, notably Hegel. Hegel's ultimate objective
was that of discerning unity behind diversity, of reaching an understanding of the one essence of religion behind its many manifestations. Kant before him had made use of the term 'phenomenon'
(from the Greek *to phainomenon*, that which shows itself) to describe
the data of experience. He had further contrasted phenomena with
'noumena' (things-in-themselves), i.e. objects and events as they
are by virtue of their own nature, independent of what our faculties
and senses make of them. Hegel went further, asserting in his first
major work, *Phänomenologie des Geistes* (The Phenomenology of
the Spirit, 1806) that the mind as it is in itself can be known through
the ways in which it experiences reality. Or, to put it somewhat
differently, essence (*Wesen*) can be approached through a study of
appearances and manifestations (*Erscheinungen*).

Gerardus van der Leeuw has claimed that at this date, the
phenomenology of religion was already in existence, although not
known by that name. Certainly there were scholars who were already

in the late eighteenth century classifying religious phenomena in order to attempt to understand the underlying essence of religion. Van der Leeuw suggests that the phenomenological line should be traced back to President de Brosses and *Le Culte des dieux fétiches* (1760), though this seems a little far-fetched. Elsewhere he cites Christoph Meiners of Göttingen as the first phenomenologist, on the strength of such statements as this :

> Since a series of the histories of all religions is either impracticable or is at least inadvisable, there remains for the historian of religion no other course than to resolve the known religions, especially the polytheistic, into their elements . . . and then observe how each essential factor of the popular religions of ancient times was, or still is, constituted.[1]

Van der Leeuw, then, considers Meiners to be 'the first systematic phenomenologist', not only because he classified various religious phenomena—fetishism, worship of the dead, sacrifice, purifications, fasts, etc.—but because 'his entire attitude . . . is in principle phenomenological', that is, he attempts by this means to discover what is essential in religion. The work of Benjamin Constant is also cited with evident approval.[2]

On such criteria as these, there are other works which might qualify for inclusion in the history of the discipline; but it is now generally agreed that the actual term 'the phenomenology of religion' (*die Phänomenologie der Religion*) was coined by the Dutch scholar P. D. Chantepie de la Saussaye, Professor in the University of Amsterdam, in a book published in 1887 under the title *Lehrbuch de Religionsgeschichte* (Handbook of the History of Religion). But although he introduces the term, he offers no philosophical justification for its use, apart from making the general observation that the task of *Religionswissenschaft* is to investigate both the essence and the empirical, visible manifestations of religion.[3] He does refer back with evident approval to Hegel as the first scholar to have recognised the close link between the conceptual and empirical aspects of religion, and states in a later passage that 'the phenomenology of religion is intimately connected with psychology in so far as it has to do with the facts of human consciousness'.[4] But he nowhere

---

[1] Van der Leeuw, *Religion in Essence and Manifestation* (Eng. tr. 1948), p. 691.
[2] ibid.
[3] Chantepie de la Saussaye, *Lehrbuch der Religionsgeschichte* (1887), p. 6 : 'Die Einheit der Religion in der Vielheit ihrer Formen ist die Voraussetzung der Religionswissenschaft.'
[4] ibid., p. 48.

gives—nor does he intend to give—the impression that he is introducing a new scientific method; all he is doing is to bring together
'groups of religious phenomena' (*Gruppen von religiösen Erscheinungen*)—the object of worship, idolatry, sacred stones, trees and
animals, nature-worship, the worship of men, the gods, magic and
divination, sacrifice and prayer, holy places, times and persons, the
community, scriptures, doctrines, mythology, dogmas and philosophies, ethics and art. Evidently in its earliest form 'the phenomenology of religion' was meant to be no more than a systematic
counterpart to the history of religion, an elementary method of
cross-cultural comparison of the constitutent elements of religious
belief and practice, as opposed to their treatment in cultural isolation
and chronological sequence.[5] In order to distinguish this from later
and more philosophical methods using the same term, we might
call Chantepie's initiative 'descriptive phenomenology'.

Oddly enough, when the second edition of Chantepie's *Lehrbuch*
appeared ten years later, the phenomenological section was missing.
This circumstance, which has caused some puzzlement among later
commentators, can in fact be explained quite simply : faced with
certain difficulties about reconciling the section in question with the
demands of philosophical method, Chantepie had determined to
devote an entire volume to the phenomenology of religion—a
volume which regrettably never saw the light of day. It has also
been suggested with some justification that Chantepie was also in
some difficulty about reaching a satisfactory synthesis of scientific
objectivity and Christian commitment.[6]

* * *

Chantepie was a theologian, and not primarily a philosopher; his
method was largely a method of systematic description. But in the
years around and after the turn of the century the term 'phenomenology' was beginning to be expounded with rather different connota-
tions by the philosopher Edmund Husserl, in his massive *Logische
Untersuchungen* (Logical Investigations, 1900–1) and later in his
Ideen zu einer reinen Phänomenologie (Ideas for a Pure Phenomenology, 1913). Husserl's major claim was that philosophy must divest
itself of all metaphysical presuppositions : it must investigate what
actually confronts it, not allowing any distorting factor to intervene

---

[5] Among recent discussions, see especially Widengren, *Religionsphänomenologie* (1969), pp. 1ff.; Hultkrantz, 'The Phenomenology of Religion :
Aims and Methods', in *Temenos* 6 (1970), pp. 68ff.; and Waardenburg,
'Religion between Reality and Idea', in *Numen* xix/2-3 (1972), pp. 128ff.
[6] Hallencreutz, *Kraemer towards Tambaram* (1966), p. 110.

and prevent it from achieving its goal of direct analysis of essences or general structures.

Husserl's influence, and that of the school he founded, was widespread, but he did not affect greatly the course of the phenomenology of religion, except in the area of general approach.[7] Few historians of religion were willing or able to follow the philosophical phenomenologists into the obscure hinterland of their thought; a partial exception was van der Leeuw, though even in this case it is difficult to be sure of the extent of the Husserlian influence. Nevertheless Husserl did provide future phenomenologists of religion with two important concepts, or principles of understanding : *epoché* and *eidetic vision*.

Epoché is derived from the Greek verb *epechô*, 'I hold back'. In effect it means 'stoppage', suspension of judgement, the exclusion from one's mind of every possible presupposition. It is also called 'bracketing' (*Einklammerung*), whereby (in John Macquarrie's words) 'an object which is present to consciousness is reduced to the pure phenomenon by 'putting in brackets' or excluding from further interest those elements which do not belong to the universal essence'.[8] Its importance in this connection is that it emphasises the need to abstain from every kind of value-judgement, to be 'present' to the phenomenon in question purely as an impartial observer, unconcerned with questions of truth and falsehood.

The term 'eidetic vision' is also derived from a Greek noun, *to eidos*, 'that which is seen', and hence 'form', 'shape' or 'essence'. In phenomenological parlance, eidetic vision is the observer's capacity for seeing the essentials of a situation, or in the case of a phenomenon, its actual essence as opposed to what it has been, might have been, or ought to be. The important thing here is that 'eidetic vision' means—and is meant to mean—a form of subjectivity. It implies, given the acquisition of objective and undistorted data, an intuitive grasp of the essentials of a situation in its wholeness. 'Objective eidetic vision' is quite literally a contradiction in terms—a circumstance which can cause a certain methodological embarrassment.[9]

* * *

[7] Waardenburg, op. cit., pp. 168ff. On Husserl generally see Ricoeur, *Husserl: An Analysis of his Phenomenology* (1967).
[8] Macquarrie, *Twentieth-Century Religious Thought* (1963), p. 219.
[9] This point has been made most forcefully by Oxtoby, in his article 'Religionswissenschaft Revisited', in Neusner (ed.), *Religions in Antiquity* (1968), pp. 590ff.

Some years were to elapse before these principles were seriously applied to the study of religious phenomena. Of more direct and immediate relevance was the wider application of the principles of biblical interpretation, or hermeneutics, to the data of comparative religion. Again the underlying question was that of the interpreter's understanding of the data.

Writing in Hastings' *ERE* in 1914, Ernst von Dobschütz traced the modern discipline of hermeneutics back to Schleiermacher, who created out of the interpretation of Scripture a philosophy of understanding (*Philosophie des Verstehens*), and maintained that :

The interpreter's task is to understand the religious personality of the writer as manifested in every single word, to look from the details to the whole, and from the standpoint of the whole to see the details in their true light.[10]

From this point of view, which has obvious affinities with phenomenology, hermeneutics is

. . . a science built upon a theory of comprehension . . . [which] proposes to explain why a given work is to be understood in one way and not another.[11]

The scholar working in this field, mainly, of course, on written documents, has not completed his task when he reaches what he considers to be an adequate personal understanding of the material under his hand. He must proceed to the task of making the material comprehensible to others : 'The decisive proof of one's having understood is the ability to reproduce with clearness.' In this connection he must learn to compare, to make every possible use of comparable material; the scholar, '. . . in order to grasp the peculiar significance of details, must assign them to their proper place in the whole, and compare them with as many similar facts as possible.'[12]

It is also significant that von Dobschütz should conclude his article by stressing the subjective element in the work of the interpreter, though again only after having emphasised to the full the scholar's need to make the best possible use of all the available material.

Exegesis is an art; and of exegesis, as of all art, it is true that its highest merit consists, not in originality, but in the sureness with which the right thing is seized . . .[13]

10 Von Dobschütz, 'Interpretation,' in *ERE* VII (1914), pp. 392a-b.
11 ibid., p. 392b.
12 ibid., p. 393a.
13 ibid., p. 395b.

It is true that hermeneutics is here being seen as a technique for use within the Judaeo-Christian tradition. But its comparative principles were those already laid down by the *Religionsgeschichtliche Schule*, and once allowed, they might in principle be applied to any body of material from any religious tradition—as many scholars had already begun to discover.

The hermeneutical line in the history of religions was developed particularly by Joachim Wach, first in Germany and later in the United States. We shall return to Wach shortly. But in the meantime, we must follow the tradition of descriptive phenomenology, as carried further by three Scandinavians, the Swede Nathan Söderblom, the Dane Edvard Lehmann and the expatriate Norwegian William Brede Kristensen.

* * *

We have already written at some length about Söderblom,[14] and here we may simply observe that all his work in the field of comparative religion was aimed at deepening a personal understanding of man's will to believe. His personal preference was for a historical approach to the material, rather than for that type of systematic approach connected with descriptive phenomenology, and he retained a generally evolutionary scale of values. But the debt owed by subsequent phenomenologists to Söderblom was incalculable. Friedrich Heiler of Marburg was perhaps his closest disciple,[15] but it was Gerardus van der Leeuw who later wrote that of all scholars, 'the great name of Nathan Söderblom' typified most clearly the phenomenological approach :

> For without his acute insight and his deeply penetrating view of what 'appears', we could not advance another step in our territory; and the change of direction in the history of religion, plainly set forth in the current phenomenological viewpoint, finds its symbol in this thinker's name.[16]

In the same year as the publication of Söderblom's major work of comparative religion, *Gudstrons uppkomst*—1914—there appeared a slim volume by the Danish scholar Edvard Lehmann (1862–1930), who had previously served in Berlin but who was now Professor of the History of Religion in the University of Lund

---

[14] cf. above, pp. 154-61.
[15] cf. above, pp. 167-8.
[16] Van der Leeuw, op. cit., p. 694.

in Sweden. The book was called simply *Religionsvetenskapen* (*The Science of Religion*). The third part of the book, based on an earlier article in the *RGG* (2nd ed.), he called *Den synliga religionen: religionens fenomenologi* (Visible religion : the phenomenology of religion).

Lehmann divided his material into three main sections, 'Sacred actions', 'Sacred words' and 'Sacred places'. In the first he dealt with magic and with ritual—the cult object, cultic actions, sanctuaries and festivals. In the second he considered, among other things, incantation and prayer, song and sermon. The third section shows the influence of Söderblom in its concentration on the phenomena of holiness (still before Otto) as associated with persons—kings, priests, prophets, mystics, pilgrims and others; it also takes up to consideration 'sacred (holy) behaviour' in ecstasy, asceticism and the like, peculiarly transferable instances of holiness (blessings, sacraments), and the complex of ideas connected with the saints and with the sacred community.

This was a very capable systematisation of the phenomena of religion, and it was not surprising that when Chantepie de la Saussaye's *Lehrbuch* was reissued in a fourth edition Lehmann should have been asked to contribute a phenomenological section, as well as a history of the development of the science of religion. In essence this later work merely recapitulates his earlier material, though on this occasion the simplified title 'visible religion' is changed to *Erscheinungs- und Ideenwelt der Religion* (The world of religious phenomena and ideas).

Shortly after the turn of the century, the academic succession at the University of Leiden, Holland, passed from C. P. Tiele to the Norwegian scholar William Brede Kristensen (1867–1953). Tiele might actually have been succeeded by Söderblom, who had already carried out a useful revision of Tiele's *Kompendium der Religionsgeschichte*; but in the event Kristensen, who had been Tiele's pupil and who had written under his supervision a doctoral dissertation on the Egyptian conception of life after death, was elected in 1901. He remained in the same post until his retirement in 1937.

Kristensen's recognition as a phenomenologist of importance was curiously delayed. During his lifetime, he was not well known internationally, though he was of course highly respected in the phenomenological strongholds of Holland and Scandinavia. Not until seven years after his death did the publication of his phenomenological lectures, translated by J. B. Carman, as *The Meaning of Religion*, bring his work to the notice of the English-speaking world. Even then, the fact that the volume had an introduction by Hendrik

Kraemer, who was widely known as a Christian theologian of an uncompromising type, caused some puzzlement.[17]

A few years earlier, there had appeared a similar book in his native Norwegian, entitled *Religionshistorisk Studium* (The Study of the History of Religion, 1954), in which equally important statements of principle are to be found.

Kristensen's main methodological concern, and one which can be traced back to his early years in Leiden, was with the problem of value judgements. The evolutionary theory he believed to have been responsible for inducing scholars to pass premature judgement on material which they had learned to understand only in part. Again and again the scholar had come to assume that his own scholarly presuppositions were adequate for an understanding of any religious phenomena. Not so, maintained Kristensen; our presuppositions are seldom as adequate as we suppose. Certainly, written sources are first-hand material, produced without a view to the needs of the outside observer; but even then we must be cautious. When such material is missing, as in virtually every case the evolutionists had used as pillars of their theories, we can do nothing but admit our own ultimate inability to understand. In either case the believer's own understanding of his faith must be given absolute priority :

> Let us never forget [he wrote] that there exists no other religious reality than the faith of the believer. If we really want to understand religion, we must refer exclusively to the believer's testimony. What we believe, from our point of view, about the nature or value of other religions, is a reliable testimony to our own faith, or to our own understanding of religious faith; but if our opinion about another religion differs from the opinion and evaluation of the believers, then we are no longer talking about their religion. We have turned aside from historical reality, and are concerned only with ourselves.[18]

[17] On Kraemer, see Hallencreutz, op. cit., passim, and cf. Waardenburg, op. cit., pp. 145ff. Kraemer's best known works are *The Christian Message in a Non-Christian World* (1938), and *Religion and the Christian Faith* (1956). In the latter work Kraemer had written that while comparative religion had graded religions on an ascending evolutionary scale, this technique had now been shown to be wrong: 'Now, strictly speaking, honest research has come to the conclusion that the many religions are *incommensurable*. . . The only meaning that the phrase 'Comparative Religion' (*Vergleichende Religionswissenschaft*) can have is : not evaluating and grading, but contrasting and elaborating the peculiar character and structure of different religions.' (p. 77f).

[18] Kristensen, *Religionshistorisk studium* (1954), p. 27.

It is perhaps necessary to emphasise in this context that Kristensen was writing about the scholar's interpretation of the religions of the past, rather than the dialogician's interpretation of the religions of the present. But the principle is an important one. If it is true, as Kristensen claims, that we can never experience someone else's religious tradition as the believer experiences it (a point of view with which it is difficult to argue), what then is left for the phenomenologist of religion, other than tamely to acknowledge that 'the believer is always right'—even though the believer may on an occasion appear to have been disastrously wrong?

What he must do, according to Kristensen, is to respect the integrity of the believer, to refrain from imposing on him his (the scholar's) own value-judgements—but then to aim at the ideal of integral objective knowledge and total understanding, however well he may know that the ideal is an unattainable one.

It is true that our own historical understanding never is, and never can be, perfect; but that is precisely the path we must follow, continually working in the direction of a realistic understanding of the forces of religion in history. Every historian of religion, whatever his individual abilities, can contribute towards the attainment of this goal.[19]

Religionshistorisk studium is in no sense a work of Husserlian phenomenology; but it is a work of hermeneutics, the testimony of a historian of religion tired of labouring under the burden of evolutionary value-judgements. Perhaps, too, it is the work of a believer who is concerned to protect the integrity of other believers against the unintentional distortions of scholars who, while not unfriendly, had never learned to understand.

* * *

In considering this work of Kristensen's, produced at the very end of a long and fruitful life, we have passed over the contribution of the man who was long, and rightly, considered to be the doyen of the phenomenologists. We must therefore now retrace our steps slightly.

Between 1925 and 1950, the phenomenology of religion was associated almost exclusively with the name of the Dutch scholar Gerardus van der Leeuw (1890–1950), and with his book *Phänomen-*

ologie der Religion (1933; Eng. tr. *Religion in Essence and Manifestation*, 1948). Van der Leeuw is in many ways reminiscent of Söderblom, whom he admired greatly. Both were historians of religion and Christian theologians; both were public personalities (one an Archbishop, the other Minister of Education); both had a great gift of imaginative sympathy, perhaps resting ultimately on highly developed aesthetic faculties, in which music played a large part. The parallels cannot be extended indefinitely—for instance, Söderblom was more the historian and van der Leeuw more the philosopher—but in both cases it is well-nigh impossible to sum up their work in a few sentences, and a variety of distortions have been perpetuated by those who have tried to do so.

Similarly, it is difficult to estimate 'influences' on van der Leeuw, since he had a vast gift of assimilation. Some there undoubtedly were, however : in Holland, his teacher Brede Kristensen, under whom he began his career (like so many other Dutch scholars) as an Egyptologist,[20] and Chantepie de la Saussaye; in Germany, Rudolf Otto, Edmund Husserl and Wilhelm Dilthey, the modern father of the science of hermeneutics, whose views underly a great deal of van der Leeuw's phenomenology. Mention should also be made of the close friendship between van der Leeuw and the New Testament scholar Rudolf Bultmann, who assisted materially in the preparation of van der Leeuw's *magnum opus*, and who may well have received fruitful impulses in return. Van der Leeuw also acknowledged his debt of gratitude to Rudolf Otto, to Nathan Söderblom and his disciple Friedrich Heiler, and to the French anthropologist Lucien Lévy-Bruhl.[21]

Van der Leeuw was appointed Professor of the History of Religion at Groningen in 1918, and (again like Söderblom) devoted his inaugural lecture to a discussion of the relationship between comparative religion and Christian theology.[22] In this lecture he stressed—in generally evolutionary terms—that it is necessary to

[20] On van der Leuw, see Waardenburg, op. cit., pp. 161ff. Van der Leeuw wrote of Kristensen that he, '. . . possédé par l'idée aussi profonde que grandiose de la vie spontanée surgissant de la mort, le cherchait et trouvait un peu partout et m'inspirait pour toujours l'amour de l'histoire des religions' ('Confession Scientifique', in *Numen* I, 1954, p. 9). It is also interesting to note in this connection that Waardenburg is of the opinion that van der Leeuw knew Husserl only slightly, from secondary sources, and that Husserl's influence on him has often been overrated.

[21] Van der Leeuw counted himself a defender of the views of Lévy-Bruhl (cf. above, pp. 190-4). This is especially clear from his book *L'Homme primitif et la religion* (1940).

[22] *Plats en taak van de godsdienstgeschiednis in de theologische wetenschap* (1918). For Söderblom's inaugural, see above, pp. 155-6.

arrive at some form of Christian theological understanding of religious phenomena. The influence of Lévy-Bruhl is especially evident in this paper. In later years he was to moderate his evolutionary position somewhat, particularly under the influence of comparative religion and philosophical theology. This may seem at first sight to be incompatible in principle with what is generally taken to be the ideal stance of the phenomenologist, and it may be freely admitted that there were always certain tensions in van der Leeuw's work, which were never satisfactorily resolved. However, to attempt to discuss these in this context would lead far beyond the bounds of this survey. The problem, though, was that which always faces the committed adherent of one religious tradition when he attempts to cross the frontiers of his own tradition in a quest for understanding (*Verstehen*), particularly when that quest involves a consideration of 'religion-as-such'.

It was in this quest, he later wrote, that he followed the example of Chantepie de la Saussaye and Edvard Lehmann in attempting to blaze a trail through the multiple phenomena of religion in order to give a systematic description of 'religion' :

> In doing this I realised that this phenomenology of religion consisted not merely in making an inventory and classification of phenomena as they appear in history, but also a psychological description which necessitated not only a meticulous observation of the religious reality, but also a systematic introspection; not only the description of what is visible from outside, but above all the experience born of what can only become reality after it has been admitted into the life of the observer himself. In other words, I realised that in carrying on the magnificent, but essentially unphilosophical, work of Chantepie and Lehmann, I was in the very centre of the great phenomenological stream which was at that time flowing through philosophy, psychiatry and other sciences.[23]

With this in mind, we may turn to a brief consideration of some of the principles underlying *Religion in Essence and Manifestation*.

Van der Leeuw is not writing merely descriptive phenomenology—a systematic catalogue of religious 'things'; to him, a phenomenon is emphatically not a 'thing' : it is 'what "appears" ' (*dasjenige, was sich zeigt*), 'an object related to a subject, and a subject related to an object' (*ein subjektbezogenes Objekt und ein*

---

[23] *Confession Scientifique*, p. 10. cf. what he says about 'der Religionsgeschichte des Verstehens' in *Die Religion in Geschichte und Gegenwart* (3rd ed.), IV, col. 1897.

objektbezogenes Subjekt).[24] A phenomenon, therefore, is given in the interplay and interpenetration of subject and object, in the very act of understanding : 'The phenomenon . . . is not produced by the subject, and still less substantiated or demonstrated by it; its entire essence is given in its "appearance", and its appearance to "someone". If (finally) this "someone" begins to discuss what "appears", then phenomenology arises.'[25] He goes on to claim that phenomenology is neither metaphysics nor the comprehension of empirical reality; it is 'man's vital activity . . . standing aside and understanding what appears into view'.[26] The conditions on which such understanding can take place never vary in essence; van der Leeuw acknowledges that perhaps we can know nothing, and understand very little; still, it is no harder in principle to understand an ancient Egyptian than it is to understand one's next-door neighbour—assuming that the data are present to one's consciousness. In order that sufficient data may be obtained, the phenomenologist must continually submit to historical correction; if phenomenology is to do its job properly, he wrote,

. . . it imperatively requires perpetual correction by the most conscientious philological and archaeological research . . . as soon as . . . [phenomenological understanding] withdraws itself from control by philological and archaeological interpretation, it becomes pure art or empty fantasy.[27]

But he stresses that the phenomenology of religion is something more than pure history nevertheless; when the phenomenologist ceases to understand the material under his hand, his work is at an end, but when the historian ceases to understand, he can still go on recording and cataloguing for the sake of others.[28]

Nor, despite the fact that van der Leeuw always held himself to be a theologian above all, is the phenomenology of religion identical with theology. For theology speaks about God, and this the phenomenologist cannot do—for theological reasons, oddly enough. Because God, to be grasped by phenomenology, would have to be either subject or object; and he is neither. So to the phenomenologist, though he may study religious experience (and in fact does so constantly), and may observe men and women responding (or claiming to respond) to divine revelation, the revelation itself

[24] *Religion in Essence and Manifestation*, p. 671.
[25] ibid.
[26] ibid., p. 676.
[27] ibid., p. 677, cf. *Confession*, p. 9.
[28] ibid., p. 686.

remains inaccessible. As van der Leeuw has written, 'We can never understand God's utterance by means of any purely intellectual capacity: what we can understand is only our own answer. . . .'[29] This is, of course, a theological statement, claiming as it does to define an aspect of 'God's utterance', and it is apparent from whole tracts of van der Leeuw's phenomenology that, although he may not be 'doing theology' in the narrower dogmatic sense, his whole approach is basically theological (quite apart from his treatment of Christianity). Again, to take an illustrative statement from his fragment of autobiography :

> I have never felt the need to forget that I am a theologian, and naturally I have attempted to enable theology to profit from phenomenological method. Certainly not in order to make a science of religion out of theology, but on the contrary, the better to show forth theological method, which is in my opinion absolutely autonomous. Nevertheless, theology is concerned with history, since it is history which gives theology both its foundation and point of departure : revelation. Now phenomenology can assist theology to organise facts, to penetrate their sense, to find their essence, before theology is able to evaluate and use them for its doctrinal conclusions.[30]

Phenomenology, then, while not *per se* concerned with theological evaluations, may be regarded as a form of theological propaedeutics.

Not specifically theological, but fully understandable from within the Christian tradition, is this statement, in which he epitomises the understanding attitude as :

> the loving gaze of the lover on the beloved object. For all understanding rests upon self-surrendering love. Were that not the case, then not only all discussion of what appears in religion, but all discussion of appearance in general, would be quite impossible; since to him who does not love, nothing whatever is manifested. . . [31]

Clearly for van der Leeuw, the exercise of love and the exercise of *epoché* were in no sense mutually exclusive. It seems to be the case that *epoché* serves largely to guard against the making of premature and unfounded truth-claims (another point, incidentally, on which phenomenology and theology differ), as well as eliminating the need for the phenomenologist to concern himself with questions

29 ibid., p. 68of.
30 *Confession*, p. 13; cf. Waardenburg, op. cit., p. 183.
31 *Religion in Essence and Manifestation*, p. 684.

of origin and development in religion. Religion is neither more nor less than *given*. And this being so, the total task of the phenomenologist resolves itself into the following five stages :

1. To assign names to groups of phenomena—such as sacrifice, prayer, saviour, myth, etc.
2. To interpolate the experiences within one's own life and experience them systematically—a point which seems at first sight hard to reconcile with the claim that the aim of phenomenology is 'pure objectivity'.
3. To exercise *epoché*, i.e. to withdraw to one side and observe.
4. To clarify and comprehend.
5. To confront chaotic reality and testify to what has been understood.[32]

It is evident that van der Leeuw's phenomenological work can be understood on a number of different levels. It *can* be taken and used merely as a collection of materials. As a work of hermeneutics, on the other hand, it has been more admired than imitated, entirely on account of the subtle methodological principles on which it is based—principles which few subsequent scholars have shown any real wish to assimilate. But *Religion in Essence and Manifestation* is a superb compilation, and to very many students has long been a stimulating guide through the world of religion. Its basic religious category of 'holiness' (in which van der Leeuw acknowledged profound indebtedness to Söderblom and Otto alike) is one which *homo religiosus* himself at once understands, but one which the academic mind has always regarded with some doubt, feeling that here he is invited to embark upon a hazardous voyage on a metaphysical ocean. But to van der Leeuw, phenomenological scholarship was not to be sharply differentiated from metaphysics or from theology.

We have already seen that van der Leeuw was a resolute defender of Lucien Lévy-Bruhl, and in *L'Homme primitif et la religion* (1940) he not only defends Lévy-Bruhl and his theory of 'primitive mentality' against the remarkable number of misrepresentations to which both have been subjected over the last sixty years, but he also undertakes a valuable criticism of 'modern' culture. Van der Leeuw rejects out of hand the idea that 'primitive mentality' is a term which can be understood only on the basis of unilinear evolu-

---

[32] This important relationship—between understanding and testimony to what has been understood—is treated in Hermelink, *Verstehen and Bezeugen* (1960), with reference to van der Leeuw's theology. Once more it must be stressed that to attempt to interpret van der Leeuw other than in theological terms is ultimately a self-defeating procedure.

tion. He points out that Lévy-Bruhl himself had repeatedly insisted that 'primitivity' and 'logical' thought coexist on all cultural levels— a circumstance easily verifiable. Where he does criticise his mentor is in the latter's unspoken assumption that there is a monolithic 'modern' mentality which must of necessity be normative for all anthropological, social and religious studies. This modern mentality is an abstraction. Consisting as it does in removing the subject as far as possible from the observed object, it may well, thinks van der Leeuw, be regarded as pathological and aberrant, and he cites an impressive array of modern thinkers, from Nietzsche and Kierkegaard to G. K. Chesterton, who share this view in some form. To think in 'primitive' forms is to experience reality directly, subjectively, intuitively—and is ultimately to find one's Self.[33]

He concluded that no religious phenomenon can be understood without reference to 'primitive' structures in the mind of man. When the attempt is made to study religion solely on the basis of logical and social categories, the whole enterprise so often moves in the sphere of abstractions, revealing nothing of the mind of *homo religiosus*, and failing at any point seriously to make contact with the personality of the researcher. Perhaps this goes some way toward accounting for what some have held to be the disturbingly subjective elements in van der Leeuw's phenomenology. Hultkrantz, for instance, has written, concerning van der Leeuw's *magnum opus*, that although it is still the classic study in its field,

. . . it is too speculative, in some places even incomprehensible, to be of much use to the seriously working empirical religious researcher . . Van der Leeuw's phenomenology comprises— maybe—an 'Einklammerung', a parenthesis, in the development of the phenomenology of religion.[34]

The crux lies perhaps in this word 'empirical'. To be thoroughly empirical was, in a manner of speaking, the foremost symptom of what van der Leeuw held to be the typical twentieth-century sickness. He did not, as we have seen, look down upon empirical research. Far from it. But to be narrowly and exclusively empirical was to deny one's own wholeness, and hence to fail at the scholar's most vital and most sensitive point, the point of genuine understanding.

*   *   *

[33] In this particular book van der Leeuw does not cite C. G. Jung, but as a participant in the *Eranos* Conferences he was clearly receptive to the general message of the 'Jungians'.

[34] Hultkrantz, in *Temenos* 6 (1970), p. 72f.

Among van der Leeuw's successors in the Dutch phenomenological tradition, the most influential has been C. Jouco Bleeker (b. 1899); as well as being Professor in the University of Amsterdam, he served for twenty years as Secretary-General of the International Association for the History of Religions (1950–1970), and still remains Editor of the Association's journal *Numen*. Like van der Leeuw, Bleeker's specialist field is Egyptology.

Statements of Bleeker's approach to the phenomenology of religion are to be found in a variety of publications; typical are, however, the essays collected and published in 1963 as *The Sacred Bridge*. The first of these is entitled 'The Phenomenological Method'. In this essay, Bleeker admits that the problem of the subject is that it appears to many to be a hybrid between the history and the philosophy of religion; but, he insists, it is 'an empirical science without philosophical aspirations',[35] which should make as little use as possible of philosophical of psychological terminology, in order not to be fettered by their own peculiar presuppositions. He recognises that at this point he is departing from the position occupied by van der Leeuw—for whom he otherwise shows respect tempered by healthy criticism. Phenomenology, he insists, can never consider the 'philosophical' question of the truth of religion; all it can do is to take religion seriously, observing and recording what it sees :

> It only maintains its position of impartiality by demanding that all religion should be understood as what it stands for, namely as a serious testimony of religious people that they possess a knowledge of God.[36]

Perhaps it is not possible to go beyond this approach to the multiple phenomena of religion :

> If there exists a chance of reaching the sole aim, deserving the hard labour of painstaking research, namely a profound understanding of foreign religions, it is solely by means of this method.[37]

Bleeker's method does not in fact differ greatly from that of his mentors, save, as we have seen, in his express rejection of any 'philosophical' claims. But he does use a distinctive vocabulary to express his views. Like van der Leeuw, he speaks often of *epochê* and eidetic vision, insisting that both are 'objective' criteria (a point on which more than one opinion is possible); but he uses three other

---

[35] Bleeker, *The Sacred Bridge* (1963), p. 7. cf. Waardenburg, op. cit., pp. 183ff.
[36] Bleeker, op. cit., p. 9.
[37] ibid.

technical terms. The phenomenologist, he says, must be concerned with *theôria*, the implications of aspects of religion; with *logos*, the structure of different religious traditions; and with *entelecheia*, 'the course of events in which the essence is realised by its manifestations'.[38] The latter term is particularly interesting, since it is an attempt to coin a replacement for 'evolution', a term which recognises that religious traditions are not static, but which refuses to be bound by the specific assumptions of evolutionism, unilinear or otherwise. *Entelecheia*, says Bleeker, is not evolution; rather it seems to work according to a law of challenge and response. And he concludes :

Each relapse seems to evoke in religious people strong desire for and an attempt at restoring religion. Actually this effort results in a rising of the religious level. The phenomenology of religion is man's inseparable companion. It is an invincible, creative and self-generating force. So there is good reason for applying the old proverb : *magna est veritas et prevalebit*.[39]

Thus far the mainstream of the Dutch-Scandinavian phenomenological tradition. From Chantepie de la Saussaye to Bleeker, most of its representatives were Christian theologians, for whom phenomenology appeared to provide a theoretical justification for their work in religious traditions other than Christianity. Theologians in such a position are always open to the criticism that they cannot possibly 'understand' any tradition to which they are not personally committed; the contention of the phenomenologists was that they had found a means of removing, or at least of suspending, the value-judgements (at first theological, but also evolutionary) which had previously stood in the way of full understanding. They had adopted at least some of the vocabulary of Husserlian phenomenology, but their aims were simple. They wished to combine complete accuracy of scholarship with complete sympathy of treatment to ensure complete understanding of the religious beliefs and practices of other human beings.

*   *   *

The period which saw the rise of phenomenology in Holland was not one of Germany's most productive intellectual periods, and the history of religions in particular was carried out in an idiosyncratic manner. But before 1933, considerable interest was shown among

[38] ibid., p. 14.
[39] ibid., p. 24.

German scholars in the parallel field of hermeneutics, along the lines which we have already associated with von Dobschütz. Representative of this trend, first in its German form and subsequently in its transplantation to America, was Joachim Wach (1898–1955). Wach has found a faithful and sympathetic commentator in Joseph M. Kitagawa, and we shall not attempt here to do more than give the briefest outline of his career.[40] Of Jewish extraction, Wach was descended both from Moses Mendelssohn and Felix Mendelssohn-Bartholdy. He was however a Christian. Educated at the University of Leipzig, he was introduced to the comparative study of religion by Friedrich Heiler, and counted among his mentors Troeltsch, Harnack, Söderblom, Weber and Otto. In 1935 the Nazis deprived him of his teaching post at Leipzig, and he emigrated to the United States, where he taught for the rest of his life, first at Brown University, Providence, Rhode Island, and after 1945 at the University of Chicago. Among the most important of his publications are *Religionswissenschaft* (1924), *Das Verstehen* (1926–1933), *Sociology of Religion* (1944), *Types of Religious Experience* (1951), and two posthumous works, both edited by Kitagawa, *The Comparative Study of Religions* (1958), and a collection of essays, *Understanding and Believing* (1968).

In an article first published in German in 1935, and subsequently translated into English as 'The Meaning and Task of the History of Religions', Wach attempts to delineate the ethos of his subject, and particularly to consider the scholar's motives for entering into the study. The idea of scholarship for its own sake he dismisses out of hand : '. . . if *Religionswissenschaft* is only an aesthetically interesting or purely academic matter, then, indeed, it has no right to exist today.'[41] But if it is not 'purely academic', then what is it? Wach answers that the discipline serves to broaden and deepen the *sensus numinis*, to deepen the scholar's own faith (if he has one), and to encourage 'a new and comprehensive experience of what religion is and means'.[42] Religious traditions must be seen, using the very best techniques that scholarship can offer, as living totalities; and all the living relationships within those totalities must be seen and evaluated. But in the last resort, '. . . the central concern of *Religionswissenschaft* must be the understanding of other religions'.[43]

---

[40] The full details will be found in Wach, *The Comparative Study of Religions* (ed. Kitagawa, 1958), Introduction, pp. xiii-xlviii. See also Kitagawa, *Gibt es ein Verstehen fremder Religionen?* (1963).
[41] Wach (ed. Kitagawa), *Understanding and Believing* (1968), p. 126.
[42] ibid., p. 127.
[43] ibid., p. 130.

But how does the scholar 'understand'? It seems that there is no absolute guarantee that he ever will. For in the last resort there must be a creative intuition, which cannot be counterfeited : either the scholar possesses this, or he does not. Wach seems to want to say that any scholar *could* possess such an intuition, however :

. . . in principle there could resound in each of us something of the ecstatic, the spectral, the unusual—something of that which to us, the children of another age, of another race, and of other customs, appears strange among the religious expressions of distant lands. Where this natural disposition is developed through training, there also the prerequisite for an actual understanding of foreign religiosity exists.[44]

Hermeneutics therefore demands a religious instinct—and there, perhaps, lies one divergence from phenomenology. For while the phenomenologist is liable to attempt to discount his own subjectivity, the hermeneut accepts and uses his. This extends to the question of values, for while the phenomenologist attempts to eliminate judgements of value, Wach is able to say that 'we now have found again the right and the courage to evaluate.'[45] Presumably, however, the hermeneut would not object to being asked to state the precise criteria on which his values were based.

Wach adhered strongly to his fundamental hermeneutical principles throughout his career. In his *Sociology of Religion*—a work, incidentally, in which he claims to be supplementing van der Leeuw—he speaks of the need for such principles, and states that 'the inquirer must feel an affinity to his subject, and he must be trained to interpret his material with sympathetic understanding'.[46] And in his book *The Comparative Study of Religions* he sets out the ethos of the comparative study as being to complement the insights of theology, writing that 'a comparative study of religions such as the new era [has] made possible enables us to have a fuller vision of what religious experience can mean, what forms its expression may take, and what it might do for man.'[47]

It was this latter book which called forth such a scathing criticism from R. J. Zwi Werblowsky, who stated in effect that Wach neither knew nor cared where comparative religion ended and theology began. We shall consider this review later.[48] In the meantime, we can do no more than suggest that the methodological diffi-

[44] ibid., p. 135.
[45] ibid.
[46] Wach, *The Sociology of Religion* (1944), p. 10.
[47] *The Comparative Study of Religions*, p. 9.
[48] cf. below, pp. 275-6.

culties raised by Wach's hermeneutics are essentially those which have plagued the comparative study of religion from its very beginning—how, if at all, to balance a profound commitment with an equally profound desire to do justice to that to which the scholar is *not* specifically committed.

* * *

Following Wach's death, the hermeneutical tradition was carried on at the University of Chicago by Wach's disciple and interpreter Joseph M. Kitagawa, and by Mircea Eliade.

In a 1968 article entitled 'The Making of a Historian of Religions',[49] Kitagawa remarks on the 'strange popularity' of the history of religions in American colleges and universities, but is also forced to say that '. . . there seems to be rather widespread ambiguity about the nature of the discipline in spite of, or because of, its popularity'.[50] While dismissing the idea of a perpetual interfaith conference as naive, and lamenting that the history of religions is coming to be understood only as the history of non-Western religions, he aligns himself with the hermeneutical position of Wach, pleading for accurate scholarship allied to breadth of vision. He writes :

We must . . . be crystal clear concerning the basic distinction between the study of specific religions and the history of religions. We are all aware, of course, that in the popular mind the history of religions [comparative religion] is often thought of as a convenient semantic umbrella that covers all the independent studies of specific religions. But the objective of the history of religions (*Religionswissenschaft*), in the technical sense in which we use this term, must be nothing short of scholarly inquiry into the nature and structure of the religious experience of the human race and its diverse manifestations in history.[51]

We have already spoken of Eliade's work in the context of new developments in the psychology of religion. Here, for the sake of continuity, we may simply quote a representative statement, from the Foreword to *The Two and the One* (Eng. tr. 1965) :

Now, the proper frame of mind for discovering the meaning

[49] Kitagawa, 'The Making of a Historian of Religions', in *Journal of the American Academy of Religion* (September 1968), pp. 191–202.
[50] ibid., p. 191.
[51] ibid., p. 199.

of a typical human situation is not the 'objectivity' of the natural-ist but the intelligent sympathy of the exegetist (*sic*), the inter-preter. . . . The will properly to understand the 'others' is re-warded . . . by an enrichment of the Western consciousness. The encounter might even lead to a renewal in the philosophical field, in the same way that the discovery of the exotic and primi-tive arts half a century ago opened up new perspectives for European arts.[52]

It will be clear from this brief quotation even that Eliade's commit-ment is not identical with that of Wach; Eliade's 'new humanism' differs somewhat from Wach's Christian idealism. Yet the value of the hermeneutical exercise remains—enriching the human condi-tion by means of an interpretative exercise of the very highest order.

*   *   *

We must again retrace our steps, this time to Great Britain be-tween the wars. There, evolutionary comparative method had hardly as yet been seriously challenged, and comparative religion, perhaps partly owing to the strength of accepted religious tradition, was passing through lean years. Of the prophets and pioneers, Frazer and Marett were among those still writing.

At the outbreak of war, the burden and heat of the day was being borne by two of their heirs and disciples, both Anglican clergy-men, E. O. James (1888–1972) and A. C. Bouquet (b. 1884). The debt which scholarship in Britain owed, and owes, to these two men is quite incalculable. James was an anthropologist and historian of religion, a man of great erudition and breadth, who already had many solid works to his credit—a list which was to be substantially complemented in the post-war years. His technique might perhaps be characterised as that of descriptive phenomenology allied to straight history. His earliest phenomenological works such as *Christian Myth and Ritual* (1933), *The Origins of Religion* (1937) and *The Origins of Sacrifice* (1937), represent a continuation of the Frazerian line and method, albeit greatly refined. The same method-ological presuppositions are evident in his brief work *Comparative Religion* (1938), which differs only in respect of material (not in method) from earlier handbooks by Menzies, Carpenter and Geden. That this approach genuinely represented the position of British scholarship at the time is further shown by A. C. Bouquet's popular work *Comparative Religion*, which began its long and useful life in 1941. This is not so much phenomenology as a series of brief regional characterisations of the history of religion, with a Christian *logos* theology (which Bouquet expounded at length in his later book *The Christian Faith and Non-Christian Religions* (1958)) at no great depth beneath the surface. But it should be remembered that intellectual commerce between the English and German-speaking worlds was at this time less extensive than formerly, and certainly less extensive than it was subsequently to become; there was still only one chair of comparative religion in Britain, and the subject as such was scarcely in the forefront of debate, historical, anthropological or theological.

Thus when in 1940 Eva Hirschmann evaluated the current position of the phenomenology of religion in her book *Phänomenologie der Religion*, no scholar from the English-speaking world found a place in it. Of the thirteen scholars dealt with, four were Dutch, two Scandinavian and the remainder (not all of whom have been considered in this chapter) Germans.[52a]

Since 1945, a number of developments have taken place, some healthy, some perhaps less so. On the most obvious level, there have been a number of books published which have analysed the data provided by the history of religion into themes and types—substantially on the same lines as Chantepie's *Gruppen von religiösen Erscheinungen*, though according to methods and orders of classification dictated by the presuppositions and background of the scholars concerned.

Chronologically, the first of these to appear after the war was by the Swedish historian of religion Geo Widengren : *Religionens värld* (1945 and later eds.; Ger. tr. *Religionsphänomenologie*, 1970). Widengren, who succeeded Tor Andrae at the University of Uppsala in 1943, was (and has remained) an outstanding representative of the Scandinavian branch of the 'Myth and Ritual School'. He is passionately opposed to evolutionism in the study of religion, and a great deal of his research has centred upon the question of high gods, on the sacral kingship, and on myth and ritual patterns in the Ancient Near East. All these matters are dealt with in outline in *Religionens värld*, in an order which makes plain the author's priorities in the study and exposition of religion. Beginning with a statement of the distinction between religion and magic, Widengren then deals, in order, with high gods; pantheism, polytheism and

[52a] Hirschmann, *Phänomenologie der Religion: Eine historisch-systematische Untersuchung von 'Religionsphänomenologie' und 'religionsphänomenologischer Methode' in der Religionswissenschaft* (1940). The scholars treated in this book are: Chantepie de la Saussaye, Tiele, Söderblom, Lehmann, Pfister, Scheler, Wobbermin, Winkler, Wach, Otto, Frick, Mensching and van der Leeuw.

monotheism; myth; ritual; sacrifice; sacral kingship; death and burial, spirit and soul; eschatology and apocalyptic; Gnosticism; individual and group; and finally, mysticism (these are the chapter headings in the first edition; later editions expand somewhat). To Widengren, the phenomenology of religion is a classificatory science, the science of the various forms in which religion manifests itself, and thus the systematic counterpart of the history of religion, with which, however, it should not be confused :

> While phenomenology deals with all the expressions of the religious life, wherever they may appear, the history of religion, with its purely historical discipline, examines the development of separate religions. The phenomenology of religion attempts to give a coherent account of all the various phenomena of religion, and is thus the systematic complement of the history of religion. The history of religion gives the historical analysis, while the phenomenology of religion provides us with the systematic synthesis.[53]

We have already seen that Widengren is one of the most powerful advocates of the 'purely historical' approach to the study of religion, and he emphasises again and again that no phenomenologist can ever claim to abandon historical method. Nevertheless in his very selection of types and patterns for his phenomenology he has moved some steps beyond plain and unadorned historical exposition; there is a higher degree of subjectivity in this procedure than he would perhaps want to allow. But it is no part of our present purpose to decry that element in phenomenology; indeed, it is hard to see how phenomenology could otherwise exist at all, if there is to be even the slightest trace of the 'eidetic vision' involved in its conception and execution. We would merely remark that it is at this point that the phenomenologist who wants at the same time to claim objective status for his work may well find himself in something of a dilemma.

* * *

The dilemma is perhaps less acutely felt in the phenomenologies that have emerged from post-war Germany, partly because the tendency there has often been to acknowledge the subjective element. For instance, Gustav Mensching in *Die Religion* (1949), follows substantially the van der Leeuw line. Similarly Alfred Bertholet, *Grundformen der Erscheinungswelt der Religion* (1953) and Kurt

[53]Widengren, *Religionens värld* (1st ed. 1945), p. 9.

Goldammer, *Die Formenwelt des Religiösen* (1960). But the full
range of the difficulties facing the phenomenologist are epitomised
in Friedrich Heiler, *Erscheinungsformen und Wesen der Religion*
(1949), which forms a methodological prologue to the massive
Kohlhammer historical series *Die Religionen der Menschheit*.
Heiler's work is certainly a *tour de force* : more than 600 pages long
and copiously documented. But in the attempt to include everything
of significance, Heiler is apt to induce acute intellectual indigestion
in his readers (those, that is, who do not take the easy way out and
read selectively, *via* the indexes). Certainly the systematic outline
is clear enough, but within the framework of sacred objects, sacred
places, the sacred word, sacred scriptures, and so on (in which one
can still sense the influence of Söderblom, Otto and van der Leeuw),
the sheer mass of material is simply overwhelming. Again, although
in his introduction Heiler states that 'there is no science which is
free from presuppositions', nevertheless 'every philosophical *a
priori* must be excluded'—prompting the reflection that the dividing
line between a presupposition and an *a priori* attitude may be a very
delicate one. In Heiler's view, it is necessary to find the *right* presuppositions, viz., those that are contained in the use of a strictly
inductive method. One must immerse oneself in the totality of
religion before one begins to construct theories or frame hypotheses.
This is all very well, but is such an encyclopaedic ideal not self-
defeating? And in reality, Heiler's own presuppositions (which some
might want to call a form of *Apriorismus*) stand out with uncommon
clarity, even from amid the forest of 'facts' that go to make up his
book.[54]

The difficulties facing the phenomenology of religion are, as we
have said, essentially those that have faced comparative religion
throughout its hundred-year history. They concern the limits of
scholarly objectivity above all. We may establish that the vast
majority of phenomenologists are concerned, as far as is possible,
to apply the principle of *epochê*, and to ensure that their material
is gathered and verified according to the strictest principles of historical scholarship. All would agree with Heiler, that the phenomenologist must be a philologist,[55] and that he should have that total

[54] Ultimately he acknowledges this, in effect, when he writes on p. 559 :
'Die mannigfalten religiösen Erscheinungsformen, Vorstellungen und Erleb-
nisse wiesen über sich hinaus; sie richten sich auf eine letztes Gegenständ-
liches das transzendent ist, das hinter und über allen sinnlichen und geist-
lichen Phänomen liegt. Diesen Gegenständliche ist das Heilige . . .' For
another view of substantially this problem, see Goldammer, 'Faktum, Interpretation und Verstehen,' in *Religion und Religionen: Festschrift für Gustav
Mensching* (1967), pp. 11ff.
[55] Heiler, *Erscheinungsformen*, p. 15.

mastery of some specialist field of research which enables him to judge other specialisms with sympathy and accuracy. But supposing him to be capable of this, how does he then proceed?

Whatever he does, in writing (or teaching) the phenomenology of religion he is doing something other than 'straight' chronological history, historian though he may be. He selects, systematises, interprets. He establishes types, patterns, morphologies—all with a view to penetrating the 'essence' of religion. He then arranges whatever material he happens to have available (and no one can have *all* the material) around those patterns. Now clearly there is very little reason here for the scholar to claim an ideal (an in any case wholly unrealisable) state of freedom from presuppositions. Presuppositions are writ large across the whole phenomenological enterprise. Materials have been acquired under strictly scientific conditions, and the phenomenologist may wish to claim that his systematising activity is equally scientific. But in this respect at least, science must be content to acknowledge its affinity with art.

It is this tension between scientifically acquired 'facts' and subsequent interpretation of those facts which has given rise of late to a certain amount of rather inconclusive methodological debate, partly between adherents of varying subjectively-determined schools of thought, but also to some extent involving those who wish at all costs to defend the objective and empirical status of the phenomenology of religion. It is this tension which prompts Bleeker to write that to some, the phenomenology of religion appears to be a hybrid between the history of religion and the philosophy of religion, but that in his opinion, 'the phenomenology of religion is an empirical science without philosophical aspirations'. It is furthermore an impartial science, demanding nothing more (or less) than that 'all religion should be understood as what it stands for, namely as a serious testimony of religious people that they possess a knowledge of God'.[56] It saves the scholar from barren specialisation, and has the further advantage that it provides the only means of reaching 'a profound understanding of foreign religions'. Thus the ideal is of impartiality striving to understand. Overt *a priori* judgements are abandoned, and the resultant activity cannot therefore be classified as either theology or philosophy. It must be science.

One cannot, however, altogether avoid the feeling that the debate has been unnecessarily confused by a fundamental failure to clarify the terms in which it is being conducted. 'History' and 'philosophy' are used as though they referred only to the proper activities of separate university departments. But they are not the

[56] cf. above, pp. 236-7.

radically, eternally separate sciences that they have sometimes been made to appear; after all, the historian cannot even begin to be a historian (though he may be a chronicler) unless he is prepared, first, to ask the right questions, and secondly, to interpret (creatively) his material so as to provide cogent answers to those questions. And this is suspiciously like a type of philosophy!

* * *

There is, however, one species of 'phenomenology' which perhaps escapes from the methodological dilemma by refusing to concern itself too deeply with 'religion-as-such'. The species in question is perhaps best characterised as the 'comparative monograph', in which a study of one phenomenon, or one group of phenomena, is undertaken 'across the board'. In the English-speaking world the trend was set in the early part of the century by the thematic articles in Hastings' *Encyclopaedia of Religion and Ethics*, since when there have been very many such studies, in most of the European languages. A well-known German example would be Heiler's *Das Gebet* (1918), while in England, E. O. James was for many years a specialist in this type of study—covering kingship, sacrifice, high gods, and so forth. Also in this category come several books by S. G. F. Brandon (1907–1971), among them *Time and Mankind* (1951), *Man and his Destiny in the Great Religions* (1962), *History, Time and Deity* (1965) and *The Judgment of the Dead* (1967).[57] It is true that all these works, and the first and third of them in particular, involve a particular theory of the origin of religion in man's developing time-consciousness, and of the nature of religion as consisting in man's response to the awareness of the passing of time; nevertheless the treatment throughout is historical and thematic, and the series as a whole is an epitome of what we might call 'selective phenomenology'.

The present writer has in his possession the original manuscript of Brandon's first book, *Time and Mankind* (dated 1949). Its first page contains the moving story of how its author, then serving in the army in North Africa, visited the ruins of the ancient city of Hippo Regius. There, '. . . an overwhelming sense of the enigma of Time's interweaving of human affairs possessed him. Had the

[57] On Brandon, see Simon, 'S. G. F. Brandon (1907–1971)', in *Numen* XIX (1972), pp. 84ff.; Sharpe, 'S. G. F. Brandon (1907–1971)', in *History of Religions* 12/1 (August 1972), pp. 71ff.; and cf. Sharpe and Hinnells, *Man and his Salvation: Studies in Memory of S. G. F. Brandon* (1973), which contains personal appreciations by H. C. Snape and E. O. James, and a bibliography of Brandon's works.

curious complex any meaning?' As a trained historian, he saw a pageant of the ages pass before him, bringing together 'Libyans, Phoenecians, Romans, Vandals, Byzantines, Arabs, French, Germans, British, Americans—what connected them all across the ages with this place?'

This intellectual vision prompted Brandon to undertake the scholarly task of tracing out the various ways in which mankind had reacted to the awareness of the passage of time. This task occupied him throughout his career, and gained him the respect of the scholarly world.[58] Brandon was content to call himself only a historian; and there were those who felt that greater acquaintance with alternative modes of phenomenological and hermeneutical inquiry would have deepened still further his treatment of this theme. As it was, his conclusions in *Time and Mankind* were, as he said, 'austere and perhaps not very original'—that man has been obsessed by the passage of time and has sought various ways to overcome its terrors. He was unwilling to pass beyond the evidence as it presented itself to him. In Palaeolithic religion he saw the attempt to overcome time by the ritual perpetuation of the past (a line of inquiry which had points in common with Eliade's theory of the eternal return). In Ancient Egypt he saw a struggle to defeat time; in Ancient Mesopotamia an act of resignation to time's annihilation; in Ancient Israel a belief in history as the revelation of Divine Providence—and so on, throughout the religions of the ancient world. He was subsequently to sum up in the words:

> Because of its fundamental, or primordial character, man's reaction to his awareness of Time has been single and constant in its primary impetus; but the forms in which that awareness has found expression and man has sought solution of the problems he has sensed, have been various, being conditioned by many differing psychological and cultural factors.[59]

Those factors he traced out with great energy through the sources of the ancient world.

With the 'modern' material Brandon was less happy; indeed, to all intents and purposes his hermeneutical exercise came to an end in the High Middle Ages. He believed religion to have reached a climax at that time, and that the subsequent history of religion can only be a record of decay and compromise. But the problem remains.

---

[58] This was marked particularly by his appointment as General-Secretary of the International Association for the History of Religions in 1970. It is strange that Brandon should find no place whatever in Waardenburg's symposium *Classical Approaches to the Study of Religion* (1973).
[59] Brandon, *History, Time and Deity* (1965), p. 2.

Thus the problem of Time abides, confronting all our seeking for significance with its chilling logic of the inevitability of decay and death. From the existential philosophy of life which it thus seems to thrust upon us our instinct still is to turn and seek other and transcendental values. Hence the continuous effort, finding expression in an unceasing series of books, to explain the nature of history or to make sense of mankind's past.[60]

*   *   *

It seems that the phenomenologist of religion must, if he is honest, confess that the enterprise on which he is engaged cannot but involve the subjective faculty of interpretation if it is to avoid degenerating altogether into a barren catalogue of what are taken to be religious 'facts'. But this once having been admitted, it seems that the would-be phenomenologist is plunged into unfathomable depths of epistemological theory. But he may not always realise this. Since van der Leeuw and perhaps also Joachim Wach, few specialists in the field have shown any inclination to attempt to pursue the findings of the philosophical phenomenologists; and additionally, as Oxtoby has said, 'the philosophically non-technical masses are fair game for initiation into the rites of the phenomenology of religion'[61]—which is to say that there has arisen of late a regrettable tendency to seize on the term 'the phenomenology of religion' and use it in all manner of approximate senses, some of which may suit the present 'age of approximation' in their general lack of clarity, but few of which bear any real relation to the work of any of the scholars we have been discussing.

An example would be an anthology called *The Phenomenology of Religion* collected and published by J. D. Bettis in 1969. Bettis distinguishes three types of phenomenology of religion : first, philosophical phenomenology; secondly, the application of phenomenological method to the history of religions; and thirdly, the application of general phenomenological methods to the whole spectrum of religious ideas, activities, and so on. Phenomenology, he says, is descriptive; and one may agree in part. But after having observed that the selections include, as well as pieces of van der Leeuw and Kristensen, morsels of Maritain, Feuerbach, Schleiermacher, Tillich, Malinowski, Eliade and Buber, and having read Bettis' 'definition'—'Phenomenology of religion is an effort to focus

---

[60] ibid., p. 210.

[61] Oxtoby, 'Religionswissenschaft Revisited', in Neusner (ed.), *Religions in Antiquity* (1968), p. 596.

the perception of religious symbolic data to the degree of clarity demanded by the sharply focussed questions of the inquiring modern intellect'[62]—there is little that one can say, except that either the door has been thrown open to random subjectivity, or that a respectable scholarly ideal has disappeared behind a verbal mist. The aims of the book are so unclear that either interpretation seems equally feasible. Phenomenology may be more of an approach than a method, but there is no excuse for such treatment.

Turning, finally, to wiser counsels and saner opinions, among the many recent methodological explorations are two coming from opposite sides of the Atlantic. From America Willard G. Oxtoby draws attention to the extreme fragmentation of the field; this he holds to be an inevitable consequence of a consistent application of the principle of eidetic vision, which, as he puts it, 'suspends objectivity'. And he goes on :

> The phenomenologist is obliged simply to set forth his understanding as a whole, trusting that his reader will enter into it. But there is no procedure stated by which he can compel a second phenomenologist to agree with the adequacy and incontrovertibility of his analysis, unless the second phenomenologist's eidetic vision happens to be the same as the first's. For this reason phenomenological expositions of religion are in fact very personal appreciations of it, akin more to certain forms of literary and aesthetic criticism than to the natural or even the social sciences. As an approach phenomenology can be characterised, and yet when it is used for presenting phenomena there appear to be as many phenomenologies as there are phenomenologists. . . .[63]

Oxtoby has in mind here the type of phenomenology which passes far beyond the early descriptive ideal—that type exemplified by van der Leeuw and still more by Mircea Eliade's *Patterns in Comparative Religion*. And there can be little doubt that he is right. If Husserlian principles are consistently applied, then this must be the consequence; and there must be a similar consequence if the historical approach is used with sensitivity. But it is significant that from the American horizon, phenomenology has these implications.

Returning to Europe, Åke Hultkrantz of Stockholm is by training an ethnologist as well as a historian of religion. He sees the phenomenology of religion as consisting essentially in the systematisation of given material within its own appropriate cultural context (here using methods derived from Frobenius, via Jensen).

[62] Bettis (ed.), *The Phenomenology of Religion* (1969), p. 4.
[63] Oxtoby, op. cit., p. 597f.

This he calls typological, or morphological comparison. And he writes :

> I believe that it is possible to find a common attitude among many religious researchers of the present day, perhaps especially in the Nordic countries and in Italy, toward the aims and methods of the phenomenology of religion. As I see it only a strict, positive research along the lines which these researchers have drawn up has prospects of forming durable scientific results. Characteristics of this phenomenology are firstly the seeking of objectiveness and neutrality in questions of value, and secondly the connection with the problems within anthropology (including ethnology) and folklore. . . The phenomenology of religion is thus the systematic study of the forms of religion, that part of religious research which classifies and systematically investigates religious conceptions, rites and myth-traditions from comparative morphological-typological points of view. In principle the phenomenology of religion is identical with the older term 'comparative religion' . . .[64]

So it would appear that in some sense the wheel of comparative religion has come full circle. But at the same time, comparing this statement with that of Oxtoby, there are obviously some profound disagreements of method dividing, say, the United States from 'the Nordic countries and Italy'. We shall return to these in our final chapter.

[64] Hultkrantz, in *Temenos* 6 (1970), p. 74f.

XI

Toward a Dialogue of Religions?

At the Tokyo Congress of the International Association for the History of Religions, held in 1958, Friedrich Heiler of Marburg delivered a paper on 'The History of Religions as a Way to Unity of Religions', in which he called the 'bringing to light' of 'the unity of all religions' one of the most important tasks of the science of religion. The science's inquiry into truth, he stated,

> . . . bears important consequences for the practical relationship of one religion to another. Whoever recognises their unity must take it seriously by tolerance in word and deed. Thus scientific insight into this unity calls for a practical realisation in friendly exchange and in common ethical endeavour, 'fellowship' and 'cooperation'.[1]

Heiler was here putting into words what has become a widespread popular assumption in recent discussion about comparative religion (the science of religion) : that the only ultimately justifiable reason for engaging in this study is to improve relations between the adherents of different religious traditions. If the student of comparative religion, it may be asked, does not hold the key to better understanding between Christians and Hindus, Muslims and Jews, what can be the purpose of all the effort he has put into his studies?

Those who ask such questions as these may be depressed, or puzzled, that the academic specialist in this area will often answer that the study is its own justification, and that the introduction of such 'subjective' and emotionally loaded categories as 'dialogue' into the discussion will inevitably mean the loss of precision and quality, and that actually to engage in dialogue is no part of his calling. As a rule his time will in any case be taken up with the study of the past, rather than the present, of religions. Shortly we shall see just how much of recent discussion has revolved around this vexed question; but first we must inquire briefly into the conditions which brought the debate into being, and created the positions which are currently being attacked or defended.

There is another reason for examining this material. An impres-

---

[1] *Proceedings of the XIth International Congress for the History of Religions, Tokyo and Kyoto 1958* (1960), p. 19. cf. below, pp. 271-3.

sion common among orthodox Christians (and perhaps others) is that the student of comparative religion is by nature only comparatively religious, that is, that he is committed to religious relativity and syncretism and hence not to be trusted. Again, the reason—if one reason can be isolated—is to be sought in the same area of inter-religious *rapprochement* and dialogue. The association of 'comparative religion' with certain religious attitudes of an ultra-liberal nature lies behind this argument. We shall examine some of the relevant material, less to take sides in a current debate than to account for it, and for the acerbity still to be found on both sides.

We may begin by recalling that the founding fathers of comparative religion—men like C. P. Tiele, Max Müller, J. G. Frazer and P. D. Chantepie de la Saussaye—were 'liberals', in that they were uncommitted to any very specific external seat of authority in religion. To these men, the only religious authority was the authority of truth discovered by a process of free inquiry. And although they were mainly concerned with problems of religious origins, the problems of living religion were not foreign to most of them. Max Müller in particular engaged repeatedly in the politics and debates of the borderlands. They were therefore quite happy that comparative religion should be an applied, as well as a pure, science. Some were entirely willing to have their names associated with such public manifestations as the Chicago World's Parliament of Religions in 1893—again Max Müller is the outstanding example. Their views on what might result from this kind of exercise varied. The more orthodox probably looked forward to the ultimate triumph of Christianity, though a Christianity enriched by the insights of the Sacred Books of the East. The less orthodox anticipated a synthesis of religions, in which all sects, schisms, denominations and parties would be swallowed up. But that comparative religion was at root a *practical* activity would not be challenged in these circles.

But not all scholars held such views, and at the subsequent congresses—Stockholm 1897 and Paris 1900—we have been able to see the field being gradually taken over by the advocates of comparative religion as a pure historical science. The eirenic enthusiast was not welcomed, and soon came to realise that his interests would only be served by an entirely independent kind of gathering devoted to the goal of the final unity of all believers. The separation became more and more marked as time went on, and the scholarly climate of opinion began to turn away from unilinear evolution and world-wide comparison, and towards culture history, culture circles and the uniqueness of religious traditions. Thus by the 1920s the two paths had become almost entirely separated.

Unfortunately for subsequent students (not to mention historians), both parties continued to speak of their field as 'comparative religion' : the scholars used it to describe a type of historical scholarship, cool and uncommitted; the enthusiasts used it to describe a means to an end. How much later confusion might have been avoided, had the parties been able to devise independent terminologies, can only be imagined.

* * *

Concentrating now on the enthusiasts, the line from Chicago proceeded first of all to a 'continuation committee', and then to a series of meetings of the International Council of Unitarian and other Liberal Religious Thinkers and Workers, which were held between 1901 and 1913 in London, Amsterdam, Geneva, Boston, Berlin and Paris, under Unitarian auspices.[2] Attempts were made in the immediate pre-war years to extend this kind of work by calling conferences in India, Ceylon, China and Japan, but the war intervened. Subsequently Jabez T. Sunderland, who had attempted to organise these Asian conferences, described his objective :

> Believing that there is one God over all the world, and that all religions contain truths that are of vital and permanent importance to men, representatives of all faiths were invited to come together to confer with one another as brothers, on the broad basis of the Universal Fatherhood of God and the Universal Brotherhood of Man.[3]

More specifically, the conferences were expected (i) to promote better acquaintance between adherents of different religious traditions; (ii) to emphasise 'the universal elements in all the religions'; and (iii) to try to create in all the religions 'the conviction that they have a great work to do together for the moral uplift of the world'.[4]

It is not surprising to read that Sunderland's proposals were most

---

[2] The first President of the Council was J. Estlin Carpenter (cf. above, pp. 129-30), who wrote in connection with the Berlin meeting of 1910: 'Freedom and progress were throughout the inspiring watchwords of the Congress. . . Beneath all varieties of thought and expression lay the conviction of the profound importance of religion as a moral and spiritual force in human life. Among the themes which excited the most eager interest were its place in education, its share in the social order, its influence on peace.' Herford (ed.), *Joseph Estlin Carpenter* (1929), p. 130f.

[3] Weller (ed.), *World Fellowship* (1935), p. 520.

[4] ibid., p. 521.

warmly welcomed by groups in India, for by this time the dogma that all religions are of equal value as *sādhanas*, that is, as spiritual disciplines and ways to God, had come to be almost universally accepted among intellectuals.

This is not the place to trace out the emergence of this view in its entirety, but some mention must be made of its most outstanding advocates in modern times. Rāmmohun Roy (1772/4-1833), founder of the Brāhma Samāj, was a Hindu who had learned theism from Islamic sources, and who developed into an eirenic Deist, convinced of the oneness of God and the rationality of faith. He had had close contacts with both Unitarians and Evangelicals among Christians; had published in 1820 *The Precepts of Jesus, the Guide to Peace and Happiness*; and had defended himself vigorously when attacked by Evangelical missionaries on points of doctrine. In his belief that all great religious traditions embody essentially the same truths and are liable to fall into distinctive and individual errors, he paralleled the European Deists. In his advocacy of a multi-faith approach to religious problems, he anticipated (as certain Western minds also anticipated) the subsequent Hindu doctrine of the equality of religions.[5]

But it was not until later in the century that the doctrine began seriously to gain ground, as a direct result of the well known work of the Bengali mystic Sri Ramakrishna and his two disciples Keshub Chunder Sen and Swami Vivekānanda.

Ramakrishna (1834-1886) had, in his attempts to explore every available means for the attainment of spiritual insight, experimented with what he took to be the *sādhanas* of Islam and Christianity; he had seen visions of Jesus and of Muhammad, and had claimed that the differences between the spiritual disciplines were of no real significance; the Bengali, Urdu and English languages have different words to describe water, he once said, but the substance itself is one, not three. In the same way competing and apparently contradictory views of religion refer to one attainable spiritual vision of reality. All *sādhanas* lead finally to the same goal, and the only ultimate heresy is to fail to realise that fact. Conversion, or the attempt to convert, is a waste of time, an exchanging of one path up the mist-shrouded mountain for another; indeed, it may be worse, since there are sound cultural reasons for remaining within one's own ancestral fold. So while Ramakrishna could say that 'every man should follow his own religion. A Christian should follow Christianity, a Muslim should follow Islam, and so on,' he could immediately add: 'For the

---

[5] On Rammohun Roy, see Hinnells and Sharpe (ed.), *Hinduism* (1972), pp. 8off.; Farquhar, *Modern Religious Movements in India* (1915), pp. 29ff.

Hindus the ancient path, the path of the Aryan Rishis, is the best.'[6]

The diffusion of Ramakrishna's teachings, and their extension into a fully-fledged theory of inter-religious fellowship and co-operation, was accomplished by two of his disciples, Keshub Chunder Sen, and Swami Vivekānanda.

Sen, as leader of the Brāhma Samāj, as the heir of Rāmmohun Roy and the disciple of Ramakrishna, made the doctrine of the complementarity of religions (*sādhanas*) into a practical programme, and in the New Dispensation (the eclectic offshoot of the Brāhma Samāj), he was able to put these teachings into practice. It has been said that the three chief notes of the New Dispensation were immediacy, synthesis and subjectivity, and all are present in such a statement as this, dating from the early 1880s :

> Come, then, to the synthetic unity of the New Dispensation. You will see how all other dispensations are unified in this, a whole host of churches resolved into a synthetic unity. In the midst of the multiplicity of dispensations in the world there is a concealed unity, and it is of the highest importance to us all that we should discover it with the light of logic and science. For science and salvation are one thing, and the highest Unity and Deity are identical . . . If there is science in all things, is there no science in the dispensations of God?[7]

Unlike Ramakrishna, who never left Bengal, Sen visited Europe, where he met, among others, Max Müller, and made a striking impression. But Sen's impact on the West was slight compared to that of Swami Vivekānanda, on the occasion of the Chicago World's Parliament of Religions in 1893. We do not need to retell this particular story.[8] As an immediate disciple of Ramakrishna, Vivekānanda claimed to speaking with 'his master's voice'; and undoubtedly this was so : most of his teaching on the equal value of religions was genuinely derived from Ramakrishna. But he reached the ear of the Western world as Ramakrishna had never done, and on his return, hailed as he was as India's first 'missionary' to the West, he became a national hero.[9] He himself died in 1902, having helped to create a new Hindu orthodoxy—that all religious traditions are good and true, and that the highest wisdom consists in recognising that fact.

[6] On Ramakrishna, see Hinnells and Sharpe, op. cit., pp. 86ff.; Farquhar, op. cit., pp. 188ff.

[7] Quoted in Parekh, *The Brahma Samaj* (1929), p. 164f.

[8] cf. above, p. 138f.

[9] Sharma, *Studies in the Renaissance of Hinduism in the Nineteenth and Twentieth Centuries* (1944), p. 281.

The final act of apostasy is to attempt (whether successfully or not) to proselytise. There was in fact a polemical edge here, aimed in the general direction of Christianity; but for our purposes, it is enough to note that it helped at the same time to create precisely the right climate of opinion in India for a certain kind of comparative religion—that which furthers, and is intended to further, a living dialogue of religions, and to aim ultimately at the acknowledged unity of all believers.

The process was materially assisted by the work of the Theosophical Society. Founded in New York in 1875, by the early years of the twentieth century its headquarters had been moved to Madras, where the affairs of the society were presided over by Mrs. Annie Besant. Two of the three avowed aims of the society were, first, to further the brotherhood of man, and secondly, to promote the study of comparative religion (originally the phrase used here had been 'Aryan religion')[10]—with the obvious implication that the study of comparative religion does contribute to the creation of a sense of universal brotherhood.

* * *

The Eastern and Western branches of this movement did in fact meet in the inter-war years, in an atmosphere considerably sobered by the events of 1914–18. Anglo-German scholarly mistrust, already marked, was growing apace, a feeling which the events of the immediate post-war years did little enough to dispel.

But there were some optimists. There was President Wilson, and there were the members of the League of Nations; and in the Wilsonian dawn there were other international movements sponsored from the United States. In 1918 a 'League of Neighbors' began to work for racial unity; in 1924 a 'Fellowship of Faiths' began to work for spiritual unity. In 1928 there was founded a 'Threefold Movement—Union of East and West, League of Neighbors, Fellowship of Faiths' which became in 1929 the *World Fellowship of Faiths.*[11]

Meanwhile, in Europe, proposals were afoot for a 'World Conference for International Peace through Religion', with preliminary conferences held in the 1920s and early 1930s. And in 1921 no less

[10] Besant, 'Theosophical Society', in *ERE* XII (1921), pp. 300ff. The objects of the society are there stated as: (1) To form a nucleus of the Universal Brotherhood of Humanity, without distinction of race, creed, sex, caste or colour; (2) To encourage the study of comparative religion, philosophy, and science; (3) To investigate the unexplained laws of Nature and the powers latent in man. cf. Farquhar, *Modern Religious Movements in India* (1913), pp. 208ff.

[11] *World Fellowship*, p. 502.

a person than Rudolf Otto inaugurated an Inter-Religious League (*Religiöser Menschheitsbund*), the programme of which began by asking :

> Who will save the world out of its common and enormous want and distress, into which we are sinking deeper and deeper? Politics, Science, Economics? They avail nothing with the vital thing. And what is the vital thing? The vital thing is the unanimous, strong and common will or responsibility of the entire cultural civilisation to master evil through mutual effort and a mutual aim, through a reciprocal responsibility and a well planned interchange of purpose. . .[12]

Only 'religion with its organisations, its education, its pronouncements, its chosen leaders and standard bearers' is capable of fulfilling this purpose. And so, if the churches and other religious institutions of the world could only be enlisted on the side of this type of quest for understanding, what might not be achieved? Perhaps '. . . a spiritual foundation would be created for a general conviction . . . out of which enduring forms could develop into powerful interstate [international] organisations of nations and classes'.[13]

In 1928–9, Otto went to Ceylon and India to gain support for his *Menschheitsbund*. From the highly detailed report of this journey written by his Swedish companion Birger Forell, it is clear that Otto was extremely well received throughout the subcontinent.[14] But it is equally evident that Hindu leaders were for the most part accepting Otto on their terms, rather than on his. Otto was certainly not interested in creating a synthetic, Esperanto-type religion; he wanted merely to enlist the support of religious leaders to combat worldwide negation of the principles of morals and religion. But many Christians believed him to be on the verge of selling the pass altogether, and his active involvement in the dialogue of religions was not shared by many of his fellow-scholars. Nathan Söderblom, for instance, when invited in 1930 to attend the World Religions for Peace Conference at Geneva, wrote to his assistant Herman Neander, 'You must go, but I wish to die a Lutheran.' Söderblom was similarly critical of Otto's ideas and initiatives, which he considered syncretistic.[15]

Otherwise it was typical of the religious stresses and strains of the period that a synthetic faith such as Baha'i should have enjoyed a great vogue during these same years. The most popular of Baha'i

[12] ibid., p. 504.
[13] ibid., p. 505.
[14] Forell, *Från Ceylon till Himalaya* (1929).
[15] Sundkler, *Nathan Söderblom* (1968), p. 422ff.

books, Esslemont's *Bahā'u'llāh and the New Era* (1923), in fact stated the aims of Baha'i as being, among other things:

The unification of the world of humanity, the welding together of the world's different religions, the reconciliation of religion and science, the establishment of universal peace...[16]

Otto wanted not so much a world faith as a world forum, in which representatives of different traditions could meet together in opposition to the common enemy, variously called 'materialism' or 'secularism'.

Many religious leaders of the inter-war period were prepared to accept such a position. It made its presence felt, for instance, at the 1928 conference of the International Missionary Council in Jerusalem;[17] and dominated the report, published four years later, of the Laymen's Foreign Missions Inquiry, *Rethinking Missions*.[18] And indeed it was a position on which the liberals of all religious traditions proved able to agree without difficulty; but what was its relation to comparative religion?

* * *

Among those who most unhesitatingly identified the concerns of comparative religion with the concerns of world peace, international harmony and universal brotherhood, a peculiarly influential place was occupied—and continued for many years to be occupied—by Sarvepalli Radhakrishnan (b. 1888).[19]

Born a Telegu Brahmin, taught philosophy in Madras by the brilliant A. G. Hogg, early influenced by the precept and example of Vivekānanda, between 1909 and 1926 Radhakrishnan had occupied teaching posts in Madras, Mysore and Calcutta. In 1926 he visited the West for the first time on the invitation of L. P. Jacks, then Editor of the *Unitarian Hibbert Journal*, to lecture at Manchester College, Oxford. These lectures were afterward published as *The Hindu View of Life*. In 1929 he took the post vacated by J.

[16] Esslemont, *Bahā'u'llāh and the New Era* (1973 ed.), p. 258.

[17] *Report of the Jerusalem Meeting of the International Missionary Council* 1: The Christian Life and Message in relation to Non-Christian Systems (1928). The most important paper was perhaps that by the Quaker Rufus Jones, 'Secular Civilisation and the Christian Task', pp. 284ff.

[18] *Re-thinking Missions : a Layman's Inquiry after One Hundred Years*, by the Commission of Appraisal: William Ernest Hocking, Chairman (1932). Rufus Jones was one of the leading members of the Commission. Hendrik Kraemer's book *The Christian Message in a Non-Christian World* (1938) was very largely a counterblast to this report.

[19] Schilpp (ed.), *The Philosophy of Sarvepalli Radhakrishnan* (1952); cf. Sharpe and Hinnells, *Hinduism* (1972), pp. 102ff.

Estlin Carpenter as Professor of Comparative Religion at Manchester College. Returning to India for a brief period as Vice-
Chancellor of Andhra University, in 1936 he came back to Oxford
as Spalding Professor of Eastern Religions and Ethics, a post which
he held until the outbreak of war. Subsequently his career led him
into politics rather than religion and philosophy; ultimately, from
1962 until his retirement in 1967, he was president of the Republic
of India.

Radhakrishnan's view of the task and responsibility of comparative religion to assist in the unification of mankind can be distilled
from virtually all his many books; but we may take one of the most
explicit statements, a lecture on 'Comparative Religion' delivered
at Manchester College in October 1929, and published in *East and
West in Religion* (1933).

The scientific student of religion, says Radhakrishnan, is required
'to treat all religions in a spirit of absolute detachment and impartiality'.[20] But Radhakrishnan's impartiality is not the impartiality
of the phenomenologist, attempting to accept the believer's own
faith-stance whatever that may be; it is predetermined. Impartiality,
in his view, is virtually bound to make us 'surrender our exclusive
claims', that is, to accept the view of religion which a particular
philosophy of religion prescribes for us. Comparative religion, however, will teach us that religion is a 'universal phenomenon', 'native
to the human mind', and 'integral to human nature'; and it will show
us that behind all the expressions of religion there is '. . . the same
intention, the same striving, the same faith'.[21] Such a realisation as
this is especially valuable now, in the present disarray of the world.
In the midst of world disorder (and we must remember the period
in which this is being written) there is a growing sense of unity and
co-operation, and those who can read the signs of the times are
urging more contact, more exchange, more mutual understanding.
And he goes on :

> The keynote of the new attitude is expressed by the word
> 'sharing'. The different religious men of the East and the West
> are to share their visions and insights, hopes and fears, plans and
> purposes. Unhappily, just as in the political region, so here also
> this is more an aspiration than an actuality. Comparative Religion
> helps us to further this ideal of the sharing among religions which
> no longer stand in uncontaminated isolation. . . They are fellow
> workers toward the same goal.[22]

[20] Radhakrishnan, *East and West in Religion* (1933), p. 16.
[21] ibid., p. 19.
[22] ibid., p. 26.

It is not without some significance in the history of ideas that a later edition of this book includes here an appreciative reference to the Laymen's Report of 1932, *Rethinking Missions*.

To this belief in comparative religion as an instrument of sharing Radhakrishnan then adds a belief in comparative religion as a prophylactic against exclusiveness, saying (as he was to say throughout his career) that 'the absolute claim' of any tradition to uniqueness is disproved by comparative religion. One can only comment that comparative religion *can* do this, but not as a science; it can do it only if the student begins with this presupposition, in which case it can certainly confirm what is already believed. But this is scarcely science. And 'comparative religion' as we have been following its development in these pages, can fulfil a function of this kind at most implicitly; it can never be an explicit concern, or a plank in its public platform.

One of the last major public appearances made by Radhakrishnan before his retirement was to deliver an address at the inauguration of the Harvard University Center for the Study of World Religions. This address, entitled *Fellowship of the Spirit*, was published in 1961, and reprinted in L. S. Rouner (ed.), *Philosophy, Religion, and the Coming World Civilisation* (1966)—a collection of essays in honour of W. E. Hocking, the architect of *Rethinking Missions*. Here Radhakrishnan is once more affirming his faith in mankind and his pessimism about human beings, his anticipation of something better which the study and practice of religion will help to bring about, and his trust in the mutual appreciation which study brings. The argument is essentially that of the lecture of the 1920s, and we need not recapitulate it. But we may quote the peroration :

> **The different religions are to be used as building stones for the development of a human culture** in which the adherents of the different religions may be fraternally united as children of one Supreme. All religions convey to their followers a message of abiding hope. The world will give birth to a new faith which will be but the old faith in another form, the faith of all ages, the potential divinity of man which will work for the supreme purpose written in our hearts and souls, the unity of all mankind. It is my hope and prayer that unbelief shall disappear and superstition shall not enslave the mind and we shall recognise that we are brothers, one in spirit and one in fellowship.[23]

* * *

[23] Rouner, op. cit., p. 296.

Returning now to the pre-Second World War period, there took place during the 1930s a number of inter-faith conferences, on both sides of the Atlantic. In the United States, the most comprehensive of these appears to have been the 1933 International Congress of the World Fellowship of Faiths.[24] In Britain, 1936, 1937 and 1938 saw three meetings of the World Congress of Faiths, at London, Oxford and Cambridge, all under the chairmanship of Sir Francis Younghusband.

To judge from the records of the third of these,[25] the entire proceeding must have served to confirm, in the eyes of the academic authorities, that this was the direction in which comparative religion was pointing. Three years previously, Radhakrishnan (one of the main speakers on this occasion) had been appointed Spalding Professor of Eastern Religions and Ethics at Oxford, the first appointee of this kind since the days of Max Müller. And it was well known that notwithstanding his eminence as a Hindu philosopher, he was at best a tendentious *Religionsgeschichtler*. Previously, it may be recalled, 'comparative religion' had been associated, as far as Oxford was concerned, with Dissent, being taught only at Manchester College (Unitarian) and Mansfield College (Congregational). Radhakrishnan had come to Oxford rather in the guise of a latter-day Rammohun Roy, as an exotic Unitarian. Some limited support he certainly had from the liberal wing of the Anglican establishment. But as it was, these developments had made it difficult for comparative religion to achieve genuine academic status as a historical discipline, free from theological (or for that matter anthropological) ties. And the World Congress of Faiths, coming to Oxford and Cambridge when it did, may have served to deepen the suspicion in some minds that comparative religion was not to be taken seriously as an academic discipline.

But on this occasion, C. E. Raven, addressing the assembly as Regius Professor of Divinity, expressed his appreciation for the work of the Congress, which he called 'this movement of ours':

... if this movement of ours is to make its proper impression upon the history of our time, sooner or later it will have to be acclimatised, planted in the universities, and for that the work that Professor Radhakrishnan is doing in Oxford has set a standard and given us here something to look forward to.[26]

[24] Weller (ed.), *World Fellowship: Addresses and Messages by Leading Spokesmen of all Faiths, Races and Countries* (1935).
[25] *The Renaissance of Religion: Being the proceedings of the third meeting of the World Congress of Faiths, Cambridge University 1938* (1938).
[26] ibid., p. 5.

Otherwise this same speaker touched upon an issue which in coming years was to assume greater and greater importance when he observed that the student of theology ought to be given the opportunity of first-hand knowledge, 'not only of his own religion but of those other great faiths whose history goes back into so remote a past, and whose connection with the religious experience of mankind is so intimate'.[27] And he added that the task of the Congress as a whole was '. . . to help us to clear away misunderstandings; it is to deepen . . . our understanding both of religion in general and of our own particular faiths; to deepen that understanding by enlightening us by the flint and steel method . . .'[28] One might perhaps observe that while some comparative religionists would certainly have agreed with this assessment, many more would have been totally at a loss to know how to conduct such a prospective 'flint and steel' encounter! Field-work and 'participant observation', though by now well-established in anthropology and the infant social sciences, had scarcely as yet penetrated the academic study of religion. Only the much maligned missionaries were likely to be really at ease in such a situation of encounter; but their priorities were not necessarily those of World Congresses or World Fellowships of Faiths.

* * *

It could be argued that the World Congress of Faiths, and similar movements, were carrying out a useful function in attempting to bring together adherents of different religious traditions. Certainly there were a great many misunderstandings between believers which then needed, and to a great extent still need, to be cleared up. But another group were arguing at the same time that the externals and the observables of religion are of no real value, and that close examination of the data of comparative religion reveals a core of truth common to all (or perhaps to most) of the major religious traditions, a core which can be accepted and revered even by those alienated from specific traditions and their accretions.

In some ways this movement was simply neo-Deist; in other ways it owed allegiance to the mystical tradition, and in particular to that part of it which had been passed through the prism of neo-Hinduism. As its watchword it took the title *philosophia perennis*, the 'perennial philosophy'. It falls outside the scope of this survey to consider this approach in detail, but we may mention that its most energetic advocates included Ananda K. Coomaraswamy and his disciples Frithjof Schuon and René Guénon.

[27] ibid., p. 6.
[28] ibid., p. 7.

The most widely read manifesto of the school was Aldous Huxley's book *The Perennial Philosophy* (1946), which contains the statement that this philosophy '. . . is primarily concerned with the one divine Reality substantial to the manifold world of things and lives and minds'.[29] Among acknowledged scholars who privately confess allegiance to the perennial philosophy we may mention the Buddhologist Edward Conze (b. 1904), while among its opponents particular significance attaches to Radhakrishnan's successor as Spalding Professor of Eastern Religions and Ethics at Oxford, R. C. Zaehner (1913–1974).

At his inaugural lecture, delivered in November 1953, Zaehner paid tribute to Mr and Mrs H. N. Spalding, who had endowed the Chair 'with the aim of bringing together the world's great religions in closer understanding, harmony, and friendship', and suggested that the Professorship had three main functions. First came the furthering of interest in the world's great religions; then the interpretation, comparison and contrasting of those systems; and thirdly the bringing of them together in closer 'understanding, harmony, and friendship'. Only the first two of these he felt to be legitimate. And in somewhat drastic terms he went on :

> The third—the promotion of understanding between the great religions—can hardly be pursued in a British university where the non-Christian religions can scarcely be said to be represented at all. Nor do I think that it can be a legitimate function of a university professor to attempt to induce harmony among elements as disparate as the great religions of mankind appear to be, if, as seems inevitable, the resultant harmony is only to be apparent, verbal, and therefore fictitious. Such a procedure may well be commendable in a statesman. In a profession that concerns itself with the pursuit of truth it is damnable.[30]

In fact Zaehner's period at Oxford saw a total *volte-face* in the Spalding chair from the position held by Radhakrishnan to a method of comparison by means of radical contrast. Among his many books mention may be made of *Zurvan, a Zoroastrian Dilemma* (1955), *Mysticism Sacred and Profane* (1957), *At Sundry Times* (1958), *Hindu and Muslim Mysticism* (1960), and his Gifford Lectures of 1967–9, *Concordant Discord* (1970).

As a Roman Catholic layman, Zaehner showed himself to be totally opposed to the perennial philosophy in any form, save perhaps as a mere description of the teaching of the non-prophetic religions. The prophetic religions, Judaism (from which are derived

[29] Huxley, *The Perennial Philosophy* (1946), p. 10.
[30] Zaehner, *Concordant Discord* (1970), p. 429.

Christianity and Islam) and Zoroastrianism, he saw as working on such fundamentally different principles that any attempt to subsume them under a blanket term such as *philosophia perennis* is utterly mistaken. 'Mystics make no demands,' he wrote in *At Sundry Times*, 'they merely point a way : prophets make insistent demands, they demand obedience. They are extremely uncomfortable people.'[31] Thus while one aim of comparative religion may well be to increase the mutual understanding of believers, it in no way follows that a further aim is either to create a synthetic religion out of the dismembered fragments of the world's faiths, or to pretend that all paths lead to the same goal. And in a confession of faith in his Giffords, he adopts a clear and unambiguous position :

> In all my writing on comparative religion my aim has been to show that there *is* a coherent pattern in religious history. For me the centre of coherence can only be Christ. It could scarcely be otherwise since I have freely accepted the 'bondage' of the Catholic Church, and I would scarcely have done this if I had not thought that in that very bondage there was also 'release' and that this was in fact the true religion—for me.[32]

It must remain a moot point to what extent Zaehner did fulfil the literal requirements of the Spalding Chair; but that his writings have in fact greatly illuminated the Zoroastrian and Hindu traditions in particular goes without saying.

* * *

We began this chapter by noting the puzzlement felt by some in the present situation that there are scholars who, while claiming to be concerned with the comparative study of religions, appear to wish to avoid committing themselves in the matter of the actual encounter of believers. We have traced in a summary fashion a line of tradition which has been very much involved in that encounter, and we have hinted at the kind of opposition it has aroused. There remains to be said, however, that the tide of *popular* opinion has for some years been running strongly in favour of 'dialogue'.[33]

[31] id., *At Sundry Times* (1958), p. 26.
[32] *Concordant Discord*, p. 16f.
[33] Sharpe, 'The Goals of Inter-Religious Dialogue', in Hick (ed.), *Truth and Dialogue* (1974), pp. 77ff. In this essay I have attempted to show that the term 'dialogue' is used in a number of different ways, determined largely by the goals to which the process is expected to lead, and that blanket use of the term is seldom other than misleading.

Popular interest, particularly among students, in the religious traditions of the East is intensive, and is often coupled with a degree of alienation (which may be merely fashionable, but which is none the less real) from Western religious traditions. As a result of these and other pressures, scholarship has found it progressively harder to maintain an attitude of aloofness, however that attitude may be motivated; particularly in Britain and America, it is expected of the comparative religionist that he will at least have something to say on these issues. What he says will be inseparable from his own private presuppositions; and these still vary greatly, as we shall see in our final chapter. But what he may not do is to remain unaware that the problem exists.

There is one final point which must be made, or rather reinforced. We have already noted how confusing it can be that people use the words 'comparative religion' in different ways, and mean different things by it. It happens that at the present time the words 'studies in comparative religion' refer to three separate publications.

The first comprises a series of thirty-nine pamphlets, first published in the 1930s by the Catholic Truth Society, and reissued in the 1950s, under the editorship of E. C. Messenger.[34] Each deals with a specific religious tradition or a part thereof, and the series as a whole reminds one of the *Religionsgeschichtliche Volksbücher* of the turn of the century, except that its intention is purely apologetical. In this perspective, the study of comparative religion is wholly a (Catholic) Christian apologetical exercise, in which it is shown how each 'religion' is either replaced or fulfilled by 'the Catholic Religion in its three historical stages : Primitive, Judaic, and Christian'.[35]

The second publication is a journal, which commenced publication in the 1960s, and which is dedicated to 'Metaphysics, Cosmology, Tradition, Symbolism'. It stands firmly on the ground of a belief in the *philosophia perennis*, and much space is taken up by articles from the great triumvirate of Ananda Coomaraswamy, Frithjof Schuon and René Guénon. Here, comparative religion is the process by which the individual attains to this particular form of intellectual enlightenment.

The third is called 'Stockholm Studies in Comparative Religion', and up to 1968 it comprised eight monographs, each of a highly specialised and impeccably scholarly nature. Among them are Ivar

---

[34] Messenger (ed.), *'Studies in Comparative Religion (1953–1956)*. Among the authors of the pamphlets are Wilhelm Schmidt, L. de la Vallée Poussin, A. J. Carnoy and Christopher Dawson.

[35] Messenger, *A Philosophy of Comparative Religion* (vol. 39 of the series), p. 26f.

Paulson, *Schutzgeister und Gottheiten des Wildes in Norderasien* (Guardian Spirits and Deities of the Wild in Northern Asia, 1961); Åke Hultkrantz, *Les Religions des Indiens primitifs de l'Amérique* (1963); Andrejs Johansons, *Der Schirmherr des Hofes im Volksglauben der Letter* (The Protector of the Farm in Latvian Folkbelief, 1964); and Walther Eidlitz, *Kṛṣṇa-Çaitānya* (1968). To the Scandinavian scholarship represented here, 'comparative religion' has been re-adopted as an internationally acceptable term in replacement of 'history of religions' or *Religionswissenschaft*, but retaining the absolute demands for objectivity and scholarly precision which have run like a golden thread throughout the hundred years we have been studying. The actual emphasis is anthropological and ethnological, however.

It is perhaps arguable that a term capable of being used in such widely differing meanings—irrespective of the issues of 'dialogue'—is no longer usable at all. But in fact it is still used, against a background of methodological uncertainty, produced by all the varying impulses we have passed in review. We shall proceed now to try to bring our survey to a conclusion by giving an account of some of the methodological discussion of the last twenty years.

XII

Twenty Years of International Debate, 1950–1970

An attempt will be made in this last chapter to pick out some of the issues which have been debated among historians of religion since the early 1950s, and to give a summary account of a few selected methodological discussions during that time. A comprehensive account is of course not possible. A vast amount of material has accumulated during the past two decades, much of it directly or indirectly relevant to the methodological debate, and merely to catalogue it would be an onerous task. In addition, the debate has been carried on in many countries and languages, and in response to local, as well as general, stimuli. Again there is no way in which one reporter can have his finger on all the relevant pulses, and a process of selection is absolutely necessary. A third problem is simply that the debate is still in progress, and that it is hard to step outside it in order to gain perspective. Eventually, with all the wisdom of hindsight, we may be able to tell what has happened; but for the moment, it is sometimes the hardest thing in the world to tell exactly what is happening.

In 1959 an American historian of religion, E. R. Goodenough, summed up the climate of opinion as he then saw it in the words : 'This generation wants either an assurance that its true existence is not in the scientific world, or it wants analytical precision.'[1] This of course expresses in a nutshell the perennial choice, the either/or which has faced the comparative study of religion from the very beginning. Scholarship, as we have seen in so many ways, has had the choice of being 'pure', striving after a historical and analytical understanding of religion as a human phenomenon; or of channelling all its energies into its own religious quest, thus becoming an 'applied' science almost to the verge of soteriology. Perhaps there is no alternative. Certainly, the demand for analytical precision has very often been heard against the background of the noise of solemn assemblies. Equally, soteriology may be a reaction against what is believed to be a destructive analysis. But in our day, when the old soteriologies have weakened and opened the way to so many new and ephemeral forms of religion, scholarship has tended to assert

[1] Goodenough, 'Religionswissenschaft', in *Numen* VI (1959, p. 84.

its own identity principally by burrowing more and more deeply into fragmented specialist study.

Thus the comparative religionist (or *Religionswissenschaftler*, or historian of religions) today is seldom an encyclopaedic personality. He is as a rule a historian, who cultivates philological and archaeological techniques; he may have more or less familiarity with psychology, philosophy or phenomenology. Probably he combines features of a number of these. And it is still more probable that he will have little or nothing, save a name, in common with the pioneers who first began to speak of 'comparative religion' a century ago. Even the name may have gone. Comparative religion, he may argue, was a splendid Victorian science, but one which the passage of time has simply rendered redundant.

But as we have seen, the abandonment of one method in the study of religion has not meant its automatic replacement by another. For many years now the question of method has been wide open, and despite the high seriousness which has always been found in the study of religion, the scholarly community has not always been able to agree on the terms or conditions on which that study ought to be pursued. And therein lies our present problem, as we shall now try to show.

*　　*　　*

The last twenty-five years have seen the methodological discussion carried on in a variety of journals and conferences; but a convenient focus is provided by the International Association for the History of Religions, which was founded in 1950.[2]

The first initiative toward the setting up of such an organisation came from a Dutch society of historians of religion, *Genootschap van Godsdiensthistorici.* This society sent out in the late 1940s an invitation to scholars in the field, which pointed out that the last international congress had taken place as long ago as in 1934, and suggested that the time might now be ripe for reinvigorating that tradition. The invitation was signed by A. Bertholet of Basel, G. van der Leeuw of Groningen and C. J. Bleeker of Amsterdam. A list of 29 names of 'Members of an Organising Committee' was circulated at the same time. Of these, twenty were continental Europeans; two were British (S. A. Cook and E. O. James), three Swedes (J. E. Holmberg, M. P. Nilsson and Geo Widengren) and only four Americans (W. F. Albright, A. D. Nock, R. H. Lowie and Joachim

---

[2] The following account is based in part on unpublished letters and papers, part of the equipment of the IAHR Secretariat.

Wach). But this represented very adequately the position of international scholarship in the field at that time, which was proportionately much stronger in Holland and Sweden than in almost any other country (except France, but the French played little initial part in the organisation).

The Conference met, mustering a total of 193 delegates, and the International Association for the History of Religions was officially constituted, with Gerardus van der Leeuw as its first President and C. Jouco Bleeker as its first General Secretary. Sadly, before the year was out van der Leeuw had died; he was replaced as President by Raffaele Pettazzoni of Rome. Subsequent Presidents were Geo Widengren of Uppsala and the present incumbent, Marcel Simon of Strasbourg. The Secretaryship continued to be held by Bleeker until 1970, when he was succeeded by S. G. F. Brandon of Manchester, and following Brandon's tragic death in the following year, by the present writer.

The theme of the Amsterdam conference was 'The Mythic-Ritual Pattern in Civilisation'—a highly controversial subject, on which opinions and theories differed radically.[3] While some scholars, notably in Scandinavia, were apt to stress the interdependence of myth and ritual at every opportunity, and to see 'myth and ritual patterns' everywhere in the Ancient Near East, other scholars remained notably sceptical.[4] Already an extensive polemic had been carried on in the scholarly press, and this was to continue, at least into the 1960s. For our purposes, however, it is enough to note that no consensus was aimed at, that differences of opinion were expected and noted, and that the conference therefore served (as subsequent conferences were also to serve) as a scholarly barometer, not a rudder.

It is also interesting, in view of later controversies, to find the Secretary General, Bleeker, noting in an address that the conference was not fully representative; gaps in personnel needed to be filled for the sake of the discipline as a whole. There was, said Bleeker, a striking lack of scholars from the Oriental world at this conference; in the past Western scholarship had been instrumental

[3] Bleeker, Drewes and Hidding (eds.), *Proceedings of the 7th Congress for the History of Religions, Amsterdam, 4th–9th September 1950* (1951).
[4] I had originally planned that this book should include a chapter devoted to the debate surrounding the questions of myth, ritual and kingship, partly in order to give some more concrete indication of the type of question which modern research in comparative religion busies itself with. Much of the chapter was in fact written, but had to be omitted for reasons of space. See Edsman, 'Zum sakralen Königtum in der Forschung der letzten hundert Jahre,' in *The Sacral Kingship* (Supplements to *Numen* IV, 1969), pp. 4–17.

in opening up the East, but 'it may be foreseen that the spirit of . . . rising selfconsciousness in the East will stimulate many scholars there to study their spiritual heritage : a next congress should include a well chosen delegation from the East.'[5] To this it is perhaps necessary to add that much was to depend on the precise definition of 'scholar' in this context, and that a well chosen delegation presupposed someone to do the choosing. Again criteria are involved, on which individuals might conceivably not agree. At all events, there were seeds here of dissent, or at least of misunderstanding.

The sole object of the IAHR was 'the promotion of the academic study of the history of religions through the international collaboration of all scholars whose research has a bearing on the subject'. This seemed straightforward enough, and in fact most of the scholars who took part in the early meetings of the Association were, and remained, content with such a general formulation. The ideals it expressed served to support not only various series of congresses and study conferences, but an extensive programme of publishing, notably involving the journal *Numen* (from 1954, first under Pettazzoni's and later under Bleeker's editorship) and an international bibliography (also from 1954). But the phrase 'the academic study of the history of religions' was in some ways a loaded expression. The word 'academic' in particular implied, though it did not say, that only certain standards of scholarship were acceptable in *IAHR* circles. These were the historical and philological standards established around the turn of the century, partly in reaction to any form of theological treatment of religious data; and the phenomenological method, particularly as practised by van der Leeuw, Bleeker and Widengren. Thus the Association was at first largely a society of specialists, mostly employed by European universities; their ethos was that of the secular historian, though applied to the data of religion, and in their work they might possibly move into the wider field of the phenomenology of religion from time to time. However, we may recall that in our last chapter we pointed to the existence in the West of another, less stringently historical approach. The affinities of this we saw to be with reformed Hinduism, and with the dreams of idealists generally. Gradually the two positions were to meet under the IAHR umbrella, but not immediately.

The second post-war congress, in Rome in 1955, dealt with another purely historical question, that of the sacral kingship (an issue which was then closely linked with that of myth and ritual).[6]

---

[5] *Amsterdam Report*, p. 85.

[6] cf. Hooke (ed.), *Myth, Ritual and Kingship* (1958). As a student at Manchester I attended the series of lectures which were published as this volume.

Though historically controversial, there was little to cause methodological excitement here. But a turning-point, as far as the IAHR was concerned, came in the years 1958–60.

In 1958 the IAHR held an international congress in Tokyo.[7] This was actually the ninth in overall sequence since the 1900 congress in Paris, but it was the first to be held outside Europe. Appropriately the theme chosen for the meeting was 'Religion and Thought in East and West : A Century of Cultural Exchange'.

What the organisers expected to emerge from this meeting is not quite clear. The historian knew—or ought to have known—that the 'cultural exchange' between East and West over the past decades had been less than ideal. And on the matter of religion, there was a considerable gulf fixed between Eastern and Western interpretations of both the essence and the manifestations of religion. The West had generally tended to look upon religion for scholarly purposes as something static, a collection of data, or alternatively as an organism to be dissected. Typically the West had long been accustomed to spending most of its labours on the ancient religious traditions. Perhaps by the 1950s its approach was no longer purely genetic; but well-established conventions die hard. The East, on the other hand, could as a rule conceive of no purpose for the study of religion other than to deepen one's apprehension and understanding of Reality; certainly it could never look upon religion merely as a passive object stretched out on the scholar's operating table. Religion is there to be lived, and if study does not help the student to live better or more fully, then there can be little or no point in it.

But this was approximately what one group of scholars and others had been saying in the West, at least since the days of Schelling and Emerson and the other romantics—that religion is to be *lived*, and that the comparative study of religion can only be motivated as a life-enhancing discipline. But of the IAHR leadership, few would have been prepared to affirm this much. They might privately have agreed; but in public they refused to compromise their scholarly reputation by such 'subjectivism'. Therein lay the seeds of fresh conflict, which the conference in Tokyo began to reveal.

The conference report, when it appeared in 1960, comprised almost a thousand tightly-packed pages, and by far the greater part of the papers therein contained are eminently scholarly; the problem was not one of scholarly standards. But the organisers felt it appropriate to place first in the volume an address by Friedrich Heiler

[7] *Proceedings of the IXth International Congress for the History of Religions, Tokyo and Kyoto 1958* (1960).

of Marburg on 'The History of Religions as a Way to Unity of Religions'.[8]

The Western religious traditions, said Heiler, are traditionally exclusive in their attitudes to other faiths, ascribing to themselves an ultimate validity. There is, however, a tradition of tolerance in the world, stretching from Aśoka to the fathers of comparative religion ('. . . men like Friedrich Max Müller, Nathan Söderblom, Rudolf Otto, Tor Andrae, Alfred Loisy, Gerardus van der Leeuw, Raffaele Pettazzoni'), and which has given us '. . . a host of insights by which century-old prejudices have been removed'.[9] The scholar sees how close religions are to one another : by comparing their structure, beliefs and practices, he is led to a 'transcendent' which overarches all and yet is immanent in human hearts. Study, then, is the best prophylactic against exclusiveness, because it teaches love; and where there is love, there can be—indeed there must be— unity in the spirit. And he concluded :

> One of the most important tasks of the science of religion is to bring to light this unity of all religions. It thereby pursues only one purpose, that of pure knowledge of the truth. But unintentionally there sprouts forth from the root of scientific inquiry into truth not only a tree with wondrous blossoms, but also with glorious fruit. When Helmholtz discovered the eye-mirror a century ago, he was pursuing no practical medical purpose but only a theoretical research purpose. But through his research zeal he brought help to millions who suffer with eye-disease. The same is true of the scientific study of religion. Its inquiry into truth bears important consequences for the practical relationship of one religion to another.
>
> A new era will dawn upon mankind when the religions will rise to true tolerance and co-operation on behalf of mankind. To assist in preparing the way for this era is one of the finest hopes of the scientific study of religion.[10]

Now among scholars in the history of religions, questions like

---

[8] *Tokyo Report*, pp. 7–22.
[9] ibid., p. 9.
[10] ibid., pp. 19, 21. It is worth noting that at this congress, Bleeker welcomed the broadening of the IAHR's horizons which it marked. He said : 'I am not exaggerating when I say that I have the feeling that we have come to a turning-point in the history of the IAHR, perhaps in the study of the history of religions.' (p. 834). In another address, R. L. Slater was wise to observe that '. . . the unity which pertains to vital religion cannot be equated with intellectual unanimity and may even exist apart from it.' 'World Peace and World Order', ibid., p. 612f.

these were normally avoided altogether, as being hopelessly subjective; and many found it an embarrassment that Heiler should have seemed to speak in this way on behalf of the IAHR—which in fact he did not. The general feeling of uneasiness was compounded by the knowledge that the next IAHR congress was to take place in Marburg, on Heiler's home ground.

* * *

Before we proceed to consider what happened at Marburg in 1960, we must look once more across the Atlantic, to the founding in April 1959 of the American Society for the Study of Religion. An important address was delivered on that occasion by Erwin Ramsdell Goodenough (1893–1965) of Yale, the society's first President. Goodenough's field was the meeting-ground of Jewish and Christian in the Hellenistic period, and his major work *Jewish Symbols in the Greco-Roman Period* (1953–1968), which was, incidentally, published by the Bollingen Foundation and shows Jungian influence. But his interests were wider and ranged over the whole *Problematik* of ancient and modern man in search of a soul. His 1959 address was called simply 'Religionswissenschaft'—an attempt to speak of a broad science of religion without tying the attempt down to any of the existing terminologies, and an attempt to outline the possible scope of the (scientific) study of religion.[11]

Goodenough began by saying that he could see no other value in 'the history of religions' than its contribution to *Religionswissenschaft*. The modern world is subject to all manner of disintegrating influences, and we are trying to found new societies out of the pieces. Even the much-mooted contribution of religion to national and international peace and goodwill (in the perspective of the 1950s) was unlikely to help, since '. . . it is precisely Religionswissenschaft in any meaningful sense that the religious leaders of our generation have rejected'.[12] To be sure, there is a faithful remnant, but they are scattered over the face of the earth, in a variety of academic fields. And often enough these fields are uninterested in religion. Again the demand is for wholeness, integration, mutual recognition between competent workers :

[11] Goodenough, 'Religionswissenschaft', in *Numen* vi (1959), pp. xxff.
[12] ibid., p. 82. cf. Michaelsen, *The Scholarly Study of Religion in College and University* (1964), p. 22 : 'Above all, the scholars in this area are insisting on approaching religious phenomena directly and insofar as possible (*sic*) from within.'

K

The hope of reviving study of the science of religion lies, I believe, not in courting the traditionalists and theologians, but in coming to recognise that science itself is a religious exercise, a new religion, and that science and religion have fallen apart largely because traditionalists have done what they have always done, failing to recognise a new approach to religion as it has formed itself in their midst.[13]

In this task, literally anything may serve as material, and before integral understanding is achieved, a great deal of close and detailed work will be necessary. The important thing is not to believe that in religion, the necessary microscope-work is an end in itself :

> We hope to clarify the larger problems by solving the smaller, but in simply solving the smaller we are technicians and antiquarians, not people adding to scientific knowledge at all.[14]

These technicians Goodenough called 'the Pharisees of science'. They have their place, however, and since one must learn to walk before one can run,

> At the present stage of the Science of Religion, we would do well to ask small questions until we have established a methodology we can all approve and use.[15]

In this important paper, Goodenough was calling for some kind of integral understanding of religion-as-such, and for the science of religion (*Religionswissenschaft*) to address itself *ultimately* to this end. The techniques—philological, historical, archaeological and the rest—on which this work had of necessity to be based, were to be cultivated, conscientiously and accurately. They were not, however, to be regarded as ends in themselves. Without this wider application, they were useless. But on the other hand, premature pontificating about cosmic issues would be even more useless :

> *Religionswissenschaft* writes no popular books, no simplified summaries for sophomores. Perhaps we must make our living doing this, but we must recognise in it no part of our real business.[16]

Goodenough's presidential address was really a plea for a humanised study of religion. It was clear that he was echoing not only the words but also the innermost impulses of Joachim Wach; it was equally clear that these were the tones which scholarship would

[13] Goodenough, op. cit., p. 85.
[14] ibid., p. 93.
[15] ibid., p. 94.
[16] Loc. cit.

have to be prepared to hear from the USA for some time to come. We have already mentioned Wach's book *The Comparative Study of Religions*, and it is unnecessary at this stage to spend further time explaining his desire for an 'integral understanding' of religion.[17] But it is perhaps important to remind ourselves that although his work in a way contributed to the weakening of historicism in the study of religion, it equally invited students to abandon certain less defensible positions, notably the position of the dweller in an ivory tower totally isolated from value-judgements and subjective presuppositions. The student had in Wach's view to be a scholar. But he had to be more : he had to have 'an adequate emotional condition' before undertaking his task. Whether this emotional condition inevitably involved the acceptance of the validity of religious experience is a question which we will not attempt to answer. It is nevertheless necessary to note that for Wach, the comparative study of religions offers not only 'a clear vision of what religious experience can mean' and 'what forms its expression may take', but also, and more importantly, 'what it might do for man'.

Thus from all sides the American position seemed to be crystallising into one in which the old historicism was being weighed in the balance and found seriously wanting, because it was incapable of answering even its own deepest questions. We must consider now how European scholarship reacted to this fresh approach.

In the autumn of 1959, *Judaism: a Quarterly Journal of Jewish Life and Thought* printed a review of Wach's book by the Jewish scholar R. J. Zwi Werblowsky, a prominent member of the IAHR.[18] Werblowsky's view was that Wach's book had seriously confused *Religionswissenschaft* with theology; and that in purporting to answer questions appropriate to the comparative study of religion, it was really addressing itself almost entirely to theologians, or at least to readers sympathetic to a certain range of theological values. The difficulty, according to Werblowsky, was created by a situation in which

. . . the theologian, committed to an exclusive religion claiming absolute value, at the same time also accepts certain liberal values which do not allow him simply to write off other religious forms as sheer humbug or error.[19]

[17] cf. above, pp. 238–40.
[18] Werblowsky, 'The Comparative Study of Religions—A Review Essay', in *Judaism* 8/4 (1959), offprint pagination 1–9.
[19] He goes on to say that 'however fascinating this problem may be, it has obviously very little to do with the comparative study of religion as such. It is a purely theological problem' (ibid., p. 1).

Wach was apparently just such a theologian, and his book seemed to have been addressed to other theologians. That was the trouble, for 'comparative religion' or *Religionswissenschaft* could never permit itself to be compromised in this way. The problems of the book, similarly, were not those of 'Comparative Religion proper', but of 'theology struggling towards a positive approach to Comparative Religion'. And again : 'The confusion between theology and *Religionswissenschaft* is characteristic of the book as a whole.'[20]

Werblowsky's view was that of the strict, scientifically 'objective' school of scholarship. Every true scholar, he wrote, '. . . eliminates his religion from his studies, whatever the 'religious' character of the motives and drives that make him study religion at all'.[21] And undoubtedly the majority of scholars then involved in the work of the IAHR would have agreed with him, and would have shared the view that any intrusion of 'personal religion' into a scholarly debate was only to be deplored.

This was, of course, not a debate, since Wach was no longer in a position to respond. One suspects, however, that he would have been less than happy with the distinction which Werblowsky was proposing to draw between the two modes of religious understanding—not least since he had (as Werblowsky pointed out) previously maintained that religion should be studied by 'objective' means, and hence may have felt that he had simply outgrown the objectivist view. Perhaps, too, he might have asked what other adequate reason there might be for *wanting* to study in this way, than the attainment of a better understanding of the work of God in the world. But this is merely conjectural. What is relatively certain is that viewed from this perspective, the debate had not moved forward very far from the position it had reached in 1914. The same alternatives were being presented; only the relative weight of the protagonists had changed.

*   *   *

Now, however, we must return to the IAHR, and to the Marburg Congress of 1960.[22] It is difficult for one who was not himself involved in this congress to gain a full and satisfactory impression of its proceedings; the papers were printed only in summary form, and little can be deduced from a mere list of those taking part. But

[20] ibid., p. 5.
[21] ibid., p. 3.
[22] *X. Internationaler Kongress für Religionsgeschichte*, 11–17. September 1960 in Marburg/Lahn, Herausgegeben vom Organisationsausschuss (1961).

it is clear that Marburg was in many ways to be a watershed, for the simple reason that there methodological discussion established itself for the first time as an integral part of IAHR procedure. Previously method had been discussed only incidentally, perhaps because scholars were too busy to give much thought to it; but the Far-Eastern experience, and the general climate of opinion of the period, had changed things.

On 17 September, Bleeker addressed the congress on the subject 'The Future Task of the History of Religions'—the first methodological pronouncement of its kind at a congress. The IAHR, said Bleeker, is now more fully international than hitherto; but that has given rise to problems, since 'everybody who knows the Orient even superficially will realise that the subjects of the history of religions are approached in a different way in the East from that in the West.'[23] But does this mean that neither is able to learn from the other? The Tokyo experience had taught scholars in the West that religion can still be a live option; further, the Tokyo theme could not be judged '. . . in the spirit of complete disinterestedness which is normally characteristic of the history of religions'.[24] Indeed there was a difference of outlook involved :

> On the one hand the oriental student is inclined to contend that the very heart of religion can best be reached by intuition and that the ultimate result of the study of religious phenomena must be a deeper insight into the actual value of religion. On the other hand the western student of the history of religions is convinced that his sole task consists of a painstaking study of greater or minor segments of a certain religion in order to understand their religious meaning in a tentative way and that he has to refrain from pronouncing any kind of value judgements.[25]

However, Bleeker was at once forced to admit that the problem was not only one of East *versus* West; the 'intuitive' attitude was also represented in the West (perhaps he was thinking of the Marburg tradition, though he did not say so), and the pressures on scholars to play some part in 'the reconstruction of cultural and religious life' were growing. Indeed they were—perhaps more than even Bleeker realised at the time. But in the meantime Bleeker urged caution; the scholar must not compromise his scholarly conscience : he must keep his distance from the transcendent (as against what

---

[23] Bleeker, 'The Future Task of the History of Religions', in *Numen* VII (1960), p. 223.
[24] ibid., p. 225.
[25] ibid., p. 226.

Goodenough and Wilfred Cantwell Smith were urging) and concern himself only with his trade. As for international understanding, it might be a pleasant by-product of the scholar's work, but it could never become a matter of primary concern.

Bleeker was despite everything attempting to maintain the eirenic position appropriate to a Secretary General. A more outspoken representative of the scholarly tradition was R. J. Zwi Werblowsky, whose highly critical review of Joachim Wach's *The Comparative Study of Religion* we have already considered. On this occasion he put forward a short statement of what he called the *basic minimum presuppositions* of the kind of study aimed at by the IAHR; this statement, signed by scholars as diverse as Brandon, Eliade, Goodenough, Kitagawa, Simon and Zaehner, urged that there was no question of an 'East versus West' situation arising.[26] The history of religions is a branch of the humanities, not of theology and still less of international politics; it is simply there, to be discussed as dispassionately as possible on the principle of truth for its own sake : '. . . whatever the analysable sociological function of scientific activity in any specific cultural and historical situations the *ethos* of our studies is in themselves'. And it follows that whatever ideals the individual scholar may choose to cultivate in private, these are his own concern, '. . . and must under no circumstances be allowed to influence or colour the character of the IAHR.'[27]

A certain amount of inconclusive discussion there was, of course; after it all Werblowsky returned to the fray in a *Numen* article, 'Marburg—and after?' in which he urged that the IAHR must protect itself from invasion by dilettantes, theologians and idealists equally.[28] Studies are scientific and scholarly—or they are not. *Tertium non datur.*

* * *

The Marburg debate had shown that there might be scholars in the West whose priorities were not altogether identical with those of the IAHR. This was well enough known. What was less easy to decide was precisely where the dividing line went between what was academically respectable and what was not. The term 'phenomenology of religion' in particular was a source of confusion. In 1961 Friedrich Heiler, who had done so much to precipitate the debate,

---

[26] cf. Schimmel, 'Summary of the Discussion', in *Numen* vii (1960), pp. 235ff.
[27] ibid., p. 237.
[28] Werblowsky, 'Marburg—and after?' in *Numen* vii (1960), pp. 215ff.

published his *Erscheinungsformen und Wesen der Religion*—a phenomenological study on the grand scale, which said virtually nothing about inter-religious *rapprochement*, though it implied a great deal. But it kept to the phenomenological rules. So too did Mircea Eliade's *Patterns in Comparative Religion*, which had appeared two years previously, in 1958.

Eliade had signed Werblowsky's manifesto; as had his University of Chicago colleagues Joseph Kitagawa and Charles Long. Eliade, as Wach's successor, and Kitagawa, as one of his notable disciples, clearly in some sense carried on that particular Chicago tradition; but in other ways they were altogether independent, and maintained a flourishing school of graduate study much more reminiscent of that of the continent of Europe than of North America.[29]

In 1961 Chicago began the publication of a new journal, *History of Religions*, which quickly gained status as the American equivalent of *Revue d'histoire des religions* and *Numen*. It began, and continued, as a medium of straightforward historical research. But it had a further dimension in that it concerned itself from the very first with the problems of hermeneutics (interpretation)—a subject which for many Europeans in the field was perhaps somewhat less than respectable. The first article published in the new journal set its tone.[30]

Mircea Eliade, writing on 'History of Religions and a New Humanism', stated that one of the aims of the journal would be to improve 'the hermeneutics of religious data'—a subject neglected by historians of religion :

Like it or not [Eliade wrote], the scholar has not finished his work when he has reconstructed the history of a religious form or brought out its sociological, economic, or political contexts. In addition, he must understand its meaning—that is, identify and elucidate the situations and positions that have induced or made possible its appearance or its triumph at a particular historical moment.

It is solely insofar as it will perform this task . . . that the science of religions will fulfil its true cultural function. For whatever its role has been in the past, the comparative study of religions is destined to assume a cultural role of the first importance in the near future . . .[31]

The East-West cultural dialogue has already started (the Tokyo

[29] cf. above, pp. 238-41.
[30] The article in question was reprinted in *The Quest* (1969), pp. 1ff.
[31] *The Quest*, p. 2.

memory), and the history of religions has its role to play in it—in which process the historian 'will inevitably attain to a deeper knowledge of man'. This, in a term, is 'the new humanism'. Erudition is important—indeed it is indispensable—but erudition unsupported by creative hermeneutics, as the attempt is made to understand religions and religious expressions 'in their own plane of reference', is woefully incomplete. This is of course a similar point of view to that of the phenomenologist, calling for *epoché* and the eidetic vision. And Eliade does indeed refer to the two approaches of the historian and the phenomenologist; but he maintains that whatever tension there may be between them is a creative tension, by which the history of religions as a whole will escape dogmatism and stagnation.

The Chicago hermeneutical programme was not meant as a counterblast to the IAHR's five principles, but it certainly widened the scope of the historian of religion considerably. Most important, it acknowledged that the historian of religions might find himself playing an active role in the world's cultural dialogue, rather than merely sitting on the sidelines as a disinterested observer; also it committed the scholar to a search for the inner meaning of religion, and not only to a quest for historical fact and circumstance. The 'objective' historian of religions was in danger, one feels, of being acknowledged as a skilled craftsman whose work might be admirable in itself, but who would have to learn new concerns and new techniques if he were to be of real significance in the new world. That some of the historians in question found difficulty in even understanding this position, much less in adopting it, is further evidence of a growing gulf between them and the new hermeneuts.

But by the early 1960s the American schools were moving firmly into the acceptance of this wider role. There were of course external reasons for this.[32] A long period of American isolationism in world politics, disturbed by the Second World War, was now at an end, with the spiralling tragedy of Vietnam; an increasing volume of questioning voices was being heard: Western institutions and methods were being weighed as never before in the balances, and not infrequently found wanting. Students in Western institutions were beginning once more, as in other periods of frustration and disillusion, to look for light from the East, and the American educational community, always sensitive to the climate of opinion among its customers, had begun to develop a new sensitivity to what the

---

[32] cf. Kitagawa, 'The History of Religions in America', in id. (ed.), *The History of Religions: Essays in Methodology* (1959), pp. 1ff.

students were saying and thinking. In Europe and America alike, traditional standards of disinterested and objective, philologically-based scholarship, while not rejected altogether, were being eroded by this wider, utilitarian approach. And even in the theological colleges and seminaries, staff and students, many of whom had traditionally shown an interest (though not necessarily a specialist or even very highly informed interest) in the methods and materials of comparative religion, were finding Kierkegaard reigning almost alone among the Christians, flanked by the Buddha, Śankara, and the Zen and Taoist teachers in a new eclectic academy. The issue was further complicated, as far as America was concerned, by that feature of the Constitution whereby no religious instruction might be given in any educational institution supported by public funds. However, since the original aim of this law had been to eliminate the danger of sectarianism, and since comparative religion was nothing if not unsectarian, openings began to be found for the teaching of comparative religion under the Chicago programme, not as religion in any traditional sense, but as the 'new humanism' Eliade claimed it to be. All in all, then, the climate of popular opinion was changing fairly rapidly during the late 1950s and early 1960s, but changing subtly *away from* the stated ideals of the IAHR.

For contrast, we might look briefly across the Atlantic to a 1962 book from behind the Iron Curtain : Kurt Rudolph's *Die Religionsgeschichte an der Leipziger Universität* (The History of Religions at the University of Leipzig). Here the ideal of pure, objective scholarship is pressed to its absolute limits, and hard words are spoken against those who would compromise these standards for any reason whatever.[33]

* * *

The 1965 International Congress of the IAHR was held at Clare-

---

[33] Rudolf writes (op. cit., p. 118): 'Whether the study of religion enriches or furthers religious life depends upon the scholar's subjective attitude and views, and upon his religious faith, which must not be made into a condition or presupposition of scientific research. Religions are *historical* entities, and hence objects for historical research; this, however, is independent of religious faith and in no way bound to it. Thus the *Religionswissenschaftler*, unlike the theologian, cannot speak of a "reflection of the divine in the human soul"; the most he can do is to report statements of faith relative to these matters. As far as he is concerned, religious manifestations and forms are data of *Geistesgeschichte* or *Glaubensgeschichte* (the history of the spirit, or of faith), which belong to social reality, and hence are accessible to every historian and philologist according to the measure of his techniques and his scientific

L

mont, California—the first of these international congresses to be held on the American Continent.[34] But before we look at its impact, we may note that in the previous year, 1964, an invitational conference on the study of religion in the state university had been held in Indiana.[35] At both, major papers were delivered by Wilfred Cantwell Smith of Harvard.

Smith had already made a considerable impact on the field of religious studies generally with his book *The Meaning and End of Religion* (1963)—a passionate plea for Western scholarship to come to terms with its own past, to see how easily intellectual convention can become fossilised into apparently eternal law, and to take seriously *homo religiosus* in his wholeness. In this book, as well as analysing the concept 'religion' in the context of the history of ideas, Smith had suggested that the problem might be solved by the use of two alternative concepts, 'cumulative tradition' and 'faith'. Cumulative tradition is the tradition which each individual or group receives, which it may or may not modify, and which it then passes on to the next generation. 'Faith' is the individual's attitude to whatever he conceives the Transcendent to be. In this way one may at least dismiss from the debate a great deal of redundant talk about 'religious systems'; and much more *might* be achieved.[36]

---

skills. Whether there has been an adequate scientific recognition or a misinterpretation of a religio-historical phenomenon cannot be scientifically established by faith (*Glaube*) and subjective emotions (*Gefühl*), but only by means of a scientific judgement oriented toward objective reality. In *Religionswissenschaft* the interpretation of accessible historical sources must take place on a basis of universally valid historical and critical method. If *Religionswissenschaft* is to be kept uncontaminated, it is necessary that it be sharply separated from theology.' cf. Bianchi, *Problemi di storia delle religioni* (Swedish translation, *Religionshistoriska problem*, 1966), p. 25: 'The history of religion is . . . a science which, using accepted historical method and with the support of psychology, sociology and phenomenology, establishes and examines facts in order to identify historically integrated religious worlds and to study their respective characteristics.'

[34] Schneider and van Proosdij (eds.), *Proceedings of the XIth International Congress of the IAHR. . .* Claremont, *California*, 6–11 September 1965, I–II (1968).

[35] Michaelsen (ed.), *A Report on an Invitational Conference on the Study of Religion in the State University* (1964).

[36] Cantwell Smith's work has aroused considerable interest in recent years. Among recent articles, mention may be made of Gualtieri, 'Faith, Tradition and Transcendence: a study of Wilfred Cantwell Smith', in *Canadian Journal of Theology* (1969), pp. 102ff.; Sharpe, 'Dialogue and Faith', in *Religion* 3 (1973), pp. 89ff.; and Pruett, 'History, Transcendence and World Community in the work of Wilfred Cantwell Smith', in *Journal of the American Academy of Religion* xli/4 (1973), pp. 573ff. cf. also Baird, *Category Formation and the History of Religions* (1971), pp. 91ff.

His Indiana paper was entitled 'Non-Western Studies: the Religious Approach', and carried on this line of thought. The fragmentation of 'disciplines', Smith maintained, was a bad thing: perhaps we have found that we can chop up our lives in this way, but what right does this give us so to treat the lives of others? The subordination of 'religious' to other factors in Non-Western Studies is the unimaginative reaction of secular Western man to a complex of phenomena which he neither understands nor wishes to understand. 'What is needed, on the religious plane, is the ability to see the religious traditions from the inside—and that means, not alongside the other "factors" in a man's life, but over-arching them.'[37] And this means, among other things, that our analytical understanding of living religious traditions other than our own cannot be improved, and may be destroyed by, distance and the quest for objectivity. For instance, 'We can understand the faith of Hindus only when, like them, we can use the religious traditions of Hindus to enable us to see all of life . . . through Hindu eyes.' And he summed up, almost programmatically:

> To understand human life in the Orient, we must endeavour to do so neither in terms of analysis only without any integration nor in terms of analysis with Western integrations tacitly presupposed, but in terms of analysis and of the integration that is appropriate to those concerned, and to which the analysis must be subordinated.[38]

—a clumsy statement, but one which implied allowing the East to speak for itself. Perhaps it is not altogether irrelevant to recall at this point that when the Harvard University Center for the Study of World Religions (over which Cantwell Smith then presided) was inaugurated in 1961, the inaugural address had been delivered by Sarvepalli Radhakrishnan—a striking example of the policy of allowing the Eastern tradition of religious studies to 'speak for itself'.[39]

The Claremont Congress, like that at Tokyo, was conducted in

[37] Smith, 'Non-Western Studies: the Religious Approach', in *Indiana Report*, pp. 50ff. The quotation is from p. 51.

[38] ibid., p. 57. cf. his remark on p. 56: '. . . Western social scientists also cannot come to an authentic understanding of life outside Western civilisation except at the price of being willing to revise *their* basic presuppositions and convictions, such as the sacrosanct concepts of "discipline" and "objectivity"—and fairly few social scientists are willing to pay that price. There are more dogmatism and unexamined premises in a social science department these days than in a divinity faculty!'

[39] cf. above, pp. 258 60.

separate sections, one being devoted to a purely academic theme, 'guilt or pollution and rites of purification', one to 'the impact of modern culture on traditional religions', and the third to 'the role of historical scholarship in changing the relations among religions'. Space does not, of course, permit anything like a review of the proceedings as a whole; but in a great deal of what was said and done at Claremont it was clear that the ideal of disinterested, objective scholarship *for its own sake*, while not abandoned, had been relegated to a position of only relative importance.

Six addresses were delivered at plenary sessions, by O. H. de Wijesekera, Jean Filliozat, Wilfred Cantwell Smith, P. N. Dandekar, Manuel Sarkisyanz and E. Geoffrey Parrinder, dealing with the impact of modern cultures on religious traditions in various parts of the world. Of these, we may again note the contribution of Cantwell Smith.

Speaking on 'Traditional Religions and Modern Culture', Smith appeared almost to be thinking aloud, approaching the set problem from a variety of angles in turn, worrying the problem, shaking it to make it shed its last drop of meaning. His paper is therefore almost impossible to characterise briefly; but the following statement is significant. After saying that the question of the relationship of religion to culture is 'momentous', 'crucial' and 'cosmic', he gives an example :

'Religion and modern culture' may not be a cosmic issue for us . . .; but we cannot handle it even as a 'scientific' question (in the European sense) if we do not understand that, and how, it is a cosmic question for those whom we are studying, for those because of whom it is a question at all.

Let no one imagine that the question of what is happening to Islam in Pakistan is anything other than the question of what is happening to man in Pakistan. And even this does not mean only, what is happening to Pakistanis in Pakistan : it is rather, what is happening to mankind in Pakistan. Let no one imagine that the question of the cow in India, is anything less than the question of how we men are to understand ourselves and our place in the universe. The Buddhist's involvement in politics in Vietnam is a political question but also a question of our relation to eternity— yours and mine as well as his. Every time a person anywhere makes a religious decision, at stake is the final destiny and meaning of the human race.

If we do not see this, and cannot make our public see it, then whatever else we may be, we are not historians of religion.[40]

---

[40] *Claremont Report*, p. 64f.

Reactions to this approach—and indeed reactions to the overall programme of the congress—varied considerably. The Europeans in particular, still concerned with the adequate problems of historical study, and remembering the debates of Marburg, were somewhat troubled at the turn events seemed to be taking. Part of the trouble on this occasion was that a section of the conference had been set aside for discussion of the subject 'The Role of Historical Scholarship in Changing the Relations among Religions' (volume 3 of the conference report). And a number of papers were delivered on themes connected with this subject—by Horace L. Friess, Ernst Benz and others. However, the standard of these papers was not outstanding, and no record was published of the discussions; all that appeared in retrospect to have emerged was the unremarkable judgement that the serious student of religion is more likely to be sympathetic to representatives of other traditions than the person who has no such training. It was really unnecessary to set apart a section of an international congress to say that.

An interesting reaction to the conference as a whole came from S. G. F. Brandon of the University of Manchester, writing in *The Times* (London).[41] Brandon, as a historian, was more in tune with the European than with the American extremities of this discussion. Nevertheless he wished to report both positions fairly.

Brandon began by noting that the emphasis of the Claremont conference was on 'the present and future significance of religion in human culture', and not on the traditional genetic and evolutionary questions. 'This new orientation was welcomed by many scholars; but it stirred misgivings among others, particularly those nurtured in the academic tradition of Europe.' He mentioned Cantwell Smith's paper as being particularly significant in this context, adding that Smith's failure to mention Christianity might be important, since Christianity cannot be understood 'without reference to its historical beginnings'. On the whole, though : 'Such advocacy of the sociological approach to comparative religion ['sociological' here is simply the antithesis of 'historical'] seemed to reflect the American predisposition to concentrate on the existing situation.' But Brandon did not feel that the dialogical approach ought to be permitted to usurp the critically historical approach to religion. A variety of motives for comparative study is one thing ('. . . difference of motivation attests a new appreciation of the importance of comparative religion'), but in the final analysis, 'it is unlikely that the European concern with the history of religions will succumb to the

41 *The Times*, 20 September 1965.

American sociological approach. The dialogue between the two will doubtless stimulate greater interest and increase the importance of the subject in the curriculum of humanistic studies.'

Before leaving the subject of Claremont 1965, there is one further point which, regrettably, must be made. Partly as a result of a genuine conflict of principles of method, partly due to personal incompatibilities, the conference was followed by the resignation from the International Association of one of the Claremont conference organisers. I do not propose to dwell on this unfortunate episode, except to note that for a few years thereafter, the history of religions in America and on the continent of Europe tended to drift apart.

Europe continued on the official level to be dominated by the purely historical approach—an approach which found further expression in such works of scholarship as Ringgren and Ström, *Religionerna i historia och nutid* (2nd ed. 1959) from Sweden, the three volumes of Asmussen and Laessøe, *Illustreret Religionshistorie* (1968) from Denmark, and a work of international collaboration, the two volumes of Bleeker and Widengren, *Historia Religionum: Handbook for the History of Religions* (1970-71).

In America during the years following Claremont, there were few startling developments. E. R. Goodenough having died in 1965, in 1968 a memorial volume was published, in which Willard G. Oxtoby (then of Yale, subsequently of Toronto) looked back to Goodenough's article *Religionswissenschaft*.[42] He conducted in the process a survey of the years 1959-68 in respect of the problem of method in the study of religion. Pointing out that in Goodenough's day (very recently), *Religionswissenschaft* had scarcely even been a respectable university discipline in the eyes of many American scholars, he suggested three goals which the study of comparative religion might well bear in mind : first, that no theoretical limits ought to be set to the type or range of data to be dealt with. Secondly, that no chronological limits could be set, either. This was of some significance in view of recent tendencies to historicise or to sociologise, and to regard the two approaches as mutually exclusive. And thirdly, that the overall attitude of the student of comparative religion might well be summed up as one of 'non-pragmatic cosmopolitanism', in which the contributions of anyone at all might be respected : '*Religionswissenschaft* rightly conceived,' wrote Oxtoby, 'is not the religious indoctrination of the young, nor a bland, laudatory inter-faith panel, but a quest for new descriptive formu-

---

[42] Oxtoby, 'Religionswissenschaft Revisited', in Neusner (ed.), *Religions in Antiquity* (1968), pp. xxff.

lations in which the trained outsider might—just might—have something to say.'[43]

*   *   *

Until this time, British scholarship had provided very little grist for the methodological mill. For one thing, there were distressingly few British scholars of international standing in the field. In 1950, a dominant position was still occupied by two Anglican clergymen, E. O. James and A. C. Bouquet, an anthropologist and a theologian respectively, neither of whom had made any notable contribution to the methodological debate, though both had done sterling work in other areas. Some sign of the dearth of scholars in the field can be gained from the fact that when in 1951 the chair of comparative religion in Manchester came to be filled, the appointee was a regular army chaplain with no previous university teaching experience, S. G. F. Brandon. The solid achievements of Brandon's subsequent career notwithstanding, the field lacked depth; and Brandon himself, though he had an important theory about religion, was a pure historian in point of method.[44] Typically, then, when a methodological pronouncement was made—by James—it took the form of a British compromise. In the first issue of *Numen*, James wrote :

> The study of religion, be it for academic purposes, as a way of life, or in the interests of inter-religious understanding and international peace, demands both a historical and scientific approach and a theological and philosophical evaluation, if it is to be understood in its essential nature and ever-developing content, and its foundations are to be well and truly laid.[45]

This was of course true, though calculated to appeal to neither extreme wing of the debate at the time.

However, the subject of comparative religion, which had included so many British scholars among its pioneers, was passing through a lean period, as we have said. I recall only too well the general lack of following which the subject had, even in the University of Manchester, its oldest stronghold in the country; in 1956–7 a 'special' course mustered only three students, and before its end one-third of the class had fallen by the wayside. But a remarkable revival of

---

[43] ibid., p. 608.
[44] cf. above, pp. 246–8.
[45] James, 'The History, Science and Comparative Study of Religion', in *Numen* I (1954), p. 105.

interest was in the offing, here as in the United States, and the size of classes increased over the next decade by up to ten times their 1956 level. This trend was of course reflected in publications. A new demand for popular works of comparative religion was met in a variety of ways, and the few scholars who taught in the field found themselves much in demand as writers of *oeuvres de vulgarisation*, as well as carrying on their own specialist studies.

In Britain, the subject had three centres in the 1950s and early 1960s. At Manchester, S. G. F. Brandon was assisted by the Sinologist D. Howard Smith, and after Smith's retirement in 1966, by the present writer. At Leeds, comparative religion was represented by a Buddhologist, Trevor Ling (who was to succeed Brandon at Manchester on the latter's death in 1971), and William Weaver, who specialised in African studies and Islam. In London, the grand old man of the subject, E. O. James, had retired, being replaced by the philosopher of religion Hywel D. Lewis, who was associated with the Africanist and Indologist E. Geoffrey Parrinder, one of the most effective and prolific writers in the field. But up to this time, few of these scholars had concerned themselves with problems of method. Lewis had collaborated with R. L. Slater of Harvard to produce a small book, *The Study of Religion*, in 1966, in which some problems of method were discussed; but generally speaking the British tendency was at that time to leave the problem of method to take care of itself. And when method was discussed, as by Trevor Ling, in the introduction to *A History of Religions, East and West* (1968), its treatment tended to be perfunctory. Ling saw the essential function of comparative religion as being '. . . the relating of the findings of two separate disciplines, the philosophy of religion and the sociology of religion, *each pursued in a world context*',[46] and indicated that he might even have considered calling the discipline 'the comparative philosophy and sociology of world religions', had the title not been so clumsy.[47] He saw the problem, in other words, as being that of relating meaning (the work of the philosopher) and function (the work of the sociologist). But Ling was clearly not *au fait* with earlier methodological discussions; his options were too narrow, though unexceptionable in themselves; and the impression of reduction is unavoidable.

This same general impression—that the small number of comparative religionists in Britain in the late 1960s were generally unconcerned with anything beyond their immediate spheres of specialist interest—was felt by me most forcefully when I returned

---

[46] Ling, *A History of Religions, East and West* (1968), p. xix.
[47] ibid., p. xxi.

to Britain in 1966, after eight years spent in Sweden and the United States. But the situation was not static. A very important new local factor was introduced with the setting up in 1967 of a Department of Religious Studies in the new University of Lancaster.

The headship of the department was not allocated to any of the traditional 'disciplines'. But its first Professor, Ninian Smart, combined in a manner fairly typical for Britain but untypical for Europe generally, comparative religion with the philosophy of religion. He had previously worked at such diverse centres as Aberystwyth, London, Benares Hindu University, Yale, the University of Wisconsin, and Birmingham. His publications already included *Reasons and Faiths* (1958), *Doctrine and Argument in Indian Philosophy* (1964), *A Dialogue of Religions* (1960), and *The Religious Experience of Mankind* (1969).

For one who has himself been a member of the Lancaster department since 1970 to attempt to evaluate publicly either the contribution of the Department or its head to the methodology of comparative religion would be invidious, and perhaps dangerous. But some points may be made. First, that, as Ninian Smart wrote in a 1968 publication, *Secular Education and the Logic of Religion,*

> Since the study of man is in an important sense participatory— for one has to enter into men's intentions, beliefs, myths, desires, in order to understand why they act as they do—it is fatal if cultures including our own are described merely externally, without entering into dialogue with them.[48]

This did not imply a rejection of history, linguistics and the other traditional disciplines; rather it implied a bringing of them together into a conscious team effort, aimed at the understanding, as far as possible, of *homo religiosus* at least as well as he understands himself. Not surprisingly, then, the Lancaster position is that the study of religion must be polymethodic and interdisciplinary—not *faute de mieux*, but as a matter of absolute necessity.[49]

It must be pointed out, however, that the Lancaster department is a department of 'religious studies', and not of comparative religion (or the history of religions) only. Courses are offered

[48] Smart, *Secular Education and the Logic of Religion* (1968), p. 104.
[49] Smart, *The Principles and Meaning of the Study of Religion* (1968), p. 11: 'The student of religion . . . needs to have historical knowledge and expertise, sensitivity and imagination in crossing cultures and time, and analytical grasp. He has to be a latter-day Leonardo. This shows why Religious Studies is neither the Queen of Sciences nor the Knave of Arts; but it is one of the foci of the humanities and social sciences. In it some of the most engaging and perplexing problems in these disciplines have a meet-

in modern religious and atheistic thought, in Christian studies, in the recent history of ideas, in the psychology of religion, as well as in what might be termed 'world religions'. Outside the classroom (a place where many comparative religionists have in the past spent far too little time), a journal began publication in 1971 (*Religion: a Journal of Religion and Religions*), the interdisciplinary aim of which was explicit from the first. There have been difficulties and tensions, but if the size of a graduate school is of any significance, and if imitation be the sincerest form of flattery, then 'the Lancaster approach' to the study of religion may well take its place among the more significant trends of recent years in our subject.

* * *

At the end of our hundred years of comparative religion stands the twelfth international congress of the IAHR. It took place in Stockholm, and was devoted to a consideration of the varieties of 'Belief in God'—at least ostensibly, though many of the papers were on only marginally relevant themes.[50] Geo Widengren and C. J. Bleeker delivered the introductory and valedictory addresses, both somewhat in the minor key, warning the scholarly community against an undue relaxation of standards.[51] But both were now retiring, and the active leadership of the Association passed into the hands of Marcel Simon of Strasbourg, who assumed the Presidency from Widengren, and S. G. F. Brandon of Manchester, who became Secretary General—this latter appointment aimed specifically at healing the breach which had developed since Claremont (or perhaps since Tokyo) between different approaches and emphases.

1970 did, then, represent a turning point in the international debate; rather like a musical cadence, it marked both an end and a

---

ing point. For to tell the truth, we are all of us far from having anything but a rather superficial grasp of the multiple structures of religious faith, myths and institutions.' Among later books in which this approach has been elaborated we may mention *The Concept of Worship* (1972), *The Phenomenon of Religion* (1973) and *The Science of Religion and the Sociology of Knowledge* (1973). cf. Goldammer, *Religion und Religionen* (1967), p. 17: Religion is '. . . ein verwickeltes Ganzheitsphänomen und nur als solches verstehbar'.

[50] The report of this conference has not yet been published (May 1974).

[51] Widengren also recorded his intense disappointment that so many specialists in the various fields which go to make up the history of religions show so little interest in the larger activity: 'Here I have to express my regret at the fact that so many scholars, active in our field, but chiefly possessed of a philological education, do not even visit any congresses of the history of religions.'

beginning. What had ended was perhaps the period in which scholars had locked themselves into a rigid methodological 'either-or', and had failed to recognise the essentially complementary character of alternative approaches. What had begun we cannot yet know : we can only hope, and work.

Since the story told so summarily in this chapter has included such a large and invaluable contribution from Widengren and Bleeker (or from the tradition of exact scholarship they represented), it may be appropriate to give a penultimate word to Bleeker, reviewing Widengren—the German translation of his phenomenology, *Religionsphänomenologie*. Writing in the Dutch periodical *Bibliotheca Orientalis*, in a review dated June 1971, Bleeker said :

> My generation has been deeply concerned with the phenomenology of religion, but no longer possesses the imagination and creative energy to produce anything new along the lines of Widengren's *Religionsphänomenologie*. A younger generation must now carry on the work. The first condition for phenomenological success must be for the scholar to collect precise knowledge, being possessed by the same passionate love for truth in the history of religion that has possessed men like Kristensen, Heiler, James, Eliade and Widengren. Secondly, no one will ever be able to write massive tomes again [*Zweitens wird man keine dicken Wälzer mehr schreiben können*]. As in modern literature, the form will be that of the short story. But they must be short stories which from the point of view of method and content are still more factually and critically built up than has been the case up to now.[52]

Of course Bleeker was right, that no synoptic enthusiasm can ever compensate for exact knowledge. That lesson has to be learned over and over again, but it still stands. To that extent, comparative religion will always be bound by the precise standards of philosophy, archaeology and ethnology. But it will hope to pass beyond their confines, perhaps on a successful venture of exploration into the mind of man, perhaps into ambiguity and enigma.[53] Again and again

[52] *Bibliotheca Orientalis* xxviii (1971), p. 307.
[53] Butterfield, *Man on his Past* (1969), pp. xi-xii: 'We may say that we will lock ourselves in some local topic, or burrow in a special field, or isolate a single aspect of history; but the mere act of "digging ourselves in" is not the thing which qualifies us to establish even our own subject in its external relations and its wider significance . . . [Further] we cannot even escape having a general history which in a certain sense must preside over the works of multiple specialists and co-ordinate them with one another.' cf. Clavier, 'Problème de méthode en histoire des religions', in *Numen* xv (1968), p. 110: 'Le vice commun à toutes ces théories qui se battent et qui se contre-battent, c'est leur dogmatisme initiale.'

the student of comparative religion will overreach himself; he really does not need to be warned against that particular danger, least of all by his more fearful or professionally nervous colleagues. But what Bleeker called *leidenschaftliche Liebe zur religionsgeschichtlichen Wahrheit* is a hard driver—and ultimately, perhaps, a safe guide.

In September 1970 I ended a paper delivered to the British section of the International Association for the History of Religions with these words—and with them I bring this survey to a close.[54]

There can be no doubt that we are faced at this present time in religious studies with a profound conflict of ideals, and that this conflict is not going to be easily or cheaply reconciled. There are diversities of gifts, temperaments and inclinations, and it is simply impossible to attempt without more ado to isolate scholarship from national and traditional factors. What we have to do first of all is to try to understand the present situation as it is; only then are we going to be in a position to bring our own presuppositions, and the presuppositions of others, into the full light of day. Clavier has recently called for competence, sincerity and impartiality as the three conditions on which the study of religion can proceed. I think he is right, though I would perhaps go further, and say that the scholar may express any opinion, provided that he always nails his colours to the mast and makes it quite clear on what criteria he is passing judgment. I am also convinced that trans-Atlantic or trans-world polemics can serve no useful purpose whatsoever.

Perhaps in the last analysis what the comparative study of religion needs in these days is not a rigid methodological 'either-or', though there will certainly be those who will continue to cultivate one method rather than another; far more will be

[54] Sharpe, 'Some Problems of Method in the Study of Religion', in *Religion* 1/1 (1971), p. 12. Methodological pronouncements of one kind or another are becoming fairly frequent. From the mass of such pronouncements I may perhaps pick out three in particular: the valuable introduction to Pye, *Comparative Religion* (1972); van Baaren and others, *Religion, Culture and Methodology*: Papers of the Groningen working-group for the study of fundamental problems and methods of science of religion (1974); and Lanczkowski (ed.), *Selbstverständnis und Wesen der Religionswissenschaft* (1974), a collection of essays by Hardy, Wach, Steffes, van der Leeuw, Frick, Baetke, Pettazzoni, Latte, Werblowsky, Bleeker, Benz, Clavier, Widengren, Simon, Edsman, Hultkrantz and Bianchi. Special mention must also be made of Waardenburg's valuable (but not exhaustive) compilation *Classical Approaches to the Study of Religion* (1973), which came into my hands only after almost the whole of this book had been written; and Hultkrantz, *Metodväger inom den jämförande religionsforskningen* (1973), which I have not been able to utilise.

achieved if scholarship refuses to stagger from one methodological extreme to another, and resists the temptation to anathematize currently or locally unfashionable approaches. The study of religion must remain the meeting-ground of complementary (not competing) methods—historical, sociological, phenomenological, philosophical, psychological. Great harm has been done to the study in the past by those who have insisted that their approach excludes every conceivable alternative. Let us hope that such dogmatism is a thing of the past. Only as methods and approaches meet can we hope to understand and appreciate religion in all its complexity. . .

XIII

From Comparative Religion to Religious Studies

Reviewing the first edition of this book in the *Times Literary Supplement* (3 September 1976), Christopher Clausen observed, after cataloguing a number of issues with which the previous chapters had *not* dealt—among them the nineteenth-century quest for a 'post-Darwinian alternative to Christianity' and the recent vogue for various forms of 'oriental mysticism' in the West—that my 'neglect of such matters gives the impression that [I am] somewhat uncomfortable about the religious effects and uses of [my] discipline'.

This rather bore out the observation I had myself made, that it is at least confusing when a term like 'comparative religion' is used in different ways to mean different things.[1] There is a certain difference between 'altogether overlooking' issues (as Clausen thought I had done), and deliberately choosing not to deal with them, at least not in any very great detail, in a book designed with other ends in view. Comparative relition, as I have tried to chronicle it in the preceding chapters, has operated mainly in an academic setting in the attempt to reduce the study of religion to 'scientific' principles. Had those involved always been able to agree on the nature and limits of those principles, and had they been able to distance themselves completely from those other students of religion for whom the study is subordinate to the following of a Way, then much of the debate I have chronicled need not have taken place. But neither of these conditions was fulfilled. On the 'scientific' front, greatly diverse approaches and methods were brought to bear on the material, having little in common save a determined refusal to submit to the control of those whose reading of the world's religious evidence led to predetermined results. On the 'religious' front—and this was a much more difficult and subtle issue—there was the phenomenon of religious liberalism to be taken into consideration. Readers of the earlier part of this book can hardly have failed to be struck by the wide overlap between comparative religion and liberal Christian (and

*Compared to the previous chapters in this book, this chapter is more in the nature of a discussion than a straightforward chronicle. This is due partly to the sheer mass of material that has accumulated in recent years, though it is also hoped that this account may itself contribute in some small way to the continuing debate, for which reason issues have tended to take precedence over publications and personalities.

[1] Above, p.265.

other) theology. From the 'founding fathers' of comparative religion, C.P. Tiele, Max Müller, Nathan Söderblom and W. Brede Kristensen in the years around the turn of the century by way of Rudolf Otto and Friedrich Heiler down to Wilfred Cantwell Smith in our own day, the involvement of liberal religion in the comparative enterprise has been fairly constant. We might perhaps add that this involvement has been an irritant to those scholars who have been jealous of their own scientific integrity as dispassionate investigators and empiricists.

I am however not at all 'comfortable' about this, nor about the 'religious effects and uses' of comparative religion. On the contrary, I have grown more and more convinced over the past few years that *as a matter of historical fact*, comparative religion has done at least as much to shape liberal Christianity as the reverse. There is always something of the chameleon about liberal religion, which has a bewildering ability to melt into its background and social setting (in recent years liberal Christianity at least has shown itself nothing if not adaptable to external circumstances) and incidentally to absorb a great deal of the findings of comparative religion on the general level (for instance, in today's ready assumption that whatever the nature of divine revelation, at least it is not to be limited in principle to the deliverances of only one religious tradition).

There are on the other hand those who find any 'religious' involvement in the 'scientific' study of religion distasteful and improper. They are, it is safe to say, relatively few in number, and they have a variety of reasons for their anti-theological stance. We shall have more to say about this subject later, but for the moment it will be enough to say that the debate between those who are and those who are not prepared to affirm that the comparative study of religion has some transcendental point of reference is still in progress in 1986. This is of course still the 'pure-versus-applied' controversy with which our previous chapter concluded, and one might be forgiven for supposing that on this level, that of fundamental presupposition, little has changed over the past fifteen or so years. However, this would not be an altogether correct assumption, since a number of factors have come into play since 1970 which have had the effect of changing the relative weight and influence of the protagonists.

*   *   *

In 1970 the comparative and non-confessional study of religion had reached a parting of the ways, and a change of direction provoked in part by what was happening in Western religion generally at the same time.[2] Of course the change did not take place overnight. It had been preparing for a number of years before, and arguably still is by no means complete. Nor was it a simple matter, being rather the product of a number of factors acting together, some of them political and economic, others intellectual, and almost all of them in one sense or another open to sociological analysis. Two factors in particular influenced the study of religion in the universities and colleges of the West.

The first was the realignment of patterns of power in the world, with the dismantling of most of the remnants of the European empires, British, Dutch, French and Portuguese, and the consolidating of the present-day power blocks, American and Soviet. This had the effect of bringing a new status to those many parts of the world that for so many years had served as suppliers of the raw material of religion to the intellectual mills of the Western world. 'Aboriginal' religion (using the word in its widest sense) was no longer an assembly of fossils, but living and powerful tradition, and demanding to be treated as such. Similarly with the great traditions of the non-Western world, Hinduism, Buddhism, Islam and the rest: the renaissance which had begun under colonial pressure in the late nineteenth century achieved an altogether new self-awareness in the late twentieth. Although especially marked in the Muslim world, the reaction against Western influence and Western judgments of value grew very rapidly from about the mid-1960s on, and did much to persuade at least the more sensitive members of the Western scholarly community to attempt to re-think their previous positions.[3]

The second factor was not unconnected with the first, though somewhat more theoretical. Down to the mid-1960s, it had seemed to the greater part of religious scholarship that the process of secularisation was both inevitable and indeed irreversible.[4] Adaptable as always, the liberal theological community had gone to great lengths to explain this inevitability as, in effect, the will of God.[5] By the early 1970s, however, it was becoming evident that secularisation theory was simply inadequate to explain what was happening in the world of the religions. Not only were there such manifestations as the Islamic renaissance to be taken into account.[6]

---

[2] Above, p.290f.
[3] On the recent inter-religious dialogue debate, see Sharpe, 'The Goals of Inter-Religious Dialogue', in Hick (ed.), *Truth and Dialogue* (1974), pp. 77-95; idem, *Faith meets Faith* (1977), especially pp. 118-49.
[4] cf. Sharpe, *Understanding Religion* (1983), pp. 108ff.
[5] Expressed most forcefully by Cox, *The Secular City* (1985), though Cox himself has since moved some way from this position.
[6] cf. Hjärpe, *Politisk Islam* (1980). On the Iranian revolution, see most recently Aneer,

Equally there were appearing in the West a plethora of 'new religious movements' (otherwise 'cults' or 'sects'), some of them of Western, but mostly of Eastern, Hindu or Buddhist, origin. Before 1970 the academic community had paid very little attention to what most scholars clearly regarded as a flash in the pan, religiously speaking, as well as being so far removed from their parent traditions as to be scarcely worthy of serious attention.[7] Even today that attitude of superiority if still very common in departments of religious studies.

Nevertheless the 'new religious movements' phenomenon—and this of course includes the remarkable rise to power and influence of conservative evangelical forms of Christianity in the last twenty years[8]—has exercised a powerful, if indirect, influence on the academic study of religion. At least we can see clearly now that the secularisation process is by no means massively unilinear, and that when dammed up in one direction the religious impulse is entirely capable of cutting new channels in another. And where one's own students are themselves engaged in private, 'alternative' religious quests of their own, it requires a high degree of insensitivity on the teacher's part not to take those quests—and their results—seriously.[9] In 1986 this trend may have passed its peak. Not all the prophets and gurus of the early 1970s were what they pretended to be. But the study of religion today carries the mark of what transpired in this area during 1965-1975 period—one is tempted to add, whether it likes it or not.[10]

✻   ✻   ✻

Imâm Rûhullâh Khumainî, Šâh Muhammad Rizâ Pahlaví and the Religious Traditions of Iran (1985).

[7] One of the first attempts to locate a 'new religious movement' in its tradition was Judah, *Hare Krishna and the Counter Culture* (1974). Of the masses of recent literature, mention may be made of Needleman and Baker (eds.) *Understanding the New Religions* (1978), Barker (ed.), *New Religious Movements: a Perspective for Understanding Society* (1982) and Wilson (ed.), *The Social Impact of New Religious Movements* (1981). See also the entries by Turner and Melton in Hinnells (ed.), *A Handbook of Living Religions* (1984), pp. 439-74, with bibliographies. The new religious movements of, for instance, Japan, Africa and the Pacific region have seldom been fully related to their Western counterparts. See however Werblowsky, 'Religions New and Not So New', in Barker, op.cit., pp. 32ff.; Sundkler, *Zulu Zion* (1976); Trompf (ed.), *Prophets of Melanesia* (1981); and Loeliger and Trompf (eds.), *New Religious Movements in Melanesia* (1985).

[8] The 'Christian right' has been very little studied from within the religious studies community, or vice versa. Neither is prepared to accept the credentials of the other, the result being a fairly constant level of polemics. cf. Barr, *Fundamentalism* (1977). But see the valuable volume edited by Marsden, *Evangelicalism in Modern America* (1984), written largely by Evangelicals – though not those of the extreme right – and showing a high level of critical awareness.

[9] cf. Cox, *Turning East* (1977).

[10] It is now hardly possible to regard the secularisation process as either inevitable or

The most obvious effect of the re-evaluation of the study of religion in a secular direction that took place during these same years was the setting up throughout the Western world of numerous new university and college departments of (usually) 'religious studies'. Already in 1970 the term 'comparative religion' was falling into disuse, though more as a matter of fashion than as a deliberate policy. In North America it had generally been replaced as a label by 'the history of religions', and this had carried over into the international forum of the International Association for the History of Religions (the title of which still survives, despite occasional objections).[11] History could, however, be seen as only one possible approach to the study of religion, alongside sociology, ethnology, anthropology, psychology and the rest; and 'religious studies' at least had the advantage of having no obvious limitations. In particular, it did not exclude in principle anyone engaged in the study of religion, and in intention at least took with the utmost seriousness the *desideratum* that the study of religion should be multi-disciplinary and poly-methodic, the meeting place of complementary approaches to a given body of material. What was hoped for, and sometimes achieved, was a transposition to the academic level of the dialogical approach to religion itself, in which subject specialists would share insights and compare findings to their mutual benefit.[12]

Although there is much that might be said about the extent to which these ideals have or have not been realised in practice, here I shall restrict myself to the new phase of methodological discussion that was precipitated by these developments. Let us be quite clear on a couple of points. First, that the new departments of religious studies were unable to, and were never intended to provide a single methodological pattern for the study of religion: they gave highly diverse companies of scholars an *organisational* canopy under which to shelter, and in many cases that was all. And secondly, that not even religious studies can be both multi-disciplinary and a single coherent discipline at one and the same time. Students of religion, and particularly those who have been through the PhD mill (which is to say every tenured university teacher of the younger generation, and all but a very few of the older), have made their way as specialists in a

---

irreversible, as it seemed in the early 1960s. On this subject, see Greeley, *The Persistence of Religion* (1972) and most recently Hammond (ed.), *The Sacred in a Secular Age* (1985).

[11] The argument has been against the term 'history', which it has frequently been argued might profitably be replaced by 'study'. See Wiebe, 'A Positive Episteme for the Study of Religion', in *The Scottish Journal of Religious Studies* (1985), p. 95 n. 42.

[12] cf. above, p. 289.

narrowly circumscribed area, the methods and approaches of which they have mastered, and on the strength of which they have been hired. In the circumstances, it is only to be expected that communication between subject specialists—between, say, a textually orientated Buddhologist and a field-working anthropologist—might prove difficult, despite their occupying adjacent offices on the same corridor. Certainly both are contributing to the study of religion. The common ground between them may on the other hand prove at best elusive, and at worst non-existent. Only the introduction of the 'transcendental' element can complicate matters still further, but I shall return to that contentious subject at a later stage.

*   *   *

Passing from generalities to specifics, the five-year period from 1970 to 1975—in IAHR terms, between the Stockholm and Lancaster International Congresses—saw the appearance in print of a number of volumes of methodological review and reflection, the mere comparison of which might well form the subject of an extended essay. Some took a firm stand on a particular approach or set of approaches, and were the products of individual scholars working separately. In this category belong Michael Pye's *Comparative Religion* (1972), Åke Hultkrantz's *Metodvägar inom den jämförande religions-forskningen* (1973, regrettably still available only in Swedish), Ninian Smart's *The Phenomenon of Religion* (1973), and a new English translation of Ugo Bianchi's 1966 book *Problemi di storia delle religioni* (*The History of Religions*, 1975).

Methodological diversity could be seen more easily in the composite volumes—collections of independent essays or conference reports—that also began to appear with some regularity in these same years. Of these, the conference reports were generally the more illuminating, since they gave room for response and debate, and not merely for unrelated individual statements of principle, such as we find, for example, in Lanczkowski's compilation *Selbstverständnis und Wesen der Religionswissenschaft* (1974). In the early 1970s the study of religion had reached a point at which those involved in it clearly felt the need to bring their perplexities, hopes and misgivings out into the open, and 'methodology' conferences, consultations, symposia and working parties became fairly common. Some of these were of course gatherings of specialists within a narrow historical area—for instance Iranian and Roman Mithraism, to take only one example[13]—and as such cannot concern us here. From among those

---

[13] cf. Hinnells (ed.), *Mithraic Studies* I-II (1975).

in which wider questions of method and approach were considered, we may select four representative examples, from Italy, Finland, the USA and the Netherlands respectively.

The Italian volume, *Problems and Methods of the History of Religions* appeared in 1972, though the conference of which it was the report had actually been held in Rome in December 1969. Called to commemorate the tenth anniversary of the death of Raffaele Pettazzoni, it perhaps may be seen as the last occasion on which the historical empiricists of the Continental tradition (chiefly Italian, though with the significant presence of Bleeker and Widengren) were able to affirm their own position without serious contradiction. None of the main speakers was prepared to pass beyond the historical study of the religions of the past, except to a cautious rearrangement of the historical material under the label of 'phenomenology'.[14] Comparative method, to Widengren, was to be placed 'between philology and phenomenology'. Speculation—philosophical, psychological, most of all theological—was ruled out in principle. Bleeker may or may not have been ironical when he stated that

> It is a well known fact that historians of religions do not bother their heads much about the presuppositions of their work. No wonder, for they are empirics [sic] ...[15]

Bleeker was not saying either that historians of religions have no presuppositions, or that whatever presuppositions they might have, can simply be ignored. But it was hard to see how these might be uncovered and corrected without venturing into non-historical, and therefore dangerous, territory. The duty of the historian of religions is to uncover and interpret 'facts'—texts and monuments, myths and rituals—allowing his or her own personality to intrude as little as possible. The phenomenology of religion therefore he restated as being ' ... not a philosophical discipline, but a *systematisation of historical facts* [my italics] with the intent to study their religious meaning'.[16] Whether historical technique as the empiricists understood it was capable of meeting these demands was at least open to question, however.

In August 1973 there took place in Turku, Finland, the first IAHR-sponsored conference devoted entirely to questions of method and approach in the study of religion. It was fairly small-scale, numbering less than 50 active participants in all (which is to say that it brought together most of those scholars in Europe and North

---

[14] Above, Chapter X.
[15] *Problems and Methods* ..., p. 43.
[16] ibid., p. 51.

America who were actively concerned with questions of method at the time), and was extraordinarily well documented.[17] In keeping with the traditionally high level of Finnish and Scandinavian scholarship in the circumpolar and Ancient Near Eastern fields, much attention was paid to the scholarly methods appropriate to each—ethnological and folkloristic in the former case, historical and philological in the latter. A group of contributions was devoted to 'The Future of the Phenomenology of Religion', but these gave little firm direction. A disappointment to those present (myself included) was that Mircea Eliade, attending what would seem to have been his last international conference in the history of religions, chose not to contribute to this or any other discussion. It is perhaps invidious to select one paper for special comment, but it was Walter Capps of the University of California (Santa Barbara) who raised a question of more than local significance. Pointing out that 'the science of religion is ripe for ground-clearing, for it is not always clear about its conceptual basis',[18] he went on to suggest that it would be helpful to concentrate more on the history of the discipline, or what he called 'second-order' studies:

> ... if a sense of a second-order tradition is to be recovered [he pointed out], one cannot expect to look for a chain of communication that bears any resemblance to apostolic succession. Instead, it is disparate, disjointed, flexible, and accumulated or even created rather than discovered ... But no matter how difficult it is to recover, the field cannot get along without a sense of an underlying, second-order tradition ... It cannot pretend to find its way until it can relate to its past in narrative form.[19]

To digress for a moment: Capps' observation was more important than most of those present at Turku perhaps realised. Twenty years or so earlier Alvin Gouldner had written that 'A science ignorant of its founders does not know how far it has travelled, or in what direction ... ',[20] and in 1974 the comparative study of religion was still very poorly equipped to estimate its own past. The last comprehensive account of the history of the discipline had appeared in French in 1929; there was a Dutch volume from 1932, and a smallish German work from 1948.[21] None of these was available in

[17] Honko (ed.), *Science of Religion: Studies in Methodology* (not published until 1979, although the conference had taken place six years earlier).

[18] ibid., p. 179.

[19] ibid., p. 179f.

[20] Quoted in O'Toole, *Religion: Classical Sociological Approaches* (1984), p. 209.

[21] Pinard de la Boullaye 1929, Bellon 1932, Mensching 1948 (details in bibliography). The long-planned history of the discipline in the German Kohlhammer series has not yet appeared.

English. The English-speaking student had only Kees Bolle's translation of the Dutch scholar Jan de Vries' *The Study of Religion: a Historical Approach* (1967), which was slight and left many gaps in the narrative. However, between 1973 and 1975 matters improved with the appearance, first, of Jacques Waardenburg's *Classical Approaches to the Study of Religion* (1973-4), followed by the first edition of this present book in 1975, which was cast more in the narrative mode than Waardenburg's person-by-person account.

It would be too much to claim that in the early 1970s a transition was being effected 'from comparative religion to religious studies' entirely without knowledge of how the various partners in the merger had come to the positions they then occupied. But it would seem to have been the case that few of the partners were in a position to know where some of the others had been. The reconstruction of 'second-order' studies is still far from complete,[22] and nowhere less so than in the troublesome encounter of comparative religion and theology, of which we shall have more to say shortly.

*   *   *

From Turku the 'method conference' sequence passed across the Atlantic to the University of Iowa, where in April 1974 Robert D. Baird presided over a small but extremely important gathering devoted to *Methodological Issues in Religious Studies*.[23] We may note the terminological shift: Rome 1969 had considered method in 'the history of religions', Turku 1973 had used the term 'the science of religion'—both of course reflecting a generally empiricist position. By 1974 in North America the broader 'religious studies' network was very largely in place (as indeed it was on a much smaller scale in Britain; it was just beginning to be assembled in Australia and New Zealand),[24] and it was imperative to try to establish a *modus vivendi* among its highly diverse participants.

Where Iowa 1974 differed from most religious studies conferences, whether occasional or seasonal, was in having only three major

[22] Today we are relatively well informed on the work of generalists and theorists in the field. There remain many gaps to be filled in respect of our knowledge of subject specialists. cf. however, Waardenburg, *L'Islam dans le miroir de l'Occident* (3rd ed. 1969), Welbon, *The Buddhist Nirvāna and its Western Interpreters* (1968) and Sharpe, *The Universal Gītā* (1985).

[23] Proceedings published in 1975.

[24] See the area surveys published in the British journal *Religion* (special congress issue) in 1975. For subsequent developments, see e.g. the Nordic surveys in *Temenos* 17 (1981), pp. 151ff. and 18 (1982), pp. 147ff., and the Australian survey by Hayes, *AASR in Profile: a Tenth Anniversary Report of the Australian Association for the Study of Religion* (1985).

speakers, Wilfred Cantwell Smith, Jacob Neusner and Hans Penner. Smith delivered only one paper, Neusner and Penner two each. However, the approaches of the three participants were distinctive, and together provided an impressive demonstration of the diversity of the newer religious studies enterprise, not least when compared with some of what was being said elsewhere in the world in these same years. Neusner's two papers reasoned outward from the study of Judaism to the study of religion, arguing that ' ... place is to be found in the history of religions for those who, like myself, think much of consequence is to be learned from the history of the growth and continuity of a given religious tradition'.[25] One cannot but agree, while perhaps lamenting that of the vast company of those who like Neusner have spent their academic lives in investigating the history of one religious tradition, so few have been prepared to draw more general conclusions from their detailed findings.

Hans Penner's two papers were of a more theoretical nature, and both argued strongly that in the interpretation of religious data, and particularly of myth and ritual, structuralism is potentially a far more fruitful approach than that of either the phenomenologist or the functionalist. This was to introduce a new element into the methodological debate, but one to which (it is fairly safe to say) very few scholars in the field of the study of religion had so far paid very much attention, except perhaps in connection with linguistic or anthropological exercises.[26] The overlap between structuralism in linguistics and religious studies was small, while Edmund Leach's attack on Mircea Eliade was still fairly fresh in the religious studies mind.[27] But the subject was and is important, and I shall return to it at a later stage.

There remained the contribution of Wilfred Cantwell Smith to the Iowa conference, entitled 'Methodology and the Study of Religion: Some Misgivings'. Chief among Smith's misgivings was the danger of methodology becoming a useless substitute for the real study of religion, or rather (for Smith had for years been arguing against the concept of 'religion')[28] of people in their various interactions with the transcendent.

> Manifestly something is wrong [he said] when virtually all my friends, and many persons obviously much more intelligent than I, are stalwart methodologists, whereas I feel that methodology is the massive red herring of modern scholarship, the most

---

[25] *Methodological Issues* ..., p. 45.
[26] cf. above, p. 217f.
[27] cf. above, p. 218 n. 49.
[28] Smith, *The Meaning and End of Religion* (1964), passim.

significant obstacle to intellectual progress, and the chief distraction from rational understanding of the world.[29]

This was not to say that the student of religion has no need of a method. But academic method ('critical, analytical, systematic, deliberate, comparative, public, cumulative ... inductive and in some sense empirical') is 'generic for *all* university studies; it is not particular, differing from discipline to discipline'.[30] What the student of religion *does* need, on the other hand, is a high level of personal commitment to those whom he is studying: ' ... in the study of religion, I would distrust any scholar of the Hindus who did not love India, or any interpreter of Islamics who had no Muslim friends'.[31]

In the course of his provocative—and to some, no doubt, irritating—paper Smith made one other observation to which we might well pay attention. It seemed to him, he said, that some of his friends

> ... talk about methodology when they mean not something pertaining to method but what I would call, rather, conceptual framework, ideology, presuppositions, or the like ... Often ... a given method is almost predictably derived from the preconceptions of the person using it.[32]

This is undoubtedly the case, and it has been this which has brought so many troubles upon the newer religious studies enterprise, in departments assembled from among historians, anthropologists, philosophers, psychologists, theologians and the rest—each individual having inherited the methods and approaches, the language and above all the presuppositions of his narrower (and more coherent) professional guild.

*　　*　　*

Last in this short sequence from the early 1970s we may mention briefly the Dutch publication *Religion, Culture and Methodology*, produced in 1974 by 'the Groningen working-group for the study of fundamental problems and methods of science of religion', which took a severely 'scientific' and detached attitude to the question of scholarship in the field. It was not mono-methodic, though it did insist that personal predilections must not be allowed to influence the course of 'science' in the area. Jacques Waardenburg of Utrecht

---

[29] *Methodological Issues* ..., p. 2.
[30] ibid., p. 3.
[31] ibid., p. 11.
[32] ibid., p. 16.

stated the matter as follows: the student

> ... has, in his field of research, the absolute everywhere around: yet, as a student, he has himself to work without absolutes. His concern is the man for whom something appears to have an absolute quality, not the absolute itself.[33]

Of course the scholar does *not* work 'without absolutes', and what Waardenburg perhaps ought to have said was that in investigating religion, the scholar's absolute generally cannot be those of the believers under investigation. But this was less a matter of method than an ideal stance which may or may not be achieved. The Dutch point, in common with that of scholars of the Bleeker-Widengren generation, was otherwise that 'scientific' methods and approaches ought not to be used to bolster a confessional religious argument, nor can the study of religion submit to control from any religious quarter. By the mid-1970s, however, such control was more a fear than an actuality, confessional and secular studies having achieved an almost complete organisational separation. For Holland's part that separation had been effected a century before, in 1877,[34] though many Dutch historians of religions had sustained something of a dual citizenship as theologians and 'scientists'.[35]

In the 1970s Jacques Waardenburg was consolidating his position as spokesman of Dutch scholarship in the field. In 1971 he had begun the publication of an English-language monograph series, *Religion and Reason*, devoted to 'method and theory in the study and interpretation of religion', the first volume of which was Robert D. Baird's study of Wilfred Cantwell Smith, *Category Formation and the History of Religions* (1971). The fifteenth volume of the series was Waardenburg's own *Reflections on the Study of Religion* (1978), in which he characterised the Dutch position as one in which stress was laid on freedom from confessional control, on a high level of impersonality in research and on the elevation of theory over 'factual positivism'.[36] The scholar's attitude he insisted should be 'sincere and unprejudiced'.[37] His search should not be for 'timeless essences' in religion, as earlier generations of scholars had generally assumed, but for 'meanings inside time' and the patterns of belief and

[33] *Religion, Culture* ..., p. 135.
[34] cf. above, pp. 120ff.
[35] Although the example of Gerardus van der Leeuw immediately springs to mind, even a determined empiricist like C.J. Bleeker, though by no means a professional theologian, in 1966 had published *Christ in Modern Athens*, in which he had gone some way beyond the empiricist position he professed as a scholar.
[36] Waardenburg, *Reflections* ..., p. 61f.
[37] ibid., p. 147.

behaviour to which these have given rise. The gods, Waardenburg asserted, have lived in the faith of believers, 'and we have no other way of knowing what these gods have meant to man than by reconstituting the religious universe' in which they once occupied a central position.[38]

*　　*　　*

The second volume in Waardenburg's *Religion and Reason* series was edited by Johannis (Hans) Mol, *Western Religion: a Country-by-Country Sociological Inquiry* (1972), a composite work mainly constructed on demographic and statistical principles. Although Dutch by birth, Mol has worked chiefly in the USA, Australia, New Zealand and most recently Canada. His first major sociological work was *Religion in Australia* (1971), and since then he has contributed further studies of religion in New Zealand, Australia and Canada, and a major theoretical work, *Identity and the Sacred* (1976).[39] All have a common theme, centred on the conviction that 'religion defines man and his place in the universe'.[40] Religion, according to Mol, is in effect 'the sacralisation of identity', operating through the mechanisms of objectification, commitment, ritual and myth.[41] In 1985, when the International Association for the History of Religions met for the first time in the Southern Hemisphere, in Sydney, Australia, it had as its theme 'Religion and Identity', and Mol was its main speaker. This may perhaps serve as an epitome of an important shift of focus that has taken place in the study of religion since 1970, a shift in a generally sociological direction.

In the pre-1970 period there was little reason to stress the sociological dimension of comparative religion, save in the early beginnings among the theories of totemism and social origins.[42] Social theory and comparative religion for many years followed different (though occasionally overlapping) paths, and operated on different assumptions. Even in the 1960s the social sciences were only marginally interested in religion, and in some sociological quarters the sociologist of religion was held to be 'an academic deviant living

[38] ibid., p. 87. Most recently, Waardenburg has produced a valuable 'systematic methodology', *Religionen und Religion: Systematische Einführung in die Religionswissenschaft* (1986), which considers the study of religion from the historical, comparative, contextual and hermeneutical angles.

[39] On New Zealand, *The Fixed and the Fickle* (1982); on Australia, *The Firm and the Formless* (1982) and *The Faith of Australians* (1985); and on Canada, *Faith and Fragility* (1985).

[40] Mol, *Identity and the Sacred* (1976), p. x.

[41] For definitions of these terms, see ibid., p. 15.

[42] cf. above, pp. 72ff.

by a non-existent subject',[43] since 'religious' behaviour is simply human behaviour operating in peculiarly defined communities. Comparative religionists for their part often rather prided themselves on their lack of sociological interest, arguing that sociology was 'reductionist' (whatever that pejorative term might be taken to mean, in this case perhaps that the sociologists were interested only in the machinery, and not at all in the 'essence' of religion).

Much the same argument was used to justify the comparative religionists' relative lack of interest in the newer forms and approaches of anthropology—roughly speaking, anthropologists worked in non-Western societies while sociologists concentrated on the home base: in theoretical terms, there was a broad overlap.

Occasionally the anti-sociological bias of comparative religion in its classical period could lead to odd omissions and distortions, for instance, in the suspicion of the work of the great French scholar Georges Dumézil shown by all but a very few of his fellow Indo-Europeanists down to the early 1970s.[44] The trouble was that Dumézil had related the structure of Indo-European mythology to the 'tripartite' functional structure of ancient Indo-European society. Although Dumézil's long sequence of immensely erudite publications began in the 1920s and continued down to the 1960s, the first translations into English did not appear until 1970 (with the two volumes of *Archaic Roman Religion* and *The Destiny of the Warrior*). At about the same time Dumézil seminars were held at the University of California (Santa Barbara), resulting in the volumes *Myth and Law among the Indo-Europeans* (ed. Puhvel, 1970) and *Myth in Indo-European Antiquity* (ed. Larson, Littleton and Puhvel, 1974) C. Scott Littleton provided an 'anthropological assessment' of his work in a book entitled *The New Comparative Mythology* (revised ed. 1973), which demonstrated Dumézil's indebtedness to Durkheim, Mauss, Granet and others of the French sociological tradition in point of theory, while using philological technique as his primary tool.[45] The rediscovery of Dumézil is still far from complete, and in any case

[43] David A. Martin, writing in the *British Journal of Sociology* (Dec. 1966), p. 354. For an admirable survey of developments in the field of the sociology of religion, see O'Toole, *Religion: Classical Sociological Approaches* (1984) and numerous journals, of which *Journal for the Scientific Study of Religion* and *Sociological Analysis* are worthy of particular mention. See also Eister (ed.), *Changing Perspectives in the Scientific Study of Religion* (1974), and Wilson, *Religion in Sociological Perspective* (1982).

[44] Dumézil once taught French at the University of Uppsala, and played a not unimportant role in the formation of the 'Uppsala school' of the 1950s and 1960s (see Widengren's Introduction to the Swedish translation of *Mythes et dieux des Germains*, 1959, Sw. tr. *De nordiska gudarna*, 1962, pp. 5-8). Both the Dumézil and the Uppsala connection are at present well represented at Santa Barbara.

[45] Littleton also provides an excellent working bibliography.

limited to Indo-Europeanists. But there can no longer be any question of excluding this variant of historical sociology as a matter of principle.

Most sociology, however, is historical in the sense of being concerned with recent and for the most part close-at-hand history—again in sharp contrast with classical comparative religion, which so often functioned as a specialised kind of ancient history.[46] It goes without saying that its stance is purely empirical, and that the sociologist as a sociologist is unconcerned with 'transcendental' meanings. He has on the other hand a high level of commitment to theory. Bryan Wilson has written that the sociologist's approach to religion

> ... differs from what I take to be that of comparative religionists because the sociologist has ultimate commitment to explain religion by reference to broad theoretical propositions about society ... [The sociologist] seeks to find, beneath the overlay of specific cultural style and content, social structural principles.[47]

This is perhaps another way of saying that the sociologist (or social scientist) will always have a high level of commitment to methodology, and may indeed become obsessive on the subject. To the extent that the study of religion has moved in a sociological direction, this may go some way towards explaining the higher level of methodological discussion that has become evident in our field since the 1970s. Social scientific methods are just as explicit as those of the historians and philologists who formerly dominated the field; added to which, they are equally agnostic in respect of 'transcendental' interpretations, leaving each individual scholar to make up his or her own mind on such issues privately. Professionally, the only appropriate stance is that of 'the detached, neutral, and objective investigator'.[48]

It has become increasingly important in recent years for religious studies to affirm its right to academic recognition in what has sometimes been an unfriendly environment, and this has generally involved a greater approximation to the methods and approaches of the social sciences. I do not wish to suggest that this has been determined only by the demands of *Realpolitik*, however. Today it is hardly possible for a religious studies department to ignore the work of at least some sociologists and anthropologists. I do not have the

[46] On the necessity of a close working relationship between sociology and history, see Berger, *Invitation to Sociology* (1963), p. 168f.

[47] Wilson, *Religion in Sociological Perspective* (1982), p. 20.

[48] ibid., p. 23 – perhaps *contra* that species of 'sociology' that analysed society, the better to be able to influence it in a Christian direction.

space to consider these in any detail, though in anthropology the names of Mary Douglas, Victor Turner and Clifford Geertz,[49] and in sociology those of Peter Berger, Thomas Luckmann, Robert Bellah, Bryan Wilson, Roland Robertson, Roger O'Toole and (as previously mentioned) Hans Mol may be counted among those whose works have become 'required reading' in the broader religious studies field.[50] These developments may perhaps be seen as returning the field to something like the breadth it possessed eighty or so years ago.

Concerning the consequences of this broadening process, we must again be brief. One consequence has certainly been the turning of the study of religion more in the direction of contemporary social (and political) concern. The 'new religious movements' of the late 1960s and early 1970s came as a challenge to students of religion. Some responded, though admittedly more did not.[51] The investigation of the historical origins of the great religions of the world was not discontinued, but came to be seen as only one element in a far more complex process, of which the most recent stages were arguably the most important. The historian and the sociologist were able, further, to find common ground in the theory of the 'sociology of knowledge'.

Coined in the 1920s, the term 'sociology of knowledge' (*Wissenssoziologie*) became current again in America in the 1950s and 1960s. According to Peter Berger,

> ... [it] rejects the pretence that thought occurs in isolation from the social context within which particular men think about particular

---

[49] Among the many relevant titles, mention may be made of Douglas, *Purity and Danger* (1966), *Implicit Meanings* (1978) and *Natural Symbols* (1982); Turner, *The Ritual Process* (p.b. 1974) and *From Ritual to Theatre* (1982), cf. also the special edition of the journal *Religion* 15/3 (July 1985); for Geertz, *Islam Observed* (1971) and *The Interpretation of Cultures* (1973).

[50] cf. Berger, *The Social Reality of Religion* (1969); Berger and Luckmann, *The Social Construction of Reality* (new ed. 1971); Bellah, *Beyond Belief* (1970); Wilson, *Magic and the Millennium* (p.b. 1975) and *Religion in Sociological Perspective* (1982); Robertson, *The Sociological Interpretation of Religion* (1970). By far the best survey is O'Toole, *Religion: Classical Sociological Approaches* (1984), described by one reviewer as ' ... a near encyclopedic review ... [and] a comprehensive analysis of the classical sources, against which other efforts will be judged' (Robert Blumstock in *Sociological Analysis* 46/1 (1985), p. 89f.).

[51] cf. note 7, above. Mention might also be made here of the international conferences sponsored by the Unification Church of Rev. Sun Myung Moon, which have attracted a considerable following among scholars, while also giving rise to some controversy. Conference volumes include Wilson (ed.), *The Social Impact of New Religious Movements* (1981) and Sontag and Bryant (eds.), *God: The Contemporary Discussion* (1982).

[52] Merton, *Social Theory and Social Structure* (1957), pp. 437-508; Berger and Luckmann, *The Social Construction of Reality* (1966), pp. 13-30; Smart, *The Science of Religion and the Sociology of Knowledge* (1973).

things. Even in the case of very abstract ideas that seemingly have little social connection, the sociology of knowledge attempts to draw the line from the thought to the thinker to his social world.[53]

Religious studies can scarcely function without some such awareness. The 'empirical' wing of the discipline has always attempted to bring together sequence and system, the history of religions and the phenomenology of religion, into some form of synthesis. The sociology of knowledge would not deny the synthesis, but would insist that behind the thought there is the thinker, and behind the thinker the demands, expectations and fashions of his society—a line or argument passionately resisted by the idealist. Put somewhat differently, both the history of religion and the history of the study of religion must be regarded as social history. E.W. Said's study *Orientalism* (1978) may serve as an example of the consequences in respect of the Western study of Islam. My own book *The Universal Gītā* (1985), in which I tried to survey what two centuries of Western readers of the *Bhagavad Gītā thought* that it meant on a basis of their varied expectations, might also fall into this class.[54]

*   *   *

I would not wish to give the impression that the present-day religious studies enterprise is no more than the older history of religions line (historical, philological, archaeological) forced into an administrative (and secular) marriage of convenience with the social sciences. A third, and more contentious, element was brought into the alliance with the re-entry of theology into the comparative field.[55]

Theology (and it must be remembered that there are Jewish, Muslim and Hindu theologies as well as the Christian varieties dominant in Europe and North America) in principle elucidates, not human behaviour, but divine revelation as mediated by prophet, lawgiver, seer or saviour and communicated along a line of authoritative tradition. But there are more conservative and more liberal theological traditions, of which the former have almost always been ill-disposed towards comparative religion, the latter being more positive, though still in many ways ambivalent. Here I wish to make only one point: that scholars trained in one or other liberal religious

---

[53] Berger, *Invitation to Sociology* (1963), p. 111.

[54] I should however prefer to locate *The Universal Gītā* in the category of 'comparative hermeneutics', that is, the interpretation of scriptures belonging to a tradition other than one's own.

[55] A considerable part of the staff of religious studies departments has been recruited from among those trained in divinity schools and faculties of theology.

tradition have come to occupy a prominent position in the newer religious studies enterprise since the early 1970s, from which position they have argued that the transcendental dimension of religion must always be taken with the utmost seriousness. The fact that such liberals have to a large extent rejected old confessional notions of authority in religion does not, obviously, mean that they have none of their own. It might well be argued that there has in fact arisen in recent years among liberal Christians (I do not venture to speak of others) a subtly new form of confessionalism, based more on implicit than explicit values, more on convention than precept, and that this has given rise to certain tensions *vis-à-vis* other scholars of a more 'empiricist' persuasion. Such tensions may well be creative, however.

* * *

Of the countries in which religious studies has developed most strongly in recent years, Canada has provided one of the most interesting examples of a local debate having much wider implications. At the centre of the debate stands Wilfred Cantwell Smith, described by one reviewer in the bilingual Canadian journal *Studies in Religion/Sciences Religieuses* as without doubt 'the largest figure on the Canadian horizon in the field of religious studies'.[56] Having made his mark in the early 1960s with the magisterial book *The Meaning and End of Religion* (1963) and with various interpretations of Islamic history, including *Islam in Modern History* (1957) and *Modern Islam in India*, Smith has for more than two decades been the most articulate of 'theological' comparative religionists: for instance, his *Questions of Religious Truth* (1967) concludes with the words:

> Religious life begins in the fact of God: a fact that includes His initiative, His agony, His love for all of us without exception, without discrimination, without favor, without remainder. Given that fact—and it is given; absolutely, and quite independently of whether or how we human beings recognise it; given that irremovable fact, religious life then consists in the *quality* of our response.[57]

In the late 1970s and early 1980s Smith developed his position in a trilogy of books, *Belief and History* (1977), *Faith and Belief* (1979) and *Towards a World Theology* (1981), the burden of which was that religion is one, because humanity is one and God is One, and that the study of religion (whatever else it may be) is the study of the ways of God with humanity.

---

[56] *SR* (1976-7), p. 456.
[57] *Questions* ..., p. 123.

In some ways, Smith's position closely resembles that of, say, Nathan Söderblom earlier this century, though with a shift of emphasis from the theological category of revelation to the human category of faith as the factor unifying the otherwise confusing religious panorama of the world.[58] And over the past ten years the Canadian debate has circled around Smith to a very considerable extent, while also involving many other North American and European scholars. The international debate sequence perhaps began with a conference convened in Birmingham, England in April 1970 by John Hick, the papers of which were subsequently published as *Truth and Dialogue* (1974).[59] Here the focus was more on inter-religious dialogue than on Smith himself, though the starting-point of the discussion was Smith's *Questions of Religious Truth*. Incidentally there was also much debate on this occasion over the question of religious 'truth-claims'—an unfortunate term and often a red herring, though one which the 'philosophical' wing of religious studies has seldom been able to resist pursuing.[60]

In subsequent years the discussion has kept pace with the appearance of Smith's books, with one wing generally favouring and the other opposing his position, in terms not greatly dissimilar from those of the IAHR method controversies of the early 1960s. I do not propose on this occasion even to attempt to chronicle the debate, which by now has reached considerable proportions and generated a certain level of acrimony in some quarters.[61] It is worth noting, on the other hand, that it has centred almost entirely on the question of the 're-theologising' of religious studies, that it has in many ways been provoked by the encounter of idealistic and empirical studies under the common religious studies canopy, and that it has involved relatively few historians of religions in the narrower specialist sense. At its most acute, the Canadian debate has been between those who, like Charles Davis, have welcomed the emergence of 'a theology of

[58] Söderblom, *Uppenbarelsereligion* (originally 1903) drew a distinction between 'general' and 'special' revelation, the latter bringing the former to completion. A marked shift to the 'faith' category took place in the 1920s, with such works as A.G. Hogg, *Redemption from this World* (1922) and D.S. Cairns, *The Faith that Rebels* (1928).

[59] The participants were, apart from Smith, R.C. Zaehner, Ninian Smart, Trevor Ling, S.C. Sengupta, Geoffrey Parrinder, Kenneth Cragg, John Hick and myself. The British edition of the proceedings carries the title *Truth and Dialogue: The Relationship between World Religions*, and the American *Truth and Dialogue in World Religions: Conflicting Truth-Claims* (both 1974).

[60] In his 'rejoinder', Smith said: 'I am ill at ease … with the notion of "truth-claims". This unhappy neologism is part of the armoury used in the attack by analytic philosophers upon religious statements generally. It distorts, I venture to suggest' (*Truth and Dialogue*, p. 158).

[61] cf. the contributions of Charles Davis and Donald Wiebe in *SR* 13/4 (1984), pp. 393-422.

the religious history of humankind'[62] and those who, like Donald Wiebe, have been dismayed that 'the hidden theological agenda present in religious studies has now, so to speak, come out of the closet'.[63] Part of the trouble, however, has undoubtedly been caused by the fact of antithetical approaches—empirical and transcendental—to the study of religion having found themselves by force of circumstances occupying the *same* closet.

*   *   *

We cannot pursue this debate further on this occasion. It is still in progress, and still unresolved. Between the extremes there are many intermediate positions, and some which do not sort neatly into either category. One such is that of 'structuralism'.

At the 1974 Iowa conference Wilfred Cantwell Smith had asked, evidently in some perplexity, 'What is it that a person knows, who knows structuralism?'[64] I am myself too little of a structuralist to know in any detail what the answer to this might be, though structuralism presents itself rather as a mode of interpreting previously acquired data than as data source. In its beginnings it aimed at nothing short of the construction of a scientific method for the elucidation of practically all human phenomena. Its first premiss was and is that 'the nature of every element in any given situation has no significance by itself, and is in fact determined by its relationship to all the other elements involved in that situation.'[65] Its basic methods are those of linguistics and semiotics/semiology ('the science of signs'), and its most obvious overlap with classical comparative religion is to be found in the area of myth and ritual. Founding fathers aside, in recent years its most celebrated advocates have included Claude Lévi-Strauss, Edmund Leach, Roland Barthes and Umberto Eco, otherwise famous as the author of *The Name of the Rose* (1980, Eng. tr. 1983).[66]

In the religious studies field, in recent years the most consistent advocate of the structuralist approach has been the American scholar Hans H. Penner. A participant at both the Turku and the Iowa methodology conferences, at the latter he had delivered a paper on 'The Problem of Semantics in the Study of Religion', in which he had

[62] *SR* 12/1 (1983), p. 95.
[63] *SR* 13/4 (1984), p. 411. On p. 420 Wiebe wrote that 'The influence of Wilfred Cantwell Smith on the Canadian scene is almost all-pervasive and it is most certainly an influence favouring the "re-theologizing" of religious studies.'
[64] Baird (ed.), *Methodological Issues* ..., p. 17.
[65] Hawkes, *Structuralism and Semiotics* (1977), p. 18.
[66] cf. above, p. 218. Eco, *A Theory of Semiotics* (Eng. tr. 1976).

lamented the general lack of theory in the study of religion,[67] and ventured a forecast for the future:

> A well-formed theory of meaning will, I am certain, provide us with the proper framework for the study of religion. A theory of religion, if this is desired, will become a subdivision of semantic theory.[68]

But still in 1985 he was writing in the optative mood:

> ... I think that theoretical developments in the study of religion which advance our knowledge of this subject will come from developments in linguistics: *the study of linguistics is the necessary foundation for explanations of religion* [my italics].[69]

On one level this may well be so—at least for those who have been initiated into the *arcana* of the structuralist approach and its frequently sybilline language. Myth, ritual and religion need to be interpreted from as many angles as possible. The danger is perhaps that of superimposing the mind (and *its* structures) of the observer upon the mind of the believer in such a way as to produce a pattern—or a structure—totally foreign to the believer's own perceptions and intentions. Comparative religion has always been prone to behave in this way, however inadvertently. Repeated attempts have been made to overcome the tyranny of historical, geographical and cultural distance, not least through the phenomenological enterprise. Whether structuralism will succeed where history and phenomenology have allegedly failed still remains to be seen.

*　　*　　*

It is by no means easy to assess the present position of comparative religion/religious studies either in the world of scholarship or as a factor contributing to a better understanding of the larger community. As to the latter, it has been seriously hampered by its chronic difficulty in communicating satisfactorily with the world outside its own narrow frontiers. The ideals that inspired the academic expansion of the early 1970s have in large measure dissolved, and retrenchment has followed expansion, disastrously in Britain, seriously in other parts of the world. As to the former, the volume of scholarly writing on various aspects of the study of religion

---

[67] Baird (ed.), *Methodological Issues* ..., p. 81.
[68] ibid., p. 92.
[69] Penner, 'Language, Ritual and Meaning', in *Numen* XXXII/1 (1985), p. 8.

has shown no signs of diminishing.[70] Its quality has varied very little over the past two decades. What does appear to have changed, on the other hand, has been the balance between 'general' and 'specialist' studies, as academic specialists have become increasingly disinclined to venture too far afield from their specialisations. The methodological debate has been pursued with some energy by a smallish number of individuals at successive conferences of, notably, the American Academy of Religion (1984) and the International Association for the History of Religions (1985), and in articles in the professional journals.[71] Few however would want to claim that it has registered any notable advances over the meetings of a decade earlier. Today such themes as the overall structure and functions of religion—as opposed to its myriad local expressions—are dealt with rarely and often unconvincingly, in sharp contrast to the never-ending supply of articles and monographs, theses and dissertations in which questions of detail are discussed. The new religious movements have left less of a mark than some were inclined to predict a decade ago, perhaps in part because their *clientèle* has been severely reduced of late by the pressures of economic necessity. Some writers have continued to tackle the larger themes, including matters of approach (if not explicitly of method): here we may give pride of place to the long sequence of publications of Ninian Smart, now of the University of California, Santa Barbara.[72] Mention may also be made in this connection of Peter Slater's *The Dynamics of Religion* (1978), Frederick J. Streng's *Understanding Religious Life* (3rd ed. 1985) and my own *Understanding Religion* (1983).

The compilation of textbooks containing selections of significant facts about the religions of the world continues. On this front, however, the present position is not altogether encouraging, due perhaps to the difficulty of steering a middle course between what is acceptable to the specialist and what is capable of being understood

[70] Bibliography is problematical on the international level. Adams (ed.), *A Reader's Guide to the Great Religions* (2nd ed. 1977) is still useful as a basic source. The IAHR-sponsored *International Bibliography of the History of Religions* covers the years 1954-1973, but has now been discontinued. Among volumes of abstracts of scholarly articles, special mention may be made of the Amsterdam-based quarterly *Science of Religion: Abstracts and Index of Recent Articles* (originally *Science of Religion Bulletin*, since 1976).

[71] cf. Wiebe, *Religion and Truth* (1981), Pettersson and Åkerberg, *Interpreting Religious Phenomena* (1981), Platvoet, *Comparing Religions: a Limitative Approach* (1982), Whaling (ed.), *Contemporary Approaches to the Study of Religion* I-II (1984-5); Smart, 'Beyond Eliade: The Future of Theory in Religion', in *Numen* 25 (1978), pp. 171-83, Reat, 'Insiders and Outsiders in the Study of Religious Traditions', in *Journal of the American Academy of Religion* 61 (1983), pp. 457-76.

[72] cf. Smart, *The Phenomenon of Religion* (1973), *The Phenomenon of Christianity* (1979), *Beyond Ideology* (1982) and *Worldviews* (1983).

by the undergraduate market at which most are aimed. At the present time there would seem to be only three serious competitors in the English-language area: Ninian Smart's *The Religious Experience of Mankind* (2nd ed. 1976, 3rd ed. 1984), John B. Noss's *Man's Religions* (5th ed. 1974, 6th ed. 1980, 7th ed. with David J. Noss, 1984), and a team effort, Nielsen, Reynolds, Miller, Karff, Cochran and McLean, *Religions of the World* (1983). The Germanist reading Noss and Nielsen *et al.* notes that the short Germanic sections in these two books (Smart, wisely, does not tackle the Germanic sources) contain something like forty errors of fact between them! This I take to be symptomatic of the problem facing whoever would introduce a complex specialist area to a 'popular' readership—the risk of alienating the subject specialist altogether. There is less risk attached to the dictionary and the encyclopaedia, and in recent years there have been a number of these. S.G.F. Brandon began the sequence in 1970 with *A Dictionary of Comparative Religion*, and the Brandon tradition has been carried on by John R. Hinnells, with *A Handbook of Living Religions* and *The Penguin Dictionary of Religions* (both 1984). Most impressive of all, however, will be the *Encyclopaedia of Religion*, presently in course of preparation. Containing some 2,500 articles written by a vast team of specialists from all over the world, this work will certainly come to occupy a position comparable to that of Hastings' *Encyclopaedia of Religion and Ethics* in years past.

Interestingly enough, the new *Encyclopaedia* will contain relatively few articles on general methodological or (in the academic sense) 'disciplinary' issues.[73] This is perhaps a healthy sign, to the extent that it shows that the vast majority of scholars in the field of religion are quietly going about their main business of investigation and analysis, though it may be less so if it means that important issues are being bypassed or ignored.

Methodological debates do not, and should not, serve the purpose of trying to impose uniformity of approach on what cannot be other than a highly diverse field. Were we to try to do so, we should be in great risk of heresy trials. It may also be that the sense of insecurity which it is very hard *not* to notice here and there in our field is partly of our own making, in that we have gone through a period of unplanned expansion during which—previously reported methodology debates notwithstanding—we have done far too little to

---

[73] I have contributed an article on 'Methodological Issues' to the *Encyclopedia*. Written in May 1985, it identifies a number of foci of current concern, among them: judgments of value, the vocabulary of the study of religion, the 'response threshold' (crossed when the believer's right to pronounce on his own tradition is taken at least as seriously as that of the scholar), problems of translation, transmission and tradition, and the relationship between 'religion' and 'culture'.

justify ourselves *to* ourselves. Above all, comparative religion/ religious studies has reflected far too little on its own history. For although in a sense each one of us has to create his or her own identity, the question of heredity is not without importance. I feel that the present uneasy relationship between the various members of the religious studies family could be greatly illuminated if teachers and students alike were to look up various family trees. The history of ideas, with or without the sociology of knowledge, will not solve all our problems. It might on the other hand prove to be a useful diagnostic tool.[74]

Of the importance of the enterprise there can be absolutely no question, not least as a gathering point of matters of the most profound human concern in a more and more fragmented academic world. Jacob Neusner has described it as ' ... the quintessential form of humanistic learning', going on to affirm that

> Religious Studies cast a net over land and sea and everywhere find treasure. Whether or not there is a discipline distinctive to the study of religion I do not know. I am certain that there is no discipline of the academic curriculum in humanistic and social studies which Religious Studies can afford to neglect.[75]

There is of course no one discipline 'distinctive to the study of religion'. Comparative religion has always been multidisciplinary, and as comparative religion has broadened out into religious studies, the extent and variety of the available disciplinary options have increased to a bewildering extent. Some still retain the wistful hope that there just might be a master key capable of opening every one of religion's innumerable locks, or some vantage point high enough to enable one to view the whole of the labyrinth. I very much doubt the attainability of either, while being convinced (and in this I agree in large measure with Wilfred Cantwell Smith) that the only way actually to gain an understanding of religion is to study it, long and hard, in its actual living impressions—and perhaps by implication to spend less time (at least to begin with) puzzling over the ways in which others have studied it. No examination of photographs, portraits, sketches and cartoons can ever replace contact, however brief, with the person or persons they represent.

This is however not to say that we can, or should, neglect the 'second order' enterprise. For as well as knowing (or attempting to know) the believer, we must learn to recognise the process by which we have

[74] Much of this paragraph is taken verbatim from a so far unpublished paper, 'Religious Studies, Religion and the Humanities', delivered at the University of California, Santa Barbara, in April 1986.

[75] Neusner, *Stranger at Home: the Task of Religious Studies* (1979), p. 6.

formed our images of the believer: that is, we must also know ourselves as believers, unbelievers, observers, analysts and critics. Knowing—or understanding, or explaining, or comparing—the forms and functions, the ideals and actualities of religion is almost as much a matter of acquiring images indirectly as it is obtained through first-hand observation (of which comparative religion has always had far too little). Religion is simply *there* as an identifiable factor of human experience.[76] The comparison or the study is something that *we* do on a basis of the images and impressions we have formed in interplay with the values we hold. Very seldom are those images undistorted. By the time they reach us, they will have passed through many minds and along chains of tradition, some of them shaped by the sanctuary and others by the academy, while some remain practically unclassifiable. Whether we call the enterprise 'comparative religion', 'the history of religions' or 'religious studies' has very little bearing, and perhaps no bearing at all, on these conditions. In every case we are confronted both by our own presuppositions and those of the societies, communities and cultures to which we belong. The fact that we are currently unable to reach a satisfactory consensus as to the range of admissible presuppositions in the study of religion can on occasion induce what almost amounts to mental paralysis. But there is no reason why it should. Knowledge of where we have been may at least convey a sense of proportion, and can hardly fail to communicate a sense of the lasting importance of the wide-angle approach to the study of religion and religions.

*　　*　　*

In a book published in 1983 I ventured certain reflections of my own on the difficulties involved in 'understanding religion', and I shall therefore end, as I ended in 1975, by quoting myself. The newer religious studies enterprise, I wrote,

> ... is not a quest for intellectual understanding carried out from a great height, as though the student were totally immune to the religious imperative. On the contrary: because it recognises that in matters of religion, human variety is human first and varied only incidentally, it believes that the student can by this means find his or her own place in the human religious panorama, while acknowledging 'the others' less as competitors than as fellow human beings. But because in this sense, no *total* religious tradition enjoys 'most favoured religion' status, it is still met with

---

[76] cf. Sharpe, *Understanding Religion* (1983), p. 47.

less than full approval from the side of those whose religious commitment is sharply focussed ... I am not going to be so rash as to identify this exercise as an art or as a science; it contains elements of both. But it certainly involves the mastery of a craft ... It is the misfortune of the student that he or she is faced with more hard work than any, since there are so many human beings, and they all have a right to be listened to. To listen is an art; to grasp what they are saying involves both a craft and a science. But unless the student feels the force of arguments on more than one side, it is likely that a point somewhere has been missed."

" ibid., p. 32.

Bibliography

The purpose of this bibliography is to provide the reader with a check-list of some of the major books and articles in which are discussed the history, principles and methods of the comparative study of religion, and which I have used in the preparation of this book. Other primary and secondary sources will be found cited in the text and footnotes. Detailed bibliographical references covering the field of comparative religion as a whole will be found, for the earlier period, in H. Pinard de la Boullaye, *L'Étude comparée des religions* I (4th ed. 1929), and for recent writings, in *International Bibliography of the History of Religions*, published since 1954 by the International Association for the History of Religions.

ALAND, K. *Die Arbeiten der deutschen Akademie der Wissenschaften auf dem Gebiet der Religionsgeschichte.* Berlin 1957.

ALLEN, E. L. *Christianity among the Religions.* London 1960.

ANDRAE, T. *Mystikens psykologi.* Stockholm 1926.

——, *Nathan Söderblom.* Uppsala 1931.

——, 'Nathan Söderblom som religionshistoriker', in KARLSTRÖM, N. (ed.), *Nathan Söderblom in Memoriam*, pp. 25ff. Uppsala 1931.

VAN BAAREN, Th. P. and DRIJVERS, H. J. W. (eds.), *Religion, Culture and Methodology.* The Hague 1973.

BAILLIE, J. *The Interpretation of Religion.* London 1928.

——, *The Belief in Progress.* London 1950.

BAIRD, R. D. *Category Formation and the History of Religions.* The Hague 1971.

BARROWS, J. H. (ed.), *The World's Parliament of Religions* I-II. New York 1893.

DE LA BEDOYÈRE, M. *The Life of Baron von Hügel.* London 1951.

BELLON, K. L. *Inleiding tot de vergelijkende Godsdienstwetenschap.* Nijmegen 1932.

BENDIX, R. *Max Weber: an Intellectual Portrait*, London 1959.

BIANCHI, U. 'Après Marbourg (Petit discours sur la méthode)', in *Numen* 8 (1961), pp. 64ff.

——, *Problemi di storia delle religioni.* Torino 1966. Swedish translation : *Religionshistoriska problem.* Stockholm 1968.

——, BLEEKER, C. J. and BAUSANI, A. *Problems and Methods of the History of Religions.* Leiden 1972.

BIGG, C. *The Christian Platonists of Alexandria*. Oxford 1968 (1st ed. 1913).

BISHOP, D. H. 'Religious Confrontation, a Case Study: The 1893 Parliament of Religions', in *Numen* 16 (1969), pp. 63ff.

BLEEKER, C. J. 'The relation of the History of Religions to kindred religious sciences . . .', in *Numen* 1 (1954), pp. 142ff.

——, 'The future task of the History of Religions', in *Numen* 7 (1960), pp. 221ff.

——, *The Sacred Bridge: Researches into the Nature and Structure of Religion*. Leiden 1963.

——, 'Wie steht es um die Religionsphänomenologie', in *Bibliotheca Orientalis* 28 (1971), pp. 303ff.

BOEKE, R. 'Rudolf Otto, Leben und Werk', in *Numen* 14 (1967), pp. 130ff.

BRANDON, S. G. F. *Time and Mankind*. London 1951.

——, *Man and his Destiny in the Great Religions*. Manchester 1962.

——, *History, Time and Deity*. Manchester 1965.

—— (ed.), *A Dictionary of Comparative Religion*. London 1970.

BROWN, A. W. *The Metaphysical Society: Victorian Minds in Crisis, 1869–1880*. New York 1947.

VON BUNSEN, C. C. J. *Gott in der Geschichte*. Leipzig 1857–8. English translation: *God in History*. London 1868.

BURNOUF, E. L. *La Science des religions*. 2nd ed. Paris 1872. English translation: *The Science of Religions*. London 1888.

BURROW, J. W. *Evolution and Society*. London 1966.

BURY, J. B. *The Idea of Progress*. London 1920.

BUTTERFIELD, H. *Man on his Past: The Study of the History of Historical Scholarship*. Cambridge 1955.

CARMAN, J. B. 'The Theology of a Phenomenologist: an Introduction to the Theology of Gerardus van der Leeuw', in *Harvard Divinity School Bulletin* 29 (1965), pp. 13ff.

CARPENTER, J. E. *The Place of the History of Religion in Theological Study*. London 1890.

——, *Comparative Religion*. London 1913.

CHANTEPIE DE LA SAUSSAYE, P. D. *Lehrbuch der Religionsgeschichte*. Freiburg 1887.

——, *Die vergleichende Religionsforschung und der religiöse Glaube*. Freiburg 1898.

CHRISTY, A. *The Orient in American Transcendentalism*. New York 1932.

CLAVIER, H. 'Resurgences d'un problème de méthode en histoire des religions', in *Numen* 15 (1968), pp. xxff.

[CONFERENCE] *A Report on an Invitational Conference on the*

Study of Religion in the State University, Indianapolis, 1964. New Haven 1965.

[CONGRESS] *Religionsvetenskapliga Kongressen in Stockholm 1897*, edited by S. A. FRIES. Stockholm 1898.

——, *Actes du premier Congrès international d'histoire des religions, Paris 1900*. Paris 1901–2.

——, *Verhandlungen des* II. *internationalen Kongresses für allgemeine Religionsgeschichte in Basel . . . 1904*. Basel 1905.

——, *Transactions of the Third International Congress for the History of Religion* (Oxford 1908), edited by P. S. ALLEN et al. Oxford 1908.

——, *Actes du* IVe *Congrès international d'histoire des religions tenu à Leide . . . 1912*. Leiden 1913.

——, *Actes du Congrès international d'histoire des religions tenu à Paris . . . 1923*. Paris 1925.

——, *Actes du Ve Congrès international d'histoire des religions à Lund . . . 1929*. Lund 1930.

——, *Proceedings of the 7th Congress for the History of Religions, Amsterdam . . . 1950*, edited by C. J. BLEEKER et al. Amsterdam 1951.

——, *Proceedings of the IXth International Congress for the History of Religions, Tokyo and Kyoto 1958*. Tokyo 1960.

——, *X. Internationaler Congress für Religionsgeschichte 11–17. September 1960 in Marburg/Lahn*. Marburg 1961.

——, *Proceedings of the XIth International Congress of the IAHR at Claremont, California . . . 1965*. Leiden 1968.

COOK, S. A. *The Study of Religions*. London 1914.

DANIEL, G. *A Hundred Years of Archaeology*. London 1950.

——, *The Idea of Prehistory*. Harmondsworth 1964.

DECHARME, P. *La Critique des traditions religieuses chez les Grecs*. Paris 1904.

DILLENBERGER, J. *Protestant Thought and Natural Science*. London 1961.

DORSON, R. M. *The British Folklorists: A History*. London 1968.

DOWNIE, R. A. *James George Frazer: the Portrait of a Scholar*. London 1940.

——, *Frazer and the Golden Bough*. London 1970.

EDSMAN, C.-M. 'Zum sakralen Königtum in der Forschung der letzten hundert Jahre', in *The Sacral Kingship*, pp. 4ff. Leiden 1959.

——, 'Religionsforskning i går och i dag', in *Finsk tidskrift* 169/170 (1961), pp. 111ff.

——, 'Ur Nathan Söderbloms arbetsverkstad', in *Religion och Bibel* 25 (1966), pp. 18ff.

——, "Nutidstillvänd' religionshistoria', in *Religion och Bibel* 28 (1969), pp. 39ff.

——, 'Theologie oder Religionswissenschaft', in *Theologische Rundschau* 35 (1970), pp. 1ff.

——, 'Värderingar inom den allmänna religionshistorien', in *Svensk teologisk kvartalskrift* (1972), pp. 3ff.

——, 'Theology or Religious Studies?' in *Religion* 4 (1974), pp. 59ff.

ELIADE, M. 'The History of Religions in Retrospect: 1912 and After', in *The Quest*: History and Meaning in Religion, pp. 12ff. Chicago 1969.

——, 'Crisis and Renewal in History of Religions', in *History of Religions* 5 (1965), pp. 1ff.

——, 'Cultural Fashions and the History of Religions', in KITAGAWA, J. M. (ed.), *The History of Religions: Essays on the Problem of Understanding*, pp. 21ff. Chicago 1967.

ELLIOTT-BINNS, L. E. *Religion in the Victorian Era.* 2nd ed. London 1946.

EVANS-PRITCHARD, E. E. *Theories of Primitive Religion.* London 1965.

FARRAR, A. S. *A Critical History of Free Thought in reference to the Christian Religion.* London 1862.

FERM, V. *Religion in Transition.* London 1937.

FORDHAM, H. *An Introduction to Jung's Psychology.* Harmondsworth 1956.

FREUD, S. *An Autobiographical Study.* London 1935.

GALLING, K. et al. (eds.). *Die Religion in Geschichte und Gegenwart.* 3rd ed. Tübingen 1957–62.

GEDEN, A. S. *Comparative Religion.* 2nd ed. London 1922.

GLOVER, W. B. *Evangelical Nonconformists and Higher Criticism in the 19th Century.* London 1954.

GOBLET, E. (COUNT D'ALVIELLA) *Introduction à l'histoire générale des religions.* Bruxelles 1887.

GOLDAMMAR, K. 'Faktum, Interpretation und Verstehen', in *Religion und Religionen* : Festschrift für Gustav Mensching. Bonn 1967.

GOLDENWEISER, A. A. 'Religion and Society: A Critique of Émile Durkheim's Theory of the Origin and Nature of Religion', in *Journal of Philosophy, Psychology and Scientific Method* (1917), pp. 113ff.

GOODENOUGH, E. R. 'Religionswissenschaft', in *Numen* 6 (1956), pp. 77ff.

GREEN, R. L. *Andrew Lang: A Critical Biography.* Leicester 1946.

VAN HAMEL, G. 'L'Enseignement de l'histoire des religions en Hollande', in *Revue de l'Histoire des Religions* 1, pp. 379ff.

HARDY, E. *Die allgemeine vergleichende Religionswissenschaft im akademischen Studien unsere Zeit.* Freiburg 1887.

——, 'Zur Geschichte des vergleichende Religionsforschung', in *Archiv für Religionswissenschaft* 4, pp. 45ff., 97ff., 193ff.

VON HARNACK, A. 'Die Aufgabe der theologischen Fakultäten und die allgemeine Religionsgeschichte', in *Reden und Aufsätze* II, pp. 159ff. Giessen 1906.

HASTINGS, J. (ed.) *Encyclopaedia of Religion and Ethics.* 12 vols. Edinburgh 1908–21.

HAYDON, A. E. 'History of Religions', in SMITH, G. B. (ed.), *Religious Thought in the Last Quarter-Century*, pp. 140ff. Chicago 1927.

HEILER, F. 'En härold för de heligas samfund', in THULIN, S. (ed.), *Hågkomster och livsintryck* XIV, pp. 209ff. 2nd ed. Uppsala 1933.

——, 'Die Religionsgeschichte als Wegbereiterin für die Zusammenarbeit der Religionen', in *Theologische Literatur-Zeitung* 78 (1953), sp. 727ff.

HERFORD, C. H. (ed.) *Joseph Estlin Carpenter: a Memorial Volume.* Oxford 1929.

HERMELINK, J. *Verstehen und Bezeugen: Der theologische Ertrag der 'Phänomenologie der Religion' von Gerardus van der Leeuw.* München 1960.

HERSKOVITZ, M. J. *Franz Boas: The Science of Man in the Making.* New York 1953.

HIRSCHMANN, E. *Phänomenologie der Religion.* Würzburg 1940.

HODGEN, M. T. *The Doctrine of Survivals.* London 1936.

HOLSTEN, W. *Christentum und nichtchristliche Religion nach der Auffassung Luthers.* Gütersloh 1932.

HULTKRANTZ, Å. 'North American Indian Religions in the History of Research', in *History of Religions* 6/2 (1966), pp. 91ff., 6/3 (1967), pp. 183ff., 7/1 (1967), pp. 13ff., 7/2 (1967), pp. 112ff.

——, 'The Phenomenology of Religion : Aims and Methods', in *Temenos* 6 (1970), pp. 68ff.

JAFFÉ, A. *From the Life and Work of C. G. Jung.* Eng. tr. New York 1971.

JAMES, E. O. 'The History, Science and Comparative Study of Religion', in *Numen* I (1954), pp. 91ff.

JASTROW, M. *The Study of Religion.* London 1901.

JEPSON, A. 'Anmerkungen zur Phänomenologie der Religion', in *Festschrift für A. Bertholet*, pp. 267ff. Tübingen 1950.

JORDAN, L. H. *Comparative Religion: Its Genesis and Growth.* Edinburgh 1905.

—— and LABANCA, B. *The Study of Religion in the Italian Universities.* Edinburgh 1909.

——, *Comparative Religion: a Survey of its Recent Literature*. 2 vols. Edinburgh 1906–1910.

——, 'The History of Religions, and its Introduction into the German Universities', in *The Expository Times* 22 (1910–11), pp. 198ff.

——, 'The Study of the History of Religions in the German Universities', in *The Expository Times* 24 (1912–13), pp. 136ff.

——, *Comparative Religion: Its Adjuncts and Allies*. London 1915.

JUNG, C. G. *Memories, Dreams, Reflections*. Eng. tr. New York 1961.

KITAGAWA, J. M. 'The History of Religions in America', in ELIADE, M. and KITAGAWA (eds.), *The History of Religions: Essays in Methodology*, pp. 1ff. Chicago 1959.

——, *Gibt es ein Verstehen fremder Religionen?* Leiden 1963.

—— (ed.), *The History of Religions: Essays on the Problem of Understanding*. Chicago 1967.

—— and LONG, C. H. (ed.) *Myths and Symbols* : Studies in Honor of Mircea Eliade. Chicago 1969.

KITTEL, G. 'Kring Söderbloms Leipzigtid', in THULIN, S. (ed.), *Hågkomster och livsintryck* XIV, pp. 110ff. 2nd ed. Uppsala 1933.

KRISTENSEN, W. B. *Religionshistorisk studium*. Oslo 1954.

——, *The Meaning of Religion*. Eng. tr. The Hague 1960.

LANCZOWSKI, G. (ed.) *Selbsverständnis und Wesen der Religionswissenschaft*. Darmstadt 1974.

VAN DER LEEUW, G. *Phänomenologie der Religion*. Tübingen 1933. Eng. Tr. *Religion in Essence and Manifestation*. London 1938.

——, 'Confession scientifique', in *Numen* I (1954), pp. 8ff.

LEHMANN, E. *Religionsvetenskapen* I : *Inledning till religionsvetenskapen*. Stockholm 1914.

LEHMANN, F. R. *Mana*. Leipzig 1922.

——, 'Versuche, die Bedeutung des Wortes "Mana" . . . festzustellen', in *Festschrift Walter Baetke*, Leipzig 1966.

LEIBOVICI, M. 'Méthodologie et développement de l'histoire des religions', in *Studies in Religion* I (1972), pp. 339ff.

LEUBA, J. H. 'The Making of a Psychologist of Religion', in FERM, V. (ed.), *Religion in Transition*, pp. 173ff. London 1937.

LÉVI-STRAUSS, C. *Le Totémisme aujourd'hui*. Paris 1962. Eng. tr. *Totemism*. Harmondsworth 1969.

LING, T. O., 'Max Weber in India', in *The University of Leeds Review* 16 (1973), pp. 42ff.

LOVEJOY, A. O. *The Great Chain of Being*. Cambridge, Mass. 1936.

LOWIE, R. H. *The History of Ethnological Theory*. London 1937.

326   *Bibliography*

MACQUARRIE, J. *Twentieth-Century Religious Thought.* London 1963.

MARETT, R. R. *A Jerseyman at Oxford.* London 1941.

——, *Tylor*, London 1936.

MARSHALL, P. J. (ed.) *The British Discovery of Hinduism in the Eighteenth Century.* Cambridge 1970.

MATTHIESSEN, F. O. *American Renaissance: Art and Expression in the Age of Emerson and Whitman.* New York 1941.

——, *The James Family.* New York 1961.

MENSCHING, G. *Geschichte der Religionswissenschaft.* Stuttgart 1948. French translation *Histoire de la science des religions.* Paris 1955.

MENZIES, A. *History of Religion.* London 1895, 4th ed. repr. 1922.

MICHAELSEN, R. S. *The Scholarly Study of Religion in College and University.* New Haven 1964.

——, *The Study of Religion in American Universities.* New Haven 1965.

MOULTON, J. H. *Religions and Religion.* London 1911.

MOULTON, W. F. *James Hope Moulton*, by his Brother. London 1919.

MÜLLER, F. M. *My Autobiography: A Fragment.* London 1901.

MÜLLER, G. A. (ed.), *The Life and Letters of the Right Honourable Friedrich Max Müller* I-II. London 1902.

NEILL, S. C. *The Interpretation of the New Testament, 1861–1961.* London 1966.

NILSSON, M. P. 'Letter to Professor Arthur D. Nock on some fundamental concepts in the science of religion', in *Opuscula Selecta* III, pp. 345ff. Lund 1960.

NISBET, R. A. *Émile Durkheim.* Englewood Cliffs 1965.

——, *The Sociological Tradition.* London 1967.

NYBERG, H. S. 'Nathan Söderbloms insats i utforskandet av den iranska religionshistorien', in *Religion och Bibel* 2 (1943), pp. 1ff.

OXTOBY, W. G. '*Religionswissenschaft* Revisited', in NEUSNER, J. (ed.), *Religions in Antiquity*: Studies in Memory of Erwin Ramsdell Goodenough, pp. 590ff. Leiden 1968.

PAILIN, D. A. 'Some Eighteenth-Century Attitudes to "Other Religions"', in *Religion* 1 (1971), pp. 83ff.

PARSONS, T. Introduction to MAX WEBER, *The Sociology of Religion*, pp. xix ff. Eng. tr. London 1965.

PAUCK, W. *Harnack and Troeltsch: Two Historical Theologians.* New York 1968.

PEAKE, A. S. (ed.) *Inaugural Lectures Delivered by Members of the*

Faculty of Theology During its First Session, 1904–5. Manchester 1905.

PETRE, M. D. *Alfred Loisy: his Religious Significance*. Cambridge 1944.

PETTAZZONI, R. *Essays on the History of Religion*. Leiden 1954.

——, 'Aperçu introductif', in *Numen* 1 (1954), pp. 1ff.

——, 'Il metodo comparativo', in *Numen* 6 (1959), pp. 1ff.

PINARD DE LA BOULLAYE, H. *L'Étude comparée des religions* 1. 4th edition Paris 1929.

Problèmes et Méthodes d'Histoire des Religions. Paris 1968.

VAN PROOSDIJ, B. A. *A Century of the History of Religion in the Netherlands*. Leiden 1970.

PRUETT, G. E. 'History, Transcendence and World Community in the Work of Wilfred Cantwell Smith', in *Journal of the American Academy of Religion* 41 (1973), pp. 573ff.

PUMMER, R. *Religionswissenschaft* or Religiology', in *Numen* 19 (1972), pp. 91ff.

PYE, E. M. *Comparative Religion*. Newton Abbott 1972.

——, Comparative Hermeneutics in Religion', in PYE and MORGAN, R. C. (ed.), *The Cardinal Meaning: Essays in Comparative Hermeneutics*, pp. 9ff. The Hague 1973.

RAISON, T. (ed.) *The Founding Fathers of Social Science*. Harmondsworth 1969.

RÉVILLE, J. 'La situation actuelle de l'enseignement de l'histoire des religions', in *Actes du premier congrès . . . Paris* 1900, I, pp. 165ff.

RICKETTS, M. L. 'In Defence of Eliade', in *Religion* 3 (1973), pp. 13ff.

RICOEUR, P. *Husserl: An Analysis of his Phenomenology*. Evanston 1967.

ROSE, H. J. *Andrew Lang: his Place in Anthropology*. Edinburgh 1951.

RUDOLPH, K. *Die Religionsgeschichte an der Leipziger Universität und die Entwicklung der Religionswissenschaft*. Berlin 1962.

——, 'Religionsgeschichte und "Religionsphänomenologie",' in *Theologische Literaturzeitung* 96 (1971), cols. 241ff.

SCHMIDT, W. *Ursprung und Werden der Religion*. Münster 1930. Eng. tr. *The Origin and Growth of Religion: Facts and Theories*. London 1931.

VON SCHROEDER, L. 'Über die Entwicklung der Indologie in Europa', in *Reden und Aufsätze*. Leipzig 1913.

SCHÜTTE, H.-W. *Religion und Christentum in der Theologie Rudolf Ottos*. Berlin 1969.

SELBIE, W. B. *The Life of Andrew Martin Fairbairn*. London 1914.

SHARPE, E. J. *J. N. Farquhar: A Memoir*. Calcutta 1962.

——, *Not to Destroy but to Fulfil: The Contribution of J. N. Farquhar to Protestant Missionary Thought in India before 1914*. Lund 1965.

——, 'Nathan Söderblom and the Study of Religion', in *Religious Studies* 4 (1969), pp. 259ff.

——, 'The Comparative Study of Religion in Historical Perspective', in HINNELLS, J. R. (ed.), *Comparative Religion in Education*, pp. 1ff. Newcastle 1970.

——, 'Some Problems of Method in the Study of Religion', in *Religion* 1 (1971), p. 1ff.

——, 'S. G. F. Brandon (1907–1971),' in *History of Religions* 12 (1972), pp. 71ff.

SIMON, M. 'S. G. F. Brandon', in Numen 19 (1972), pp. 84ff.

SMART, N. *Secular Education and the Logic of Religion*. London 1968.

——, *The Principles and Meaning of the Study of Religion*. Lancaster 1968.

——, *The Phenomenon of Religion*. London 1973.

SMITH, J. Z. 'When the Bough Breaks', in *History of Religions* 12 (1973), pp. 342ff.

SMITH, W. C. 'Comparative Religion : Whither—and Why?' in ELIADE and KITAGAWA (eds.), *The History of Religions: Essays in Methodology*. Chicago 1959.

——, *The Meaning and End of Religion*. New York 1963.

——, 'Traditional Religions and Modern Culture', in *Proceedings of the XIth International Congress of the IAHR*, I, pp. 55ff. Leiden 1968.

SÖDERBLOM, N. *Natürliche Theologie and allgemeine Religionsgeschichte*. Stockholm and Leipzig 1913.

——, 'Holiness (General and Primitive)', in HASTINGS, J. (ed.), *Encyclopaedia of Religion and Ethics* VI (1913), pp. 731ff.

——, *Gudstrons uppkomst*. Stockholm 1914.

——, *Ur religionens historia*. Stockholm 1915.

——, *Studiet av religionen*. 3rd ed. Stockholm 1916.

SPENCER, H. *An Autobiography*. London 1904.

STARBUCK, E. D. 'Religion's Use of Me', in FERM, V. (ed.), *Religion in Transition*, pp. 201ff. London 1937.

SUNDÉN, H. *Religionen och rollerna*: Ett psykologiskt studium av fromheten. 2nd ed. Stockholm 1960.

SUNDKLER, B. G. M. *Nathan Söderblom*. London 1968.

TROELTSCH, E. *The Absoluteness of Christianity and the History of Religions*. Eng. tr. of *Die Absolutheit des Christentums und die Religionsgeschichte*. London 1972.

TRUMPF, G. W. 'Friedrich Max Müller: Some Preliminary Chips from his German Workshop', in *Journal of Religious History* 5 (1968–1969), pp. 200ff.

VAN VEEN, J. M. *Nathan Söderblom, Leven en Denken van een Godsdiensthistoricus.* Amsterdam 1940.

VOIGT, J. H. F. *Max Müller: The Man and his Ideas.* Calcutta 1967.

DE VRIES, J. *Forschungsgeschichte der Mythologie.* München 1961.

——, *The Study of Religion: A Historical Approach.* Eng. tr. New York 1967.

WAARDENBURG, J. J. *L'Islam dans le miroir de l'Occident.* 3rd ed. The Hague 1969.

——, 'Religion between Reality and Idea: A Century of the Phenomenology of Religion in the Netherlands', in *Numen* 19 (1972), pp. 128ff.

——, *Classical Approaches to the Study of Religion* I. The Hague 1973.

WACH, J. *Religionswissenschaft: Prolegomena zu ihrer wissenschafts-theoretischen Grundlegung.* Leipzig 1924.

——, [ed. KITAGAWA, J. M.] *The Comparative Study of Religions.* New York 1958.

——, *Sociology of Religion.* Chicago (1944) 1962.

——, [ed. KITAGAWA, J. M.] *Understanding and Believing.* New York 1968.

WELBON, G. R. *The Buddhist Nirvāna and its Western Interpreters.* Chicago 1968.

WERBLOWSKY, R. J. Z. 'Revelation, Natural Theology and Comparative Religion', in *The Hibbert Journal* 55 (1957), pp. 278ff.

——, 'The Comparative Study of Religions—A Review Essay', in *Judaism* 8 (1959).

——, 'On the Role of Comparative Religion in Promoting Mutual Understanding', in *The Hibbert Journal* 58 (1959).

——, 'Marburg—and After?' in *Numen* 7 (1960), pp. 215ff.

WHITNEY, W. D. *Max Müller and the Science of Language: a Criticism.* New York 1892.

WIDENGREN, G. 'Religionshistoria och religionsfenomenologi', in *Religion och Bibel* 1 (1942), pp. 21ff.

——, *Religionens värld.* Stockholm 1945. Second edition 1953, third edition 1971. German translation: *Religionsphänomenologie.* Berlin 1969.

——, 'Evolutionism and the Problem of the Origin of Religion', in *Ethnos* 10 (1945), pp. 57ff.

——, *Tor Andrae.* Stockholm 1947.

——, 'Die religionswissenschaftliche Forschung in Skandinavien', in

Zeitschrift für Religions- und Geistesgeschichte (1953), pp. 193ff., 320ff.

——, [and others] *The History of Religions in Swedish Universities.* Uppsala 1970.

WILKINSON, J. T. *Arthur Samuel Peake.* London 1958.

WILLEY, B. *The Eighteenth-Century Background.* Harmondsworth 1962.

WILSON, J. F. 'Developing the Study of Religion in American Colleges and Universities', in *The Journal of General Education* 20 (1968), pp. 190ff.

——, Introduction : 'The Background and Present Context of the Study of Religion in Colleges and Universities', in RAMSEY and WILSON (eds.), *The Study of Religion in Colleges and Universities.* pp. 3ff. Princeton 1970.

Supplement (post-1974)

ADAMS, C.J. (ed.), *A Reader's Guide to the Great Religions.* 2nd ed. New York 1977.

BAIRD, R.D. (ed.), *Methodological Issues in Religious Studies.* Chico, Calif. 1975.

BARKER, Eileen (ed.), *New Religious Movements: A Perspective for Understanding Society.* New York 1982.

BARRETT, D.B. (ed.), *World Christian Encyclopedia.* New York 1982.

BIANCHI, U. *The History of Religions.* Leiden 1975.

[Congress], *Proceedings of the XIIth International Congress of the International Association for the History of Religions* (Stockholm 1970), edited by C.J. BLEEKER, G. WIDENGREN and E.J. SHARPE. Leiden 1975.

——, *History of Religions: Proceedings of the Thirteenth Congress, International Association for the History of Religions* (Lancaster 1975), edited by M. PYE and P. McKENZIE. Leicester 1980.

——, *Traditions in Contact and Change: Selected Proceedings of the XIVth Congress of the International Association for the History of Religions* (Winnipeg 1980), edited by P. SLATER and D. WIEBE. Waterloo, Ontario 1983.

——, *Identity Issues and World Religions: Selected Proceedings of the Fifteenth Congress of the International Association for the History of Religions* (Sydney 1985), edited by V.C. HAYES. Adelaide 1986.

DAVIS, C. 'The Reconvergence of Theology and Religious Studies', in *Studies in Religion/Sciences Religieuses (SR)* 4 (1975), pp. 205ff.

——, 'Theology and Religious Studies', in *Scottish Journal of Religious Studies* 2 (1981), pp. 11ff.

——, 'Wherein there is no ecstasy', in *SR* 13 (1984), pp. 393ff.

EISTER, A.W. *Changing Perspectives in the Scientific Study of Religion.* New York 1974.

ELLWOOD, R.S. Jr. *Introducing Religion: from Inside and Outside.* Englewood Cliffs, NJ 1978.

GILKEY, L. and SMITH, H. 'Wilfred Cantwell Smith: Early Opus and Recent Trilogy', in *Religious Studies Review* 7 (1981), pp. 298ff.

GLADIGOW, B. and KIPPENBERG, H.G. *Neue Ansätze in der Religionswissenschaft.* München 1983.

GREELEY, A.M. *The Persistence of Religion.* London 1973.

———, *Religion: A Secular Theory.* New York 1982.

HEBBLETHWAITE, B. *The Problems of Theology.* Cambridge 1980.

HONKO, L. (ed.), *Science of Religion: Studies in Methodology.* The Hague 1979.

INGRAM, P.O. 'Method in the History of Religion', in *Theology Today* 32 (1976), pp. 382ff.

KEGLEY, C.W. 'Theology and Religious Studies: Friends or Enemies?', in *Theology Today* 35 (1978), pp. 273ff.

KITAGAWA, J.M. 'Theology and the Science of Religion', in *Anglican Theological Review* 29 (1975), pp. 33ff.

———, *The History of Religions: Retrospect and Prospect.* New York 1985.

KLOSTERMAIER, K.K. 'From Phenomenology to Metascience: Reflections on the Study of Religions', in *SR* 6 (1977), pp. 551ff.

MOL, J.J. *Identity and the Sacred: A Sketch for a New Social-Scientific Theory of Religion.* Oxford 1976.

NEEDLEMAN, J. and BAKER, G. (eds.), *Understanding the New Religions.* New York 1978.

NEUSNER, J. 'Religious Studies: The Next Vocation', in *CSR Bulletin* 8 (1977), pp. 117ff.

———, *Stranger at Home: The Task of Religious Studies* (inaugural lecture). Tempe, Arizona 1979.

OGDEN, S.M. 'Theology and Religious Studies: Their Difference and the Difference it Makes', in *Journal of the American Academy of Religion* 46 (1978), pp. 3ff.

O'TOOLE, R. *Religion: Classical Sociological Approaches.* Toronto 1984.

PAILIN, D.A. *Attitudes to Other Religions: Comparative Religion in Seventeenth- and Eighteenth-century Britain.* Manchester 1984.

PENNER, H.H. 'Language, Ritual and Meaning', in *Numen* 32 (1985), pp. 1ff.

PETTERSSON, O. and ÅKERBERG, H. *Interpreting Religious Phenomena: Studies with Reference to the Phenomenology of Religion.* Stockholm 1981.

PLATVOET, J.G. *Comparing Religions: A Limitative Approach.* The Hague 1981.

PUMMER, R. 'Recent Publications on the Methodology of the Science of Religion', in *Numen* 22 (1975), pp. 161ff.

RASCHKE, C.A. 'The Future of Religious Studies: Moving beyond the Mandate of the 1960s', in *CSR Bulletin* 14 (1983), pp. 146ff.

——, 'Religious Studies and the Default of Critical Intelligence', in *Journal of the American Academy of Religion* 54 (1986), pp. 131ff.

REAT, N.R. 'Insiders and Outsiders in the Study of Religious Traditions', in *Journal of the American Academy of Religion* 51 (1983), pp. 457ff.

RILEY, P.B. 'Theology and/or Religious Studies: A Case Study of *Studies in Religion/Sciences Religieuses*, 1971-1981', in *SR* 13 (1984), pp. 423ff.

SHARMA, A. 'Playing Hardball in Religious Studies', in *CSR Bulletin* 15 (1984), pp. 1ff.

SHARPE, E.J. *Religions and Cultures* (inaugural lecture). Sydney 1978.

——, *Universal Religion for Universal Man* (The Charles Strong Memorial Lecture for 1978). Melbourne 1978.

——, 'Comparative Religion at the University of Manchester, 1904-1979', in *Bulletin of the John Rylands University Library of Manchester* 63 (1980), pp. 144ff.

——, *Understanding Religion*. London 1983.

SMART, N. 'Beyond Eliade: The Future of Theory in Religion', in *Numen* 25 (1978), pp. 171ff.

SMITH, J.Z. *Map is not Territory: Studies in the History of Religions*. Leiden 1978.

SMITH, W.C. *Belief and History*. Charlottesville, Va. 1977.

——, *Faith and Belief*. Princeton 1979.

——, *Towards a World Theology: Faith and the Comparative Study of Religion*. Philadelphia 1981.

STRENG, F.J. *Understanding Religious Life*. Encino, Calif. 1976.

TYLOCH, W. (ed.) *Current Progress in the Methodology of the Science of Religions*. Warsaw 1984.

WAARDENBURG, J.J. *Reflections on the Study of Religion*. The Hague 1978.

——, *Religionen und Religion: Systematische Einführung in die Religions-wissenschaft*. Berlin 1986.

WERBLOWSKY, R.J.Z. 'On Studying Comparative Religion', in *Religious Studies* 11 (1975), pp. 145ff.

——, *Beyond Tradition and Modernity: Changing Religions in a Changing World*. London 1976.

WHALING, F. (ed.), *Contemporary Approaches to the Study of Religion* I-II. Berlin 1984.

WIEBE, D. 'Is a Science of Religion Possible?', in *SR* 7 (1978), pp. 5ff.

——, 'The Role of "Belief" in the Study of Religion: A Response to W.C. Smith', in *Numen* 26 (1979), pp. 234ff.

——, 'Theory in the Study of Religion', in *Religion* 13 (1983), pp. 283ff.

——, 'The failure of nerve in the academic study of religion', in *SR*

13 (1984), pp. 401ff.

WILSON, B. (ed.), *The Social Impact of the New Religions*. New York 1981.

Abbreviations

DCR   Brandon (ed.), *A Dictionary of Comparative Religion.*

ERE   Hastings (ed.), *Encyclopaedia of Religion and Ethics.*

RGG   *Die Religion in Geschichte und Gegenwart.*

Index

Index to Chapter XIII

also available from Duckworth

UNDERSTANDING RELIGION

Eric J. Sharpe

Professor of Religious Studies, University of Sydney

Eric Sharpe's acclaimed work clears the ground for students who are setting out to understand, rather than just to practise, religion.

Understanding Religion discusses, among other things, the relationship between commitment to a particular tradition and the quest for intellectual understanding 'in the round'; 'holiness' as an identifying aspect of religion; functional 'modes' of religion; and finally the question of secularisation.

Assuming throughout that theology and religious studies ought not to be seen as competing approaches, but as sources of complementary insights, it offers the student a fundamental introduction to an important area of enquiry.

'Admirably fitted for its role. Its easy handling of scholarship will be welcomed by those coming to the subject for the first time, yet there is no avoiding the clear message that the study of religion is a serious academic matter.'

The Churchman

'Theologians and non-theologians alike can learn from this book.'
Journal of Theological Studies

'To be recommended to both students and teachers.'
Expository Times

£9.99   **Paperback**   **0 7156 1735 4**

A CRITICAL INTRODUCTION
TO THE OLD TESTAMENT
G. W. Anderson

This clear and succinct introduction includes a brief history of the Old Testament Canon as a whole, and a detailed examination of each book or group of books within it. An account of literary forms and literary history, and a discussion of the place of the Old Testament in the Christian revelation complete the work.

'This is an excellently compact and informative guide. Professor Anderson has enabled the busiest teacher to keep up to date, and at the same time maintained a sober and balanced attitude to current theories.'

Times Educational Supplement

'His excellent book, in a short compass and with admirable clarity, reviews all the latest critical work on the Old Testament...a really judicious book which will become an indispensable text-book for some years to come.'
Church Quarterly Review

£9.99   **Paperback**   **0 7156 2603 5**

A CRITICAL INTRODUCTION TO THE
NEW TESTAMENT
Reginald H. Fuller

'The art of writing "special introductions" is aptly demonstrated in this volume. In less space than that accorded Feine-Behm-Kümmel, Professor Fuller has made careful selection from a broad base of opinion, to produce a balanced and unified picture of NT literary and historical-critical scholarship today. Ministers, teachers, graduate students, and scholars alike will find this artful volume critically helpful and theologically instructive.'
Journal of Biblical Literature

£6.95   **Paperback**   **0 7156 0582 8**

THE APOSTOLIC AGE

G.B. Caird

'A useful and well-documented account of the Apostolic age which reveals sound judgment and a wide acquaintance with the relevant literature.'
British Book News

'An admirable book for all New Testament students, and there is nothing so good or so cheap anywhere else available.'
Methodist Recorder

'At once an excellent text book and a book of interest and profit for the general reader.'
Expository Times

'An event of some importance, especially to teachers and students.'
Theology

£10.99   **Paperback**   **0 7156 1680 3**

THE LANGUAGE AND IMAGERY
OF THE BIBLE

G.B. Caird

WINNER OF THE COLLINS RELIGIOUS BOOK AWARD

'An immensely rich book to which the reader will want to return again and again...All students of the Bible will find their understanding enlarged.'
Expository Times

'Learned, profound, exciting.'   Randolph Quirk, *The Times*

'Dr. Caird has a genius for selecting the apposite example, and for drawing parallels between texts. His commentary is learned and illuminating and never dull.'
Times Literary Supplement

£12.95   **Paperback**   **0 7156 1579 3**